COMPUTERS FOR MANAGING INFORMATION

Computers for Managing Information

MARLY BERGERUD

Business Services Division
Saddleback College

THOMAS KELLER

College of Business
Arizona State University

John Wiley & Sons
NEW YORK   CHICHESTER   BRISBANE
TORONTO   SINGAPORE

Developed and produced by
Visual Education Corporation,
Princeton, New Jersey

Editor:	Robert F. Waterhouse
Associate editor:	Cheryl Morrison
Editorial, writing, and research:	Daniel Schiller, Michael Landry, Marion Castellucci, Patricia Hymson, Gerald Tallon, Patricia Sullivan, Gary Schwartz, Gerald Gleason, Jodine Mayberry, John Verilli, Marie Orsini Rosen, David Tillyer, Bette Kindman-Koffler, Dan Zimmerman, Stephen Guty, Patricia Leader, Susan Muller, Sidney Zimmerman, Richard Greenwood, Joseph Desposito, Suzanne Krueger, Paul Mulshine, Morton Redner
Appendix writer:	William Freitas
Copy editor:	Nanette Bendyna
Production editor:	Paula Harris
Text design:	Robert Sugar
Photo research:	Alexandra Hontchar, Ilene Cherna
Word processing:	Sharon A. Lucas
Illustrations:	Thomas J. McCarthy, Jim Edwards

ISBN 0-471-84441-1

Printed in the United States of America

10 9 8 7 6 5 4 3 2 1

Library of Congress Cataloging-in-Publication Data

Bergerud, Marly, date–
  Computers for managing information.

  Bibliography: p.
  Includes index.
  1. Business—Data processing. I. Keller, Thomas,
Date–   II. Title.
HF5548.2.B387   1988   650'.028'5   87-20979
ISBN 0-471-84441-1

Student Preface

You are reading this book at a time of great change in the world of business and other organizations. For more than 30 years, computers have provided essential services to major companies and large government agencies. But until the last decade or so, computers have tended to be forbidding and unapproachable machines. They were housed in separate rooms, surrounded by workers with specialized knowledge who used technical terms that few others understood. Many people were involved in preparing material for the computer, and many others received reports that the computer had generated; but few except the computing staff understood what was really happening in the computer room.

There was a major exception to this tendency, however. One type of computer, the dedicated word processor, emerged from the computer room to help organizations handle the vast numbers of written documents that were generated daily. This specialized machine was far easier to work with than a traditional computer. It was designed for workers who were "users" rather than experts—they did not need to have a detailed knowledge of how their machines worked, much as automobile drivers do not need to know all the details about car engines. Instead, word processing specialists could concentrate on developing skill at the task itself, on computers that were designed to be "user friendly."

However, computer processing that involved numbers rather than words was still usually performed only by the computer staff. This was the situation when microcomputers made their debut in the late 1970s. Since that time, tremendous changes have taken place.

The new world of computing

Business applications for computers of all sizes have increased dramatically as software packages—the instructions that determine what the computer is to do—have become the focus of a major industry. Word processing is now only one among many tasks that nontechnical users can perform at general-purpose machines. Large dedicated word processors have become a thing of the past. And many computers—not just those used for word processing—are now user friendly.

The capabilities and the variety of computers available have grown unbelievably. At the same time, prices of computing equipment have plummeted. And computers of all sizes can now be linked together in communications networks. This capability is leading to powerful systems that handle the nation's information in totally new ways—more efficiently, far more quickly, and, above all, far more universally. No longer are computers mainly for governments and large and mid-sized corporations. Even very small businesses now take advantage of the tremendous organizing capability of these increasingly economical machines.

Wherever you work, therefore, you are likely to use, and may already be using, computers for any number of tasks. Understanding the computer and what it can do for organizations is fast becoming important for everyone who works in this country, and particularly for those who work in offices. Fortunately, because most computers are now more user friendly, understanding them is not as difficult as it used to be.

Computers for Managing Information is not, therefore, intended for experts or specialists, nor for managers whose jobs require them to master the details of large computer installations. Rather, it is for all users and future users who want to improve their understanding of everyday work with computers. It explores how computers are used and what they will mean to workers and organizations in the next four or five years. In other words, the book is for people who plan to do office work of any sort, whether to organize their own businesses, to find jobs as clerical workers in local companies, or to work their way up into management positions with responsibility for coordinating the work of many people.

Content of the text

Computers for Managing Information focuses on handling information, because that is the basis of much office work, and it is a major computer task that all organizations share. The book falls into five parts, each of which covers an important aspect of the world of computers today.

- Part One is an introduction explaining the basics of organizations and why the computer is so well suited to serve them. It covers the types of information tasks that computers can typically help with, and it describes some of the jobs that involve the use of computers.

- Part Two introduces the varieties of software, and particularly microcomputer software, that are available for computers today. Software is what makes computers able to perform the many different tasks that they accomplish for today's organizations.

- Part Three examines the machines themselves—the hardware. It gives you a picture of what the various elements in a computer system do and how they work together.

- Part Four explores how the computer is used in business and how organizational systems are built around the computer. It also studies how the work environment is being increasingly tailored to allow workers maximum comfort and ease for productive work.

■ Part Five takes a look at the broader implications of the computer for the world we live in—both at the good and the bad that is happening today, and at some of the developments that are likely to affect the near future.

In addition to these five parts, there is an appendix on programming, to give some insight into the way that software works; a glossary, which defines all terms that are introduced in the text; and an index.

Learning aids

The goal of a textbook is to help you as a student to understand a subject as well as possible. In *Computers for Managing Information*, each chapter opens with a general introduction to its coverage and a list of objectives, alerting you to major topics on which to focus your attention. Also, at the end of the chapter, there is a summary of the points covered, followed by four key learning aids:

■ *Terms for Review* is a simple list of the terms that were introduced during the chapter. Reviewing the list should help you to focus on what you have learned. If you cannot remember what a word means, look back at the chapter and reread the passage where that word is presented in heavy type, or check the glossary for a more precise definition. Mastering terminology is one key aspect of coming to grips with a new field.

■ *Terminology Check* is a related exercise that will help you to assess your mastery of the new terms. You are given 10 definitions, and asked to identify the terms for review to which they apply.

■ *Information Check* consists of a set of fact questions to help you review the content and concepts explained in the chapter. Again, if you find one that you cannot answer, you should review the relevant passage in the text.

■ *Projects and Problems* includes simulations, research questions, and discussion questions that will help you think through what you have learned, apply it, and build on your new knowledge.

Special features

In addition to the materials provided at the end of each chapter, several other elements are included to enrich your reading of this text. Three types of sidebar features are included: *How It Was*, which provides interesting stories and perspectives from the earlier days of computing (the text in general does not burden you with a lot of history); *The Human Touch*, emphasizing the involvement of people with computers (it is important to realize that computers reflect the work of different people, and are intended for people to use); and *State of the Art*, features which discuss recent developments in computer technology and which alert you to changes to look out for. Your reading of the text should also be enriched by the photos and diagrams which accompany the text. Frequently the captions with these pictures provide additional information, or add more depth to the explanation of concepts covered in the text.

The importance of software

Reading this textbook is obviously only one part of the course you are studying. Many other experiences will be provided, some involving written materials, some involving software, and some involving outside speakers. One experience you should try to make the most of is working with applications software. Applications software—the packages that enable you to apply the computer to different business tasks—are the cutting edge of a user's work with the computer.

Even using one or two different packages—word processing software and a spreadsheet program, for example—will help you to come to grips with the computer at a working level. If you can try out two different packages of the same type—perhaps two word processing packages—you will add further to your appreciation of how computers operate.

A general understanding of computer hardware is important—it provides background knowledge for your work, which can be helpful if things go wrong, or when equipment is being added to your system. Attempting programming can provide insights into how software really works, though in today's computer environments programming is only required of relatively few workers. The ability to work with applications software, however, is vital to all users. That is why the chapters on software appear so early in this book.

A textbook can provide one type of understanding; the types of written exercises included with it can help to confirm those types of knowledge; but only through working with computers and software can you complete your introduction to this most important invention of the last half century.

Acknowledgments

The publisher would like to thank the board of reviewers for their guidance in commenting upon the manuscript for this book:

Donald M. Donin
Kingsborough Community College
Brooklyn, New York

David Letcher
Trenton State College
Ewing Township, New Jersey

Pat Duffy
Trenton State College
Ewing Township, New Jersey

Mary Pietrowiak
Milwaukee Area Technical College
Mequon, Wisconsin

Velma Jesser
Lane Community College
Eugene, Oregon

Victon Sherrer
Trenton State College
Ewing Township, New Jersey

Brief Contents

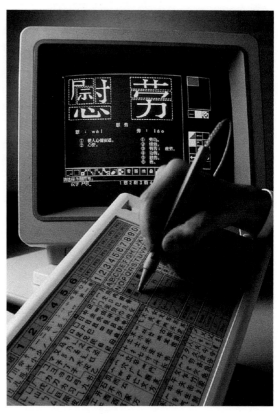

Contents

PART ONE
INTRODUCTION   2

PART TWO
COMPUTER SOFTWARE 84

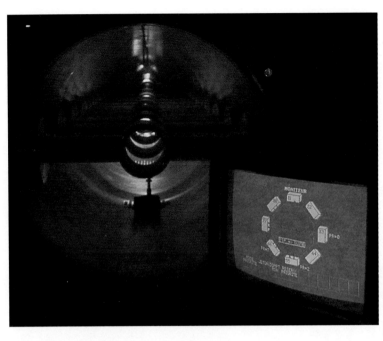

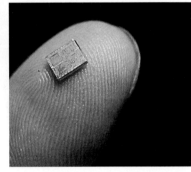

PART THREE
COMPUTER HARDWARE 204

PART FOUR
DESIGNING SYSTEMS FOR
MANAGING INFORMATION 286

PART FIVE
COMPUTERS AND THE
GENERAL PUBLIC   368

PHOTOESSAYS

COMPUTERS FOR MANAGING INFORMATION

PART ONE

INTRODUCTION

1

Organizations, systems, and the computer

It is your first day at a new job. On your desk stand a computer screen and keyboard. Your new manager is scheduled to arrive and more fully explain your duties. Suddenly you are overcome with a wave of wondering: "Why am I doing this? " You aren't questioning the money you will earn, but as you wait, you wonder why anyone would pay you to use a computer for a good part of the day.

This book will help you answer this question and others by explaining what computers do and how they do it. Many terms relating to computers will be explained. The people who work with computers—the programmers, systems analysts, operators, managers—will be introduced. But mainly, you will see the computer from the point of view of nontechnical **users**—people like yourself who use the computer because it performs tasks efficiently and helps manage information. In addition, you will discover the computer's appeal to the organizations where you may work. This will help you see why people are being paid to work with a computer and how the computer and you as its user fit into the overall work world.

Many tools in energy, communications, and transportation—from the neon light to the laser, the television to the satellite, the automobile to the space shuttle—have been produced in the twentieth century. One of the most powerful and increasingly commonplace of these is the computer. Most tools perform only physical labor. The computer performs mental labor. It imitates mental activities, processing large quantities of information at incredible speeds, with a high degree of accuracy. And, when a computer is connected to a printer or is part of a robot, it also does physical labor, printing checks and other documents at high speed or performing tasks on a factory assembly line.

What is revolutionary about the computer is how well it helps people accomplish tasks. Physically testing the effects of a new design on an automobile's fuel economy takes an engineer weeks; doing the same task on a supercomputer may take only minutes. And the effects are just as dramatic in the office. Using an adding machine to recalculate amounts in a financial plan can take an accounting assistant hours of tedious effort; a microcomputer lets the user accomplish the same task in seconds. Taking rough dictation and turning it into an effective letter at the type-writer can occupy much of an administrative assistant's day; a computer workstation using word processing allows the assistant more time to handle other tasks.

About half the money spent to operate today's organizations goes to administrative, or office, tasks. In businesses such as banks and insurance companies, office costs sometimes amount to 85 percent of their operating budgets. With such sums of money being spent, no wonder organizations welcome ways to increase the amount of office work accomplished. Using computers to help perform routine tasks has proved to be the key to increased efficiency.

This book is therefore about the use of the computer as a tool for efficiency in organizations, particularly for efficiency in handling information. Chapter 1 begins with a general introduction to organizations, systems, and computers. When you have finished reading this chapter, you should be able to:

- describe several typical settings in which computers are used today

- name four classes of computers

- describe five types of organizations and compare them

- describe five elements in a system's operation

- explain how organizational systems work at several levels

- identify the important elements and components of computer systems

Computers in organizations

Computers are increasingly becoming a part of the work environment in all sizes of organizations. The organizations range from small boutiques to huge conglomerates, large corporations composed of a number of businesses. They range from profit-minded private businesses to charitable organizations like the Red Cross and to government agencies whose primary task is to provide public services. And the computers also vary, from small microcomputers on individual desks to huge supercomputers that handle vast quantities of information and connect to many desktop computers throughout an organization.

USES OF COMPUTERS

Computers perform organizational tasks in finance, manufacturing, entertainment, sales, management, and police work. In fact, the computer has affected virtually every area of business and government.

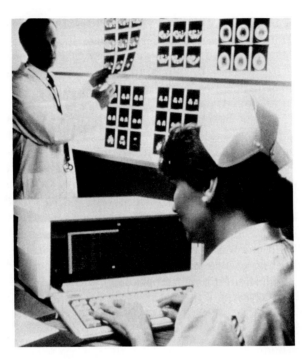

Figure 1.1 Computers for Health
Patient records are a vital resource at any hospital. They range from the names and addresses of patients, to any special dietary restrictions needed, to doctors' interpretations of important tests. Computers provide a convenient and well-organized way of keeping records—and of analyzing them too. (Photo courtesy of Compaq Computer Corporation)

Consider these examples. Kings County Hospital has a large computer system, with many computer workstations throughout the hospital. Among other information, the computer system contains records on all present and past patients for the last five years. In the past when a person was admitted to the hospital, the admissions clerk had to write down a lot of information. Then the hospital records staff searched the files to see if they had any prior information on the patient. Now the computer does most of this work. At admission time, the clerk need only enter the patient's name, and if there is information on file in the computer, it will be shown on the screen. The patient's computer record includes previous medical, insurance, and necessary personal information. A great deal of time is saved. Later, when the medical staff finds out more about the patient, that information too is added to the computer record from a different workstation. By more efficient management of all the information available for each patient, the hospital has the best possible chance both of providing appropriate care and of doing so more economically.

Johnsons' Recording Studio, a small family business on the East Coast that serves several major clients, uses a single desktop computer to keep track of all its accounts. The computer informs the owner of what any client owes the company at any time. It also provides data on how much business has been done with each client, their payment records, and other important details necessary for doing business. In addition, it takes care of writing collection letters—letters reminding clients that their payments are now overdue. All of this work used to take the Johnsons several hours each weekend. Now it can be accomplished in 15 minutes at the end of one workday.

Rustler Jeans salespeople carry portable computers when visiting retail store customers across the country. They can connect these portables to the telephone, which links them to the large central computer at headquarters. This allows them to immediately check on inventory—the number of jeans of different styles available in the company's warehouses. The salespeople can then write sales orders confidently, knowing that the product their customer wants is available. And they also know that it will not be sold to someone else, because they can send the order in and have it immediately recorded by the central computer. Before they used the portables, their sales were never totally secure. On several occasions a salesperson would have to return to the client saying that the particular item ordered was no longer available. If the client did not wish to accept a substitute, the order—and the salesperson's effort—would be lost.

When Mary Lou Peters returned to work as a clerk at the Department of Transportation after being away from the workplace for 20 years, she was amazed at the differences she found. An expert typist, she had worked in a traditional secretarial pool when younger, preparing letters and reports for the many officials in her department. During her time at home, she kept up her keyboarding skills in many ways—by helping the children with their work, taking care of family business at the typewriter, and, more recently, by taking in medical transcription work. Now as-

**Figure 1.2
Automating
Organizational Tasks**

Computers can easily automate an organization's routine tasks, like data checking, filing, and traffic monitoring at this police station. Released from these tasks, workers contribute more to an organization's efficiency by applying their skills to higher-level responsibilities. (Courtesy of Honeywell Bull Inc.)

Figure 1.3 Computers in All Shapes and Sizes
Some companies rely largely on desktop computers and terminals in the office. But others may require portable units for site inspections and other purposes. (Courtesy of Hewlett-Packard Company)

signed to the document production department, she quickly became enthusiastic about the new equipment she was being trained to operate. Using her computer workstation, she could now prepare and revise letters in a fraction of the time that it took before, and she could change the appearance of a report without having to retype the entire document.

TYPES OF COMPUTERS

As you can tell from what you have just read, computers come in all sizes. Some are small enough to carry on a plane and work with on your lap. Others are so big that it takes a large room to house all their components. Size is not the only consideration with computers; computer technology is developing so quickly that last year's computers could often be replaced by machines that are both smaller and more powerful. In fact, today's portable computers are more powerful, and faster, than the largest computers of 30 years ago. It is usual, however, to speak of computers according to their size: as microcomputers, minicomputers, mainframes, or supercomputers.

Microcomputers. Often referred to as personal computers, **microcomputers,** also called **micros,** are the smallest computers in size and capacity and the least expensive. Though usually limited to a single user, microcomputers perform many business tasks successfully, such as preparing documents, storing and accessing information, and budgeting. Portable computers are one type of micro. So are typical home computers,

How It Was

Today's Miracles, Tomorrow's Dinosaurs

Mechanical computing devices have been around for centuries, but electronic computers didn't exist before World War II. Every few years since then, major advances in electronic technology have produced a new "generation" of computers. Each generation has been more powerful, smaller, less expensive, and easier to use than its predecessor. Computers that were state of the art just a few years ago are now as extinct as dinosaurs.

The first fully electronic computer, ENIAC, was built for the U.S. Army in 1946. ENIAC weighed 30 tons. Its electrical circuitry included 18,000 vacuum tubes, which resemble light bulbs. ENIAC could not store information, and it had to be rewired by hand for each task. However, by the end of the 1940s, scientists came up with a method of storing information that made computers easier to use.

This opened the way for the mass production of computers for governments, schools, and businesses. The first mass-produced computer was called UNIVAC, which stood for Universal Automatic Computer. These first-generation computers were very large and expensive, and they were unreliable because the thousands of vacuum tubes they contained made them overheat and shut down.

The invention of the transistor led to the second generation of computers, which was introduced in 1960. Instead of containing vacuum tubes, these computers used transistors, which function similarly but generate far less heat and are more reliable. They also cost less and required less space. Researchers also developed two computer languages—FORTRAN and COBOL—that allowed people to communicate more easily with second-generation computers.

The development of integrated circuit boards led to a still more powerful third generation of computers, first produced in 1965. Unlike the circuitry for earlier computers, integrated circuit boards could be mass produced rather than built by hand. Third-generation computers were also the first to use magnetic disks, which allowed them to store great volumes of information in small spaces.

The fourth generation of computers appeared in 1972, following the invention of the silicon chip, which can house thousands of transistor-like elements on a piece of silicon smaller than a dime. This generation includes the microcomputer. Because of the silicon chip, a fourth-generation computer packs a tremendous amount of power into a small space. A fourth-generation computer the size of an attaché case can outperform a machine that filled a large room 30 years ago!

Scientists are now developing the next generation of computers, which will have even more processing power. Fifth-generation computers may approximate human reasoning skills more closely than earlier models so that they can evaluate information much as people do. Current trends are also pointing toward computers that can accept spoken instructions from people in simple human language. As computer technology continues to advance, fourth-generation machines may soon seem as primitive as UNIVAC and ENIAC.

as well as the many desktop computers used by organizations. Introduced in the late 1970s, microcomputers made computer power as accessible as the automobile and enabled even the smallest organizations to share the advantages of computing. They also transformed the way that many large organizations use their computing facilities.

Minicomputers. **Minicomputers,** or **minis,** are usually more powerful than micros and somewhat larger. They can accommodate several users. They can handle more data than typical microcomputers. Minis can also be linked to more external devices than micros can, so that there are several keyboards and screens, and perhaps more than one type of printer, attached to a single mini. Very large minicomputers, called **superminis,** are faster and more powerful than minis and even some mainframes. Minis began to appear in the late 1960s. They are quite common in schools and mid-sized businesses. However, minis cost more than micros—often in the range of tens of thousands of dollars.

Mainframe computers. **Mainframe computers** are very large, powerful machines, with greater storage capacity and usually greater processing speed than minis. Unlike micros and minis, they usually need a team of computer professionals to run them. They were the first kind of computer produced. Because of their great power, mainframes are usually the most versatile computers, and they cost in the hundreds of thousands of dollars. For this reason alone, they are found primarily in large corporations and government agencies.

Supercomputers. **Supercomputers** are currently the most powerful and fastest operating mainframe computers. They can perform more than one billion calculations per second. Supercomputers cost in the millions of dollars but are very efficient in doing some specialized work such as weather forecasting, oil exploration, and military intelligence work.

What are organizations?

Before taking a closer look at how organizations use computers, you should consider the nature of organizations. Organizations can be as simple as a local parent-teacher organization. They can be as complex as the federal government. Although there are many types, businesses and government make up the bulk of these organizations.

TYPES OF ORGANIZATIONS

What distinguishes business and government organizations from each other is their ownership and purpose. Businesses are owned by private citizens, either individually or in groups. Their main objective is usually to make a profit for their owners; of course, they could not do this if they did not also produce useful goods or services. Government organizations are owned and financed collectively, by taxpayers; their main purpose is to provide goods or services for the overall benefit of the people, but they also need to pay their workers and use their budgets efficiently.

Sole proprietorships.   The simplest type of organization is the **sole proprietorship,** a business owned and controlled by one person. About three quarters of all businesses in the United States are sole proprietorships. The owner spends money on the operation, takes risks, and personally owns all the profits after taxes; but he or she also has unlimited liability (responsibility) for any debts incurred. If the business is sued for a large amount of money, the owner may have to sell personal possessions or even declare personal bankruptcy. Computers, particularly microcomputers, have made it possible for many sole proprietors to run their businesses more efficiently.

Partnerships.   Doctors, lawyers, and others may work alone as sole proprietors of their businesses, or they may set up practice in **partnerships.** Partnerships are the least common form of business in the United States. Like sole proprietors, partners start their businesses in the hope of earning profits, which they share, usually according to a legal agree-

Figure 1.4 Expanded Work Horizons
Some people want to be their own "boss." Some need flexible work hours. And some just need a job. Today people are finding it easier to start their own businesses with the help of computers. Some of these computer-based businesses have become so profitable that their owners have incorporated out of their own homes! (Courtesy of Hewlett-Packard Company)

ment. Once again, most partners face an unlimited liability for debts that the partnership incurs. The size of computers used by these organizations varies greatly, as does the size of the organizations.

Corporations. When business organizations become large, they usually set up as corporations. **Corporations** are organizations that exist as legal entities in themselves. Their assets—buildings, equipment, and money—legally belong to the corporation, not the owners or managers. However, when there are debts, the corporation is responsible; therefore, the owners are in less danger of facing personal ruin if the company is sued.

Corporations make up a small fraction of the businesses in the United States, but because many are large, they account for most of the money earned by business. The owners do not regain their rights over the assets unless the business is terminated and all debts are paid. Instead, owners possess a share of the corporation itself, which has a value that depends on how successful the business is.

Thousands of people, called **shareholders,** may jointly own a corporation. In this case, they commonly elect a board of directors to appoint and supervise the officers who actually run the business. These officers must keep careful track of the corporation's finances. They must not only control its profitability, but also inform the shareholders, and the government, of its financial situation. Once again, computers are extremely helpful for this task.

Government agencies. In addition to the types of businesses already mentioned, there are many less profit-minded organizations. Chief among these is the federal government, a huge organization that can also be viewed as a number of smaller agencies, each with its own purpose. State and local governments also provide plenty of employment for workers with different talents.

The federal government handles many services around the nation, with offices in most large cities and in many smaller ones too. These offices include the United States Postal Service, the Internal Revenue Service, the Small Business Administration, the Veterans Administration, and the active armed services. All of these organizations, and many others in the federal government, use computers to handle more information more efficiently.

State and local governments also provide many useful services to the community. One agency with which most citizens have contact is their state motor vehicle department, where computers are used to produce drivers' licenses and vehicle registrations, as well as to do many record-keeping and analytic functions. At the local level, school systems and local police departments commonly use computer power to keep track of relevant information.

Other organizations. In addition to businesses and government agencies, many other organizations are at work in this country and across the world. Some, such as charitable organizations, are quite large and handle a considerable amount of money. Several not-for-profit, or non-profit, organizations such as private colleges and universities also make considerable use of computers to run their operations efficiently, with a minimum amount of waste. Other nonprofit organizations are quite small and may be run by only a few people, but they too can benefit from the savings that appropriate use of computers can bring.

DIFFERENCES BETWEEN ORGANIZATIONS

As you have seen, organizations can differ greatly, both in legal status and in size. These differences cover some even more basic distinctions, which have to do with the purposes for which they were started. Organizations differ in their goals and in the priorities that they attach to these goals.

Different goals. Organizations clearly exist for different goals. A dentist's practice is for fixing people's teeth—and, of course, for earning the dentist a living. A college is to educate people—and to train them for

Figure 1.5   Job Completion—And Job Creation, Too
Handling data efficiently for huge organizations, like government agencies, is just what large computer systems do best. But the use of these systems has affected these organizations another way: new job opportunities have been created especially to operate the computer systems. (Courtesy of U.S. Census Bureau)

different careers. The Internal Revenue Service collects taxes so that there is enough money to fund the federal budget. A Little League organization exists to give youngsters an opportunity for organized sport— and to promote baseball. Most organizations have more than one goal. But the sets of goals differ widely depending on the individual organization.

Different priorities. Even when organizations share goals, they may give them different priorities, meaning that they may consider some more important than others. Consider, for example, the goal of making money, which is vital to most organizations. For some businesses, making money is the primary goal; what the business produces even changes according to public demand. Contrast this with religious organizations. They too need to make money so that they can pay their employees for the work that they do, but their overriding goal of working for the betterment of mankind may lead them to sacrifice financial considerations for other causes.

Figure 1.6 Efficient, Productive, and Effective

Meeting goals on the job is easier when employees interact with computers. For example, matching inventory with shipping orders is achieved accurately and promptly in this automated warehouse. Computers more than justify their costs because, in meeting goals, they help organizations be efficient, productive, and effective. (Courtesy of Hewlett-Packard Company)

SIMILARITIES BETWEEN ORGANIZATIONS

With such clear differences in the structures, goals, and priorities of organizations, it may seem difficult to pinpoint what organizations have in common. But groups that are planning a new building, manufacturing automobiles, or running a city government clearly share characteristics that are not present in an unorganized group enjoying a vacation or listening to a street musician on their way to lunch.

The first characteristic common to organizations is that each has clearly defined goals that are shared by its members. Second, all organizations are interested in reaching their goals in the most efficient manner possible. And third, all organizations use a systematic, or planned, approach to reaching their goals.

Clearly defined goals. Though the goals of organizations may differ, all organizations have clearly defined goals toward which their members work. In fact, it is the job of the organization's management to spell out these goals so that the workers know what is expected of them.

Efficient business organizations are not content with saying that they want to make a profit or that they wish to sell many products. They state that they are looking for a 15 percent return on investment or that they have projected their profit based on total sales of 15,000 units in a six-month period. Similarly, government organizations may specify that they seek to process 30,000 tax returns in a given period or that they will patrol each street in a community once an hour. Even the most informal organization's members have a clear idea of what the goals of the organization are—otherwise it could hardly be called an organization. One effect of having clear goals is that people in the organization are able to work more efficiently.

A concern with efficient use of resources. Even though organizations occasionally spend money inefficiently to achieve some more important organizational goals, no organization can exist for long if it continues to ignore its financial responsibilities. No organization would invest in expensive computers, for example, unless it was confident that they will pay for themselves over a period of time by saving money and by increasing the organization's capabilities. If the organization purchases resources unnecessarily or uses them poorly, owners and employees are both affected.

Therefore three related goals are of great importance to all organizations and their workers: efficiency, productivity, and effectiveness. **Efficiency** means producing goods and services with a minimum of waste and expense. **Productivity** means producing as much as possible for every hour that is worked. And **effectiveness** means ensuring that what is produced is as well suited to the purposes of the organization as possible. All three of these goals are often mentioned when describing the advantages that computers can bring to an organization. Efficiency, productivity, and effectiveness can ensure that the organization will have the best chance possible of staying in existence, achieving its overall goals, and providing continued employment.

A systematic approach. Another major similarity between organizations, not shared by all other groups, is implied by the word *organization*: they are organized. Consider what that means. Unlike an individual striving to achieve goals in a haphazard way, organizations use systematic approaches, which means that they carefully plan how to get things done and reach their goals. Then they set up organizational systems to enable work projects to be done as efficiently as possible.

Most people understand the value of using a systematic approach when tasks need to be repeated; even for household chores, it is helpful to use appropriate equipment and develop routine methods so that each task can be performed as quickly and efficiently as possible. These methods can be changed for variety or because a more efficient tool has been found.

Organizational systems usually include the people who do the work, tools to help them, and routine procedures for using the tools. A person working within a system uses a set of procedures that will effectively accomplish the tasks to be done. And when more than one person is involved in a project, they must divide the work effectively so that each person contributes fully to the operation and so that people do not duplicate each other's efforts.

Because organizations realize the importance of systematic approaches for reaching their goals, computers have become a valuable tool in the workplace. Take a little time here to understand further what systems are and to see how systems, organizations, and computers relate. You will learn why computers are so well suited to help with the systematic work of organizations.

Systems and subsystems

The term **system** is used very widely in many fields. It is used to describe any set of related components that work together as an integrated whole, usually for a specific purpose. Biological systems, life support systems, railroad systems, legal systems, the solar system, and, of course, computer systems are just a few that are familiar to us. What these systems share is that they work consistently, according to established principles and procedures. Systems can be upset—trains can be late, the wrong person can be convicted, computers can malfunction. But except in unusual circumstances, a successful system will produce the results you expect, over and over again.

To operate effectively, any large system works best if subdivided into smaller systems. These smaller systems are often called **subsystems** of the larger system. In fact, there may be many levels of subsystems within a large system. A city transit system, for example, may be divided into subsystems such as a bus system, a rail system, and a carpool system.

For the entire system to function properly, all its subsystems need to operate effectively.

ORGANIZATIONAL SYSTEMS

All organizations can be viewed as systems created to achieve their goals. An automobile company is a complex system that is intended to provide cars for the American public and money for the stockholders. To do this, the company is divided into many subsystems called **organizational systems,** which provide a systematic approach to accomplishing partic-

Figure 1.7 Systems, Subsystems, and People Power
Computer users often draw tremendous satisfaction from working in a small sub-system of a larger organizational system. These users get immediate feedback. They have a sense of control over their jobs. Result: Increased worker self-esteem . . . and increased motivation on the job. (Courtesy of Xerox Corporation)

ular tasks. A common division might include separate subsystems, or departments, for manufacturing, sales, accounting, and research and development. And each of these departments is usually further subdivided. For example, there is a payroll system in accounting, and also an accounts receivable system, to make sure that all the money owed to that company is actually received. Similarly, the federal government can be viewed as a vast organization or system, subdivided into departments and agencies to help it work toward its many goals. Each of these is composed of further organizational systems—administrations, publications, and personnel to name a few.

There are also organizational systems that cut across departments. If departments operated entirely separately, they might begin to work against each other as each followed its own goals. For effective cooperation between them, there needs to be a management system. Suppose, for example, that sales of new cars are booming in a particular quarter. If new orders are to be filled, the work of the manufacturing department needs to be geared up to meet this demand. That is one of the tasks of management.

The **management system** in an organization directs and coordinates the work of its other systems. It operates partly within the different departments and partly outside of them. In a typical corporation, it falls into three levels. Lower management is responsible for organizing the details of what happens in the individual departments. Lower managers are supervisors, assigning tasks and making sure that they get done. Supervisors are directed by middle managers, who are also usually within the departmental structure. It is their responsibility to coordinate the work being performed under different supervisors and to look for ways in which the work of the department could be made more efficient. Finally, top management directs the whole organization, coordinating the efforts of the different departments and setting overall goals. Consisting of the company president and departmental vice presidents, this top level may be responsible to the board of directors or shareholders. It ensures that the work of the organization continues to meet the needs for which it was originally created.

Of key importance to all levels of management are the organization's **information systems,** through which important information is generated and passed between individuals, departments, and even organizations. Information systems, like the management system, have to cut across the boundaries between different departments if they are to help coordinate the overall work of the organization.

All of these systems—the organization itself and all of its subsystems—can be thought of as devices that take in some types of material and transform them into other things. For example, an automobile manufacturer takes in money invested by stockholders, money received from car buyers, automobile parts and new materials, fuel and human energy, and many other items. From these it creates, among other things, the cars themselves, stockholder dividends, paychecks for employees, and taxes for the government. Each subsystem causes similar transforma-

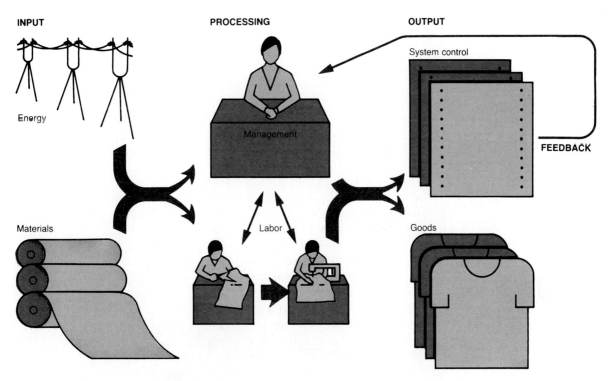

Figure 1.8 A Business System
People create systems in order to produce goods and services efficiently. Input
from sources outside the firm is turned into finished products in the processing
stage. Output consists of goods to sell and information to monitor the firm's
activities.

tions. These transformations can be looked at in terms of five elements:
input, processing, output, feedback, and environment.

Input.   **Input** means what goes into systems. Payroll systems have for
their input information on time worked and rates of pay. In other systems,
the input is different. An automobile production line can be viewed as a
system for producing cars; the input is the materials and parts needed
to make the car and also the labor and energy needed to drive the machinery.

Processing.   **Processing** is the stage at which the system "does its
work." When the auto plant production line assembles a car, it is processing the materials. The payroll system processes by performing calculations. The details of payroll processing may vary: it may involve the
use of a calculator, an adding machine, or a computer. But in each case
the math used is essentially the same.

Output.   **Output** means the end result. Clearly the finished vehicles
are important output, as are the payroll checks. But they are not the only

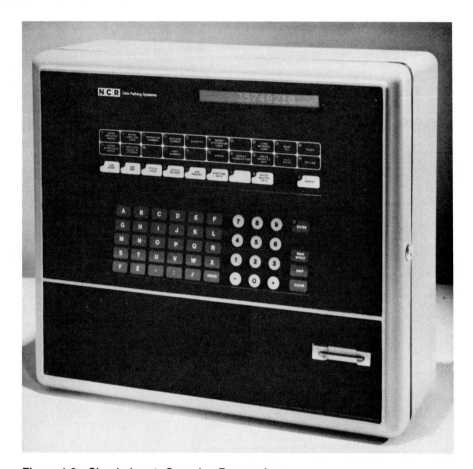

Figure 1.9   Simple Input, Complex Processing
Computers are designed to accept, analyze, organize, store, retrieve, and distribute data. They can thus take simple input (arrival and departure time punched into a time clock) and process it into the many different types of information an organization needs—gross and net pay, taxes withheld, benefits paid, and so on. (Courtesy of NCR Corporation)

output of importance. A good automobile production system will keep records of any substandard parts that had to be rejected along the way. These records are also an output of the production system. And a payroll department must also keep records, both for the organization itself and for the Internal Revenue Service.

Feedback.   **Feedback** allows a system to make adjustments in response to its own output. To be productive, any system must be flexible, able to change. When substandard parts being made by a production line are rejected, more parts are needed to ensure that enough are available to meet production quotas. If errors are found in the payroll checks, other corrective action must be taken. Feedback is, among other things, a troubleshooting mechanism; it allows the nature of the output to affect the way the rest of the system operates.

Environment. The **environment** of a system is important because it is the context in which the system works. Both the payroll department and the automobile plant might be parts of the same environment—a major automobile manufacturer. Similarly, the automobile manufacturer also works in an environment, which includes the American economy, as well as other aspects of society such as laws, competition, and prevailing wage rates. Events in the environment can continually affect a system and cause it to change or to need change. An economic upsurge could cause the automobile manufacturer to call not only for more cars from the plant, affecting the production line, but also for changes in the payroll, which will have to handle more overtime.

STATE OF THE ART
Computers Outside the Office

When the American automobile industry began to lose out heavily to Japanese competition in the early 1980s, General Motors Corporation (GM) turned to high technology to try to overcome the Japanese invasion and recover its share of the market.

GM already had computers, of course, and some robots that could perform simple, repetitive assembly-line tasks, but the computers and robots were not as productive as they could be. This was because each plant used a different computer system, and the plant's computers could not communicate with one another.

What GM wanted was a completely automated "push-button plant," where every job was performed or assisted by computers and computer-directed robots. By the mid-1980s, it had spent more than $40 billion to integrate the computer-assisted manufacturing (CAM) at many of its plants, and it is continuing the automation process at other plants.

First, GM financed the development of special silicon chips that allow computers and other electronic equipment made by different manufacturers to work together. Today, these devices enable GM engineers to design and engineer automobile parts entirely on the computer screen. Then they can program robots to perform the necessary manufacturing tasks. All of this can happen within a few hours instead of the days or weeks it took to perform the same jobs before the CAM systems were integrated.

GM's computer-controlled robots are sophisticated machines that can see, touch, and measure their work. They can be programmed to weld seams of varying widths, tighten bolts to exactly the right tension, mark identifying numbers on engines, check the dimensions of each vehicle's body, and perform many other tasks. If a human worker or robot makes a mistake, computers monitoring the assembly line quickly weed any defective parts that result and then correct the error.

Integrating its CAM systems has greatly increased GM's productivity in several ways. It has shortened the time it takes to design new vehicles and retool the plants to produce them. It has cut personnel expenses significantly, because the use of a robot costs $5 or $6 an hour, compared with $23 an hour for a human employee. In addition, GM says CAM has improved the overall quality of its vehicles.

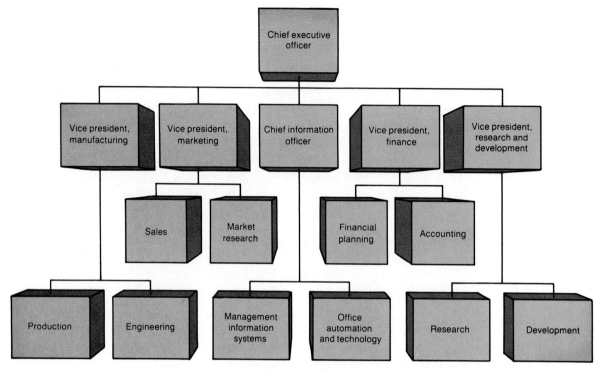

Figure 1.10 Organization of a Firm by Department
Many corporations are organized into departments by functions, as shown here.
Alternate forms of organization group departments by geographic territory or by
product. Companies typically use some combination of these three forms.

COMPUTER SYSTEMS

Each organizational system and subsystem can use a computer to accomplish its tasks and manage its information. The computer is an ideal tool to help with systematic work because it is a system itself. Computers can be organized into systems that parallel an organization's systems. From the smallest microcomputer to the largest supercomputer, these machines work in a totally logical, systematic way. They are very flexible; they work according to sets of instructions, or **software,** that can be changed to enable them to perform different tasks. But with any particular software, a computer operates totally consistently, and also very fast.

Computer systems are often described as consisting of software and hardware. **Hardware** means the machines themselves, including keyboards, screens, printers, and other devices, as well as the main units that contain the computer circuitry. This book will be about software and hardware. However, when computers and computer systems are discussed, only the hardware, plus some built-in instructions called **firmware** that cannot be changed, is being referred to. Firmware enables the computer to interpret other instructions; without it, the hardware and software would both be useless.

Like the other systems previously described, computer systems need input, perform processing, and produce output. They adapt to different events through the use of feedback. And they work in many different organizational environments.

Input. Computers receive input (besides the electrical power that keeps them operating) of essentially of two types: data and instructions on how to deal with the data. The **data**—the material the computer will work on—may be sets of numbers collected by the accounting department; it may be words entered at the keyboard by an operator using word processing; it may even be lines and colors selected and sketched by a graphic artist. The instructions may be **commands** keyed into the computer by the user, telling the computer to manipulate the data in a particular way—for example, to delete a word from a document. Or the instructions may be in the software itself, entered into the computer at high speed from a magnetic tape or disk. The software tells the computer what procedures to follow and what calculations to perform in any of a number of circumstances; in other words, it prepares it to perform a particular task.

Processing. In response to this input, the computer processes the words or numbers—the data—that have been supplied to it. Processing takes place as a result of two important elements in the computer: its memory and its processor. The **memory** is essentially an area within the computer where it can arrange the data and store the set of instructions so that both are immediately accessible. The **processor** takes each stored instruction and applies it to the data, producing results. These results are stored back into the memory, where they await output.

Output. The desired end result of computing is, obviously, the information that the user is looking for. It may be presented as a document—a completed written report or a financial summary table, for example. However, there are other important outputs. One example is the continuous screen display that many software packages present to their users. It shows the current state of the document being worked on; or it presents lists of choices to be made; or it may provide helpful advice on what to do next. Other examples include sounds that indicate some mistake has been made; records of how the computer has been used during the past week or month; lists of documents that are available for working on; and many more screen displays that can help users or computer technicians with their work.

Feedback. Feedback is a standard part of all computer systems. Often it occurs without your being aware of it—the computer checks one of its results and makes automatic adjustments to what it is doing. But, equally often, the computer waits for feedback from the user—it presents a choice and adjusts all of its subsequent work on the basis of the choice made.

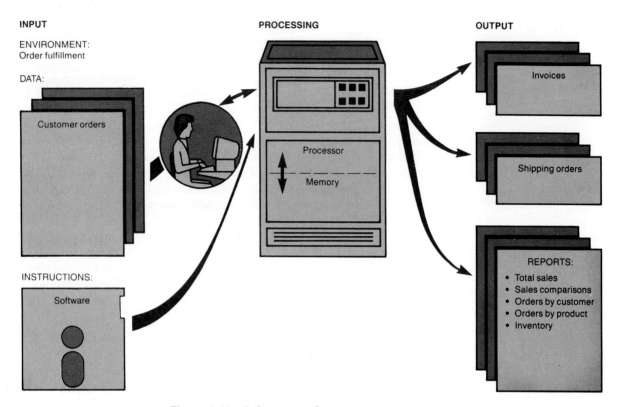

INPUT

ENVIRONMENT:
Order fulfillment

DATA:

Customer orders

INSTRUCTIONS:

Software

PROCESSING

Processor

Memory

OUTPUT

Invoices

Shipping orders

REPORTS:
- Total sales
- Sales comparisons
- Orders by customer
- Orders by product
- Inventory

Figure 1.11   A Computer System
Input in a computer system includes data, such as customer orders, and instructions on how to handle the data. Input entered by an employee at a keyboard and display screen is sent to the computer's memory and processor. The processor applies the instructions to the data to create output. In addition to final output, such as shipping orders, the processor may generate output that goes to the employee's screen. For example, a computer used in an order fulfillment environment may display a message saying that an item is not in stock. This output could influence the employee's next input. During order fulfillment, the computer may be processing data for other environments as well, such as accounting or research.

Environment.   The immediate environment in which a computer is working at any one time is the organizational system that it contributes to. Because of its flexibility, however, the computer may be working one second for the accounting system in a business, the next second on word processing. In fact, most large computers are so powerful and so flexible that they appear to be working in many different environments at the same time.

Like management systems and information systems, a computer system essentially cuts across organizational departments. It is a powerful, systematic tool, and it contributes so much to so many systems in an organization that it has become almost essential to the functioning of most major organizations in the United States today.

Tour of the book

This book will provide you with a more detailed look at computers and some of their applications, particularly how they are used to help organizations manage information. It is divided into five parts, each consisting of related chapters. The remainder of Part One provides, in Chapter 2, a broad overview of the information systems that are common in organizations and of some tools that are being used to make them efficient, including, of course, the computer. Chapter 3 will give you a picture of the types of jobs that modern information systems make possible. You will see how computers make it possible in nearly all areas of employment to work with more and more information and yet avoid much repetitive work formerly associated with information work in the office.

Part Two is about computer software. Chapters 4, 5, and 6 look at a broad range of software packages, which enable the computer to perform different tasks. These are called **applications software** because they prepare the computer for different applications. The applications include word processing, database management, communications, calculating with spreadsheets, preparing graphics, and many more specific tasks valuable to particular organizations. Chapter 7 looks at a different type of software called **system software,** which, among other things, allows users to gain more direct control over what the computer does and to prepare their own software.

Part Three, on computer hardware, will provide you with a broad overview of what computers do with the data and software instructions that they receive. Chapter 8 studies the general flow of information through

Figure 1.12 Telling a Computer What to Do

Software may be held on diskettes (shown here) or tapes; it may also be stored internally in the computer system. The software itself provides most of the computer's instructions, but you must know what keyboard commands are needed for what results. (Courtesy of Hewlett-Packard Company)

a computer system by looking at microcomputers, explaining further the way that the processor and the memory work together to generate new information. It also looks at common **peripherals,** devices such as keyboards and printers that are attached to computers for particular tasks. Chapter 9 covers larger computers—minicomputers, mainframes, and supercomputers—and discusses how their added power enables them to work on several applications for several users at once. It also describes more peripherals, which add to the computer's power as well as to its usefulness. And Chapter 10 describes how computers can be connected into networks, adding still to their power and convenience for organizing and working with information.

Part Four takes a step back from the detail of computer systems and examines how they fit into information systems and organizations as a whole. Chapter 11 returns to the topic of information systems in general, exploring how they fit into an organizational environment and who makes sure they are running correctly and helps users to work with them. Chapter 12 discusses the difficult problem of changing information systems where change is needed—how existing systems are modified and new ones created to meet the continual adjustments organizations must make. And Chapter 13 describes how systems are tailored to the needs of people who work with them and within them. Even the most powerful machine is useless if people are unable to work efficiently with it.

Finally, Part Five looks at some even broader issues—the effects of computers on society at large and the directions that computer technology appears to be taking.

SUMMARY

- Computers are tools that can help users perform complex tasks very quickly.

- Computers are increasingly a part of the standard office working environment in the United States. Varying in size from microcomputers to supercomputers, they are used in all types of organizations, from small businesses to large government departments.

- Organizations differ widely in their goals and structure. However, all have defined goals and all share an interest in the gains in efficiency, productivity, and effectiveness that systematic use of computers can bring.

- Organizations can be viewed as systems, operating according to established principles and procedures and further divided into subsystems for efficiency. Coordinating the work of related systems is the task of management and of the information systems of an organization.

- Whole organizations and departments within organizations can be understood in terms of input, processing, output, feedback, and an environment.

■ Computers are extremely efficient systems themselves and can be understood in the same terms as organizations. Their input includes software and user commands, both of which instruct the computer how to deal with data. The data is the material to be worked on and may be words, numbers, or graphics.

■ Processing in the computer involves computer memory and a processor, which can be directed by different software to produce different types of printed output. Other outputs may include many types of screen display, including the feedback that may be provided for the user. The great flexibility of computers, as well as their great power, is what makes them so useful to organizations.

TERMS FOR REVIEW

users	efficiency	environment
microcomputers	productivity	software
micros	effectiveness	hardware
minicomputers	system	firmware
minis	subsystems	data
superminis	organizational	commands
mainframe	systems	memory
computers	management	processor
supercomputers	system	applications
sole proprietorship	information systems	software
consultants	input	system software
partnerships	processing	peripherals
corporations	output	
shareholders	feedback	

TERMINOLOGY CHECK

For each of these definitions, choose the correct term from the list of Terms for Review:

1. The area within a computer where data, and instructions, are arranged and stored so that they are immediately accessible.

2. Process by which a computer checks results and automatically makes adjustments or responds to commands from the user.

3. Organizational structure which facilitates generating important information, and passing it between individuals, departments, and even organizations.

4. Devices attached to computers that perform particular tasks of input, processing and output.

5. A set of instructions which directs a computer to perform a particular task, usually stored in magnetic form.

6. A person who utilizes the services of a computer for a particular task.

7. Software programs that direct the input, processing, and output functions of a computer for particular organizational tasks.

8. A large and versatile computer run by computer professionals and primarily used by large corporations and government agencies.

9. Any set of related components that work consistently together, according to established principles and procedures, usually for a specific purpose.

10. A specific instruction for the computer that is entered by the user through the keyboard.

INFORMATION CHECK

1. Name four classes of computers.

2. What features help you distinguish between the classes of computers?

3. List and briefly describe five types of organizations.

4. How do organizations differ from each other?

5. List three characteristics shared by different types of organizations.

6. What three words are often used to describe the benefits that computers can bring to an organization? Define each.

7. How do organizations set up systematic ways to achieve their goals?

8. What do all systems have in common?

9. What is the purpose of a subsystem?

10. What makes systems useful to organizations?

11. Briefly describe a management system.

12. What is the purpose of an information system?

13. Why are computers well suited to handle systematic work?

14. Use the description of a system presented in Chapter 1 to identify the features of a computer that make it a system.

15. Identify and describe the five important elements of computer systems.

PROJECTS AND PROBLEMS

1. Each year large corporations prepare an annual report that is sent to each stockholder. Likewise, each year your college prepares a report for its board of trustees. In both situations the document describes last year's accomplishments and outlines next year's plans.

   Obtain copies of both an annual report from a corporation in your area and your school's report to the trustees. Using the characteristics shared by all organizations (as outlined in Chapter 1), write a short paper comparing the characteristics of the corporation with those of your school.

2. Interview the chief of your school's security force and the chief or other high official of your local police force. In your interviews, ask how each system functions in terms of input, processing, output, feedback, and environment. Then write a brief report, making sure you answer the following questions: What are the similarities between the two systems? What are the differences? Are computers used to help the systems function? How?

3. Many articles have been written in recent years about management and information systems. Read an article in a recent periodical about an aspect of management and information systems that particularly interests you, and write a summary about what you have read.

2

Information systems and computer systems

To work effectively in an organization, people must be informed. Think back to the beginning of the previous chapter. You were waiting for your new manager to come and explain your tasks to you. Without information about what you are expected to do, it would be very difficult to perform effectively on the job.

Your manager may communicate this information through conversation. A lot of information is communicated this way, but in organizations, a large amount is also written down. Your manager would probably give you a package of materials to read that may include a formal job description, a little background about the company, and some basic instructions for using the computer system. You may be asked to fill out forms with information for the payroll department to process your paycheck. Written information is valuable because it can be studied at leisure. There is no danger that points will be missed because the presentation was too fast. And it can be kept and reviewed later, either by studying it in depth or just by scanning it for points that might have been forgotten.

Information is needed at all levels of an organization. For people to work together, they must know what others are doing, and they must tell others what to do. In addition, people need information about the world outside their particular organization to help them make the right decisions. In fact, information is one of the most important resources an organization needs to function effectively.

Organizations handle a vast amount of information. Information comes in the mail, it is sent in by the salespeople, it comes by telephone, it is drafted by managers, it is typed up by office workers, it is stored in file cabinets and records centers. For all of this information to be handled properly, efficient information systems are needed.

The center of the information systems of any organization is usually the office. This chapter will look at types of office information systems and see how new efficiencies are being achieved through automation by the computer. Document preparation is now largely handled by computers that use word processing. Information storage and records management rely more and more on the computer, not only to keep track of records, but also to store them. Information is increasingly being distributed electronically, through the use of computers, rather than by paper. And data analysis, the processing of structured, numerical information, is a major role of the computer in any organization.

You will also learn in this chapter how these information systems can be viewed as subsystems of a larger entity—the office itself. The more that the office can combine the various systems it has for processing information, the more effectively the information can be used by the organization as a whole.

When you have read this chapter, you will be able to:

- explain the importance of systematic information handling in any organization

- describe several methods of document production

- discuss alternative ways of using computers in information storage and records management

- explain some advantages of distributing information electronically

- explain how systems for information analysis aid decision making in modern organizations

- clarify the relationship between hardware, software, people, and information systems

Information and the office

The center of all information activity in an organization is the office. This is true from the smallest business to the largest organization. It is in the office that a retail store owner totals earnings for the day, keeps track of inventory, prepares mailings to customers, and pays bills to vendors. It is in office areas that a large corporation processes the payroll, develops reports, keeps track of tax-related expenses, and handles most other information tasks. There are office areas set aside in manufacturing plants where managers and their assistants gather data, prepare reports, and write memos. There are sales offices nationwide, which receive order information from salespeople in the field, pass it on to other departments in their organizations, and perform analyses and comparisons for salespeople and management. And there are offices in government agencies where clerks process the many forms that are received from the general public so that officials can make critical decisions based on the information they have gathered and studied.

Figure 2-1 Computers Here, There, and Everywhere

The microcomputer in this restaurant serves this organization as it would a more traditional computer user, by inputting, processing, outputting, storing, distributing, and providing feedback on sales and inventory data. (Courtesy of Texas Instruments)

DIFFERENT KINDS OF INFORMATION

The major task of offices is to process information, both words and numbers. When an order is sent for equipment or supplies, the order form carries information. This is used to specify the numbers and types of equipment wanted, and it is kept for future reference, perhaps to build a general picture of equipment demand during the year. When a memo is sent to a worker with instructions on a specific project, it provides information without which the particular task could not be accomplished. Exchange of information is essential to organizations; few could exist without it.

For example, suppose an office worker mistakenly omits a sentence from a memo telling other employees how to fill out a new expense account form. The missing information might lead to hundreds of incorrect forms, giving the accounting department incomplete data. Chances are that everyone will have to fill out a new form; the time spent correcting the mistake will therefore cost the organization considerable time and money. Or suppose that an administrative assistant doesn't get around to preparing and mailing a thank-you letter to a client. The client may turn business over to a competitor who is more courteous. Such oversights can lose other clients as well, and the organization's business may suffer.

Even when information is passed on by word of mouth, the office is heavily involved. Decisions made during meetings must be recorded as written minutes. Memos are often sent to confirm the content of telephone calls. Messages must be taken if people are away from their desks. And increasingly, the telephone is being used to convey written as well as spoken messages.

SYSTEMS FOR HANDLING INFORMATION

Throughout this century, offices and office workers have played a vital part in keeping the various parts of an organization informed and in communicating with the world outside the organization. Like workers in other areas of business, they have always tried to do this as efficiently and systematically as possible.

Instead of having each person carry messages to their intended recipients, for example, a central mail room is commonly set up, with messengers delivering along organized routes. Mail rooms are systems: office mail is *input* into the mail trays, *processed* by being collected and sorted,

Figure 2-2   The Computer in the Mail Room
Alongside traditional equipment, the computer often plays an important role in shipping materials. Not only can it send its own messages electronically—it can also calculate the least expensive option for shipping particular items. And it can generate address labels by the score. (Courtesy of Hewlett-Packard Company)

and *output* when it is delivered. And if the system is inefficient and people complain, this *feedback* can lead to the mail room being reorganized to give better service.

Similarly, records management systems are often developed using file folders, file cabinets, and specialized clerks. This helps to minimize the danger of losing documents, which is almost inevitable when so much paperwork changes hands. And traditional secretarial pools used to exist in which typists could work on documents for many managers. This prevented uneven workloads and increased efficiency.

Today, the computer has been brought into office systems. Automating the office has brought significant savings to businesses and has also vastly increased the amount of information that organizations can use to reach their goals. Thus, office workers are processing far more information than before, enabling their organizations to be better informed for decision making.

Automating the office includes several areas, each of which contributes greatly to the efficient flow of information through an organization. These areas include:

- document production

- information storage and retrieval

- information distribution

- information analysis

When these areas are coordinated or connected so that information from one can be used in another, even greater efficiencies can be achieved.

Document production

The documents produced in an organization are the basic carriers of information from person to person and from organization to organization. They include letters; forms; memos; handouts and minutes for meetings; financial, inventory, and sales reports; proposals; and legal contracts, just to name a few. All these must be prepared thoughtfully and clearly so that they can be accurately and quickly understood. Handwritten documents are used only very rarely—for short notes with a personal touch or for extremely urgent communications. Sometimes they serve as input to a document production system, along with dictated material. Documents are usually produced on a typewriter, an electronic typewriter, or on more advanced equipment for word processing. Whatever equipment the document production system uses, its output is the final document.

THE TYPEWRITER

The typewriter—especially the electric typewriter—is still widely used in many organizations. How long this will remain true it is difficult to say, as major manufacturers have stopped making them. However, many

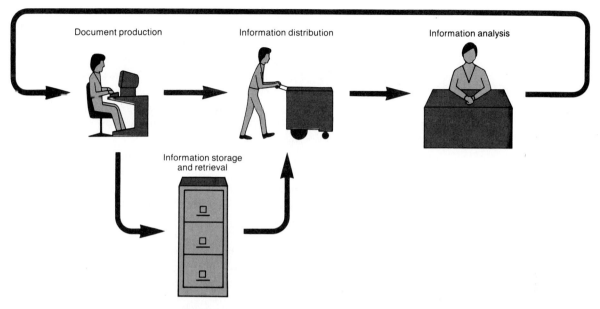

Figure 2-3   Four Areas for Office Automation
Once produced, a document can either be distributed immediately or stored for
later retrieval and distribution. When a document is received it is analyzed. Often
this analysis leads to the production of a new document.

strongly built older typewriters still survive in offices to provide added
keyboarding facilities when the need arises.

Typewriters are used in many ways. Executives with keyboarding
skills may occasionally dash off a memo directly on a typewriter. More
often they will dictate a note, either directly to an office worker at a
typewriter or to someone who takes shorthand and will type the document
later. A third option involves dictating the words onto a cassette recorder
or similar recording system, a technique also used with computerized
word processing. The message is later transcribed at the typewriter by a
member of the support staff.

But typewriters are no longer the most efficient equipment for document production, especially when repetitive typing or revision is involved. Preparing documents at the typewriter may involve doing the
same work several times, with or without minor changes. This is true
when identical but original-looking letters need to be sent to a number
of people—for example, to clients who have not paid their bills. It is also
true when a report is being prepared and needs to go through several
drafts before the writer is satisfied it is correct. Both these situations are
very common in a typical office, and both take up a lot of time when the
standard typewriter is used.

THE ELECTRONIC TYPEWRITER

Because revisions and repetitive typing are laborious to do on an electric
typewriter, the electronic typewriter is the new standard in many offices.

Document revision and rapid production of multiple copies of original-quality documents can be done easily with the **electronic typewriter.** This is a much more advanced machine than the electric typewriter because it stores keystrokes. In effect, it can "remember" a whole sequence of letters, spaces, and carriage returns that are keyboarded into it; then it can produce the same sequence over and over again. The keystrokes are electronically held in a memory, or magnetically recorded onto small floppy disks of the type used in microcomputers. Earlier versions of the computer used magnetic cards, magnetic tapes, and even punched paper tapes to store the keystrokes.

The electronic typewriter's storage capacity makes it a far more flexible and useful office tool than electric or manual typewriters. Not only can electronic typewriters store and then reproduce whole documents, but they can also handle many other repetitive, time-consuming typing tasks, such as the production of contracts, leases, insurance policies, and other standard documents. These tasks are less expensive and less tedious with the electronic typewriter's memory capabilities than with the standard typewriter. Today, a document specialist need only type the specific

Figure 2-4   Between Manual and Computer Systems
This electronic typewriter is ideal for tasks that are too time consuming for a traditional typewriter yet too simple to justify the cost of a computer. (Courtesy of Xerox Corporation)

pieces of information needed for a particular document—new names, new figures, new legal clauses. The electronic typewriter memory holds and prints out the rest of the standard document. The final result is a unique original document, but one that did not need to be typed from beginning to end.

Many electronic typewriters can also merge, or combine, form letters with mailing lists. This means that instead of stopping to allow the operator to enter a particular piece of information, the machine pauses while printing the document, retrieves a name and address from a mailing list in another part of its memory, and then continues printing the document. For the next copy of the document, it retrieves the next name in the mailing list. Thus, with almost no effort from the operator, personalized, original-quality letters can be sent to hundreds of potential customers or contributors by businesses, charitable institutions, and political organizations.

Another important feature of the electronic typewriter is its correcting ability. To a limited extent, the electronic typewriter permits text changes, so that a word, phrase, or line can be deleted or altered; the typewriter adjusts the spacing of the other words automatically. In fact, many models have small display screens that show a portion of one line of text. This allows you to see the changes as you are making them, before printing the document.

WORD PROCESSING

In the early years of computing, computers were used only for data processing—calculating with numbers and doing other logical tasks. Preparing written documents, a less logical operation relying far more on human judgment, was still done with typewriters, including early versions of the electronic typewriter.

However, computer technology was soon applied to handling language. Software was created that instructed large computers to manipulate words even more efficiently than the leading typewriters of the day. **Dedicated word processors,** computers specialized for preparing written documents, were also developed. Today, microcomputers with word processing software have become a powerful option for performing the same task. And computer technology has also been more fully incorporated into electronic typewriters, giving them almost as many capabilities as microcomputers using word processing software.

In fact, electronic typewriters are often thought of as simple dedicated word processors. However, true dedicated word processors and word processing software have much greater editing and storage capabilities than electronic typewriters. This is because computers using word processing software usually have much larger memories and faster processing speeds than typical electronic typewriters.

Dedicated word processors and word processing software use screens that allow you to view a half to a full page of text and even to compare two parts of a document at one time. They enable you to move large blocks of text from one location in a document to another. They let you type in long phrases by pressing a single key. And they have many other features, as you will read in later chapters.

Information storage and records management

Once documents are produced, they must be stored and retrieved when needed. Correspondents may need to look at earlier letters to reply to a current one; managers may want a previous month's sales report to compare with a current month's report; lawyers may wish to review earlier contract arrangements with a client to see what changes may be necessary or desirable in a new contract. These documents are **records,** information created, received, or kept for use in doing business. Office workers must be able to find records quickly and easily for the office to function smoothly and efficiently. Records can traditionally be found in office files.

FILING SYSTEMS

Most organizations, large and small, have several filing systems operating simultaneously. Usually, a central filing system contains copies of all important documents sent and received. In addition, there are departmental and individual files that contain currently used documents, or what might be called "working papers." All office personnel must have easy access to their organization's records if they are to perform their jobs properly. Records that are difficult to reach or that cannot be found cause delays, frustration, and, frequently, loss of income. Controlling an organization's records, called **records management,** helps office workers locate information quickly and easily.

Records must be stored logically if they are to be found easily. This logical arrangement of records constitutes the filing system and is usually geared to the way in which the records are used by the organization. Each file folder has a **caption** written on it—a name or number to help locate it—and the files are arranged in logical order according to their captions. In many filing systems the caption on each file is the name of a person, business, government agency, or whatever is convenient for workers in the particular organization, and the files are arranged in alphabetical order. Some systems are arranged geographically, by country, state, or region. Filing systems can also be arranged numerically. For example, legal records of court cases are filed by docket number, and government agencies, insurance companies, and banks may use social security or account numbers as file captions, arranged in an ascending or descending sequence. Another filing technique is chronological indexing, in which documents are captioned by date and arranged in the order they were sent or received.

A problem with all these filing systems is that if the key caption is not known, it is difficult or impossible to locate the record. Suppose, for example, that an insurance company receives a letter about an automobile collision that involved two of its policyholders. The file system is numerical, by policy number, but the letter identifies the policyholders only by name. Without a **cross-index** it would be impossible to find their files. A cross-index is a separate card file or list that names all policyholders in alphabetical order together with their policy numbers. Cross-indexes are often essential; however, extensive cross-indexing of paper documents

STATE OF THE ART

Information Power

Access to crucial business information can bring power and importance to a department or an individual employee. Because of this, many groups within an organization may be seeking access to—or control over—the computers that process its information. Through the years, these conflicting demands have led to several significant shifts in the way large organizations approach the control of their computer systems.

In the earliest days of business computing, the data processing (DP) department controlled the flow of information. DP was seen as an elite group of programmers and engineers; this perception was reinforced by the fact that DP staffs usually worked in isolated, glass-enclosed rooms especially designed for their computers. Because DP specialists were the only employees who understood how to operate these giant number-crunching machines, they were the only ones with complete access to their organization's computerized information.

As computer systems became more sophisticated in the 1960s and early 1970s, the pendulum began to swing away from strict control of information by the DP department. Managers wanted access to their employers' business data and demanded periodic reports. Thus, in many organizations, DP departments evolved into management information system (MIS) departments. The MIS concept recognizes that information is a valuable resource that must be available to managers, not just computer specialists.

Still, the pendulum had not swung far enough for many managers. Although MIS provided a series of systems designed to give managers timely information, managers continued to encounter backlogs that delayed the reports they requested. The expense of developing new systems also continued to frustrate managers.

For many managers, the advent of the microcomputer brought an end to many of these frustrations. Now each manager could purchase a computer and software at a relatively low cost to produce information without waiting for MIS. Processing of information became fully decentralized.

With decentralization, however, came a lack of control. Managers purchased hardware and software without consulting the MIS department. These computers were often incompatible with each other or the company's larger computers, so they could not exchange data. In addition, MIS was unable to provide training and support for the growing number of software and hardware products used in the office. In some organizations, employees using micros introduced errors in important data. The flow of information had gone out of control.

The information center represents the pendulum's swing toward a midpoint where an MIS department supports and controls decentralized computing by employees. As part of the MIS department, an information center may establish policies regarding computer use, provide training and technical support, and make the company's data available to end users with controls to safeguard its accuracy.

Figure 2-5 Managing the Paper Glut
Even a single piece of data is valuable. It can be applied to many transactions and thus can affect the bottom line. Computerized filing systems have maximized the value of that single piece of data by allowing quick and accurate cross-indexing of the contents of a file. (Courtesy of Hewlett-Packard Company)

can be very time-consuming. Consequently, it isn't always done, so retrieving documents from files can sometimes be an inefficient and difficult process.

Another major problem with preserving records on paper is that paper takes up a great deal of room—especially since several copies of a single document may be kept in different places. Given the information explosion that most organizations are now experiencing, more and more space is required to house these records. Storage areas cost money but do not directly produce income; hence, from a business point of view, they are not a good use of space. To offset this uneconomical use of space, more and more organizations are shifting their records from traditional paper files to film or electronic data banks.

MICROGRAPHICS

To save space, documents can be photographically reduced in a process called **micrographics.** The resulting **microforms**—the pieces of film which hold the tiny images—provide enormous savings in space and therefore in cost. Paper documents are photographed and reduced to as much as 1/100th of their original size; many document pages are kept on one small piece of film. The most common microforms are **microfilm,** a continuous roll of film, and **microfiche,** a sheet of film about the size of an index card. Microforms are read on special readers and reader-printers, which you may have seen or used in the library (see Figure 2-6).

The camera that produces a microform can also code the film with index marks so that specific documents can be retrieved automatically.

THE HUMAN SIDE

The Paperless Office: An Idea Whose Time Hasn't Come

When computers began to sweep through the business world, many experts envisioned a "paperless office" in the near future. Electronic technology had made it possible to create, distribute, and store all kinds of business records electronically, from personnel data to management reports to purchase orders. Therefore, the experts reasoned, people would no longer need to record most business information on paper.

So far, the paperless office has proved to be elusive. Take the case of Reliance Insurance Company. In 1979, Reliance was generating about 27 million sheets of interoffice paper per year, enough to create a paper trail 3,900 miles long! The company launched an effort to eliminate paper for interoffice information. "Paper-free by '83" became the rallying cry.

The passing of 1983 found Reliance far from paper-free. Although it had eliminated mountains of typed memos and forms, mountains of computer printouts had replaced them.

In fact, offices throughout the business world are consuming more paper than ever, and most offices automation experts today see no end to the increase. The reason for this is twofold. Organizations are generating more information than ever; and most people still want paper copies.

Computers, spreadsheets, and other new tools enable organizations to produce many kinds of business information that can't be generated without them, or, at least, that could not be generated in time to be useful. Much of this new information has become routine, and most is ending up on paper.

Moreover, business people are still demanding printed copies of memos, reports, and other documents even when they're sent through electronic mail. Experts now say that computer input microfilm (CIM) technology offers the best hope for reducing the volume of paper-based information, but even CIM isn't likely to reverse the trend.

Most people, apparently, are more comfortable with paper copies. A piece of paper has several advantages over an electronic record: you can put it in your briefcase to read on the train, make marks in the margins, and make copies for people who don't have access to computer communications. Many people have more trust in what they can see and touch, and they dislike relying solely on invisible electrical impulses to preserve vital information.

One paper company predicts that office paper consumption will increase about 5 percent a year for the next several years—and that sales of computer paper will grow much faster. Like it or not, paperwork is apparently here to stay.

Figure 2-6   Microfiche to the Rescue
Many organizations prefer micrographic records. Besides being easier to store, microforms are handled less and thus last longer than paper files. Also, they consist of reduced duplicates of original documents—whereas, for electronic storage, some documents may need to be rekeyboarded. (Courtesy of UMI (University Microfilm International), a Bell & Howell Information Company)

Many microform readers use these marks to locate a particular document page. All you need to do is enter an index number, and the page you want will be displayed on the screen.

With the help of the computer, using microform records is becoming even more convenient, through a technique known as **computer-assisted retrieval (CAR).** You indicate the caption for the document you are looking for, and the computer checks its cross-index and tells you where the microform is stored and which index number to use. Then you can locate the record on the shelf. In more complex systems, the microforms are directly accessible to the computer. The computer not only identifies the location of a particular document, but also finds it for you and displays it automatically on its screen.

Computers and microforms are used together in two other ways. Microfilm can be produced directly from a computer, using **computer output microfilm (COM)** recorders. These make a microform image of a computer document without the need to make a paper document first, which saves considerable time. The other technique is called **computer input microfilm (CIM),** in which a computer reads characters directly from microfilm and enters them into its own memory.

DATABASES AND DATA BANKS

Microforms can store large quantities of documents in a small space, but they still present indexing and retrieval problems, requiring some type of cross-index, whether from a card file or a computer. Computer technology, however, makes it possible to store documents on magnetic tapes and disks. Like microforms, these store large amounts of data in a small space, and they enable the computer to use its power even more effectively for locating information.

Much information stored by organizations is on forms. Forms are highly structured documents and are ideally suited to the systematic nature of computers. A set of forms contains many standard entries. With a paper filing system, or a micrographics system, searches can be done using only one form entry, the key caption—for example, the name or account number of a policyholder. Other entries can be found only by searching each form.

But in a computerized **database,** every entry on a stored form can be used as a key to search with, because the database consists of fully cross-indexed electronic records. Thus, the same insurance record could be located by entering the name, the policy number, the vehicle identification number, or maybe the street address of the policyholder. Lists can also be generated—all owners of a certain model of car, for example,

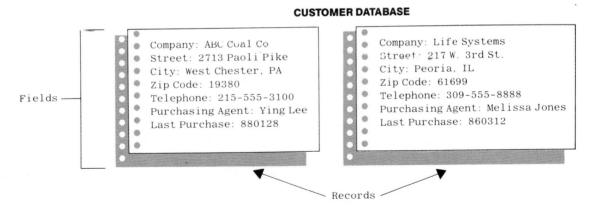

CUSTOMER DATABASE

Company: ABC Coal Co
Street: 2713 Paoli Pike
City: West Chester, PA
Zip Code: 19380
Telephone: 215-555-3100
Purchasing Agent: Ying Lee
Last Purchase: 880128

Company: Life Systems
Street: 217 W. 3rd St.
City: Peoria, IL
Zip Code: 61699
Telephone: 309-555-8888
Purchasing Agent: Melissa Jones
Last Purchase: 860312

Fields

Records

Figure 2-7   Records in an Electronic Database
A database is made up of related records. This database contains the same kinds of information about each of a supplier's customers. Each record is made up of fields. You can locate records by searching any of the fields they include. For example, you could search the Company field for the name ABC Coal Co. to locate that customer's record, or you could search the Telephone field to find all customers within area code 309. By searching the Last Purchase field, you could locate all customers who haven't placed orders since 1986.

or all people who had accidents during the month of May. And even multiple searches can be conducted—all policies with no accident record and a premium over a certain value. This complex ability to sort through and locate information in many combinations has made computer databases one of the key tools of modern information systems.

When several databases are joined, they form a data bank. **Data banks** are like vast libraries because they possess enormous amounts of cross-indexed information. But unlike the information in libraries, a data bank's information can be accessed almost instantly. There are data banks for economic and demographic statistics, stock market prices, sales figures by industry, and other numerically represented types of information. Data banks may also contain documents such as newspaper and magazine articles, court orders, patents, and book and dissertation abstracts. Access to such data banks is often sold to organizations and individuals who need specific information for business or research purposes.

Information distribution

Producing documents and developing various manual and electronic filing systems are extremely valuable activities, but only because they are linked to an information distribution system. Information distribution systems are means by which people communicate with each other—perhaps by telephone, perhaps by letter. Information is transmitted from one individual to another, and usually back again.

When a manager wants to talk to someone in her office, she can pick up the phone. When the same manager has to send a monthly report to her manager, she may send it through the mail room, which then arranges to deliver it manually, mechanically, or electronically. Each of these methods is a way of distributing information.

THE MAIL ROOM

The mail room is the traditional distribution center of an organization. Most paperwork passes through it for delivery to the appropriate places and persons. Basically three kinds of mail arrive in a mail room: mail sent to other organizations or individuals outside; mail received from outside an organization; and mail generated inside and intended for other members of the organization.

All the mail has to be sorted and then delivered. Delivery can be accomplished in several ways. Perhaps the most common is by messenger. Most organizations have staffs of messengers who deliver and pick up mail every day. Some organizations rely on mechanical devices to speed internal delivery of documents and very small parcels. A few very large organizations use automated **computerized mail carts** to pick up and deliver internal mail. The carts are programmed to visit specific locations where they can pick up or deliver mail, to ride elevators from floor to floor on their route, and to stop when they encounter obstacles.

Figure 2-8 Outmoded Automation?
Electronic technology can help to deliver messages around the office, guiding this mailmobile to different areas where workers can pick up their mail. And electronics may also make this device unnecessary. Messages can now be delivered through the computer system itself, by electronic mail. (Courtesy of Bell & Howell, Inc.)

TELEPHONE DISTRIBUTION SYSTEMS

An alternative to sending messages from department to department by messenger is using the telephone. Telephones became invaluable tools for business communications as soon as they were invented and have remained a key office fixture ever since. In fact, modern technology has made them even more valuable.

A long-standing problem with contacting people by phone has been what is commonly called telephone tag. The person you are trying to call is not at his or her desk, but when the call is returned, you are out. Telephone tag can be carried through several rounds before contact is finally made—and a letter often might have been quicker. But telephone tag can now be controlled by the answering machine, which records messages when you are out. An even newer and more powerful invention, called **voice mail,** uses a computer for the same purpose. Not only can it record calls, but it can also save you from having to listen to them all in sequence, because the computer lets you decide which calls you want to handle first. Some voice mail systems also allow you to send a voice message to several recipients at the same time, and their replies will be recorded for you to listen to at leisure.

A major problem with phone calls, however, is that, while fast, they don't leave written records, which are often vital in business. As indicated earlier, these records can be quickly scanned, studied carefully, and kept for future reference. Actually, an even older technology, telegraph, provides a written record of long-distance communication, and is used extensively in the form of **telex** service. A telex system uses typewriter-like terminals to send and receive information over the telephone lines. When the message arrives at a receiving terminal, it is printed automatically.

Another distribution system that uses telephone lines is **facsimile (FAX).** In a FAX system, the sending device scans a document and sends electronic signals to a similar device in a distant location. The electronic signals prompt the receiving unit to print an exact copy of the original document. Not only typed text can be sent by FAX, but also pictures, handwritten copy, graphs, maps, and the like. Facsimile reproduction is a much faster means of transmitting copies of documents than traditional mail service.

The general term for long-distance communications of electronic signals is **telecommunications.** Telecommunications are now handled not only by telephone wires, but also by microwave signals sent via orbiting satellites. And computers too have become deeply involved in this type of information distribution.

COMPUTER-BASED MESSAGE SYSTEMS

Work produced at the computer can be printed out and mailed. It can also be sent electronically across the office, across the nation, or across the world—to be studied on the screen, and perhaps finally printed on paper, only when it reaches its destination.

Computer-based message systems distribute information through linked computers in many ways. Whole databases of information can be sent at high speed from one computer to another. The same information that is available from a computer in New York can be made available to Europe from a London computer. **Computer conferences** take place between individuals; instead of discussing a topic over the phone, workers can link their computers and discuss the topic in writing, leaving a permanent record of their "conversation." **Communicating information processors** allow individuals in different locations to work together on a single report, exchanging words, phrases, and paragraphs as they create the document together. **Electronic mail,** which is similar to voice mail but transmits written messages, is sent via linked computers. All of these are becoming commonplace, as computers work more and more closely with telecommunications media like the telephone.

Information analysis

Much of the information generated by organizations is numerical rather than verbal. All organizations must gather and analyze numerical information. Even to write a paycheck, an employer must analyze information—how many hours did a particular employee work, what is his

Figure 2-9   Getting the Picture

Pictures have been sent by wire to newspapers for more than 50 years—the Associated Press and United Press International have long experience of this process. Modern facsimile systems are useful to many other organizations too—this FAX is portable and can transmit and receive documents on the road or in the office. (Courtesy of Xerox Corporation)

or her base rate, was any overtime involved? And larger issues must also be studied through numerical calculations. Manufacturers, for example, must determine exactly how the prices of raw materials will affect their costs and profits. Merchants need to know which items sell and which are unpopular. This information provides a basis for management decisions about an organization's day-to-day operations, such as whether to restock on a particular item, as well as longer-term decisions, such as whether to raise prices, hire more employees, or open a new branch office.

INFORMATION ANALYSIS BEFORE COMPUTERS

Until fairly recently, information workers had to perform many calculations and analyses by hand, for both simple operations such as totaling a single customer's order, and more complicated jobs, such as sorting and tallying the day's orders for a particular product. Calculations would be performed one at a time, and the answers recorded on a form or worksheet for later use. Mistakes were easy to make, difficult to find, and tedious to correct. Equipment used might include an adding machine, an electronic calculator, and a typewriter to record the figures. For very large scale calculations—for example, analysis of quarterly profits and losses—card punching and sorting machines might have been used. These used cards the size of a dollar bill and were developed by Herman Hollerith to tabulate the 1890 U.S. Census. With filled-in paper forms as input, people operating **keypunch machines** would punch holes at various locations on the cards to represent data. The punched cards were then fed into different machines that located the holes and tabulated the data automatically. The company Hollerith formed to sell these machines eventually became the International Business Machines (IBM) Corporation.

INFORMATION ANALYSIS USING COMPUTERS

When computers first became available, they were applied to the task of manipulating numerical information. Organizations that could afford computers used them to streamline systems that involved the use of numbers—for example, keeping track of customer orders or processing the company payroll. No longer did bills, receipts, and checks have to be calculated and then typed by hand. The computer needed only to be given the relevant data—for example, names, hours worked, and pay rate— and it would perform all calculations and print out the paperwork automatically. These computerized systems, which took care of many basic forms of company transactions, were called **data processing (DP) systems** and were operated by the data processing department.

Later, as computer systems became more powerful, data processing departments also began to develop **management information systems (MISs),** computerized systems that produce reports to keep managers aware of how different departments were functioning. These reports summarized much of the data processing information, providing needed overviews of sales performance, inventory movement, employee productivity, and similar trends. The information was useful to supervisors, middle managers, and top management as they developed plans for the future of the organization. In fact, managers began to demand more and more types of reports for the data processing departments; the DP staff was overloaded with work; and managers began to complain that planning and decision making were hindered by long waits for information.

Today, many organizations still have management information systems based on one or two mainframe computers. But in addition, there may be computer workstations and minicomputers located throughout the organization and linked to the central computers. Access to the management information system has become quicker and easier through this kind of decentralization. It has also become simpler as a result of new software that allows users to create reports without the help of data processing specialists.

The type of information and reports provided by today's management information systems varies greatly. One MIS may provide records of transactions and transaction summaries. This type of information can be useful, for example, to an administrative assistant, who can use a computer workstation linked to the central computer to quickly answer a customer's question about an order.

A sales manager can use data about past sales broken down by product, region, and sales representative to evaluate her department's per-

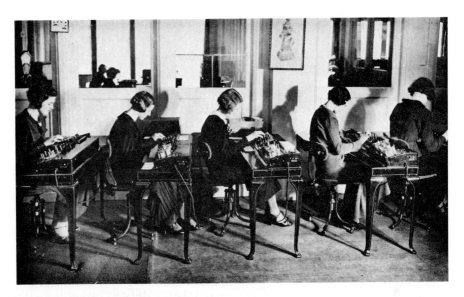

Figure 2-10   Number Crunching
Data processing keypunch operators were early workers for computerized systems. As computers have become more powerful, data processing has grown into information processing. These keypunch operators would today be data entry specialists. (Courtesy of International Business Machines Corporation)

formance over a period of time. She can use the same information to develop a strategy and sales team that will help the organization meet its goals for the year.

Top managers, whose responsibility is for the overall goals of the organization, can use a management information system to access data from linked data banks about industry trends, economic forecasts, and other information about the world outside the organization. Using this information, top managers can make decisions about whether to introduce new products, acquire other companies, issue more stock, and other matters that affect the future of the organization.

THE MICROCOMPUTER IN INFORMATION ANALYSIS

An important element in today's management information systems is the microcomputer. Microcomputer software has been developed that is extremely flexible and helpful for information analysis. Especially when linked to the organization's central computers, microcomputers enable managers and their assistants to develop many different analyses of company data.

The software that enables them to do this is usually designed to be easy to use, or **user friendly.** It does not require specialized computer skills; rather, it is designed for nonspecialists with only a little specific training. Although some packages are more user friendly than others, most microcomputer software can be used by people who have a general understanding of computers.

One of the leading types of microcomputer software for information analysis is called the **spreadsheet.** Using spreadsheets, people can process and analyze numerical information much faster than they can with calculators. A spreadsheet is an image of a large grid displayed on the computer screen, one section at a time. When you enter a new number on a spreadsheet, the computer automatically recalculates any other figures that are affected by the change. Analyses that once required hours of tedious work with an adding machine and a pencil can now be made in minutes, and mistakes can be corrected without recalculating every figure.

Another user-friendly analytic tool available on the micro is **graphics software,** which pictorialize numerical trends. People who develop and analyze numbers must often present their findings in reports or proposals to others, such as higher-ranking executives, stockholders, government officials, or clients. Increasingly, information workers are creating charts, graphs, and other images at the computer to make numerical information easier to understand. A simple pie chart or bar graph can often be used to convey in a flash the main points of a lengthy, hard-to-reach statistical table.

Graphics software, like the spreadsheet, is even more powerful when it runs on a microcomputer that is linked through the central computer to the organization's main databases. This permits data to be analyzed without the labor of keyboarding it into the microcomputer.

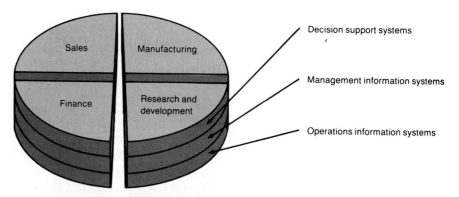

Figure 2-11   Information Systems for Managers
Managers at all levels rely on information systems. For day-to-day decisions, supervisors use operations information systems (OIS), which include records of transactions such as product sales. Traditional management information systems (MIS) produce periodic reports that summarize transactions for middle managers. And top managers making strategic decisions can use decision support systems (DSS). These are characterized by flexibility and the ability to incorporate data from various sources within and outside the organization.

Information systems, computers, and people

Most of the information systems described in this chapter depend on equipment. The computerized information systems depend on both computer hardware and software. But they consist of more than just these elements. As you learned in Chapter 1, organizational systems also involve people.

SOFTWARE, HARDWARE, AND PEOPLE

Software, hardware, and people are closely related in today's computerized information systems. Each depends on the other two. If any of the three were missing, the systems could not function properly.

Software. As discussed in Chapter 1, software instructs the computer on what to do. Most computers can be used in many different information systems and in other types of systems too. Depending on the software, a computer can become a word processing tool, a database tool, a spreadsheet tool, or a tool for any other desired application—for example, controlling a manufacturing process or analyzing marketing statistics.

Hardware. Hardware is, of course, vital to a computerized information system. The software would be meaningless unless it had hardware to instruct. The power of the hardware defines the limits of the system. A small computer can handle only a certain amount of data. Larger computers can handle much more and are powerful enough to work for many users at one time.

People. Without people, the hardware and the software in an information system would have no purpose. People interpret the output from the computer and make decisions based on it. They also make many decisions before the computer starts to run, and often while it is running, to guide the details of the whole operation. In addition, in many computerized information systems people supply essential services, like keyboarding data and words, changing disks, or connecting output devices such as printers. Without the people involved, computerized information systems would be meaningless and unable to function.

INFORMATION SYSTEMS AND COMPUTER SYSTEMS

The interdependence between software, hardware, and people in computerized information systems closely fits the definition of system that was given earlier: a set of related components forming an integrated whole. But it also underscores a difference you may have noticed—between information systems and computer systems. Input to a computer

Figure 2-12   Using and Reusing Information
This computer user, like so many others, is moving information from one system to another. The coded numbers on the merchandise tag, "read" at this point-of-sale terminal, automatically move from the pricing and revenue system at the cash register to the inventory and reordering system in the back of the store. (Courtesy of Sears Roebuck)

is provided by users, who are outside the system itself. But information workers are a *part* of typical information systems, because they handle some of the processing themselves.

In fact, the computer system acts as a subsystem in most computerized information systems. The input to a document production system, for example, is a document presented to the word processing operator, usually by dictation or through handwritten copy. The operator oversees the processing, by keyboarding the document at the computer and entering appropriate commands to change and correct it on the computer.

Similarly, though the computer may output any number of printed versions of the document, the document production system itself has only one major output—the completed document. Figure 2.00 should help you visualize how the computer can be a subsystem of the document production system.

INFORMATION SYSTEMS WORKING TOGETHER

The document production system is itself a subsystem of the overall information processing that goes on within an organization. On occasion a document may be intended for handing directly to a co-worker. More often, though, the document production system's output is turned over to other information systems. Letters and most memos are processed by the

Figure 2-13 Computerized Management

A series of black bars passes over a dark screen that reads them—and suddenly information is exchanged. When the Uniform Product Code (UPC) is passed over an optical character reader (OCR—the dark screen), computer systems interface and provide managers with a storehouse of merchandising information. (Courtesy of International Business Machines Corporation)

mail room, which is an arm of the information distribution system; documents are filed, too, by the information storage system. These systems work together to accomplish the goals of the larger system, which is the organization itself.

The places where two systems "touch" are known as the **interfaces** between the systems. When a document leaves the word processing area and is sent to the mail room, it crosses the interface and enters a new subsystem. Similarly, when a table of accounting figures is incorporated into a report, it crosses the interface between the information analysis system and the document production system.

Moving information from one system to another can involve a lot of waste. The traditional method of preparing a financial report required an office worker to retype figures provided by the accounting department. Keystrokes had to be repeated, and all of the figures had to be carefully

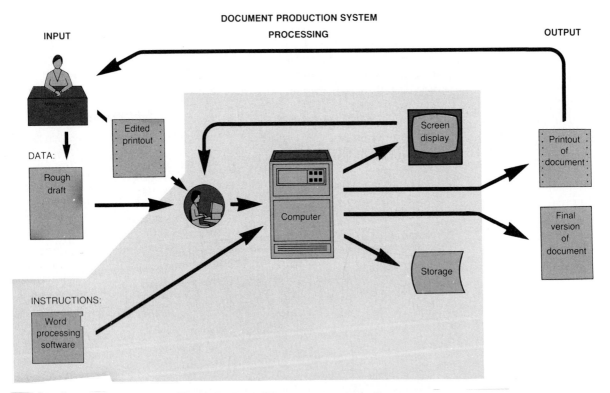

Figure 2-14   A Computer Subsystem

Increasingly, computer systems are vital parts of information systems. Both systems have input, processing, output, and feedback. A manager's rough draft serves as input for the document production system, and the finished document is the output. But for the computer subsystem input consists of the word processing specialist's keyboarding and the word processing software, and output includes a screen display and an electronic version stored on disk. Notice each system's feedback—screen display to the specialist, and draft printout for the manager.

checked. Anybody who has worked with figures knows how easy it is to make mistakes and, once made, how hard they are to find and correct.

However, computer technology can simplify these interfaces considerably. For example, when data is processed in a computer, the results do not have to be printed out and then retyped into a document. Instead, they can be output from a management information system in electronic form and input directly into the document production system. The two systems are **integrated,** or combined, and considerable time is saved.

ORGANIZATIONS, INFORMATION, AND PEOPLE

Accuracy and speed of information processing are vital to organizations. That is why the computer has so quickly earned a place at the heart of so many information systems. However, the effect has not been to lessen the amount of time spent on information work but rather to increase organization's appetites for information. Information is a very important resource for businesses and other organizations. With good information, much faulty guesswork and many misleading hunches can be avoided. Therefore, as ability to handle information has increased, the desire for information has also grown. Organizations have found that, the more information they can process, the more effectively they can reach their goals.

This increased appetite for information has made automating the office unlike automating other sites—for example, manufacturing plants. Office automation has increased the variety of jobs available. As you will read in Chapter 3, the nature of the work is changing, but it is not diminishing. People are, in fact, the only element in information systems that cannot easily be replaced. Before computers were developed, there were information systems, just as there were manufacturing systems before there were machines. Whenever people get together with a task to do, or better still, a task to repeat, they do better if they devise a system to accomplish that task. The system may involve tools, machines, even computers, but it would not function without people.

SUMMARY

■ Information of interest to organizations is traditionally handled in offices. It includes many varieties, ranging from letters to bulletins, to contracts, to basic transactional data, to financial reports. Like other elements in an organization, information is most productively handled if systems are set up to handle it. Automation of the office has brought the power of the computer to many organizational information systems.

■ Document production systems prepare business letters, memos, and bulletins, as well as such forms as legal contracts, invoices, and receipts. Traditionally handled at the typewriter and, more recently, the electronic typewriter, these tasks are today frequently done on the computer by using word processing software.

■ Information must be stored so that it can be found easily. Records management involves paper, micrographics, and electronic filing systems. Information storage is now assisted by computer technology, both in keeping track of where records are kept and in actually holding records in electronic or magnetic form rather than on paper.

■ Distribution of words and data was for a long time the exclusive business of the mail room and U.S. Postal Service (for written messages) and the telephone (for oral messages). Today computer technology is used to send written messages and data, both from one person to another and from one computer to another.

■ Information analysis, once performed by clerks with adding machines, is now usually done by the computer. Large computers were originally used to handle basic data processing and to provide management information, but now microcomputers too play an important part, using spreadsheet, graphics, and other software to analyze and present information.

■ Information systems today may rely on the computer as a component, but they also involve many people—both the workers and managers who use them and the many people who plan how they will be used and who work to make these uses possible. Thus, a modern information system involves computer hardware, computer software, and people to expedite the efficient use of information by an organization.

TERMS FOR REVIEW

electronic
  typewriter
dedicated word
  processors
records
records
  management
caption
cross-index
micrographics
microforms
microfilm
microfiche
computer-assisted
  retrieval (CAR)

computer output
  microfilm (COM)
computer input
  microfilm (CIM)
database
data banks
computerized mail
  carts
voice mail
telex
facsimile (FAX)
telecommunications
computer-based
  message systems
computer conferences

communicating
  information
  processors
electronic mail
keypunch machines
data processing
  (DP) systems
management
  information
  systems (MISs)
user friendly
spreadsheet
graphics software
interfaces
integrated

TERMINOLOGY CHECK

For each of these definitions, choose the correct term from the list of Terms for Review:

1. A set of fully cross-indexed electronic records, organized in such a way that they can be easily sorted and searched.

2. Easy to use and requiring only a little training, usually referring to software and how it is designed.

3. A computerized system that produces reports for managers and other employees of an organization, routinely analyzing trends in the functioning of different departments.

4. A computerized system for receiving phone messages when you are away from your phone, which often also allows you to send a spoken message to several recipients.

5. A worksheet or type of table displayed on a computer screen used to create, process, and analyze numerical information quickly.

6. The point at which two information systems overlap, where information passes from one to the other.

7. Computers specialized for preparing written documents.

8. Systems that permit the distribution of information through linked computers in many ways.

9. The photographic reduction and storage of documents as tiny images on film.

10. Combined in a way that they function smoothly together, often used to describe systems where the output of one becomes the input of another.

INFORMATION CHECK

1. Why is it important for an organization to handle information systematically?

2. What four major areas of office information handling have been automated by computer?

3. List three document production tools and the advantages and limitations of each.

4. What could happen if office personnel cannot locate their records easily and quickly?

5. List and briefly describe four filing systems.

6. Describe a problem associated with filing systems and the method used to resolve it.

7. Describe at least three ways computers are used in information storage and retrieval.

8. What features have made computer databases one of the key tools of information systems?

9. List and briefly describe several machine-based information distribution systems.

10. What are some advantages of distributing information electronically?

11. What kinds of numerical information do organizations typically need to analyze?

12. What are the traditional computerized systems for collecting and analyzing information? What do they accomplish?

13. What is a decentralized management information system?

14. Name and describe two types of microcomputer software used by today's managers for numerical analysis.

15. What are the key components of an information system? Why is each necessary?

PROJECTS AND PROBLEMS

1. Suppose you are an administrative assistant at one of the factories responsible for bottling Dilly Deli gourmet pickles. The demand for pickles increases tremendously three weeks before major holidays. Mr. Dill, the corporation's chief executive officer, wants to be sure that all of his factories will be ready for the Fourth of July.

   You have been asked to prepare a report for Mr. Dill demonstrating to him that your factory is prepared for the increased production load. Do not write the report now; instead, describe the types of information systems you will use to prepare the report and what you will use them for. For example, what kinds of information will you need? And what schedule will you follow—would you use word processing first, or last? You can choose whether Dilly Deli is an old-fashioned company or one with state-of-the-art technology.

2. Visit an office equipment store that sells both electronic typewriters and word processing software and equipment. Ask someone to demonstrate both. What can each do that the other can't? What types of companies typically buy each? Are certain tasks more appropriate for one and not for the other? Write a report comparing the two. Use sales literature to illustrate your report. Share your report and the literature with the class.

3. Visit a small business that uses a manual filing system. Write a short report describing the type of business and the filing system currently used. How are new files started? How are existing files located? What type of cross-reference system is used? Has the company investigated computerizing its filing? If yes, what has it tried? If not, why not?

4. Talk with a reference librarian in your school or local library. Does the library use microforms? What kind? Where are they produced? How are they filed? Does the library have access to large commercial data banks? If yes, who can use it? How much does it cost? How long has it been available? What other information and databases are available? If your college has more than one library, are the database facilities available in each?

   Tape your interview, or write a report in interview format.

3

Information careers in many fields

By altering the way organizations gather, process, and distribute the information they need for doing business, computer technology has brought about dramatic changes in the workplace. Computers have changed the way many traditional jobs are performed. In some cases they have altered the natures of those jobs. And computer technology has created positions that didn't exist when employers relied on less efficient, manual methods of handling information. Thus, computers have altered not only individual jobs but also the job market as a whole.

Computer technology has provided new tools for many traditional tasks and thus changed the ways in which organizations can accomplish those tasks. This has often shifted lines of responsibility. Once, a traditional secretary might have done all the typing and filing for one manager, for example. Today, that person might be an administrative assistant, performing these and other tasks on a computer for several managers. Also, more frequently than before, the managers themselves may work at the keyboard to draft a letter or to gain access to important information. At the same time, in some organizations, document production and information storage may be done by specialists working on special equipment in a center; this could free the administrative assistant's time for broader, and frequently more interesting, administrative responsibilities. These might include analyzing data, helping to set up a project, and performing other tasks once considered nonclerical.

Today organizations hire people to work with data in ways that did not exist or were of little practical use before the computer revolutionized information systems. As discussed in Chapters 1 and 2, computers can help organizations and their employees process important new kinds of information. Computers are also enabling employees to distribute and use the output quickly, thereby improving the organization's effectiveness.

Organizations in all fields are relying increasingly on computers. They must often hire additional people to plan, implement, and maintain their computer systems. They need workers who can make computer purchase decisions, repair computers when they malfunction, write special software, and teach other workers how to use computers for specific information processing tasks. But most of all, they need a support staff, and managers, who are able to work with computers and handle the tasks described in the previous chapter.

Not long ago, computers were used almost exclusively by large organizations, such as major corporations, large universities, and federal and state government departments. Today, organizations of all sizes are using computers to process information. In small schools as well as large ones, for example, office workers are using computers to keep track of class schedules and students' grades as well as budgets and other information. Small local businesses have computerized their payroll, inventory, and billing procedures. For example, your doctor's office assistant may use a computer to store medical information about you and other patients and to retrieve it quickly when it's needed.

This chapter looks at the range of opportunities for information workers who are at ease with computers. It will discuss the roles played by these workers in organizations large and small and describe some specific jobs that involve the use of computers.

When you have studied this chapter, you should be able to:

- name several jobs in which people work primarily with input, others where they're directly involved with processing, and some jobs that involve the use of output

- describe how general administrative support workers use computers to help them perform their tasks

- list and briefly describe specialized information processing positions

- describe the positions of workers whose responsibility is to implement computer systems for organizations

Types of information jobs

Information is the lifeblood of any organization. Employees need it to do their jobs and to help the organization achieve its goals and compete effectively in the marketplace. Therefore, information must flow through the organization smoothly and efficiently. It must be available to people when they need it, in forms that are useful to them.

Organizations usually have several systems for processing different kinds of information, as discussed in Chapter 2. There may be systems for producing verbal documents, processing the payroll, and handling customers' orders, for example, as well as for processing other kinds of business information that are important to an organization. Although each of these systems has its own kinds of input, processing, and output, the systems may, however, be integrated so that output from one can go through an interface and serve as input for another.

SALES INFORMATION SYSTEM

OTHER SYSTEMS

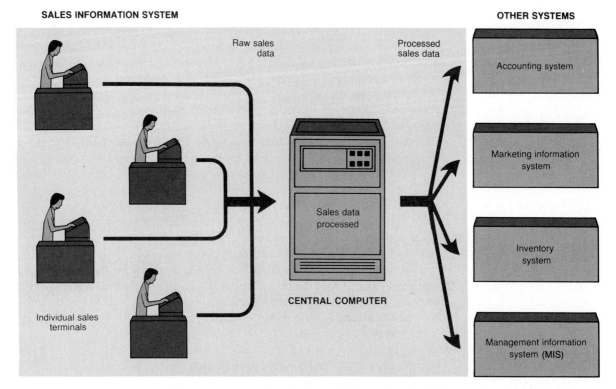

Figure 3-1 Ouput Becomes Data for Other Systems
Sales data is used by many systems in a business. Accounting uses it to calculate revenue and develop financial statements. Marketing uses it for planning and to judge the effectiveness of current campaigns. Inventory uses the data as the basis for reordering products. And MIS develops reports on the effectiveness of the organization and expected trends.

In smaller and less traditional organizations, the same workers and managers often work with several different information systems. One person may keyboard letters and memos, process customer orders, and even, in a very small organization, prepare the payroll in addition to maintaining the files, scheduling appointments, answering telephones, and greeting visitors. That person or, indeed, many members of an office staff may be involved with the input, processing, and output of information for a variety of business systems.

The larger and more traditional an organization is, however, the more likely its information workers are to be specialized, each performing a specific set of tasks within a single system. People who process payroll information, for example, have little or nothing to do with processing bills. Thus, there are a number of different jobs, each one requiring slightly different backgrounds and skills.

In addition to general and specialized jobs involving the use of computerized information systems, there are jobs that focus on the computer itself. These jobs are held by people who design, purchase, sell, maintain, and repair computer systems, write software, and teach other people how to use computers in their work. Not all of these jobs require backgrounds in programming, engineering, or other highly technical areas. Many people in these jobs started out as office workers, and through experience or training they have moved into more technical positions.

The remainder of this chapter will look at a variety of these jobs—from general office support to specialized positions. The jobs are open to workers who are familiar with computers. You will learn what tasks employees perform in these jobs and how they fit into the different information systems.

General administrative support

In many organizations, each office support worker performs a wide variety of tasks for one or more managers. These tasks may involve some or all of the computerized information systems discussed in Chapter 2. Experienced administrative support employees are in great demand in all types of businesses and have good potential for career growth.

SKILLS REQUIRED FOR ADMINISTRATIVE SUPPORT EMPLOYEES

Because administrative support positions vary greatly from organization to organization and indeed from department to department, the skills and experience required for each position will differ. Among the qualities that administrative support employees must possess are keyboarding skills; familiarity with office equipment, including transcription equipment and computers; and a comfortable feeling about learning how to use unfamiliar technology.

Language skills are just as important to job success as office skills. Many of the tasks performed by administrative support employees involve communicating with managers, co-workers, vendors, and customers. The ability to communicate clearly and accurately, using proper grammar, punctuation, and spelling, ensures that information is transmitted and understood properly so that mistakes are not made.

ADMINISTRATIVE SUPPORT POSITIONS

Openings for administrative support personnel who are familiar with computers can be found in organizations of all types and sizes. You could work for one or several managers, in a professional firm, a corporation, a government agency, or virtually any other kind of organization.

Your duties as an administrative assistant may consist of traditional responsibilities such as document production and filing or may include assisting with financial or research tasks. In some organizations, experienced administrative assistants are promoted to supervisory positions,

Figure 3-2 The Administrative Assistant's Net Worth
Computer technology has put the spotlight on administrative assistants. These computer users have mastered diversified skills. They use the computers in their workstations for word processing, accessing databases, and electronic filing, scheduling, and calendaring. (Courtesy of Wang Laboratories, Inc.)

sometimes called administrative support supervisors, or office managers, responsible for overseeing the work of a group of office support workers. Other administrative assistants who demonstrate exceptional ability may be promoted into the ranks of management.

Administrative assistant. An **administrative assistant** may produce documents, file, answer the telephone, make travel arrangements, greet visitors, and schedule appointments. In addition to using a computer for word processing tasks, the assistant may use it to prepare financial forecasts for a product or department, to retrieve information from the company's database, or to distribute information electronically. In other words, the administrative assistant performs whatever office support tasks are necessary to assist his or her managers.

Let's say you work as an administrative assistant to the northwest regional sales manager of a company that manufactures ski equipment. How might you use computer technology to assist you with your many responsibilities?

Your organization does not produce enough written documents to justify hiring specialists in word processing. Thus you are typically involved in all phases of word processing yourself. In addition to inputting your manager's letters and reports and telling the computer how to proc-

Computers at work

Plate 1

Plate 2

Computers, initially used for high-speed complex calculations, now have thousands of applications in business, government and industry. Virtually every aspect of modern life is affected by the computer.

ENIAC, the first general purpose computer, occupied a room 30 feet by 50 feet. It weighed 30 tons, and had no internal memory storage. It could do calculations a hundred times faster than the best calculators then available. However, the vacuum tubes, which provided the computing capability, burned out quickly. As a result, much time was spent locating and replacing burnt-out tubes.

Modern microcomputers, can compute at thousands of times the speed of the ENIAC at a fraction of the weight, size, and cost.

Plate 3

Plate 4

Plate 5

Plate 6

The federal government was one of the earliest users and supporters of computer technology. At first, government computers were used mainly for ballistics research and other military applications. Now, every level of government—federal, state and municipal—uses computers. They perform tasks as varied as weather prediction and mapping, transit control, processing census and tax data, scientific research, economic forecasting, and space exploration.

Plate 7

Plate 8

Industries began to use computers in the 1950s when computer-aided design and computer-aided manufacturing (CAD/CAM) technology was introduced. At first, only big manufacturers, such as the automobile and airplane industries, could use the new technology. But then robotics was introduced in the 1960s; and vastly improved and cheaper, yet vastly more powerful hardware and software were developed in the 1970s. As a result, almost all industries now use computers.

Computer applications in industry now range from planning, design, engineering, and production, to testing of the final product. In addition, computers are used to check production, to keep track of inventory of raw materials and parts, to monitor costs, and to control labor distribution and productivity.

Plate 9

Plate 10

Plate 11

Plate 12

Plate 13

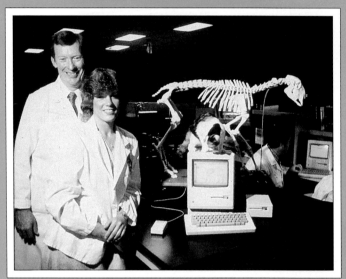

Plate 14

Since the 1970s, the United States economy has been predominantly a service rather than an industrial economy. Among the fastest growing service industries are financial services, travel, and legal services.

Plate 15

Some of the service industries that have benefitted from the use of computers include medicine, law, finance, transportation, and education. Because of the ease and speed with which information can be accessed, accumulated, and compared, the effectiveness of the individual professional is greatly enhanced.

Plate 16

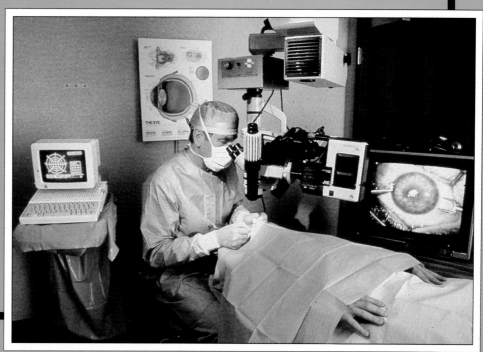

Plate 17

Plate 18

Plate 19

Not since the telephone has a piece of equipment become as pervasive in business as the computer. Over a third of all existing computers are used for customer service purposes. These applications include processing orders, checking inventory of stock, updating customer accounts, verifying credit, and analyzing sales transactions. Other business applications are in company accounting, finance, payroll, and personnel records.

Plate 20

ess them, you are responsible for making copies of the output, distributing it, and filing the disk on which it is recorded.

Even though your organization has centralized records management, you and your manager still keep some documents and other current information at your workstations. In most cases, this information is of use primarily to your department rather than to the organization as a whole. Besides sorting and filing copies of letters and other paper documents in

THE HUMAN SIDE
A Day in the Life of an Administrative Assistant

Joan Simpson works as administrative assistant to two product managers, Maria Ramirez and Kevin Murphy, at a company manufacturing specialized computers for businesses. Here is a record of the tasks she performs on a typical day in the office.

9:00 Joan sorted the mail, deciding which pieces she could handle and which ones required the attention of her managers.

9:15 Joan gave the document production center eight letters from customers requesting product information. She asked them to produce personalized copies of a standard letter she developed earlier about the company's products.

9:30 Using a word processing program, Joan wrote a response to one of Ms. Ramirez's customers who had a question about a recent order.

10:00 The receptionist called to say that a visitor Mr. Murphy was expecting had arrived. Joan escorted the visitor to Mr. Murphy's office.

10:15 Joan made travel arrangements (airline, hotel, and rental car reservations) for Mr. Murphy. Then she wrote an itinerary for him.

11:30 Joan answered phone calls for three administrative assistants while they were at lunch. (Joan's lunch was at 12:30.) The computerized phone system forwarded their calls to her phone automatically. Between calls, Joan did filing.

1:30 Ms. Ramirez gave Joan five bills she received from companies that were developing

brochures for new products. Using her micro, Joan recorded the amount of each bill in a spreadsheet that helps her keep track of budgets. She then submitted the bills to Ms. Ramirez for payment approval, pointing out that one of the bills was much higher than budgeted.

2:30 At Ms. Ramirez's request, Joan set up a meeting with the company submitting the bill that was over budget. Then she used her micro to enter the meeting in Ms. Ramirez's electronic appointment calendar.

2:45 Joan completed the paperwork for payment of the remaining bills.

3:15 Using her word processing software, Joan typed an important report that Mr. Murphy had written in longhand. Then she used other software to check the report for misspellings. Joan gave a printed copy of the report to Mr. Murphy for his approval.

4:30 Mr. Murphy added a new section to the report and made several other changes in the draft. Joan made the changes using the word processing software and printed the revised report for Mr. Murphy. This time he made no changes.

5:00 Joan made photocopies of the report, used her database software to locate the addresses of the people who were to receive copies. She then printed address labels from the database. As she left the office for the day, Joan dropped off the packages at the mail room for overnight delivery.

the department files, you manage the electronic storage and retrieval of information developed on the computers.

For example, you often prepare sales proposals, making offers of equipment to particular ski resorts at particular prices. When these are created at the computer, it is common practice to **save** an electronic version on a magnetic disk, as insurance against loss. This version is kept as an "electronic file" and can be used to generate new paper copies at a later date if they are needed. Just as with paper-based systems, however, electronic files must be systematically organized if they are to be easily located.

Therefore you must establish a system of naming these files consistently. Most computer systems allow only brief file names; these names must be carefully chosen to conform with the computer system's requirements and to enable you and your co-workers to identify any documents you want to retrieve. Then, when the manager wants to reread a proposal she sent to the company president last month, you or she can retrieve it from the electronic files quickly and print a paper copy or view the document on the computer screen.

You may also use an office computer for creating, managing, and using databases. With database management software for microcomputers, you can store and retrieve information in databases that are much smaller and less complex than those used on mainframes. For the ski equipment manufacturer's marketing and sales department, for example, you might maintain a database of information about department stores and sporting goods suppliers in your region. This database might include their names and addresses, their overall annual sales figures, and annual sales figures for your company's products. You and your manager might analyze this information to determine where you need to bolster your marketing efforts.

As an administrative assistant you may also use a micro to access information from mainframe databases. From the organization's central database, you can obtain the company's monthly sales figures broken down by geographic region for each type of equipment it makes. By analyzing these figures, perhaps with spreadsheets and other software, you and the manager could project how many of each product the company can expect to sell in Montana next September.

You might use your micro to retrieve census information from commercial databases about which locales have the largest populations of young professionals, the people most likely to buy skiing equipment. And, for making department travel arrangements, you would contact a database that provides the flight numbers and departure times of all regularly scheduled airline flights. Many kinds of business information you are likely to need, in fact, can be retrieved from a commercial database with a microcomputer.

Administrative support supervisor. Administrative assistants can gain considerable varied experience in a few years on the job. Those looking for greater challenges have several options. The first is to move to a similar position with a higher-level executive in order to be involved with the tasks of managing a company. Another option, becoming more common in recent years because of the administrative assistant's opportunity to demonstrate a wide variety of skills and to learn about the business, is to move to a more specialized position within the company. A third option, available in organizations with large departments of offices, is to become an administrative support supervisor.

An **administrative support supervisor** is responsible for overseeing the work of a group of administrative assistants and other office support staff. In addition to training the staff in work procedures, the supervisor makes sure that the workload in the department is evenly distributed. The administrative support supervisor also serves as a link between managers and administrative support staff when work priorities need to be set and problems solved.

Specialized information processing

Some organizations rely primarily on general support workers like administrative assistants for their information processing. Others make greater use of specialized workers to perform information processing tasks, often locating them in central areas—for example, a main records area—to serve several departments at once. This **centralized structure,** although widespread several years ago, is now yielding to a more flexible arrangement that combines some centralized information systems with general administrative support in the operating departments.

Centralized information processing systems offer many specialized jobs, which are described in the following paragraphs.

DOCUMENT PRODUCTION

Because computerized word processing is rapidly replacing the typewriter for producing documents, men and women with word processing skills are among the workers most sought after today by business organizations of all sizes. In addition to the same keyboard skills typists must have, jobs that use word processing require a general understanding of computers and a familiarity with word processing systems.

If you have word processing skills, you could work as a word processing specialist, perhaps in a document production center. If you have plenty of experience and "people" skills as well, you may be promoted to the position of word processing supervisor or you may become an administrative assistant.

Word processing specialist.   Large organizations, or smaller ones that require a great deal of word processing, often employ **word processing specialists.** These persons often work in centralized areas, where their duties consist solely of producing documents written by a variety of managerial employees. A few organizations have a single document production center; many others have smaller centers, each serving different departments.

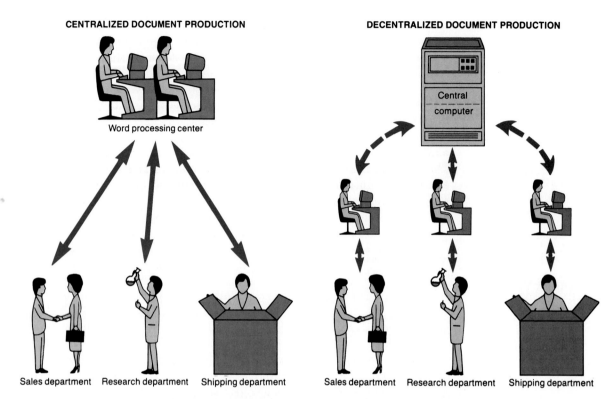

Figure 3-3 Centralized vs. Decentralized Document Production
In a centralized document production system, all departments give input to a single center, where word processing specialists produce documents for them. In a decentralized system, each department produces its own documents, keyboarded by assistants who often have other responsibilities as well. The decentralized computers may be linked to a larger central computer, enabling them to retrieve company information for use in their documents and to also distribute the documents electronically.

A typical document production center is an area where several specialists sit at workstations, which consist of desks with computers and possibly dictation/transcription machines. The center may include just a few workstations, or it may include several dozen workstations arranged in clusters or rows.

As a rule, a word processing specialist receives a manager's input in the form of a handwritten draft. Sometimes, however, the input may consist of tape-recorded dictation or a printed document. The specialist keys the input into the computer system along with formatting instructions and other processing commands and prints the document.

Word processing supervisor. **Word processing supervisors** monitor the staff's workload and distribute work among the specialists. They may also check all finished documents. These are often transmitted to the supervisor's workstation electronically so that the supervisor can check them before they are printed. Or the word processing specialists may print draft copies of the documents and hand them to the supervisor.

The supervisor, in turn, forwards the documents to the managers who wrote them, who may return them with corrections or revisions. When this happens, the supervisor returns the document to the specialist who produced it—or to another specialist—who makes the changes. A corrected paper copy of the document may then be printed, checked by the supervisor, and returned to the manager.

Other word processing positions. Large centers may employ other people in addition to word processing specialists and supervisors. Their duties may include technical writing, proofreading the output, photocopying documents, delivering documents to and from managers, and changing the paper and ribbons on printers. Otherwise, the regular specialists may handle these tasks in addition to inputting the documents.

Workplaces of word processing employees. Word processing employees are found in federal, state, and local government offices, nonprofit organizations, hospitals, and large companies of all kinds. They're often found in professional offices, too. Thus, as a word processing specialist, you could choose from a wide range of employers and work environments.

You could work for a publishing company, where you might help produce book manuscripts as well as other kinds of documents. You could work for a law firm, where you might spend most of your time producing briefs and other legal documents under intense pressure to meet court-

Figure 3-4 The Invasion of the Specialists
One way that businesses can handle the sheer volume of information the computer makes available is to create specialist jobs. Word processing specialists are experts at processing one type of information, the written documents, originated by their managers. (Courtesy of Hewlett-Packard Company)

imposed deadlines. As a word processing specialist in a hospital, you might transcribe medical reports dictated by doctors in your department. In a manufacturing company, on the other hand, the documents you produce in a single day might include letters to customers, suppliers, and government agencies as well as interoffice reports and memos and the text for advertisements and brochures.

Perhaps the most varied jobs for word processing specialists are with temporary employment agencies. These agencies send people to work for other organizations on temporary assignments, which may last anywhere from one day to several months. The more types of word processing software you are familiar with, the easier it is for the agency to find assignments for you. As a "temp," you might be working on scripts for television commercials at an advertising agency one day, then producing form letters in a government office's document production center the next day.

DATA ENTRY

Some types of information are compiled from numbers and key words like names and addresses, rather than from sentences and paragraphs. Before a computer can sort these into meaningful information, information workers must key them into the computer. This task is called data entry. Data entry clerks are indispensable to the processing of information.

Data entry clerks transfer raw data into the computer system. A variety of devices are used for data entry; but most commonly, the task

Figure 3-5   The Precision of Data Entry
Data entry specialists are precision experts. They carefully and accurately keyboard names, addresses, phone numbers, and other data into their computers, creating information that can be used again and again, in different ways, by businesses. (Courtesy of the U.S. Census Bureau)

consists of reading data written or typed on paper forms and entering it at the computer keyboard so that it appears at the appropriate place on the computer screen. Care is essential—if input is keyed in incorrectly, the information produced from it will reflect, and often magnify, the errors. Accuracy and careful attention to detail are crucial requirements for the job of data entry clerk.

Every 10 years, the U.S. government counts the country's population. The Census Bureau sends a questionnaire to every household in the nation. Recipients respond to these questionnaires by stating how many people their households include, how long they've lived there and where they lived before, how many of the adults are employed, and the age, race, education level, and sex of each person. Data entry clerks transfer all this information into the Census Bureau's computer system.

From the data, government computers are able to produce various kinds of information. The data can be sorted and calculated to show average incomes and ages in different regions, for example, or to determine how education relates to employment, household income, number of children, or geographic locale. Changes from one census to the next show migration patterns, employment prospects, educational trends, and so forth. Many government agencies use census information in forecasting the need for services such as public education. Private businesses use it to make marketing decisions, such as where they should concentrate their advertising.

The Census Bureau alone provides hundreds of data entry jobs, but a multitude of other government organizations employ data entry clerks as well. These clerks work with many kinds of input, not only in huge departments such as the Census Bureau but also in smaller divisions of government.

For example, there are local government agencies that deal with education, mass transit, drivers' licenses and vehicle registrations, highways, health and welfare, and the taxation required to finance all these agencies. Police departments, public school systems, and state universities are also government agencies. Each of these organizations gathers massive amounts of data to be processed into the information they need to meet their goals. Therefore, each of them relies on clerks to enter the data promptly and accurately.

Businesses, too, collect many kinds of data for entry into their computer systems. All businesses accumulate data about employees, customers, equipment, sales, and expenditures. Manufacturing companies gather data about raw materials, production, and shipping; and merchants maintain data on inventory. In small businesses, data entry, like document production, is often handled by general administrative support employees who have other responsibilities too. For example, much data is entered by store salespeople when they ring up a purchase at a point-of-sale terminal. But large businesses generally employ people just to do data entry. In fact, these clerks are likely to specialize in entering certain kinds of data.

Some data entry clerks work solely with customer orders. The circulation departments of magazines, for example, employ people who enter subscription orders. These clerks work from subscription and renewal forms, as well as letters, that readers have mailed in. They may also obtain data from subscribers who call on the phone. The computer processes this data into information on how many copies of the magazine to print and where to mail them. The circulation department can prepare lists of subscribers to whom it should send renewal notices. And the accounting department can use it to determine which subscribers should receive bills and which ones have paid for their subscriptions already.

Accounting departments also employ data entry clerks, who enter data about bills owed or paid by the company, expenditures on supplies or equipment, and other facts about the company's financial dealings. The information processed from accounting data helps managers to determine whether the company is making enough money to support its expenditures and, if not, where spending could be cut. A data entry clerk in accounting may specialize even further, working only with payroll, for example. As a payroll clerk, you would enter data from employees' weekly time sheets, as well as data from other company forms about changes in their pay rates or deductions. Your co-workers throughout the company would depend on you to do your work promptly and accurately so they could get their checks on time, in the correct amounts.

INFORMATION STORAGE AND RECORDS MANAGEMENT

Data entered by data entry personnel and documents prepared by word processing staff are frequently kept on file in centralized record systems. Information from these centralized systems can be made available to all authorized employees who need it to do their work. For this to take place, however, the records must be carefully managed and maintained.

Records management specialist. A large organization is likely to have a **records management center,** where a small staff of **records management specialists** controls access to the organization's centrally stored paper and microfilmed documents. In addition to the shelves and cabinets that have always dominated the decor in file rooms, modern records management centers are equipped with computers and other electronic devices that are used to create, store, and retrieve microfilms.

Some records management employees specialize in computer-aided retrieval (CAR). When someone requests a copy of a microfilmed document from the records room with a CAR system, a **CAR specialist** may look up the document's index code in a directory and then key the code into a computer. The computer scans the files until it locates the piece of microfilm that contains the document. Another electronic device conveys the record to an automatic microfilm reader, which in turn transmits the image to the CAR operator's computer terminal. The operator can then print a paper copy of the image and forward it to the person who requested it.

Other workers interested in records management may find jobs as operators of computer-output microfilm (COM) recorders. These devices create microfilms directly from computer disk files rather than from paper

Figure 3-6 Managing and Maintaining Records
Decision making—a key to all business activity—is aided by the quick storage and retrieval of documents. Enter the records management specialists, who control access to these documents. Some specialists use computers that can access hundreds of document pages a minute. (Courtesy of Nixdorf Computer Corporation)

copies of documents. A **COM operator** can record hundreds of document pages per minute. The operator may also be responsible for indexing the documents.

Database administrator. Not all information stored by an organization is kept in records centers. Much of it may be maintained in the organization's electronic database. One example of a database is the collection of Census Bureau information discussed earlier in this chapter. Large databases are generally stored on mainframe computers and designed and managed by people with technical backgrounds in computing. **Database administrators,** who are usually senior executives, control access to the information that is stored in databases. Gaining experience with a microcomputer database can be a first step in building the skills necessary for such a position. However, specialized courses are also needed to qualify for jobs at this level.

INFORMATION DISTRIBUTION

In addition to positions concerned with document production, data entry, and information storage and records management, there are many opportunities for specialists in computerized information distribution. Such jobs in large organizations tend to be highly specialized and require considerable technical training.

There are specialists who oversee the operation of an organization's computerized distribution systems, including teletypewriters, electronic copiers, and computers. And **telecommunications managers** manage

Figure 3-7   Brains Behind the Brain
One of the brains behind the "brain" of a computer is that of the programmer. Programmers write sequenced lists of commands called programs or "code." And they extensively test their work, running the software they are creating and then revising their code to improve it. (Courtesy of Hewlett-Packard Company)

the planning, installing, and operating of a large company's telecommunications systems.

INFORMATION ANALYSIS

Before computers can be used to process or distribute information, they must be told exactly what to do and how to do it. Specialized workers called **programmers** write the software, or computer **programs,** that instructs the computer to perform as the user wants. Programmers may be employed by companies that write software for computers of all sizes or by organizations that use computers, both to develop special software that may be needed and to make particular adjustments to software that the organization purchases.

To write computer programs, you must study one or more of the languages that computers can recognize. You may already be familiar with the names of some of these computer languages—BASIC, COBOL, Pascal, and C. Programming requires a particular kind of logical talent. Many computer users become fascinated by programming and acquire the specialized skills needed to work in this interesting career.

Systems implementation

Before people can use computers to retrieve information from databases, produce documents, or calculate payrolls, someone must design and create the computer systems themselves. This involves analyzing the organization's existing information systems and needs, determining what hardware and software can best meet those needs, installing and implementing these, and teaching people how to use them. The need for design and implementation has created many careers that didn't even exist before the information revolution, some within the organization and some outside it.

SYSTEMS IMPLEMENTATION WITHIN THE ORGANIZATION

Computerized information systems have created many new positions whose purpose is to help an organization use its resources in the most productive ways possible. Among the many positions focusing on the organization's use of its computer systems are the systems analyst and the trainer.

Systems analyst. Any computerized information system includes people who use hardware, software, and procedures to produce specific kinds of

Figure 3-8 Just the Design for You
Computer systems are as varied as the organizations they serve. Computer system designers must know a lot about computers and about business too, because it is their job to tailor computer systems to serve business's needs. (Courtesy of Hewlett-Packard Company)

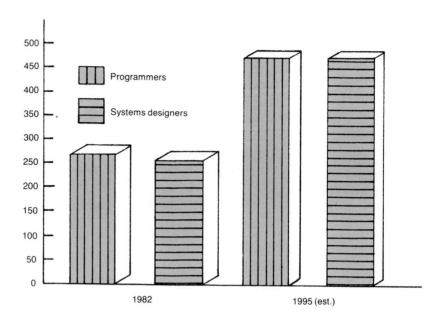

Source: Bureau of Labor Statistics

Figure 3-9   Projected Growth of Computing Jobs
Analysts say that by 1995 jobs for programmers will increase by more than 75 percent and jobs for systems designers will increase by more than 85 percent. In fact, there may even be a shortage of qualified persons, which could limit growth in the overall use of computers.

information. A **systems analyst** determines what hardware and software procedures will enable these people to do their jobs most efficiently and productively. Systems analysts design computer systems to replace less productive manual systems. And they determine how organizations that are already computerized can improve their systems so that they can process, store, and distribute more information with greater efficiency.

As the use of computers becomes more widespread, systems analysts are increasingly concerned with the ways in which computer systems can interface with each other and how they can be linked in information distribution networks. These networks may involve satellites, microwave dishes, and optical fibers, as well as telephone lines and cables. A well-designed network enables data and information to flow smoothly among departments in an office building or among numerous locations that may span thousands of miles.

Systems analysts need well-developed analytic skills for studying existing systems and determining how they can be improved. They also need oral and written communication skills, to enable them to present their findings effectively to management. Further, they must know the capabilities of many types of computers and related equipment. Although some systems analysts started their careers as computer users, most have also had extensive training in programming and the technical aspects of computer systems.

Trainer. As the computer revolution gathers momentum, more and more people in an organization must be taught how to use the new technology. And the technology is changing rapidly, so even people who already use computers often need new training from time to time to catch up with the latest developments in their fields. As a result, some of the most promising career opportunities for information workers today are in the area of training.

Although some trainers have technical backgrounds in computing, many do not. Instead, they may have become so knowledgeable about computer systems by using them in their jobs that they can now train other people to use similar systems. Many trainers once worked as word

STATE OF THE ART
How Computers Are Used in Training

One of the best ways to learn how to use a computer or a software package is through computer-based training (CBT). In CBT, the computer itself acts as a trainer, providing realistic practice situations and allowing people to learn at their own pace by simulating what they will do on the job.

Increasingly, CBT is available to teach the use of commercial software such as word processing and spreadsheet programs. In some cases, CBT tutorials are even included in the software package. CBT offers several advantages over other kinds of training. Two of these are the computer's apparent patience and stamina. Users can repeat a CBT program over and over again, until they feel that they have mastered it.

Another advantage of CBT is its ability to tailor a lesson to individual student's needs. A CBT program can take a user from one topic or lesson to another based on a user's response to questions. For example, if a user answers a set of questions correctly, a CBT lesson might move on to the next topic. If several of the answers are incorrect, the program could start a sequence of instruction that restates the material the user didn't grasp.

Many sophisticated CBT programs use not only words and simple graphic displays, but also animation, audiotapes, or videodisks or tapes to simulate real-life situations. A CBT for sales trainees, for example, may include videotaped simulations of sales calls. After presenting a tape of the call's beginning moments, the CBT offers the trainee several options on how to proceed. The trainee's response determines which videotaped scenario is shown next.

Because of the obvious advantages of the computer as a training tool, CBT is often used in situations that are unrelated to computers.

Some professional associations now provide selections of CBT courses for their members and award professional accreditation for successful completion. As each member completes a course, this accreditation can be recorded in a national database.

CBT is rapidly gaining acceptance in the business world. Thus, there is a growing demand for people who can develop effective CBT programs. Authoring systems that aid in the development of CBT are reducing the need for programming skills in developing CBT lessons. Therefore, CBT development will offer more job opportunities for computer literate but nontechnical workers.

processing specialists, as secretaries, or in other jobs where they were computer users rather than technicians.

If you have a thorough knowledge of a computer application, the organizational skills to develop a course, and the poise required to conduct a class, you will find training opportunities in large organizations as well as small ones. As a trainer, you may work with computer users at one company location or at many locations, teaching the use of one software application or a wider range of computer skills.

More and more large organizations are establishing **information centers,** where employees go for help in using computers in their jobs. At the information center, they may seek guidance about what kind of microcomputer hardware to install in their offices and what software products to use for applications such as working with databases, spreadsheets, and word processing. They may also go to the information center for training in how to use their systems. As a trainer in an information center, you can help your colleagues in an organization to use computers in ways that can make their work easier, more interesting, and more effective.

Figure 3-10   Another Kind of Training
Users need to be trained to work with difficult types of software. And now the computer itself may need to be trained—to recognize a manager's voice. Once it has learned her particular speech sounds, this computer can act on her spoken commands. (Courtesy of Texas Instruments)

Figure 3-11 Going Outside for Expertise

An option available to any organization is to get help from outside. Consultants are paid to work closely with an organization's employees, and they can be more highly specialized than a small company's training staff. They teach the same specific material at many locations. (Courtesy of Hewlett-Packard Company)

SYSTEMS IMPLEMENTATION OUTSIDE THE ORGANIZATION

Many businesses have been established in recent years whose purpose is to sell computer hardware and software to organizations. These businesses employ people who are knowledgeable about the equipment and systems they are selling and who can provide customer service to the client organizations. In addition, many small consulting firms have been established to advise organizations how best to meet their information needs. Consulting services range from planning new systems to training employees on existing systems.

Vendors. Sellers of computer systems, called **vendors,** need employees who are very familiar with their products in order to sell them to corporations and other organizations. They also employ **marketing support representatives** to provide service to their customers in the maintenance and use of the equipment and systems they sell. Vendors often hire people who have used their equipment extensively in an office support role.

Consultants and training companies. In virtually every area of the country, small consulting companies provide computer services ranging from planning systems to training employees. The trainers who work for these companies conduct classes for the client organizations' employees. Most often, these classes teach the use of specific software packages. They may be held in the consulting company's offices, at the client's office, or at some other location such as a conference center.

   As a trainer for a consulting company, you may spend a week teaching word processing software to editors in a New York City publishing house. The following week could find you teaching a database system to secretaries at the suburban headquarters of a manufacturing company. Then again, you could be teaching a class at your employer's office for people from a variety of small organizations.

SUMMARY

- By altering the way organizations process information, computer technology has brought about dramatic changes in the way people work, particularly in the office. The information revolution has changed the nature of many traditional jobs, and it has created new job categories for information workers.

- Information jobs may focus on the input, processing, or output of data or information.

- Organizations generally have distinct computerized information systems for accounting, word processing, and other business functions. However, they may have employees who use all the systems as well as employees who perform specialized tasks on only one system.

- Administrative support workers perform a wide variety of tasks for their managers. They often use computer systems for applications such as word processing and databases to assist them in their duties.

- People with word processing skills are among the most sought-after employees by organizations of all sizes. They can work as word processing specialists or supervisors.

- Data entry is another area that offers many job opportunities for information workers. From typed or handwritten forms and other kinds of input, data entry clerks key in data, which computers process into many kinds of information that can be analyzed and used by other people in the organization.

■ Computer technology has also created job opportunities in information storage and records management. Many organizations now employ records management specialists who use computers to create microform copies of documents processed on computers and who retrieve microfilmed documents from computerized filing systems. Other information jobs involve the creation and use of databases.

■ Information distribution jobs tend to be highly specialized and technical. Among them is the job of telecommunications manager.

■ Programmers are information workers who write software that directs computer systems to perform specific tasks.

■ Many new positions exist for people interested in implementing computer systems. Within an organization, systems analysts design and maintain computer systems and trainers teach employees how to use them. Equipment and systems vendors must be knowledgeable about the products they sell, and consulting firms offer organizations a wide range of computer-related services, including training.

TERMS FOR REVIEW

administrative
   assistant
save
administrative
   support
   supervisor
centralized
   structure
word processing
   specialists

word processing
   supervisors
data entry clerks
records management
   center
records management
   specialists
CAR specialist
COM operator
database administrators

telecommunications
   managers
programmers
program
systems analyst
information centers
vendors
marketing support
   representative

TERMINOLOGY CHECK

For each of these definitions, choose the correct term from the list of Terms for Review:

1. A person who manages the planning, installing, and operating of a large company's long-distance communications system.

2. A person who writes computer programs or software.

3. A person who keys raw data into a computer.

4. A place in an organization where employees can go for help in using computers in their jobs.

5. A person who monitors the word processing staff's workload and distributes work among the WP specialists.

6. A person in an office responsible for various duties some of which

may be reception work, word processing, and general office organizing.

7. To store information or documents in an electronic file.

8. A person who runs equipment that creates microfilm from computer output.

9. A person who continually analyzes information systems within an organization with a view to making them more efficient and productive.

10. An arrangement in which a particular system's facilities are located in a central area, with specialized workers, often serving several departments at once.

INFORMATION CHECK

1. How has the development of computer technology changed the relationship between management and staff workers?

2. How can a worker be part of several business information systems?

3. How do information systems in large and small organizations differ?

4. Describe the duties of an administrative assistant.

5. Describe briefly a typical centralized word processing environment.

6. What are some of the duties of a word processing specialist?

7. What types of companies employ word processing specialists?

8. What activities do data entry clerks perform in supporting information processing functions?

9. What are two important job requirements for people who work as data entry clerks?

10. List some kinds of data you might be working with as a data entry clerk in (a) a government agency, (b) a business.

11. Describe two types of jobs usually available in records management centers.

12. What are the functions of a database administrator?

13. What skills must a programmer possess?

14. What skills must a systems analyst possess?

15. What skills must a trainer possess?

PROJECTS AND PROBLEMS

1. You have been employed in the office at Garfield Township for six months. Your supervisor, whose respect and support you have gained often seeks your opinion on administrative matters. The office includes four workers, including yourself, who handle all letters, re-

ports, and documents produced by the office. There are also three records clerks, who take care of all filing, including the reports prepared by the tax assessor, the building inspector, and other departments. The township manager recently asked your supervisor to investigate placing data from these reports onto computer databases, which would require data entry but could lessen the word processing load. You have been asked your opinion on whether new data entry specialists should be hired or whether the seven current employees could handle the workload if you all began to share in the duties of the office rather than remain specialized. Make a list of the pros and cons of sharing duties—from the points of view of both the workers and the township organization. What would you recommend?

2. Visit the document production facilities in a large company. Also, visit a small company where word processing is used. Write a report comparing the two. Include in your description information about the number of people working, what their jobs are, and what kinds of hardware and software they use.

3. Get a copy of the help-wanted section of your local newspaper. Browse through the entire section. What categories of computer jobs are available in your area? What skills and/or experiences are typically required? What categories of jobs require that applicants know how to use a microcomputer? Compare the number of word processing jobs with the number of typing jobs offered.

Compile the information you have gathered into a short written report.

PART TWO

COMPUTER SOFTWARE

4

Word processing, database, and communications

A stereo system can play anything from Beethoven to hard rock. What it plays depends on the record. Similarly, a computer can do anything from writing letters to preparing a payroll. What it does depends on the software.

Software consists of a set of instructions to the computer. These instructions, originally created by a programmer, are usually stored in magnetic form—often on a **diskette** (also called a **floppy disk**), which even looks a little like a 45 rpm record. Just as the "hardware" of a stereo system—the turntable, the amplifier, the speakers—picks up information from the record and turns it into music, so too the computer hardware "reads" the software and acts according to its instructions.

When you use a computer, your actions are dictated more by the software than by the hardware. It is the software that creates the messages, or **prompts,** that the computer shows you on its screen. It is the software that interprets your commands to the computer. The software even determines what each key on the keyboard will do.

Part Two of this book is about software. You need to know very little about how the hardware works to operate a computer; if you know the names of the different pieces of equipment and have some understanding of the keyboard, that is almost enough. But if you don't understand the software you are using, you will rarely succeed in making the computer do anything useful.

Frequently, the word **program** is used to refer to a specific piece of software. The term *software package* is also used, most commonly for published programs that can be bought from a software supplier or computer dealer. But programmers also write software to order, to meet the precise needs of a particular organization. And even commercially available software can often be customized, that is, modified or adapted to make it more useful to the user.

Today's software is of two types. First, there is **applications software,** which includes the programs that make the computer perform different tasks. Some applications programs are general-purpose tools that can be used for a variety of jobs. A word processing program, for example, can be used to edit a 50-page contract, prepare a report, or write an invitation to the office Christmas party. The main classes of such general-purpose software are discussed in this and the following chapter. Other applications programs, however, are designed for more specific business tasks, such as accounting or inventory control. Applications software of this type is discussed in Chapter 6.

Second, there is **systems software,** which Chapter 7 discusses in detail. Systems software enables the computer to use the applications software efficiently. It includes programs called **operating systems,** which perform many essential tasks, like running the disk drives when they are needed. (Operating systems for microcomputers frequently include the letters **DOS** in their names, for **d**isk **o**perating **s**ystems.) Most applications programs are written to function with specific operating systems. So it is really the operating system, rather than the computer, that determines what programs you can run. Systems software also includes programs that translate computer language instructions to a form the computer can act on.

This chapter will give you some basic knowledge about the computer keyboard and other parts of the system you will be using. Then it will describe three types of applications software: word processing, database, and communications. These three applications do work that has been done in offices for decades. But they often accomplish in minutes what used to take hours or even days.

The chapter will enable you to:

- explain the concept of user interface and describe some of its components

- compare menu-driven and command-driven software

- detail some of the editing capabilities and other features that make word processing software so useful

- describe the capabilities of typical database software packages

- discuss the functions of some common uses of communications software

- describe what word processing, database, and communications software have in common and how they differ

The user interface

To use software, you need to be familiar with the user interface of your computer. *Interface* is the general term for the point of contact between two systems, or two parts of a system. **User interface** therefore means the point of contact between you (the user) and the computer—the parts

Figure 4-1   Among Computers, Less Is Often More
What makes this computer system so popular is a user-friendly device called a
mouse. Using the mouse gets users up and running with less effort. They just
move the mouse around, and presto! Words and images are manipulated; work
gets done. (Courtesy of Apple Computer, Inc.)

of the system that communicate with you, and the parts that you use to
communicate with the system.

The screen, or **monitor,** provides an image of the work you are doing.
(Home computer systems sometimes use ordinary television sets as monitors, but this is very rare in office systems.) The **printer** gives you a
paper copy of the work you create. **Disk drives,** the slots on the front or
side of a micro, let you insert disks to record your work or to load the
software you need. The **keyboard** enables you to enter data into the
computer and give it instructions.

If you are working at a terminal connected to a larger system, you
may have only a monitor and keyboard in front of you. Printers and disk
drives—often an enclosed, hard disk in this case—will be at some central
location. You may also have additional parts to the user interface—for
example, a small device called a **mouse** (see Figure 4-1), which enables
you to move words and images rapidly from one part of the screen to
another. And the software you are using affects very important aspects
of the user interface, since it controls both the prompts you see on the
monitor and the keys you must press for different purposes.

THE MONITOR

The monitor is so called because it lets you monitor, or keep track of, the
work you are doing at the computer. Monitors can range from plain black-
and-white screens to specialized displays that provide bright colors and

very clear images. The details that you see on the monitor are controlled by the software you are using, and so they differ from program to program. Most software will provide you with a **cursor** on the screen to show you where your next input will be placed. The cursor is a small mark, usually a block or a line, and often flashing. If you type an "a" on the keyboard, the "a" will appear where the cursor was located, and the cursor will usually move to accept your next input.

THE PRINTER

Printers, like monitors, come in many shapes and sizes. They are used for printing out the results of your work. They can be categorized in many ways. Two of the most common classifications are impact or nonimpact printers and draft or letter-quality printers. The first distinction refers to the way in which the image of the letters is made. **Impact printers** strike a ribbon much as a standard typewriter does. **Nonimpact printers** use different methods; for example, the laser printer uses a process similar to that of an office copying machine.

Draft and letter quality indicate the likely use of the printer. **Draft printers,** fast and inexpensive, are most often used for printing rough drafts of documents so that suggestions can be made to improve them. **Letter-quality printers** produce versions suitable for sending to a client, but these printers are more expensive and often slower. However, more and more letter-quality printers today have a "draft mode," which allows them to produce draft versions fast. And the most expensive letter-quality printers are fast enough to be used for early drafts of documents as the final versions.

DISK DRIVES

Disk drives are in one sense the electronic equivalent of a printer. They create a permanent record of your work by recording it onto a diskette or hard disk. Diskettes cannot be read directly like printed pages. However, by reinserting them into the disk drive, you can have their contents read into the computer and displayed on the monitor. You can then make further changes to the document you are working on or have it printed out by your printer.

Because disk drives can "read" diskettes as well as record onto them, they are also the means by which most microcomputer software is read into a computer. Programs often contain many thousands of instructions to the computer, but disk drives can read these instructions in a matter of seconds, preparing the computer to accept the work you plan to do.

THE KEYBOARD

The keyboard is the part of the computer that you use most. It is therefore the most important part of the user interface to understand. It looks and works very much like a typewriter keyboard, but there are important differences. One is that it is not mechanically connected to any letters or

Figure 4-2 The Ultimate Speed Reader
Disks drives, like business people, do a lot of reading. They are equipped with an electromagnetic head that allows them to read in seconds the computer language on a disk and then to write on, rewrite, or erase that same information that is displayed on your monitor. (Courtesy of Seagate Technology)

numbers; what appears on the paper or on the screen is controlled by the software. Therefore, two different programs may do different things in response to the same key. The backspace, for instance, may delete in one application but merely move the cursor in another.

Another difference between the computer keyboard and a typewriter keyboard is that the former has additional keys. These usually include keys with arrows to move the cursor, extra numerical keys for doing mathematical calculations, and various others that are described later. The reason for the additional keys is to allow you to provide specific commands. Whereas the software disk provides general instructions that determine what the computer *can* do, your commands tell the computer what to do in a particular situation.

Suppose, for example, that you have typed up a long business letter using a word processing program. You now wish to change the address at the top, but you can no longer see it because it moved up out of sight as you typed. All word processing software will allow you to move back to the top of a document, but the specific means will differ, depending on the program.

Function keys.   One approach involves the use of special keys that are set aside for commands. These are usually called **function keys.** Dedicated word processors have many such specialized keys, each key labeled with a specific function that the word processor can perform. General-purpose computers also have function keys, but these are usually numbered, and their use is different for each piece of software. If your word processing program uses a particular function key to move to the start of a document, all you need to do is press that key and the job will be done. (The software may alternatively call for you to press SHIFT and the function key together.)

CONTROL and ALT keys.   Another approach involves other keys similar to the traditional shift key. The shift key changes the "meaning" of the regular keys so that they print uppercase instead of lowercase, or special characters like the dollar sign or asterisk instead of numerals. Most computer keyboards have additional keys that provide yet more meanings for the standard letter keys. For example, there is usually a CONTROL key, which can be used together with a letter for a specific command. Pressing CONTROL and simultaneously hitting the "b" key (for beginning) could take you to the top of your business letter. This command would usually be abbreviated CTRL-b. (Pressing the "b" key alone would merely place a "b" at the cursor location.)

The control key thus adds more than 40 possible commands to the keyboard. In combination with the shift key, it can add more than 80. Some keyboards have yet another similar key, often called the alternate, or ALT, key, which makes the total possibilities still greater.

Menus.   So far we have talked about software that responds to commands—often called **command-driven software.** Another common means of conveying users' instructions to the computer involves the screen as well as the keyboard. As you can imagine, software that uses upwards of 50 commands is difficult to learn—and the commands are easy to forget if you don't use them too often. So programmers often provide menus on

Figure 4-3   The Microcomputer Keyboard
This is the standard keyboard for the IBM PC. Notice the function keys to the left, and the numeric/cursor arrow pad to the right. Other keyboards place the function keys along the top of the keyboard. Some may separate the cursor arrows from the number pad. (Courtesy of International Business Machines Corporation)

the screen to help users to control the software. **Menus** list the choices of instructions that you can use and let you select from the list, often by moving a pointer to the item you want. Thus, you give your instructions not by memorizing commands and pressing the keys but by looking at the screen and moving a pointer. This feature is particularly helpful to beginning users.

Software that uses menus is called **menu-driven software.** Using such a program to recall the start of a document, you might first press CTRL-m to call up the menu. This would show you several alternatives; a pointer may be beside one of them, or one might be highlighted. Using the arrow keys, you might move the pointer or highlighting to an option called "start of file" and then press the RETURN or ENTER key. The computer would then bring the beginning of your letter back onto the screen.

Still other software may allow you to select options from a menu by keying in their initial letters. This requires fewer keystrokes than moving the pointer does. Or you may be able to move the pointer with a mouse, again speeding up your choice.

Most menus still take more time to use than simple commands, so today's software often uses both menus and direct commands. Experienced users work with the commands, whereas novices work through the menus. Some programs, however, *require* the use of menus.

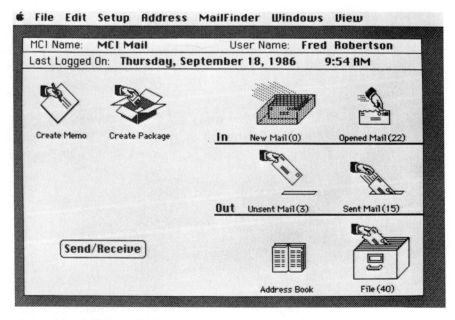

Figure 4-4 Quicker with Pictures

Some menus consist of more than a list of options. This screen shows icons, pictures designed for easy recognition. With a mouse to move a pointer across the screen, users can quickly select the option they wish to view. (Courtesy of Apple Computer, Inc.)

Word processing software

The most widely used type of microcomputer software is **word processing software.** It enables people to manipulate words efficiently so that they can communicate with each other. Clear and accurate communications are vital to business. Often this requires creating more than one draft of a document so that it can be studied and improved. And business depends heavily on the availability of permanent written records—contracts, plans, memos, financial records, personnel files, correspondence, and so on. Word processing programs allow almost anyone to write, revise, save, and print documents of all sorts. Word processing was in fact the first computerized function to leave data processing departments and enter the mainstream of the modern office. It has changed that office forever.

Imagine that you've just finished writing a 10-page report. Suddenly you see that you left out a sentence on page one. Working on a typewriter, you have to retype the first page. If you can't let the first page run a line long or find a way to delete a line somewhere else, you also have to retype the other nine pages, just because of one mistake.

With word processing software, the task is much simpler. To make a change at the beginning of your report, you merely press the appropriate keys to bring the first lines back onto the screen. Then you can easily insert new passages or change what you wrote before. The sentences that follow are automatically moved down to make room for the new material.

People who use word processing software seldom return to the typewriter willingly. It's not difficult to understand why. Typewriters turn your keystrokes into a document in a single process; after pressing the keys, you have no chance to change your mind before your words are on paper. But word processing breaks the process up into at least four stages, giving you far more flexibility to make changes:

- **keyboarding,** or entering the words into the computer's memory through the keyboard

- **editing,** or making corrections and alterations

- **formatting,** or designing the appearance of the document for printing

- **printing,** or creating the paper document

In addition, they allow **saving,** or making a permanent electronic copy on a magnetic medium such as a diskette.

KEYBOARDING

Keyboarding is the first step in word processing. Anyone who can use a typewriter already knows the basics of keyboarding words into a computer. A touch typist can quickly become a productive word processing operator. In fact, word processing is easier than using a typewriter. Each

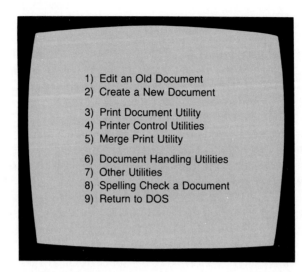

Figure 4-5   A Word Processing Menu
Steps in word processing lend themselves naturally to a menu. However, different software designers define the steps differently. In Multimate, keyboarding is called Create a New Document, edit is Edit, and formatting and printing are both viewed as Print Document Utilities.

time you press a letter, it appears on the screen, and the cursor moves a space to the right. When you reach the end of a line, the cursor automatically moves to the next line, carrying with it the word you are currently typing. This feature, known as **word wrap,** saves the need for using the RETURN key unless you wish to start a new paragraph.

When you have filled the screen, you just continue keyboarding. The first lines you keyboarded move up and off the top of the monitor one at a time to make room for the new lines you are composing. This line-by-line vertical movement is called **scrolling.**

Other features also save time. There is no need to calculate how to center a title; a simple command or menu choice will do this for you. You can specify italics and boldface type in the same way. If you leave out a word or misspell it, you can make changes instantly—or you can leave it to be "edited" later. In general, word processing allows you to work faster and more confidently, knowing that corrections will not take vast amounts of work.

SAVING

While a paragraph is held in the electronic memory of the computer, it is very easy to change, but it could also be lost. Though some computers have memories that last, memory is generally good only until the computer is turned off. The memory may also fail in the event of a power outage—a disaster if you've just spent an hour entering 12 pages and making them perfect. And memory has limits: the time may come when the memory is full, meaning there is no room for more information unless you delete some text that you entered previously.

The best way to handle all these situations is to save your work on diskettes (or the hard disk), using the commands specified for your word processing software. When you enter a "save" command, a light on the disk drive will come on, and a message on the screen will probably inform you that your work is being saved. Several word processing programs automatically save every few minutes. Otherwise, you yourself should save on a regular basis—don't wait until you've finished keyboarding. Each time you issue the save command, the record kept on your disk will be updated.

The work you save, whether from word processing or another application, is called a file. **Files** are pieces of work that your program treats as single units. They can be saved, reloaded into the computer for further use, and printed on paper. They can be copied on other disks for safety, to create a permanent **backup** in case your working diskette gets lost or damaged. They can even be sent electronically to other computers, as you will learn later in this chapter.

When you save a file, you will need to give it a **file name.** Often the computer asks you for a name before you can even begin to work. (Like manila file folders, computer files can always be renamed later.) The file name is used to help you locate your file among other files that may be saved on the same disk. To call up a file, you may be asked by some programs to enter the file's name from the keyboard. Others may show you a **directory,** or menu of the files on your diskette, and ask you to choose. As soon as you enter or select a file name, the disk drive will respond, and you'll see your work on the screen once again.

EDITING

In word processing, some of the most commonly used functions enable you to change the text on the screen. This is not only because writers make mistakes or change their minds. Another reason is that many uses of word processing involve making minor changes in standard documents, such as form letters or legal contracts.

Word processing software lets you make almost any changes you can imagine in a document. You can compose a one-page memo to your supervisor about an idea and elaborate it into a seven-page proposal for the

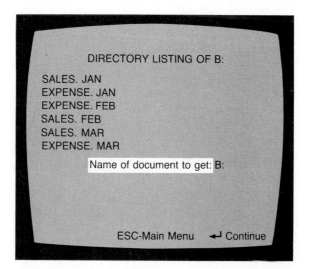

Figure 4-6 Files and Directories

A directory (this one is from PFS: write) lists files saved on your disk. If there are many, you can obtain shorter lists by using a "wild card" such as the asterisk. Ask for "B: Sales.*" and the directory will show only the Sales files. "B:*.Feb" gives the February files only.

administrative manager. You could then reorganize and condense the full proposal (keeping only the key sentences) into a two-page summary for the executive committee. Such examples demonstrate the flexibility of word processing programs. That flexibility stems from three basic powers: the power to insert, the power to delete, and the power to move blocks of text.

Inserting.   Many users consider the power to **insert** the most important function in word processing. It allows you to place new words, symbols, sentences, or paragraphs at any point in the text. To use the insert function, you simply place the cursor at the point where you want to add words and enter them. The inserted segment can be as lengthy as you desire.

Deleting.   The **delete** function is the opposite of the insert function, allowing any characters on the screen to be removed. A deletion can theoretically be performed character by character until all unwanted words are removed. But in many cases it's more convenient to remove whole words, sentences, paragraphs, or even pages. Typical word pro-

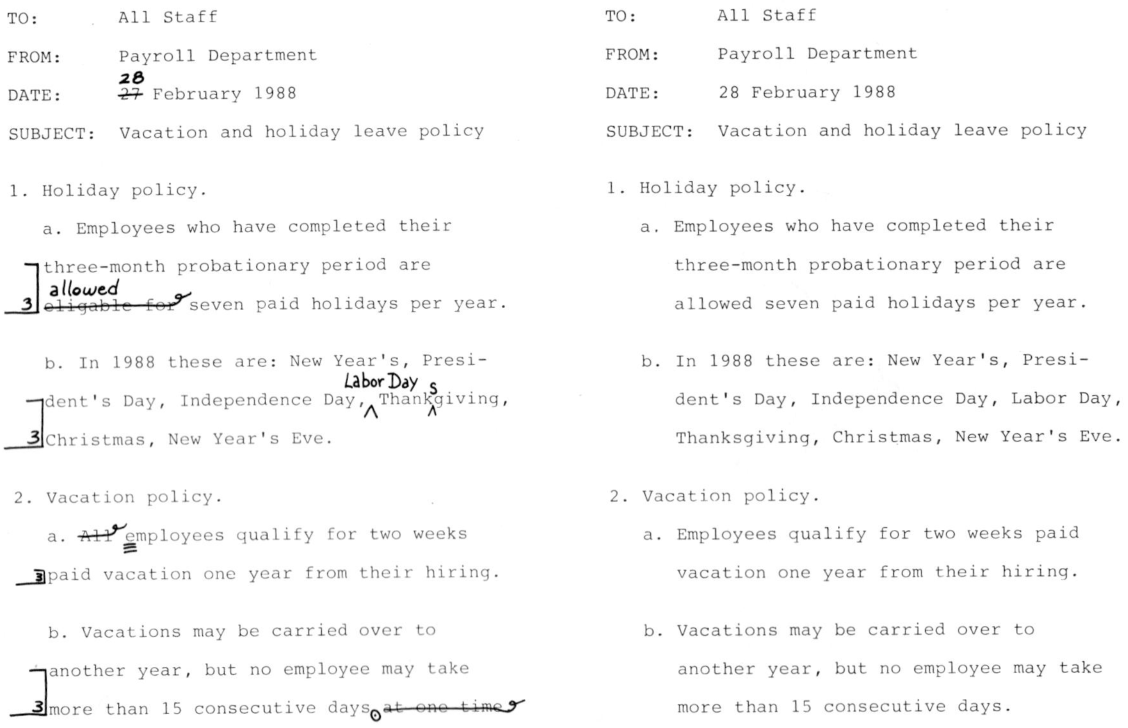

TO: All Staff

FROM: Payroll Department

DATE: ~~27~~ **28** February 1988

SUBJECT: Vacation and holiday leave policy

1. Holiday policy.

   a. Employees who have completed their
   three-month probationary period are
   3 *allowed* ~~eligable for~~ seven paid holidays per year.

   b. In 1988 these are: New Year's, President's Day, Independence Day, Thank*s*giving, *Labor Day*
   3 Christmas, New Year's Eve.

2. Vacation policy.

   a. ~~All~~ employees qualify for two weeks
   3 paid vacation one year from their hiring.

   b. Vacations may be carried over to
   another year, but no employee may take
   3 more than 15 consecutive days ~~at one time~~.

TO: All Staff

FROM: Payroll Department

DATE: 28 February 1988

SUBJECT: Vacation and holiday leave policy

1. Holiday policy.

   a. Employees who have completed their
      three-month probationary period are
      allowed seven paid holidays per year.

   b. In 1988 these are: New Year's, Presi-
      dent's Day, Independence Day, Labor Day,
      Thanksgiving, Christmas, New Year's Eve.

2. Vacation policy.

   a. Employees qualify for two weeks paid
      vacation one year from their hiring.

   b. Vacations may be carried over to
      another year, but no employee may take
      more than 15 consecutive days.

Figure 4-7   Editing a Document
Documents have always been edited to make them clearer. The difference with word processing is that they need not be fully retyped. The deletions and changes shown here could be made in less than 15 seconds, compared to four or five minutes at a typewriter.

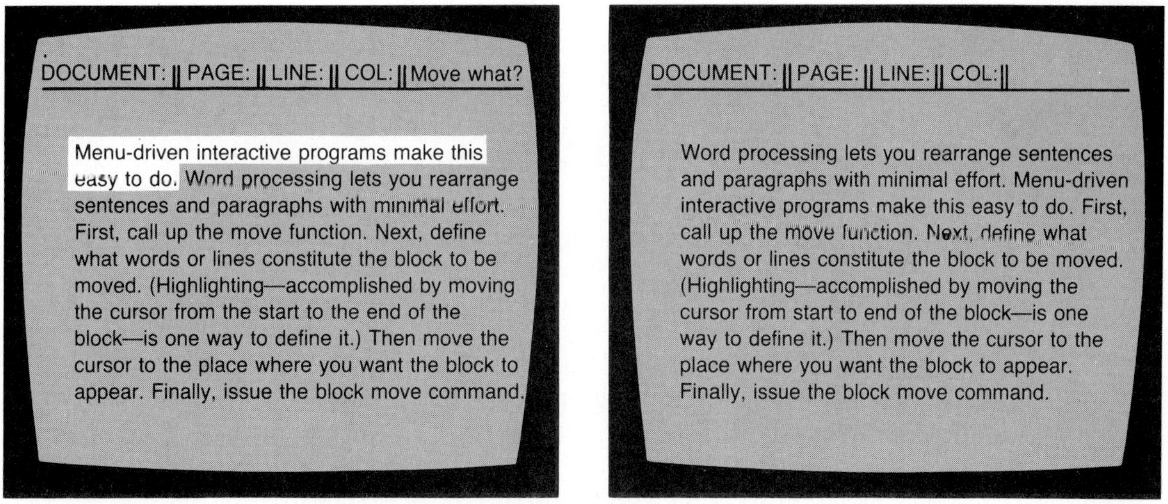

DOCUMENT: ‖ PAGE: ‖ LINE: ‖ COL: ‖ Move what?

Menu-driven interactive programs make this easy to do. Word processing lets you rearrange sentences and paragraphs with minimal effort. First, call up the move function. Next, define what words or lines constitute the block to be moved. (Highlighting—accomplished by moving the cursor from the start to the end of the block—is one way to define it.) Then move the cursor to the place where you want the block to appear. Finally, issue the block move command.

DOCUMENT: ‖ PAGE: ‖ LINE: ‖ COL: ‖

Word processing lets you rearrange sentences and paragraphs with minimal effort. Menu-driven interactive programs make this easy to do. First, call up the move function. Next, define what words or lines constitute the block to be moved. (Highlighting—accomplished by moving the cursor from start to end of the block—is one way to define it.) Then move the cursor to the place where you want the block to appear. Finally, issue the block move command.

Figure 4-8   The Block Move
Moving a sentence or other block of words is easy with word processing packages such as Multimate. First the user moves the cursor to the start of the block and presses F7 (a function key). The computer asks, Move what? The user moves the cursor to the end of the block, creating a highlight as shown; then presses F7 again. The computer asks, To where? and the user places the cursor where the block should be inserted. Pressing F7 once more makes the desired change.

cessing software therefore has separate commands for deleting by character, word, line, sentence, and paragraph. It may even have a command that deletes everything from the cursor to the end of the document.

Moving blocks.   **Block move** commands activate another function that makes word processing more versatile than typing. Often a writer will change his or her mind about the order in which material should be presented. Perhaps two paragraphs from the fifth page of a report would make more sense on the third page. The block move capability provides a quick way to make the switch. This function is sometimes referred to as "cut and paste," since that is how such revisions had to be made before the appearance of word processing.

The block of text to be moved is first defined. With most word processing software, you move the cursor to the beginning of the material and enter a command for starting the block. Then you go to the end of the material and enter a block-ending command. The block you define is usually highlighted by this process, so you can distinguish it from the rest of the text (see Figure 4-8). Next you move the cursor to the point where you want the block to appear, and you enter the command for inserting the block. It will appear in its new location.

Other block functions.   Once a block has been defined, several other things can be done with it, too. Most programs give you the option of inserting a copy of a block at one or more locations in the same document—or even in different documents—without removing the original. Alternatively, the whole block can be deleted with a single keystroke.

Many word processing programs have the power to save this deleted block on a disk so that it can be retrieved later and perhaps inserted into a different document.

SPECIAL FEATURES

In addition to these basic editing capabilities, word processing programs offer special shortcuts. For example, suppose you are a legal secretary, preparing a lease similar to previously handled leases, but with one exception: the lease is for a condominium rather than a house. You could search the lease for *every* use of the word *house* in the document and change it to *condominium*, then print out the revised document. But this would be time-consuming, and there is always a chance an important reference would be overlooked.

Search. Word processing programs typically offer features that can make this process much quicker and more reliable. One such feature offered by most programs today is called **search,** or sometimes global search. Search allows you to enter the word or phrase that you want to find—in this case *house.* The computer will then search through the lease, stopping at each use of the word *house* to let you change it.

Search and replace. Many programs have an even more convenient version of this function called **search and replace.** You enter both the word you want to change *and* the word you wish to replace it with—

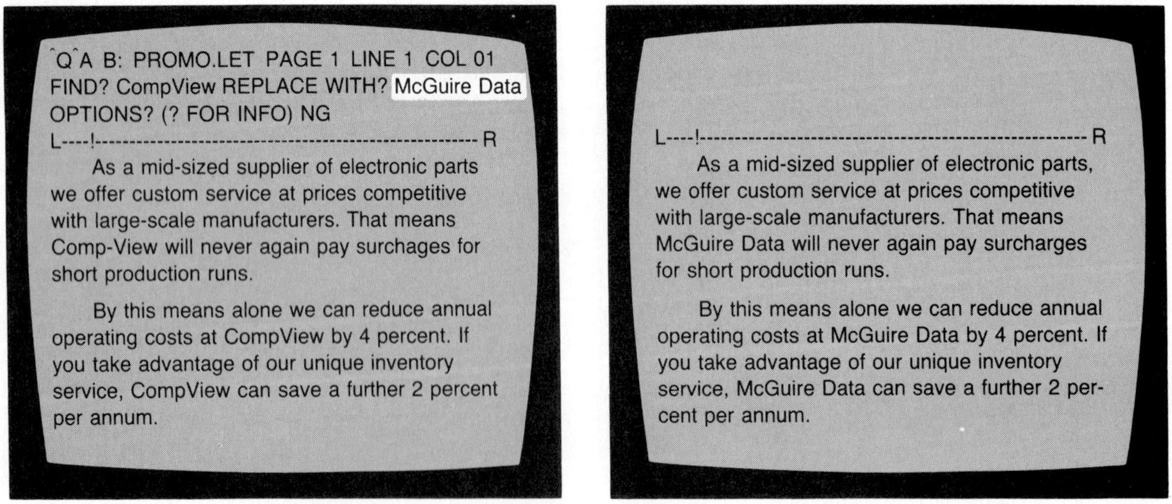

Figure 4-9   Search and Replace
A manufacturer of electronic parts is sending promotional letters to five potential clients. The letters are identical except for the name of the client, which is changed throughout the document using a search and replace function. Steps and commands are shown top left as they would be carried out with WordStar.

condominium in this example. The computer will then automatically change *house* to *condominium* throughout the lease! Alternatively, the computer may be instructed to pause at each use of *house* and ask you whether you wish to change it or not. It will obey your decision, then immediately move to the next occurrence of the word.

Spelling checker and thesaurus.

The search function is only one example of the special features you may find in today's sophisticated word processing software. Many programs now offer a **spelling checker,** which compares each word in your document with the entries in a dictionary stored on the software disk and alerts you to possible misspellings. Often you can expand the dictionary yourself, adding uncommon words or technical terms that you use in your work.

A program may even come with a computerized **thesaurus** feature. If you are dissatisfied with a word you have used in your text and wish to replace it, but can't think of the "right" one that will make your point most effectively, you need only move the cursor to your word, enter a command, and the program will give you a list of possible alternatives that have similar meanings. With many packages, you can then select from this list as from a menu, and the substitution will be made automatically. Spelling checkers and thesaurus programs can also be bought separately to use with your word processing software.

Macros and libraries.

An advanced editing feature offered by many of the more sophisticated word processing programs is the ability to create macros. **Macros** allow you to represent a term, a phrase, or even a series of commands by one or two keystrokes. Suppose, for example, that you have to prepare a report on tax-exempt municipal bonds. Your word processing program might allow you to define ALT-t as a macro, to represent *tax-exempt municipal bonds*. Whenever you entered ALT-t, the computer would spell out the full expression on the monitor screen. Similarly, you might define CTRL-h as a macro that activates all the commands needed to set up a heading, in capital letters and italics, centered, with an extra line of space above. A collection of macros is sometimes called a *glossary*.

A related time-saving feature of some programs is a **library,** where you can save phrases, paragraphs, addresses, and sometimes form letters and other documents that you use frequently. You can quickly insert library files into whatever document you are working on. Or you can use them to create a series of identical documents addressed to different people—billing notices, for example.

Merging.

When two files are combined, the process is known as **merging.** A frequently used paragraph in the library is merged into a document. Documents can also be merged with other types of files, for example, with address lists. A political candidate might wish to combine a campaign letter with the names from a list of voters so that many personalized letters are printed, each addressed to a different voter. This would require weeks or even months of work using typewriters alone.

FORMATTING

Once a document has been composed and edited, it is nearly ready to be printed. First, however, you may wish to give it a special format. Formatting has several meanings as a computer term, but in word processing it refers to designing how a printed document will look. How wide do you want its margins? If there are page numbers, where should they be placed? Is single, double, or triple spacing appropriate? Formatting controls the appearance of any document and even allows you to change it each time you print.

Most word processing packages are preset to create typical document pages—65 characters per line, perhaps, and 54 lines per page, single spaced. These are called the **default values,** because in the absence of any other instructions the program defaults to these standards. However, these standards or defaults can be changed with simple commands or menu choices. You can widen or narrow the margins. You can call for pages of 20 lines double spaced, or whatever you wish. Some programs allow you to format two- or three-column pages. And you can experiment. If you don't like the appearance of a document one way, you can change the format until you are satisfied—all without rekeyboarding a single word of the document itself.

STATE OF THE ART
Beyond Souped-Up Typing

Imagine yourself sitting in front of a computer screen. You speak into a microphone, and as if by magic, your words appear on the screen one by one. Called voice-driven word processing, this may someday be the most popular method of composing documents. Already, some companies offer equipment and software that can recognize up to 1,000 words of dictation. Others, including IBM and Kurzweil Applied Intelligence, are developing systems that will be able to recognize 10,000 words.

Some of today's most powerful word processing software incorporates voice input in other ways. IBM's DisplayWrite 4, for example, includes a "voice note" feature that can be used to add dictation or comments to a document draft. Suppose a manager reading the draft on a computer screen decides to insert a new sentence. With a system equipped for voice notes, the manager can dictate the sentence, then press a key on the keyboard to indicate where it should appear in the document. The computer marks this spot with a musical note, which signals the typist to replay the voice note.

Other innovations in word processing are helping users do a variety of writing and editing chores more easily. Some word processing software now includes style sheets, which enable the user to develop a variety of elaborate document formats by varying margins, spacing, columns, page length, type styles and sizes, and so on. These programs also store the varied formats so that you can use them repeatedly.

Several popular products, such as WordStar 2000, include features that simplify the typing of outlines. Some products have similar features for generating footnotes, glossaries, and indexes. Increasingly, computers with word processing software are much more than souped-up typewriters.

PRINTING

The process of printing with a word processing program can produce results as simple as a one-page memo or as complicated as a three-color annual report complete with charts and graphs. What is printed depends on both software and hardware. Even the least expensive microcomputer can print an acceptable letter when combined with a simple word processing program and an inexpensive printer. More complex software, computers, and printers can integrate information from database programs with word processing to create extremely sophisticated documents. You will learn more about this in the next chapter, which covers integrated software.

MAKING CHOICES

If you are using word processing software for the first time, any program will seem a vast improvement over typing or writing in longhand. Often it is only after you've used a program for a while that you can see if it best suits your purposes.

Dozens of word processing packages are available, with new ones appearing regularly. If you plan to buy a program or if you are asked to help decide which program fits your organization's word processing needs, you must determine not only which features you will use but also which will be a hindrance or not worth the extra cost. What makes a program best for one organization may make it worse for another. For example, if you are working for a scholarly press, a program that formats footnotes automatically would be a great convenience, but if you are working for a small retail store that sends out only a few letters a month, overall ease of use would be a much more important consideration.

Ease of use can mean several things, of course. Some programs are easy to use because they are very simple. They don't offer a lot of features, so they are easy to learn and easy to remember. They may meet your organization's needs for producing documents, or they may not.

Other programs are easy to use because they have excellent *documentation*, which includes the manuals that come with the software and explain its operation. Some documentation seems to assume that its readers are computer experts. However, other documentation is extremely clear and well organized. Good documentation can give you a sound overview of the software and enable you to perform specific tasks quickly.

Still other programs have special software features to help the beginning user. They provide **tutorials,** which walk you through common tasks in the software package, helping you to learn by doing. **Help messages** and **help screens** are another common feature; by striking certain keys, you can obtain an on-screen explanation of how to perform the task you've selected. And, of course, a well-designed set of menus can also guide you through the tasks you have to perform, enabling you to work more efficiently.

Evaluating software packages is a difficult task, because there are many features to consider. It is wise to get advice from people who have worked with them and to look at reviews in computer magazines. But

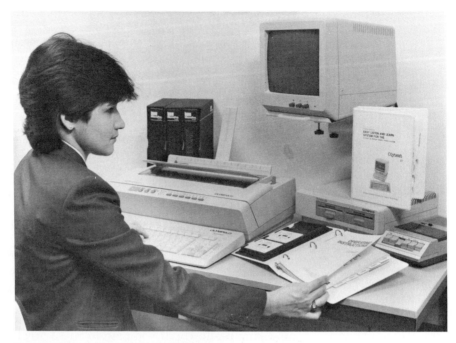

Figure 4-10 Explain It in English
Software design is a BIG business, and the marketed product is not always easy to use. To broaden the appeal of their product, software developers and technical writers provide customers with instructions (documentation), practice (tutorials), and even first aid (HELP screens). (Courtesy of Olympia USA, Inc.)

the most important items to consider are, first, whether it has the features your organization needs and, second, whether it will be easy to learn and use. These considerations apply not just to word processing programs but to all types of applications software, including database packages.

Database management software

If you are put off by the term *database*, you're not alone. For many people it brings to mind an image of thousands of facts, names, and numbers waiting to confuse a well-meaning computer user. Yet you may have watched a database being used without realizing it. Almost all of us have gone to the library to prepare a term paper or report and have asked for help in locating information. The librarian probably used a database to help us: the library's card catalog. The term *database* was not commonly used before computers were invented. But the information in a library catalog, a company's ledgers, or an encyclopedia can all be thought of as **databases:** accumulations of systematically organized information.

As suggested in Chapter 2, a computer database is a modern electronic version of that old office standby, the file cabinet. But just as word processing allows you to do many things not possible in conventional typing, computerized databases offer many conveniences not available with conventional files. Computer databases are electronic files that are created by a type of software package called a **database management system (DBMS).** Such software lets you collect a lot of information and store it in a structured, electronic form, ready to be viewed or printed out when you need it. Moreover, it can sort and reorder the information automatically, search through it to answer specific questions, perform calculations, and put together reports—all with a minimum of human help. A single DBMS may create, and consult, several unrelated databases, or it may be able to combine information from several databases in a single report.

Database software has become so convenient to use that it requires only slightly more study than word processing software. In fact, experience with a word processing package is very helpful for using a database management system. Both types of programs have similar rules for keyboarding text into the computer. And the menus and commands of database software are often similar to those used in word processing.

FILES, RECORDS, AND FIELDS

A few basic terms are used to describe the way a DBMS organizes a database. A **database file** is a full collection of data about a specific subject—often the database itself. For example, a real estate agent might save a file containing details on all the houses he has for sale. Such a database would contain a different entry for each house. Each entry would be a **record.** These records would be further broken down into categories, such as name of the seller, address, number of rooms, size of lot, and price. Each category is a **field.**

It's easy to see the value of this database to the real estate agent. If a customer asks to see every house costing less than $125,000 with at least nine rooms, the agent can go to the computer. Commands to select every record with a "price" field smaller than $125,000 and a "room" field greater than eight will quickly produce a list of all homes that might interest the buyer.

CREATING AND CONSULTING DATABASES

Database software is used both for creating and for consulting databases. The process of creating a database is a little more complex than creating a word processed document, and the process of consulting a database is also somewhat more involved than printing a document prepared with word processing software. In both cases, the complexity lies in the format or structure involved.

When you create a database, you usually need to tell the system about the fields you want to include in each record: what they should be called and how long they should be. For a real estate database, for example, you might decide to have fields titled "Name of owner," "Street address," "Asking price," and so on. Each field could be a standard length—30

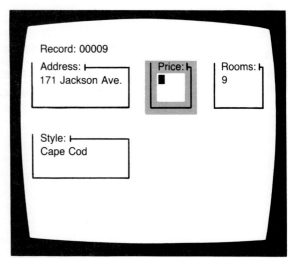

Figure 4-11   Adding a Database Record
Some DBMS packages require you to create records in a list format like the one on the left. With others, you have the option of entering data in boxes, which you can rearrange on the screen to create forms.

characters long, for example—but often, to save on memory, you'll want to limit the number of characters. Occasionally, too, you may want a longer field, to accommodate entries such as "Split level with two-car garage and finished rec room." This first step sets up your **data dictionary,** or list of fields.

The next step is to enter the data itself—the actual names, addresses, homes, and prices. Depending on your software, you may be presented with a display of several records or one record at a time (see Figure 4.11). In each case, you enter the names, numbers, or addresses at the appropriate places, then move your cursor to the next field, usually by using the RETURN/ENTER key or else the TAB key provided on some keyboards.

Once you have created a database, you can use it in a variety of ways, depending on your needs. The simplest use is probably calling up a particular record. All you do is follow the procedures appropriate for your DBMS software, as specified in its documentation. With more user-friendly packages, this will merely mean following menus and prompts. The record you want will be displayed on the screen or printed out. This operation is like searching for a particular customer's manila file so that you can study it, but the process is much faster.

A second use could involve printing the entire database, so that you can check its entries or use it to prepare a report. But this is rarely done because reports can be generated automatically. These reports select a slice of the database that is relevant to the user and may present or summarize the data. For example, you could ask for a list of all California clients in your database, with phone numbers only. Or a real estate agent could ask a DBMS for the average cost of three-bedroom houses for sale in Pittsburgh and list all houses below that average.

MODIFYING AND SORTING

Clearly, a database is of limited use if it cannot be altered. People move, prices change, new products are created. Though the electronic techniques used vary, all DBMS programs allow you to modify databases by adding new records and changing the data in individual fields. Most can also let you change a field for all records at the same time. For example, suppose that a tire retailer uses a database system to print price tags and wishes to raise prices by 5 percent across the board. Rather than go through each record and perform the calculations individually, the retailer could use a command or menu choice to instruct the computer to increase all entries in the "price" field by 5 percent. The new price tags can then be printed, and the inventory records too will be changed automatically.

Sorting is also frequently required. Are customer lists to be arranged alphabetically, by address, according to how much each customer owes, or by some other principle? Most database software will present lists organized as you choose. Just learn the appropriate commands for your software, and the list can be tailored for your purposes.

DATABASE STRUCTURES

The differences between database software packages are probably more dramatic than those between word processing programs. Most word processing software packages offer the same sets of features and all of them operate relatively quickly; but database programs vary widely in the features they offer and in the speeds at which they work. One DBMS may take a minute or more to add a new field, while another may perform this task in a few seconds. DBMS packages also differ in the time they take to generate similar reports and one program may have stricter limitations than another on the field lengths it can handle.

	Current Listings		
Address	Style	Rooms	Price
613 Lincoln Ave.	colonial	9	119,000
482 Washington Ave.	Vict.	10	105,000
2 Adams Ave.	ranch	11	95,000
278 Roosevelt Ave.	colonial	10	112,800
171 Jackson Ave.	Cape Cod	9	89,000
14 Kennedy Place	colonial	10	123,000
2281 Monroe Ave.	colonial	10	117,000
309 Garfield Ave.	Cape Cod	9	106,900

Figure 4-12   Sorting a Database
If a real estate agent's customer asked to see houses with at least nine rooms that cost less than $125,000, the agent would need to perform sorting operations on the two fields ROOMS and PRICE. This printout shows all records in which ROOM has a value of nine or more and PRICE is $125,000 or less.

Many of these differences result from the electronic organization or structure created by the particular DBMS you are using. This organization is what makes it possible to locate specific fields in the database rather than searching through every record each time a particular set of figures is needed. Four fundamental structures are used in today's databases: list or file structure, relational structure, hierarchical structure, and network structure.

List or file structure. Systems with a list or **file structure** are almost too simple to be called databases, but they are capable of many database functions. Essentially, a single list or file is kept, with different records each containing several fields. Searching these systems is often slow, particularly if there is a lot of data to process.

Relational structure. A **relational database** includes several lists or files that are related through certain fields that they share. For example, a file on purchasers and a file on product prices might both include a field that specifies "product name." This field could be used to link purchasers and prices—to generate a list, for example, of what particular customers have spent. A search in a relational database may involve searches through several files, but the net result is usually faster than searching a similarly sized file system. Relational databases can be very flexible; they can often be consulted in ways that were totally unanticipated during their design.

Hierarchical structure. **Hierarchical databases** are particularly good for speed of access and for certain types of modification. They work by progressively making a search more limited, in ways that are planned beforehand. Thus, a database of addresses might be organized geograph-

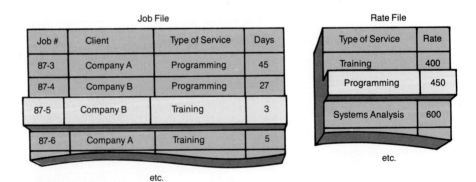

Figure 4-13   The Relational Database
Relational databases contain related lists or files that share particular fields. Here one file contains basic records of jobs a consulting firm has performed; the other has information on the firm's rate structure. A relational DBMS can relate each job record to the rate for the type of service performed. Then it can calculate the amount payable, and, perhaps, supply the client's full mailing address from another similar file. Among other advantages not mentioned in the text, a clerk would not need to look up rates and addresses when entering basic job information.

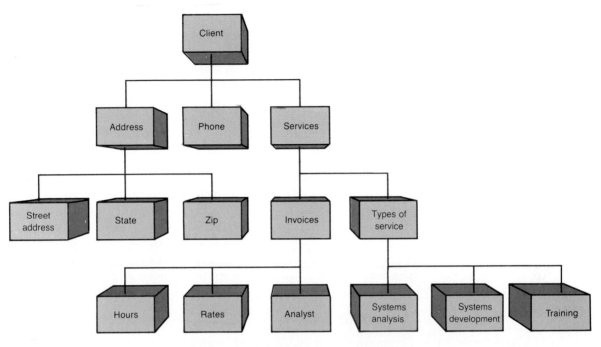

Figure 4-14   The Hierarchical Database Structure
This is how a consulting firm specializing in systems development might set up a hierarchical database organized by client. It should permit them to find all clients served by a particular analyst. However, it is not well suited to finding what services each analyst has provided to a variety of clients—that would require a detailed search of individual client records.

ically; it would first narrow a search to addresses in Texas, for example, then Dallas, and finally the client involved. This system, however, would be slow in finding a client by purchasing history. Hierarchical systems are thus relatively inflexible.

Network structure.   **Network databases** are the most difficult systems to design, though they are capable of the greatest power. They provide a type of cross-referencing system in an otherwise hierarchical structure, making for a high degree of interconnection among files, records, and fields. The result is that they can combine the speed of a hierarchical system with the flexibility of a relational system.

MAKING CHOICES

These four essentially different structures make choosing a database difficult. One may be preferable for the time it takes to plan and load the database. Another may be superior for the time it takes to access records. A third may handle modifications faster. A fourth may have a larger overall capacity for storage of data. All of the features must be taken into consideration.

With database software, as with all software, you should define your needs carefully before buying. Many simple programs that cost only a few hundred dollars are just as desirable as their more expensive relatives for many tasks. And, of course, another important consideration is the clarity and thoroughness of the program's documentation.

Communications software

Both word processing and database software produce masses of information, which can be printed in document form. In the old days, such documents had to be sent by mail or messenger—unless an organization could afford long telegrams. But in today's office, where letters and reports are created electronically before they are put on paper, they can also be

THE HUMAN SIDE

How a Video Rental Business Uses a Database System

Database programs can be customized for special purposes. When Bill Madison first established East Avenue Video Rental, he used a card file system to track which movies were rented and who had rented them. Now, he uses a computer that allows him to make much more efficient use of this data.

East Avenue Video's computer system uses Ashton-Tate's dBASE III and MicroSoft Word. It also includes a scanner for reading bar codes (similar to the codes on groceries) that Madison has placed on each videotape, videodisk, and membership card.

Madison created a database of the videos in the store. Using the database, he can create catalogs. He has one catalog that lists videos by category (comedy, horror, drama, and so on) and another that lists them alphabetically. Every week he issues a list of new releases. Madison also maintains a database of the members. East Avenue Video has two membership options, with different annual fees and rental prices. The membership database is used to print labels for special mailings to each group of members.

The system's main purpose is to track videotapes as they are rented. A clerk scans the bar code on each video being rented and then scans the customer's membership card.

The only keyboarding needed is to indicate how long the video is being rented. (If the member is not carrying a card, the clerk also enters the first three letters of the member's last name and the system searches the database for a matching record.) The correct price for the rental (depending on the type of membership) is displayed on the screen and printed on an invoice.

Using the system, Madison generates a daily late list of customers who have not returned videos. Because his database ties in with his word processing system, he can also write letters notifying customers when their memberships are about to expire.

Perhaps most important, the system allows Madison to gather information about how well his business is doing. He can find out which videos are in demand and order more copies to rent out. He also knows which categories are most popular, and least popular, and which customers rent the most videos.

Customers like the computer system, too, because it has speeded the process of renting a movie from East Avenue Video. The system has helped the business grow so much that Madison now needs to expand the system by adding a second terminal.

sent electronically. They need not be printed until they reach their destination. Indeed, they needn't be printed at all—they can be read on a monitor and saved on a disk by the recipient. All of this is done with the aid of **communications software,** which links the power of the computer to the convenience of the telephone.

A device that makes much of this transmission possible is called the **modem.** A modem changes the sending computer's output into pulses that can be transmitted over telephone lines. Another modem converts these pulses back into computer signals at the receiving end. Chapter 10 will describe in greater detail the hardware that makes up a communications system.

A typical user of communications software might be a traveling business executive with a portable computer. At the end of the workday she connects her computer, which has a built-in modem, to a phone outlet in her hotel and sends her files to the organization's central computer. Some files might be entered into the main database; others might be passed on to the word processing department to be prepared as memos or letters.

Every day, more and more files are being transmitted in this way. Computer hobbyists send messages to each other over information networks. Credit card bureaus do instant credit checks for stores. Even computer software is delivered via phone lines.

The link between computers is generally two-way: communications software can permit each computer to send data to the other. A business computer user can call up an outside system to consult a sophisticated database such as a stock market report. This is not a passive process like reading a newspaper—you can formulate your own queries to obtain, say, the latest information on a particular stock from the outside database. And some systems will even allow you to **download,** or transfer, sections

Figure 4-15 The Computer Connection
This bank officer can't leave his customer stranded while he goes to the central computer room to analyze home equity loan trends. Instead, he uses his laptop computer. Hook up its modem, and this computer—and its user!—knows just what the central computer upstairs knows. (Courtesy of Hewlett-Packard Company)

Figure 4-16   Electronics in the Service of Books
When librarians consult a database, they are frequently communicating with an outside organization's computer. Once they have made established telephone contact they can search its files on very specific subjects. (Courtesy of New York University Library/L. Pellettieri)

of a large database into your own computer. You may then analyze this data with your own software, saving some of the costs of using the large system.

FILE TRANSFERS

Communications programs are generally simple, with fewer commands than database management systems or word processing software. Their main task is to make a good connection between the two computers and then either to send or to receive the data. Learning how to use a communications program is thus relatively easy. The basic commands deal with preparing the computer, specifying the phone number, making contact, and starting data transmission.

Preparing the computer.   The computer must be prepared because there are several variables to consider when sending messages electronically. Some are technical, dealt with in Chapter 10 of this book. Others are easier to understand—for example, the speed of transmission. If one computer is sending characters at a certain rate but the other is expecting, and reading, them at a different rate, clearly no message will get through. The sender and recipient must agree on the speed and other variables before communicating, and must set them up using the software. The group of agreements for any communication is known as its **communications protocol.**

Typically, a communications protocol needs to be set only once for each computer you contact. Most communications programs can store the appropriate protocol for a particular computer, along with its phone number. You can then indicate which computer you want to contact, and the rest is handled automatically by the software.

Making contact. Once the protocol has been set, the phone connection is very easily made. The software takes care of all the details, including dialing the number, and transmission can begin. First, however, the two computers will **handshake,** or establish their connection, each one emitting a series of tones. If the contact is successful, your own computer or terminal should display a "connect" message, and data transfer can begin.

Starting data transmission. For the sender, all that's left is to tell the computer which file to send, and the software takes care of the rest. It all sounds very simple. However, planning *is* required. For example, the receiver must decide how the file should be used. Is it to be viewed on the monitor? Would it be better to get a printed copy? Or should a permanent electronic record first be made on disk? This decision is taken care of with help from the receiver's communications package.

ELECTRONIC MAIL, BULLETIN BOARDS, AND CONFERENCES

Messages can be sent electronically on a file-by-file basis, as described previously. But systems have also been developed to make the process

Figure 4-17   To Be or Not to Be—At a Computer
These stockbrokers are no computer experts, yet they are among the most frequent users of computers. Seated at their remote terminals, they use communications software to access the vast amounts of ever-changing data they need to close a financial deal. (Courtesy of Merrill Lynch)

even easier. Suppose you aren't at your desk when a message arrives for you, and your microcomputer isn't ready to receive a message. Making individual telephone contact is often difficult. But many organizations have set up **electronic mail** systems, which allow messages to be stored until the recipient is ready to study them.

In such a system, each subscriber has an electronic storage area in a larger computer, which can receive and save messages at any time. When you, the recipient, get to your desk, you contact your "electronic mailbox," find what has been delivered for you, and call it up on your screen or printer. This system allows you to receive messages fast and at your convenience. And you can often use it to send a message to many people. You key in the message and a list of recipients, and the message will be delivered to all of them—assuming, of course, that they have mailboxes on the system.

Electronic mailboxes are now a feature of many business phone systems. Organizations can also subscribe to electronic mailboxes with Western Union, MCI, and AT&T, which can be contacted by standard microcomputer communications packages. The cost is high by post office standards but competitive with telephone rates and same-day or next-day courier services.

Electronic bulletin boards are in some ways similar to mailboxes, but like real bulletin boards, they allow open access. When you contact a bulletin board through your modem, you can read messages that have been left there by prior callers or leave a message of your own. Like electronic mail, bulletin boards are often used internally by businesses.

Communications software also allows people in different locations to exchange ideas and information in a fast, efficient way known as **electronic conferencing.** The participants in such a conference sit at their computer terminals and watch their monitors. Whatever is entered by one person through his or her keyboard appears on all the monitors and can be read by everyone. Each participant has a chance to contribute his or her thoughts, questions, and suggestions. A permanent record of the exchanges can easily be made and printed for later review if desired.

INFORMATION SERVICES AND DATA BANKS

A major business use of communications software is to access commercial databases. These **information services** charge a fee to the user for the right to search their databases for whatever information the user needs. Areas covered by such services include a variety of scientific fields, medical specialties, and law as well as general news and information.

Some databases provide important financial information to businesses. There are also more comprehensive services. One provides access to more than 900 databases on topics ranging from nutrition to the weather. Users can also view catalogs and order merchandise via their terminals.

As you will read in Chapter 10, telephone lines are not the only medium for data transmission. Big businesses are pushing hardware and software designers to develop faster communications systems. Businesses frequently use microwave dishes to send signals, sometimes via satellite

Figure 4-18 Your Card, Please
Credit card transactions are a high-volume business—but the risk is high. Computerized data banks have helped reduce fraud by verifying identity, credit record, and credit line in seconds. An unexpected bonus: the goodwill of legitimate customers, whose convenience is increased while fraud is decreased. (Courtesy of International Business Machines Corporation © Gary Kufner)

relays. Because static and small signal fluctuations on the phone lines create the possibility of mistakes, complex error-checking schemes must be built into the communications software. Consequently, even the fastest experimental phone systems cannot approach the speed of direct microwave links between computers. Some experts predict that the country will eventually be totally rewired, perhaps with optical fibers, because electronic communication has become so important.

SUMMARY

- Software consists of sets of instructions to the computer. Applications software directs the computer in completing particular tasks, and systems software performs general tasks that the computer must accomplish to handle applications software.

- Software controls the user interface of a computer, which allows users to communicate with the system. It typically includes a monitor and a keyboard and often printers, disk drives, and other devices. Though details of the user interface differ from one program to another, most use commands given through the keyboard alone, or they display menus from which selections are made.

- Word processing software is heavily used by organizations, especially those that must prepare many written documents. It allows rapid revision of documents without rekeyboarding every word, as well as many features not offered by a typewriter, including word wrap and automatic centering. Nothing need be printed on paper until a document is complete and correct.

- Saving is a standard computer function with all programs involving the creation of documents. Information is typically saved as files on a storage medium such as a diskette. Files can be retrieved by the computer if they are called up by the appropriate file name.

- Word processing software allows many editing functions not available on a standard typewriter: insertion, deletion, movement and copying of blocks, and special features such as spelling checks. It also gives the user considerable control over the output, allowing a document's form to be adjusted after keyboarding is complete.

- Word processing software packages share many features but vary in complexity, ease of use, and the quality of their documentation. More sophisticated features are generally available in the more costly programs but may not be needed by many users. Organizations can benefit if they plan carefully before selecting a word processing package.

- Databases, collections of systematically organized information, are created and can be consulted by means of a database management system. They are commonly organized into files, records, and fields. A DBMS not only stores data but can also search automatically for individual records, summarize them, perform calculations, and produce reports.

- To create a database, one must first define the fields that will make up each record and then insert the appropriate data. Databases can be consulted by calling up individual records or by asking for partial listings and summaries. There are many ways to modify, or edit, a database. In addition to individual entries being changed and records added, fields can be altered systematically, and entries can be sorted or resequenced.

- The exact capabilities of databases can vary widely, depending in part on their structure. The most common types are list or file, relational, hierarchical, and network.

- Communications software enables data to be exchanged by computers at different locations, using a modem and regular phone lines. The communications software allows you to specify the protocol of how a message will be sent. It can also be set up to dial the remote computer's phone number.

- Types of communication made possible by communications software include file transfer from one business computer to another, electronic mail, storage in a central location for later retrieval by the intended recipient, electronic bulletin boards, electronic conferencing, and access to information services and other commercial databases.

TERMS FOR REVIEW

software
diskette
floppy disk
prompts
program
applications
  software
systems software
operating systems
DOS
user interface
monitor
printer
disk drives
keyboard
~~mouse~~
~~cursor~~
impact printers
nonimpact printers
draft printers
letter-quality
  printers
function keys
command-driven
  software
menus
menu-driven
  software

word processing
  software
keyboarding
editing
formatting
printing
saving
word wrap
scrolling
file
backup
file name
directory
insert
delete
block move
search
search and replace
spelling checker
thesaurus
macros
library
glossary
merging
default values
documentation
help messages
help screens

tutorials
databases
database
  management
  system (DBMS)
database file
record
field
data dictionary
sorting
file structure
relational database
hierarchical
  database
network databases
communications
  software
~~modem~~
download
communications
  protocol
handshake
electronic mail
electronic bulletin
  boards
electronic
  conferencing
information services

TERMINOLOGY CHECK

For each of these definitions, choose the correct term from the list of Terms for Review:

1. Written manual of instructions to accompany a software package. *documentation*

2. A single piece of information, like a street address, that might be contained in a database. *field*

3. Settings, in formatting, for example, that the software will use if you don't specify others that you want. *default values*

4. Device that allows data to be transmitted over telephone lines. *Modem*

5. Process of recording onto a diskette, essential for protecting and storing information. *Saving*

6. A specific instruction from the user to the computer, detailing what action it is to take. *Command*

7. Hand-held device that allows you to move the cursor quickly across the monitor screen. *Mouse*

8. Computer service that allows people to leave private written messages for each other by means of telephone lines.

9. The process of reordering records in a database. *sorting*

10. Function that allows a user to find all occurrences of a particular word or phrase in a document. *cursor*

INFORMATION CHECK

1. Distinguish applications software from systems software.

2. What are two ways of distinguishing the kinds of printers that are used with microcomputers?

3. What is menu-driven software, and why is it considered particularly useful for beginners? What are some of its disadvantages?

4. Identify and describe three advantages of word processing over typing.

5. When using word processing software, what must you do when you have finished a line of text? When you have completed a screen of text? In each case, the computer causes a movement to occur on the screen. Describe these movements.

6. What can be accomplished with the insert function in a word processing program? Why do you think it is called one of the most important features of such software?

7. Explain two very important reasons why you might want to save a word processing file.

8. Why must every document you save have a file name? What would happen if it didn't?

9. What types of files would you expect to find in the "library" of a word processing program? Why are these useful?

10. Why is good documentation important with word processing and other software packages? What is the similarity in purpose between documentation and help screens?

11. Explore the difference between a database and a database management system. Which would you describe as an applications package? Which is created by the user?

12. Why is it usually less useful to print all the data contained in a database than to print partial information from it? In what other ways can a database be consulted?

13. Why is it valuable for an organization to be able to modify a database? Why would it be useful to sort a database?

14. Explain one kind of incompatibility that communications protocols can help to overcome.

15. Describe three common uses for communications software packages.

PROJECTS AND PROBLEMS

1. Bourton and Zellers, a supplier of restaurant equipment in a rural area, employs 50 people and earns close to half a million dollars a year. Currently, all of its correspondence, inventory record keeping, and order processing is done by hand. But orders are booming, and the clerical staff is hard pressed to keep up. Because you are taking a course in computers, your supervisor, who knows very little about them, asks your help in deciding whether computers could improve the situation.

   Plan what advice you would give. What kinds of tasks could computers help with? What types of software would the company need to buy? (Don't try to recommend specific products.) What could using software do for the company? Prepare a memo to your supervisor on this topic, doing additional research in the library if you feel the need.

2. Browse through the computer magazines in your local library or bookstore and make notes on several of the latest word processing or database packages. Pay attention to both reviews and advertisements. Consider the claims made by the manufacturers, and compare the comments of reviewers in different magazines. Then write a report on your observations, indicating which particular program sounds best to you and why.

3. Visit a local computer store, and ask which are the most popular communications software packages. See if a salesperson will demonstrate one for you, and ask for the sales literature on all. What features does each offer? How easy do you think they would be to use? How much variation is there in the prices? Prepare an oral presentation to give to the class on this topic.

4. If you have access to any software of the types described in this chapter, find out what it can do for you and how to use it. Then apply it in some way that could be useful to yourself. For example, use the word processor to write a letter or a course paper. Make a database containing the names, addresses, phone numbers, and perhaps birthdays of your family and friends. Or come up with a novel use of your own. Show the results to your instructor, and be ready to explain it to the class.

5

Spreadsheets, graphics, and integrated

Why were computers originally called computers? Because they compute, or handle numbers, very efficiently. In fact, the first application of computers was mathematical calculations. And one of the earliest business uses of computers was in the accounting department, where organizations calculate the details of their financial performance.

Computer applications have come a long way since then. Word processing has surpassed mathematics as the leading business use of the microcomputer. The three applications described in the previous chapter—word processing, database management, and communications—usually involve relatively little mathematics. But in this chapter, we will look at modern software that calculates, greatly simplifying the handling and presentation of numbers.

The first type of applications software covered in this chapter is spreadsheet software. This was in fact the package that first convinced businesses to buy microcomputers. **Spreadsheet software** enables business workers to create tables of figures on the screen. The computer then performs all needed calculations and places answers in appropriate positions in those tables. If the numbers need to be changed, the answers are automatically recalculated, saving hours of work with a scratch pad or hand calculator.

Graphics software, the second type of applications program covered in this chapter, allows the user to convert numbers to graphs so that they can be understood at a glance. Has there been a rise in revenues during the past few years? Have expenses gone down? Is productivity on the increase? Enter the appropriate numbers into a graphics package, and the point can be made visually. There is no need to read and compare many numbers—nor to wait two or three days for a highly paid artist to create a chart.

Last, the chapter looks at **integrated software,** in which different applications programs are integrated, or made to work together. Integration means that numbers can be automatically taken from a database file and inserted into a spreadsheet for mathematical analysis. Then they can be displayed in graph form and finally incorporated into a report prepared with word processing. No data entry is needed after the numbers have been keyboarded into the database, and the work is done with the accuracy and speed of computers. These are some of the benefits that today's software can bring to business workers who understand computers and their uses.

When you have studied this chapter, you should be able to

- account for the value of spreadsheet software to businesses

- define rows, columns, and cells in a spreadsheet

- differentiate among values, labels, and formulas

- identify basic functions involved in entering data on a spreadsheet

- explain at least three common uses of spreadsheets and templates

- discuss the importance of graphics software to organizations

- summarize the capabilities of typical analytical graphics software and some business applications of presentation graphics

- list three categories of integrated software and discuss their advantages and limitations

Spreadsheets

Spreadsheet software is generally credited with taking the microcomputer out of the hands of computer hobbyists and mathematical/technical wizards and making it useful to the business world. Visicalc, the first spreadsheet program, came to market in 1979. It was written for the Apple II computer, which had itself been on sale for only two years, and the combination proved irresistible. The Apple gained a foothold in small business, and Visicalc was an instant best-seller. Later, Visicalc was adapted for use with other micros, including the then new IBM PC. Eventually, other more elaborate and user-friendly spreadsheets surpassed Visicalc in popularity. But spreadsheet software remains extremely useful to today's organizations. It has become a standard business tool.

WORKSHEETS AND SPREADSHEETS

Spreadsheet software is based on a very simple business form: the accountant's **worksheet.** This is a ruled paper form with rows and columns set up for the entry of numbers, especially dollar amounts. A worksheet is convenient for calculating both across the rows and down the columns. It also typically has blank spaces to the left and across the top so that rows and columns can both be labeled if necessary. Worksheet forms are

Figure 5-1   Not Only What Is—What About What If?
Successful businesses don't just exist; they plan for the future to keep profitable
and expand. Financial forecasting has always been part of business planning. In
the old days it was a tedious manual procedure, involving a great deal of paperwork. Now spreadsheet software saves much of the effort. (Courtesy of International Business Machines Corporation)

as adaptable as regular lined paper—they can be used for scratch calculations and for formal financial records.

A typical worksheet is shown in Figure 5-2. The Roy Bean Chili
Bistro, a take-out restaurant in a college town noted for cold winters, is
calculating its budget for the next week. It needs to know the cost per
serving of one of the dishes so that a price can be determined. Notice that
the second column, though ruled for numbers, is being used to record the
units of measurement. Notice, too, that the calculations are systematic.
On each row the price is multiplied by the amount, to give the cost per
ingredient. Then the cost column is totaled to permit calculations of the
price per serving.

Calculations of this type are very important to organizations of all
sorts, because they are the only way that an accurate picture can be
obtained of what has happened or will happen to the finances. How much
money was earned last week from the various items a store carries? How
much are the items in the warehouse worth today? What profits were
made during the different months of last year, and how do those amounts
compare with this year's figures? All of these questions can be answered
by preparing an appropriate worksheet.

Needless to say, preparing a worksheet by hand is a slow, painstaking task that is very prone to human error. If the bookkeeper at the Chili Bistro makes any mistakes in entering the data onto the worksheet, all the calculations will have to be redone and double-checked. That is why spreadsheet software was such an instant success—it can save a lot of this work.

Just as database management systems allow you to build databases, spreadsheet software allows you to design electronic worksheets, or **spreadsheets.** If you make errors in entering data, or if more up-to-date information becomes available, these spreadsheets, like documents prepared with word processing software, can be changed *before* they are committed to paper. Spreadsheet software can also perform, and redo, calculations automatically, without errors, in a fraction of the time that it takes a person to do them by hand.

Daily Budget for Chili

Ingredients	Unit	Amount	Price	Cost
oil	qt	.5	$ 1 49	$ 75
beef	lb	7.5	1 29	9 68
pork	lb	2.5	99	2 48
onions	20 lb	.5	3 29	1 65
green peppers	lb	3.5	69	2 42
garlic	lb	.5	2 29	1 15
vinegar	qt	.5	1 39	70
chilis	#20 jars	1	4 69	4 69
chili powder	oz	6	49	2 94
chili oil	fl oz	4	1 95	7 80
spices	cup	2	35	70
secret	cup	1	2 35	2 35
total cost				$ 37 28
cost per serving				93

Figure 5-2 An Accounting Worksheet
Worksheets let you organize data and calculations vertically (into rows) and horizontally (into columns). Here columns 1 and 2 carry labels for the three columns to the right. Columns 3 and 4 are used to record values. Most of the figures in Column 5 are derived from multiplying the figures in Columns 3 and 4. This method of organizing information is also standard in electronic spreadsheets.

A TYPICAL SPREADSHEET

Like the traditional worksheet on which it is based, a spreadsheet has areas for data to be entered, arranged in horizontal **rows** and vertical **columns.** These areas are called **cells.** A cell is typically identified by a number to indicate its row and a letter for its column. Thus, cell A1 is the top left cell, A2 is immediately below it, and B1 is to its right.

As on a worksheet, these cells can contain numbers, called **values,** or words, called **labels.** However, spreadsheet cells can carry a third type of information, which accounts for their remarkable power: they can carry **formulas.** Formulas are not visible on the completed spreadsheet: they supply numbers to take their place. But instead of working out the answer to a calculation, you, as a spreadsheet user, need only to enter the formula for that calculation. The spreadsheet software does the rest.

For example, look again at the Chili Bistro worksheet. The bookkeeper who was assigned the work had to hand-calculate each cost figure—a total of 12 calculations. To do the same problem on a spreadsheet, you need only enter the appropriate formula in each cost cell—the work is left to the computer.

E3:C3*D3

	A	B	C	D	E
1	Ingred.	Unit	Amount	Price	Cost
2					
3	oil	qt.	0.5	$1.49	$0.75
4	beef	lb.	7.5	$1.29	$9.68
5	pork	lb.	2.5	$0.99	$2.48
6	onions	20 lb.	0.5	$3.29	$1.65
7	g.ppprs.	lb.	3.5	$0.69	$2.42
8	garlic	lb.	0.5	$2.29	$1.15
9	vinegar	qt.	0.5	$1.39	$0.70
10	chilis	#20 jar	1.0	$4.69	$4.69
11	chili pwd.	oz.	6.0	$0.49	$2.94
12	chili oil	fl. oz.	4.0	$1.95	$7.80
13	spices	cup	2.0	$0.35	$0.70
14	secret	cup	1.0	$2.35	$2.35
15					
16	total cost (40 servings)				37.28
17	cost per serving				0.93

Figure 5-3   A Spreadsheet for Chili Bistro
Spreadsheets allow computer data to be organized into orderly tables of information. Data is entered into cells as labels (A1), values (C3), or formulas (E3). Note that the number shown in cell E3 was calculated from a formula, which is displayed above the spreadsheet when the cell is highlighted.

Ingred.	Unit	Amount	Price	Cost
oil	qt.	0.5	1.49	+C3*D3
beef	lb.	7.5	1.29	+C4*D4
pork	lb.	2.5	0.99	+C5*D5
onions	20 lb.	0.5	3.29	+C6*D6
g.ppprs.	lb.	3.5	0.69	+C7*D7
garlic	lb.	0.5	2.29	+C8*D8
vinegar	qt.	0.5	1.39	+C9*D9
chilis	#20 jar	1	4.69	+C10*D10
chili pwd.	oz.	6	0.49	+C11*D11
chili oil	fl. oz.	4	1.95	+C12*D12
spices	cup	2	0.35	+C13*D13
secret	cup	1	2.35	+C14*D14
total cost (40 servings)				@SUM(E3..E14)
cost per serving				+E16/40

Figure 5-4   The Chili Bistro Spreadsheet Revealed
One way to see the complete set of formulas for a particular spreadsheet is to use the reveal function available on many software packages. This function can be used to spot errors in the spreadsheet and to study its underlying structure. Here it shows how the spreadsheet in Figure 5-3 was created.

In Figure 5-4 you can see how this is done. Instead of calculating the cost of the vegetable oil by multiplying the quantity (in cell C3) by the unit price (in cell D3) and then entering the answer in E3, the bookkeeper simply keyed in a formula, C3*D3. (The asterisk means "times" in most computer languages.) This formula, placed in cell E3, provides the needed answer.

Similarly, the total cost can be entered as a formula at cell E16 and calculated automatically. So can the cost per serving at E17. Thus, although you still need to know what calculations must be done, there is no need for any actual arithmetic—that is done by the computer.

The other great advantage of using formulas is that, if one of the original values needs to be changed—perhaps because it was entered incorrectly—the computer itself can recalculate the table almost instantly. As already noted, this is the feature that sold business on the use of spreadsheets.

USING A SPREADSHEET

As with word processing software, the commands used in different spreadsheet programs differ, but they achieve similar results. To design any spreadsheet, you must carry out standard operations many times: you must move to the cell that needs work and enter or change information (a label, a value, or a formula) in the cell. Of course, other instructions must be given—for example, to indicate how large the spreadsheet is to be or to print it—but these are needed far less often in the creation of a particular sheet.

Moving from cell to cell. At any time, spreadsheet software indicates the cell it is ready to work on, usually by highlighting that cell. This highlight must be moved if figures need to be entered or changed at other locations. Such movement is very simple. Typically the arrow keys are used for short moves (for example, one cell to the right), and for longer moves a command can be issued identifying the particular cell (for example, E16) where you want to work. Other commands are also available; for example, you can use one to move to either end of the row or column you are working on or to the A1 cell, the "beginning" of the spreadsheet.

These fast moves are particularly useful when you are working on a large spreadsheet. Whereas a paper worksheet is limited by the number of areas that can be contained on a piece of paper (perhaps seven columns and 40 rows on a standard-sized sheet), spreadsheet software can provide a much larger work area: typical spreadsheets today can have more than 200 columns and rows each. Using the cursor arrows to move through

THE HUMAN SIDE
A Short-Lived Sensation

Dan Bricklin was laboriously making calculations by hand to complete a financial analysis for a course at the Harvard Business School when he had an idea. Could he, he wondered, design a computer program that would perform the same calculations much more quickly and easily? He could and he did working afternoons with a friend, Bob Frankston, in Frankston's attic.

What Bricklin and Frankston came up with was Visicalc. The two men formed a company, Software Arts, Inc., and introduced Visicalc to the business world at the 1979 National Computer Convention. Microcomputers were not even officially included at that convention, and manufacturers had to hold their own personal computer festival nearby. Visicalc would change all that.

Visicalc was the first blockbuster product of the microcomputer software industry. Today, that industry generates $5 billion a year in sales of more than 27,000 products.

Software Arts went into partnership with Dan Fylstra, who formed Visicorp to market Visicalc. The two companies enjoyed instant and enormous success, selling more than 700,000 copies of the software. But Visicalc proved to be a hard act for them to follow. While Bricklin struggled to come up with a new version, Fylstra's Visicorp began concentrating on developing and marketing its own software.

Meanwhile, in 1983, Lotus Development Corporation introduced a product called Lotus 1-2-3 that made four-year-old Visicalc obsolete. Lotus sales soared, and Visicalc sales plummeted. To make matters worse for the Visicalc team, Software Arts and Visicorp became embroiled in a costly lawsuit that sapped their resources, stalling new product development and forcing massive layoffs of employees.

Finally, in 1985, Bricklin sold the all-but-bankrupt Software Arts to its successful rival, Lotus, and went on to other things. In just six years, Visicalc had gone from leader of the pack to poor relation in the microcomputer software industry. But Bricklin can take comfort in one thing: thanks to Visicalc, today's Harvard Business School students are required to use microcomputers and spreadsheets to perform financial analyses.

such a spreadsheet would be very time-consuming. Fast cursor moves make traveling between distant cells far more efficient.

Entering information. When the highlight is located in a particular cell, you can enter or change data there. Once again, exact techniques for doing this vary. In most programs, keyboarding letters or numbers automatically activates cell entry. But if the software mistook a formula for a label, it would show the formula's symbols in the cell instead of performing the calculation. Therefore, most spreadsheet software makes some provision for identifying the type of information you are entering. With some major packages, for example, a plus sign before a formula indicates that it is not a label or value.

Like word processing programs, spreadsheet software usually includes several features to simplify entry. Individual characters can be deleted, and so can whole cells, rows, and columns. Single cell entries, blocks of cells, and whole rows and columns can also be moved from one location to another—or copied so they appear in more than one place.

Copying formulas is made especially convenient by a feature called **relative reference.** This allows the particular cells mentioned in one formula to be replaced by equivalent cells, rather than the same ones, when they are copied. Thus, if the Chili Bistro bookkeeper copies the cell at E3 (which contains the formula C3*D3) to E4, he would automatically

Figure 5-5   Data at Work

In all kinds of businesses, it frequently helps to work with a combination of printout and screen. The printout shows the data you started with—the screen shows how you have changed it. (Courtesy of Hewlett-Packard Company)

produce the formula C4*D4—the same formula relative to the new row. This makes it very easy to fill column E; for the next 10 rows, all he does is copy the cell from each location to the next.

Many other conveniences are added to make data entry easier. Most spreadsheet software provides a variety of shortcuts. For example, "@sum(E3. . .E14)" is used in more than one spreadsheet program to mean "add the block of numbers in column E between E3 and E14." On the Chili Bistro spreadsheet, this could save quite a lot of keyboarding for the grand total formula at E16. And still more keyboarding can often be saved with a technique known as **cursor pointing.** This would create the same formula by using cursor movements to highlight the block of numbers, much as you do when preparing for a word processing block move. This leads the computer to enter the appropriate letters, numbers, and symbols into the formula automatically.

Yet another convenience is **windowing,** which lets you view different parts of the spreadsheet side by side on the same screen—useful if you need to compare sets of numbers that are at opposite ends of the spreadsheet. Windowing began with spreadsheet software, but it is now avail-

E16:@SUM(E3..E14)

	A	B	C	D	E
1	Ingred.	Unit	Amount	Price	Cost
2					
3	oil	qt.	0.5	$1.49	$0.75
4	beef	lb.	7.5	$1.29	$9.68
5	pork	lb.	2.5	$0.99	$2.48
6	onions	20 lb.	0.5	$3.29	$1.65
7	g.ppprs.	lb.	3.5	$0.69	$2.42
8	garlic	lb.	0.5	$2.29	$1.15
9	vinegar	qt.	0.5	$1.39	$0.70
10	chilis	#20 jar	1.0	$4.69	$4.69
11	chili pwd.	oz.	6.0	$0.49	$2.94
12	chili oil	fl. oz.	4.0	$1.95	$7.80
13	spices	cup	2.0	$0.35	$0.70
14	secret	cup	1.0	$2.35	$2.35
15					
16	total cost (40 servings)				
17	cost per serving				

Figure 5-6   Cursor Pointing

Instead of keyboarding the formula for cell E6, the bookkeeper can begin the formula by typing @SUM and then manipulate the highlight over the cells. The spreadsheet software automatically supplies the appropriate formula to describe the highlighted cells. Cursor pointing can be used for many functions in spreadsheet programs.

able in some word processing packages, allowing you to compare different paragraphs on the screen. And you will read later in this chapter that it is also widely used to place different applications on the screen at the same time.

TEMPLATES

Spreadsheet programs are very flexible tools. They are a prime example of software that is written not just for a specific job but rather to be adaptable to many different jobs. Not only can they be used for computing costs, they can also calculate revenues, keep track of inventory, prepare budgets, and perform any number of other tasks. Spreadsheet programs can even provide simple accounting systems for business, the equal of many packages designed exclusively for this purpose. You will take a look at such special programs in the next chapter.

Of course, preparing a spreadsheet to handle each of these tasks takes time. In addition to the values—the data being processed—formulas have to be entered to indicate required calculations. And labels have to be provided so that the spreadsheets make sense to executives who will study them.

However, once a spreadsheet has been designed, it can be used again and again with different numbers. For the Chili Bistro, if the price of various ingredients changes, these can be changed on the same spreadsheet, without the addition of new labels or formulas. This is true of any prepared spreadsheet. Once saved on a diskette, the labels and formulas make it appropriate for a specific business task, and from then on it can be reused to handle different data for different situations.

The set of labels and formulas for a particular spreadsheet design is often called a **template.** Templates can be prepared for many business needs, and they can be purchased. In fact, most popular spreadsheet packages are supported by commercially developed templates that meet common business needs. Thus, if your organization owns the appropriate spreadsheet software, templates may be available for analyzing and comparing loan interest rates, for keeping track of inventory, for determining prices, or for calculating hourly wages and commissions. Instead of spending a lot of time and effort setting up the labels and formulas, you can buy the appropriate template to provide them. You merely have to fill in the numbers; the template and the spreadsheet software will do the rest.

SPREADSHEETS FOR MAKING PROJECTIONS

The great flexibility of spreadsheet software makes it useful to business in many ways. One of the most interesting is that spreadsheets can be used to forecast the future. Just as the Chili Bistro's spreadsheet can be changed to respond to a rise in the price of vegetable oil, for example, it can also be changed to show what would happen *if* there were a change in the price of oil. This is obviously of interest to restaurant managers. It is also of interest to the marketers of vegetable oil. What would happen if there were a sudden price drop of five cents per quart? Would the

	A	B	C
1	Drexel Toolmaking Company		
2	First-Year Income Projections		
3			
4	Revenue		76000
5			
6	Expenses:		
7	Rent	9000	
8	Leases	18000	
9	Wages	+C4*0.18	
10	Materials	+C4*0.17	
11	Administrative	+C4*0.12	
12	Electricity	+C4*0.08	
13	Total expenses		@SUM(B7..B12)
14			
15		Operating income	+C4-C13

Drexel Toolmaking Company
First-Year Income Projections

Revenue		$76,000
Expenses:		
Rent	$9,000	
Leases	$18,000	
Wages	$13,680	
Materials	$12,920	
Administrative	$9,120	
Electricity	$6,080	
Total expenses		$68,800
Operating income		$7,200

Drexel Toolmaking Company
First-Year Income Projections

Revenue		$87,000
Expenses:		
Rent	$9,000	
Leases	$18,000	
Wages	$15,660	
Materials	$14,790	
Administrative	$10,440	
Electricity	$6,960	
Total expenses		$74,850
Operating income		$12,150

Figure 5-7 Projections on an Electronic Spreadsheet
Spreadsheets help managers calculate the effects of variable or uncertain factors. The screen above shows a revealed spreadsheet projecting several expenses as a percentage of a sales revenue estimate. The printout on the left reflects this figure—changing the estimate from $76,000 to $87,000 produces the printout at right.

organization still make adequate profits? Is it time to diversify, to begin to carry other products to offset the anticipated downturn? A spreadsheet obviously cannot tell managers how to react. But it can tell them the full extent of the danger.

Spreadsheets are widely used for making such projections. They can also be used to find out what would happen if several events happened at the same time. What if sales were to drop by 6 percent, the price of gasoline were to rise 10 cents per gallon, and sales taxes were increased by 1 percent? Would borrowing money at 9.9 percent interest instead of 11 percent enable profits to be maintained? Spreadsheet software makes calculating with multiple variables quite easy.

Imagine if a large-scale worksheet had to be recalculated by hand each time a new possibility was considered. It would take so long that it

Computer graphics

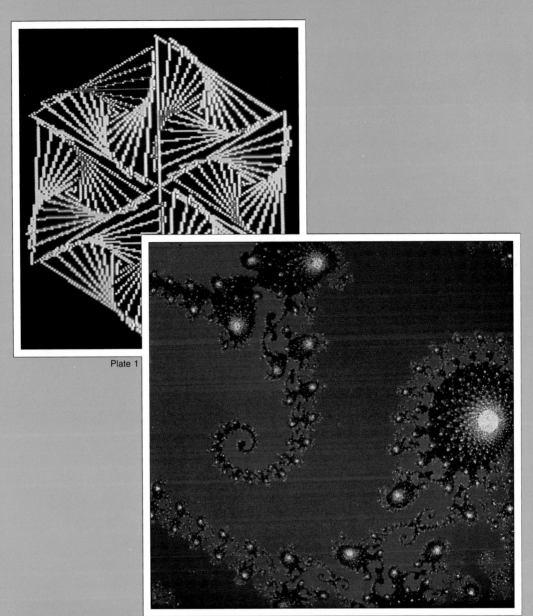

Plate 1

Plate 2

Computer graphics have progressed a long way in a remarkably short time. During the 1970s, color graphics frequently had jagged edges, and looked far more complex than they were. Today, even highly abstract equations can look deceptively simple—and beautiful. And graphics are now used for many purposes.

Plate 3

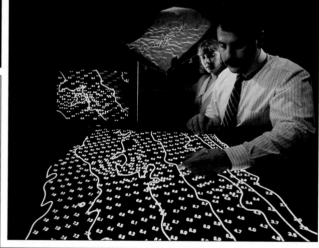

Plate 4

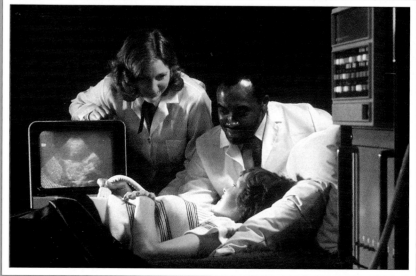

Plate 5

Plate 6

Computer graphics can now be used in nearly all fields of work. Business organizations employ them for a wide range of financial and other analyses. Oceanographers generate and then examine graphics of the ocean floor. Medical teams look at internal processes, studying the development and movement of an unborn chlld, for example, with pictures created by analysing sound echos. Artists can create, manipulate and explore shapes to help them build and analyse their work. And aerospace engineers can use computer graphics to study invisible natural processes that are important to the success of their projects.

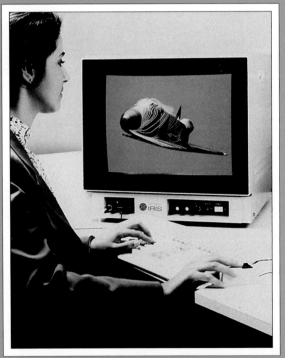

Plate 7

Plate 8

The simple pie charts, bar and line graphs used in business can be produced, and analysed, at most workstations with access to appropriate software. More sophisticated designs may need the help of special CAD equipment—for example, dual screens, digitizers, as well as the extra power of larger computers. Finished output may come from appropriate printers, or from plotters, which can even be transported to the sites where they are needed.

Plate 9

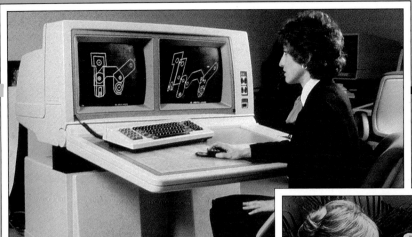

Plate 10

Plate 11

Plate 12

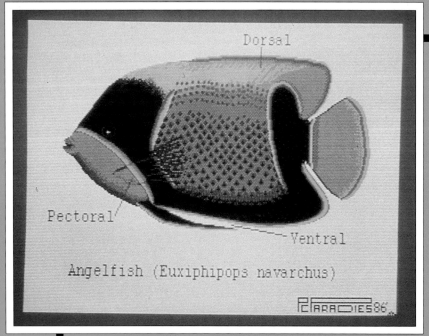

Plate 13

The vivid colors of today's computer graphics can serve several purposes, depending on what the picture is intended to accomplish. In illustrations they can range from realistic to imaginative. On graphs they can be used to enhance basic shapes and also to clarify the different elements being described. In scientific models, color can show important aspects of the objects being described; for example, changes in air pressure across a moving surface, or the processes of growth in complex natural shapes.

Plate 14

Plate 15

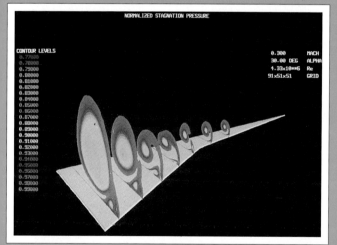

Plate 16

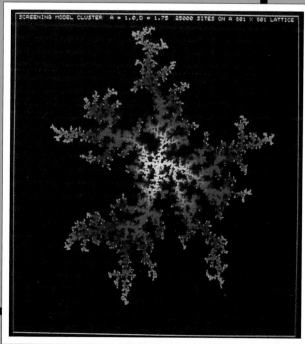

Plate 17

Plate 18

The capabilities of
the computers to create
useful visual output are
still being extended.
They are currently used
to make flat images,
which can then if
necessary be
incorporated into three
dimensional models.
But experiments are
going on to generate
holographic images
from the computer —
images formed of laser
light which can be
studied from many
different perspectives.

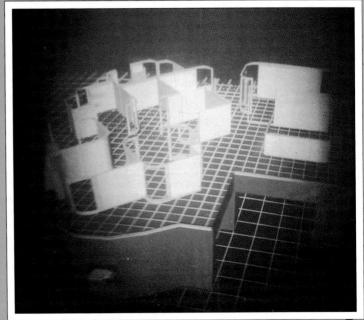

Plate 19

would probably be uneconomical and unproductive. Projections would not be done at all, and organizations would thus lose a useful tool. Spreadsheet software, however, can bring this type of forecasting even to small organizations. Managers can literally watch the calculations ripple across the screen. This software has truly brought new power to decision makers.

MAKING CHOICES

As a worker in a business office that uses more than one spreadsheet package, you may be expected to choose which software is the most appropriate for a particular task. You may also be asked to help select spreadsheet software if you are perceived as someone who knows about computers. In either case, you need to be aware that, even though spreadsheets are quite similar in overall design, there are important differences.

One is the speed with which your spreadsheet makes its calculations and recalculations. A program that is user friendly typically takes up extra space in a computer's memory. The amount of memory remaining, in turn, affects both the size of the spreadsheets that can be handled and the speed with which calculations can be done. You may have to decide whether speed, capacity, or ease of use is most important to you.

A second limitation arises from the format of spreadsheets themselves: they are by nature spread out. Although your spreadsheet might allow the use of 200 columns or more, your printer might still use 8½-by-11 paper, allowing a maximum of 132 characters per line. If you need paper printouts of your spreadsheet, you'll need software that enables your printer to handle spreadsheets.

Finally, it's worth checking whether your spreadsheet software is compatible with other applications. For example, can it lift data directly from the database your organization uses? And can the spreadsheet itself be read by other programs—if you have to present the findings as a pie chart or bar chart, for example? There may be graphics applications that enable you to tailor information on your spreadsheet for presentation to almost any audience. Will you have to rekeyboard the relevant information into the graphics software, or can the two programs be integrated? Computer graphics are becoming vital to many organizations.

Graphics

From video games to flashy TV commercials, computer graphics have become a familiar part of our world. With the appropriate software, computers can create elaborate graphic displays with carefully controlled animation. Although much of this software seems more applicable to the world of entertainment, many graphics packages are frequently used in the office, for serious business purposes.

The well-known saying "A picture is worth a thousand words" is very true in business, especially if it is restated: "A picture is worth a thousand numbers." Numbers are very difficult for most people to study. Even when they are carefully arranged in rows and columns, it can take much thought to understand their meaning. However, as organizations have known since before the first business computer was even thought of, plotting the same numbers on a simple graph can make the meaning very plain. You can grasp the details of how total sales vary from month to month far more easily from the graph in Figure 5-8 than from the table below it.

Words that might lack interest can also be made appealing by the appropriate pictures. Written reports often use illustrations, and formal

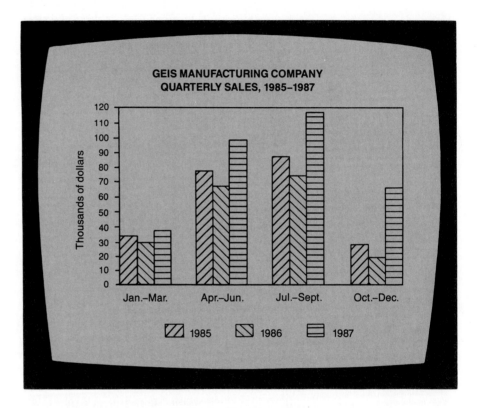

Geis Manufacturing Company Quarterly sales, 1985–1987 All dollar figures in thousands			
	1985	1986	1987
Jan.–Mar.	$32	$29	$37
Apr.–Jun.	$78	$66	$98
Jul.–Sept.	$87	$73	$117
Oct.–Dec.	$28	$18	$65

Figure 5-8 Analytic Graphics
A pictorial representation may make data more meaningful. The sales figures in the table appear to be random. The graph clearly shows two patterns: first, sales are seasonal and are always strongest in the second and third quarter; second, 1987 sales are consistently higher than those of the two previous years.

Figure 5-9 Graphics Make Better Numbers
Executives read financial reports. Employees read benefits brochures. Everyone must grasp the significance of numbers. Graphics software has made numerical information more accessible by presenting it more attractively and clearly. (Courtesy of Hewlett-Packard Company)

business presentations are frequently strengthened by the use of audio-visuals. Standard graphs may be enhanced with color and imaginative designs to give them more immediate impact. Diagrams, too, are often vital to explain new manufacturing techniques or office layouts. And at meetings, particularly, speakers are often concerned about making their message as interesting as possible, so they may use humorous slides to underscore certain points.

Such graphics traditionally take time to prepare. Speakers must plan their illustration programs well ahead of time to have the materials ready. Unfortunately, the artist may make mistakes so a graphic just isn't right for the talk—and frequently there's no time to redo it. These are some of the frustrations of the traditional approach to graphics.

Enter the computer. Computers, as you know from the other applications packages, can make you a master at last-minute changes. Written documents can be studied and refined before being put onto paper. Spreadsheets can be examined and corrected before they are printed. And it's the same with graphics. If a chart would look better with "department" along the bottom and "revenues" up the side instead of the other way around, or in color rather than shades of gray, this can be taken care of immediately. There's no need to go back to the artist with new instructions.

This part of the chapter will discuss two kinds of graphics software: **analytic graphics packages,** which take numerical data and display them for easy understanding, and **presentation graphics packages,** which can be used to design attractive visuals for a wide variety of purposes.

ANALYTIC GRAPHICS PACKAGES

Typical graphing software allows someone who is not an expert artist, and not an expert mathematician, to make effective graphs of many kinds. It allows selection of the type of graph to be used and provides for entry of the data to be represented. And it permits important labels to be added to the graph—such as the title, the meanings of the various parts, and the source of the information.

Selecting the type of graph. Many types of graphs are useful for presenting data. You are certainly familiar with line, bar, and pie charts. (They are illustrated in these pages.) These charts can be used to present a single set of data, for example, sales fluctuations during 1987. Or they

---

STATE OF THE ART

New Roles For Computer Graphics

It used to be that the only way you could get graphics out of the computer was to print them on paper. But recent technological advances have made it possible to transfer computer graphics to several different media. As a result, graphics are going places they've never been before, onto photographic slides, transparencies, videotapes, and even artists' canvases.

Many businesses use slides to make presentations to large groups of people, and they needed an efficient way to make slides of computer-generated graphs and pie charts. Bell and Howell, Polaroid, and a few other companies have come to the rescue with special cameras that either can take a photograph of the graphic on the computer screen or can record the image of the graphic on film electronically.

The transition from computer graphic to overhead projector transparency is even simpler than the changeover from computer image to slide. Most graphics programs enable you to create the labels and symbols you need to make a transparency. In addition, sign-making programs such as Overhead Express, Sign-Master, and GEM WordChart were designed specifically to make word charts for transparencies. Once you have created the graphic you want to use as an over-head transparency, you can simply print it and use a photocopier to transfer the image to a transparency sheet.

Sometimes the best way to make a presentation is by showing a video, which allows you to move smoothly from one graphic to another as you talk. Two programs, Show Partner and PC Storyboard, enable you to capture graphics from other software for use in a video. They also provide an array of special effects to blend, fade, and dissolve one image into another. Once your video is complete, you can connect the computer to a television and broadcast the results on the TV screen.

Commercial artists have long been using computer graphics to free themselves from tedious jobs, and even fine artists are experimenting with computer art by using programs such as Easel to produce high-quality artwork. At least one artist, James Couper, has gone a step further. He uses a special plotter owned by the 3M Company in Los Angeles to transform a photograph into a painting on canvas. He then paints over this computer-generated "underpainting," adding his own color palette and details to create complex, shimmering landscapes of the Florida Everglades.

can compare two or more sets of data, showing how 1987 differed from the immediately previous years. They can also, of course, be used to show projected future figures.

Which type of chart is selected depends partly on the taste of the person preparing the chart. Line charts are more often used if the figures being shown vary continuously; bar charts are more appropriate if they represent values at more widely spaced points in time (for example, monthly sales figures). Pie charts are most useful for showing how a whole amount (for example, a budget) gets divided into parts. However, there is no rule that must be followed. For this reason, it's useful to see how the same set of data would look in various graphic forms.

Selecting the type of graphic—and changing your choice—is easy on the computer. Most packages offer a menu of types; some even show pictorial representations. The types of charts offered may vary from package to package; some offer five or six varieties, and others offer as many as 30 or 40 versions of the standard business charts. All you need to do is think about the different possibilities, guided perhaps by the documentation, and then make a selection.

Putting in labels. Once the type of graph has been chosen, the software must be given more details. One key question is, what do the

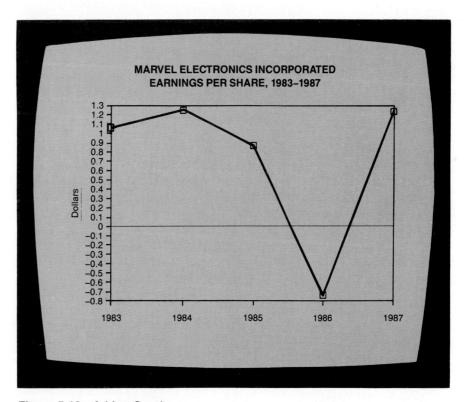

Figure 5-10 A Line Graph
Line graphs can express change over time. Analytic software packages allow users to transform data from spreadsheet format to graphics.

Labels

1. line types
2. color
3. shading
4. Hash marks/pattern

Sales

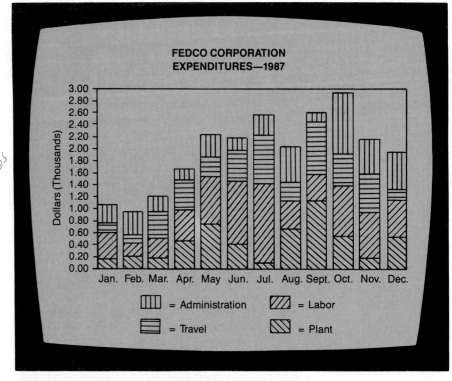

FEDCO CORPORATION
EXPENDITURES—1987

Figure 5-11   A Stacked Bar Graph
The purpose of a stacked bar graph is to compare totals of data from different sources. The height of each bar shows the total expenditure for a month. The height of each section within a bar shows what proportion of the total was paid out in each expense category.

measurements or numbers stand for? Do the bars in a bar chart represent personnel (as they might in a comparison of sick leave taken)? If so, the name of each person will have to be entered so that it can appear below the appropriate bar. Does the height of the bar mean the total sick days per year or the average sick days per week? This will have to be indicated on the chart. On a pie chart, what do the various slices signify? Such labels are needed for the chart to be clear to others, and they may be required for you to enter your data. Therefore, you are asked to provide this information, often on a second menu.

In addition, the title of the chart is very important. "Comparison of sick leave in the data entry department" turns a meaningless drawing into a telling document. A pie chart titled "Budget for office supplies, 1989" is much more useful than an unidentified circle split into segments labeled "printer ribbons," "computer paper," "copier toner," and so on. Titles, too, can be entered on a menu, to be displayed across the top of the finished product. The source from which the figures were collected is also vital information, usually printed below the graph in question. Once again, provision is made for you to supply this label to the software.

Be aware that these packages differ. Some may require you to issue a command if you want to add a title or source; in other words, they will not prompt you for this information. Others may invite you to move the cursor and enter these labels on the finished chart. Learning how different packages work is always important; that is what the documentation is for.

Entering data. No graph can be drawn, obviously, without the numbers that are to be plotted. So all graphics programs provide ways for the numbers to be entered. Some require you to enter them individually from the keyboard. The graphics software may prompt you to provide data for the vertical axis first, the horizontal axis second, vice versa, or in some other way. But the data will need to be accurately entered; otherwise the finished chart will be wrong.

Many analytic packages today allow you to input data directly from another program file—a spreadsheet, for example, or a database. This can seem complex at first, but in fact it saves a lot of work. The numbers do not have to be rekeyboarded. Often the labels too can be borrowed

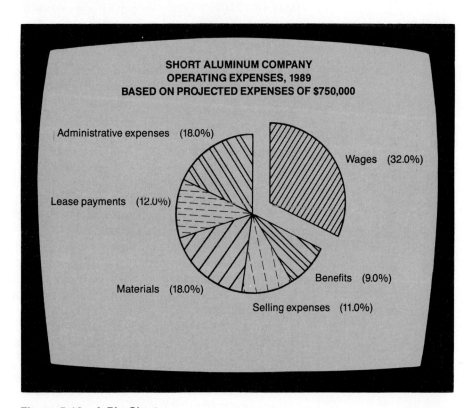

Figure 5-12   A Pie Chart
Pie charts compare the value of parts to the value of the whole. They are often used to express percentages. Some programs allow users to draw attention to a particular part by exploding it—separating it from the rest of the pie.

from the source file: if you are comparing sales totals across different months, you can use the names of the months that are already entered into the spreadsheet.

Editing and printing.   Once you have provided the information needed, the graphics software gets started, and within seconds you see the results of your work. If you are satisfied with it, the job is almost finished. But even if you aren't, most of your work need not be repeated. With a few commands or menu choices, you may be able to change the proportions of the chart, switch it from a horizontal to vertical format, add color or shading to make the bars more distinct, or even change the type of chart you are using. (Most packages include at least some of these features, but, as noted, graphics programs do vary considerably.)

Printing is also very simple, provided that you have the right hardware. However, some printers are equipped only with standard text characters and cannot print graphics. Also, even when a printer can produce graphics, you need to be sure it is compatible with the program you are using.

Finally, an office may possess a **plotter,** a device that, rather than printing through a ribbon or in some other way, actually moves pens across the paper to produce a very fine-looking, accurate picture. To use this machine, you must again check whether the graphics software is able to "drive" it.

Making choices.   Selecting analytic graphics software must take into account the wide differences among the various programs. The first question to ask is whether the package is compatible with your existing hardware. Can it drive your printer? Do you need color equipment to use the software fully—a color monitor and a color printer or plotter? Does your computer have enough memory to handle graphics? Is any additional hardware required inside the computer itself? (For example, a graphics board may be needed to provide some of the instructions for drawing the pictures, as discussed in Chapter 8.) And, perhaps as important, will the graphics package be able to work with data from your spreadsheet software or from your organization's databases?

Your choice also depends on the purpose of the charts. Perhaps they are merely to help an executive analyze data. If so, a simple line-drawn chart might be adequate. (If that executive plans to do some chart editing himself or herself, though, it may be worth considering user-friendly graphics software—that is, menu driven rather than command driven.) Suppose, on the other hand, that these are graphics for use at a sales presentation, in a report to stockholders, or at public meetings. Then you should look for a package that can run a plotter or work with a special camera that produces instant slides. With this equipment, you would also want a full range of other features, such as color, shadowing (to allow certain bars to stand out), different textures, and, perhaps, the ability to add small drawings at different places on the finished work. Such a package, of course, borders on the realm of presentation graphics software, which you will read about in the next section.

Figure 5-13 Plotting for Accuracy

Plotter printers convert output, like numbers entered on a keyboard, into graphics. This output can be drawings on paper or displays on terminals. In this engineering office, printer plotters allow users to label and add comments to the graphics illustrating their work. (Courtesy of Hewlett-Packard Company)

PRESENTATION GRAPHICS PACKAGES

Presentation graphics software is not as common in the office as analytic packages are. This is not surprising. Analytic graphics can generally be quite plain; and they may be essential to an organization. If they can be produced less expensively on a computer than by an artist and mathematician, the organization benefits. But presentation graphics packages usually require artistic talent. Drawing a human figure freehand on a computer is every bit as challenging as it is on paper.

Of course, drawings can be bought. There are electronic picture libraries, commercially available diskettes that store numbers of graphics that are commonly of use to organizations. These don't require an artist in residence. But for more advanced art, qualified artists and designers are desirable.

Drawing packages. To be able to draw, a computer must be "told" exactly where to create the lines and shadings you require. These lines and shadings are made up of dots on the screen. Each dot must be exactly positioned if the picture is to turn out right. As usual, there are several ways to achieve this precision.

The simplest (for the computer) would be to have you define where each dot is to be placed by using **coordinates.** Coordinates are the basic data that the computer must have to create a picture. Coordinates aren't difficult to understand: a set of coordinates is a pair of numbers that define a dot's position, exactly as a letter and a number define the position of a spreadsheet cell—for example, B3. But coordinates are difficult to use. A standard single screen contains more than 250,000 dots; and if each dot in a drawing had to be called up by two numbers, even the most dedicated computer artist would quit within an hour or so.

All the other methods of drawing make the computer do the hard work of defining coordinates. Users *show* the computer where to draw by moving the cursor rather than by telling it with numbers. For simple graphics, you can do this with the cursor arrows. However, additional equipment can greatly simplify computer drawing. In addition to the mouse shown in Chapter 4, which moves the cursor across the screen according to the way it is rolled over a flat surface, there is the **graphics tablet,** on which you draw with a stylus to manipulate the image, and the **touch screen,** which lets you position the cursor by touching the screen with a finger.

Using this type of equipment, together with appropriate software that offers choices of lines, colors, shading, and other features, a talented office worker can create, and change, drawings on the computer screen. Then the same displays can be drawn on paper with a color printer or plotter, or on slides with the appropriate camera interface. With even more elaborate software, these images can be made to move. Such packages require skill and a great deal of computer memory, especially if many colors and brightnesses are used. But the results can be very professional. An office worker can add effective pictures to the company newsletter, and an artist can create spectacular graphics for a stockholder report.

Integrated software

Graphics software may be one of the more "memory-hungry" applications available today, but integrating applications usually makes even greater demands on memory. Integrating common office tasks has been a concern of office automation for some time. Productivity is clearly improved by individual software applications like word processing, database management systems, and spreadsheets. But if the applications are kept separate, there can often be annoying inefficiencies.

Using a wide variety of software can lead to training problems. Office workers may have to master many different menu and command systems. A worker might remember the database command for move, use it by mistake on a word processor, and spend a lot of time wondering why it didn't work. Or worse still, he might use a spreadsheet command to save, and find that in a graphics program it meant delete. **Command consistency,** having similar operations handled by similar commands, is highly desirable in an office setting.

A second inefficiency has already been mentioned more than once in this book. When data is used in one application and again in another, it is wasteful to rekeyboard it for the second use. So efforts have been made to provide **data compatibility,** allowing data to be transported from one

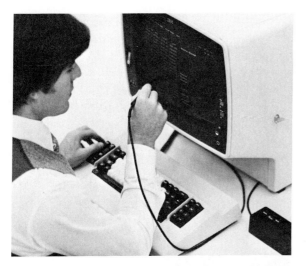 

Figure 5-14   Artists, Meet Computers
These computer-trained artists turn business data into graphics the easy way—on computer. The health care, architecture, engineering, drafting, and fashion industries rely on the results of these increasingly common joint ventures between human talent and graphics software. (Courtesy of International Business Machines Corporation and Hewlett-Packard Company)

application to another—from database to spreadsheet, from spreadsheet to graphics or word processing programs. This is another factor in integrated software.

A third feature that designers of office software saw to be desirable was **concurrency.** As you may have found out, when a piece of software is entered into the microcomputer, it usually takes over the machine, driving other programs out of the computer's memory. This means that if a manager and her assistant wish to interrupt a word processing task and turn to a spreadsheet, they have to save their files, put the word processing diskettes away in an orderly fashion, then take out spreadsheet software and wait for it to be loaded into the computer. Later, after the spreadsheet task is done, they must reload the word processing software and find their place in the document they were working on. Clearly, it is desirable to let the two programs be loaded concurrently, or together. Then they could just switch from one application to another in the computer, and be far more productive.

Three approaches have been used to provide these types of integration. The first, developed when microcomputers did not have much memory available, involved creating separate office software packages in an **integrated series.** The second, taking advantage of technological advances, produced large single programs called **integrated packages.** The third approach, which requires still more memory, takes advantage of the fact that one program can be made to control others. A basic coordinating program called an **integrated operating environment** is first loaded, then the particular applications to be used can be loaded "into" it.

INTEGRATED SERIES

An integrated series is a product family or product line. It is particularly useful for those who do not need all of the features of integration mentioned previously. By its nature it lacks concurrency: applications must be unloaded and loaded whenever you switch between them. It is, however, good for offices that use one or two software applications almost exclusively or for those just starting out and unsure of their software needs.

Integrated series software consists of separate modules for each major application. These are, however, specially designed for command consistency and data compatibility. Each module is of reasonably high quality and low cost and is easy to use; and you can purchase these one at a time, as you need them.

In an office where not everyone is a spreadsheet, or word processing, or graphics expert (in other words a typical office), having easy-to-use, inexpensive, compatible software is a definite plus. Such series may in fact offer many different applications—a popular series offers appointment scheduling, typeface design, and calculation capabilities in addition to the five applications thus far described in this book.

The disadvantage of integrated series software is, of course, that they are not fully integrated. You can exchange data between applications, but the exchange is often clumsy because the programs lack concurrency. You have to terminate one program and load the next application you need. Unless your computer is equipped with a hard disk, you must also switch program diskettes.

INTEGRATED PACKAGES

Integrated, multifunction packages were the first integrated software to enjoy the same kind of almost legendary financial success earned by Visicalc. The product that led the way for this type of software was Lotus 1-2-3, introduced by the Lotus Development Corporation in February 1983. By the end of the same year, it had delivered a quarter of a million packages and earned revenues of $55 million. Lotus 1-2-3 led weekly software sales for nearly two years. It integrates three applications: a spreadsheet program, a simple database management system, and a graphics program. These are loaded as one piece of software into the computer's memory. They share a command structure. And data can easily be moved from one application to another—it can be retrieved from a database, manipulated on a spreadsheet, and then displayed as a graph.

More recent integrated packages have added other capabilities—notably word processing and communications. Such packages enable you not only to move information from database to graph but also to include the graph in a written report and send it electronically, all within the framework of a single program. In all of them, the commands that you use in, say, the word processing application will be the same in the graphics program. Other features may be offered, too—an outlining capability that can be used to plan and build a document, for example, or the power to use files created by many other types of software.

Windowing, which you read about in connection with spreadsheets, is also a feature of many integrated packages. Windowing, you will remember, allows you to view different parts of your work together—for example, two sections of a spreadsheet or written document. In integrated packages you can also view different applications together. You can change values in a spreadsheet in one window; watch the changes appear on a graphics display in another window; and use your word processing application to write a memo about it in a third window.

The main disadvantage of most integrated packages is that they represent a compromise. They take up a lot of space in the computer memory, leaving less room for the work that is being done. Trying to solve this problem has led to another. Some of the applications are less powerful than independent or standalone packages, because in trying to save space, the software designers have left out a few special features. This is not true of all the applications, however. The spreadsheet in Lotus 1-2-3 is often viewed as *the* spreadsheet, preferred to standalone spreadsheets such as Visicalc.

Integrated packages are so large that they fill several disks. This means that on computer systems that use only floppy disks, the disks still need to be swapped. These swaps are not performed every time an application is changed. Instead, some of the less commonly used features are left stored on the disks to conserve memory; when they are needed, the program prompts you to load the appropriate disk. But such disk swapping still defeats the purpose of concurrency.

Figure 5-15 Doing Two—or Three—Things at Once

Have a deadline? Need to compare data? No need to walk over to that file and examine related documents. Use the windowing feature of your integrated software application instead. Access your spreadsheet for those figures needed in your word processed report. Meet that deadline, and increase your accuracy too. (Courtesy of Xerox Corporation)

INTEGRATED OPERATING ENVIRONMENTS

The issue of memory is even more important when it comes to integrated operating environments, which are not really designed for floppy disk systems at all. Fortunately, many business microcomputers today use hard disks, which store considerably more information than a diskette and thus make disk swapping unnecessary. And today's microcomputers are having more and more memory built in, so that memory-hungry software is now more acceptable than ever before.

Operating environments aren't exactly applications. You can't turn on your computer, run the operating environment software, and immediately write a letter or sort through a database mailing list. It is better to think of them as "windowing programs," which provide slots in which to place different applications. Once loaded, they can contain several applications programs at the same time. You can load these applications one after another, then open a window into each application as you need it. As in an integrated package, you work in one window and see current work from the same or different applications in others.

An operating environment not only offers concurrency by providing windows into a number of applications you want to use but also creates data compatibility, allowing your data to be directed from one application to another. And some can also provide command consistency; if you feel comfortable with your word processing program's commands, you can instruct such systems to let you use these commands to perform similar operations on a spreadsheet and database. Alternatively, you could work with an integrated series and use it in an integrated operating environment. You would then have the command consistency and data compatibility of the series, with the concurrency provided by the environment.

The advantage of operating environments clearly is that they allow you to choose the specific applications you want—you don't have to go with those supplied as part of the package. You can select your preferred software for word processing and spreadsheet work; neither application need be less powerful because of compromises made by the software designer.

OTHER APPROACHES

Integrating the office reaches its peak in these large programs, the integrated packages, and the integrated operating environments. But for offices with less computing power, other approaches are being offered that don't tie you into series software.

For example, many independent programs are designed to accept data from the most popular database and spreadsheet packages. This is wise marketing on the manufacturers' part; they know that if their packages are compatible with these programs, they will sell better.

In addition, many packages offer "customizable" command sets. Users can accept the menus or command sets that the manufacturer provides, or they can change those commands to conform to other programs that they are using.

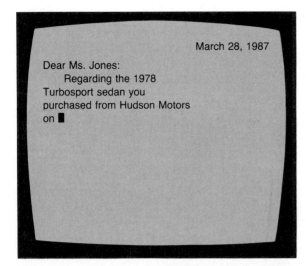 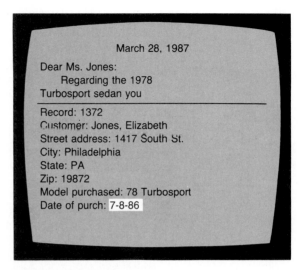

Figure 5-16   An Integrated Operating Environment
With an integrated operating environment, you can load several software packages into the computer's memory at once. For example, when writing a letter to a customer, you could load both word processing and DBMS software. Most of the time, you would use only the word processing software. But if you needed some data about a customer to include in a letter, such as a purchase date, you could open a window where you could use the DBMS software to retrieve it.

And, to provide concurrency, several support packages are available that are designed to load in a remote corner of the computer's memory, where they won't be pushed out by other programs. These programs, discussed in the next chapter as memory resident enhancements, can then be called on to provide help when you are working with your major application.

SUMMARY

- The "traditional" field in which computers excel is mathematics. Organizations can take full advantage of this capacity, both for performing complex calculations and for presenting the results visually as graphics. Software developers are also finding ways to integrate applications so that data need only be entered once in order to be worked on by different applications for various types of processing.

- The most commonly used type of mathematical program for the micro today is spreadsheet software. This general-purpose software allows you to create and manipulate tables of numbers, automatically performing necessary calculations as you work. Developing a spreadsheet involves filling cells with labels to clarify the table's meaning, numbers to represent the basic data that you are entering, or formulas to specify calculations that the spreadsheet is to perform.

■ A saved spreadsheet includes all labels and all formulas as well as numerical data. The next time it is used the numbers can be changed, and it can perform the same mathematical manipulations on a new set of data. The saved spreadsheet is known as a template. Complex templates are often produced commercially to go with the major spreadsheet packages.

■ In addition to being used for analysis of data, spreadsheets can be used for projections. Organizational planners alter figures in a spreadsheet to forecast the results of specific business decisions, changes in economic conditions, and the like.

■ Analytic graphics packages are available to help present complex data in graph form for easy comprehension. These programs start with sets of numbers and instantly create bar graphs, line graphs, pie charts, and other graphics that interpret them. Such graphics packages can often accept numbers imported from another program, so the numbers do not have to be reentered by hand. Many also allow you to enhance the display with colors, labels, and graphics devices of your own choosing.

■ Presentation graphics packages allow you to create images on the screen and, with appropriate hardware, print them on paper. Most use special devices such as the mouse to help the user create images.

■ Many software manufacturers are focusing on the problem of integrating software applications. Such integration usually involves giving the applications command consistency, arranging for data compatibility, and allowing them to run concurrently.

■ There are three main approaches to providing integration. Integrated series are sets of related software packages that can read the same user-created data files. Integrated packages are large programs that incorporate several applications into one package. And integrated operating environments allow the user to load independent software packages into the computer together and transfer data between them.

TERMS FOR REVIEW

spreadsheet software	formulas	graphics tablet
	relative reference	touch screen
graphics software	cursor pointing	command consistency
integrated software	windowing	
worksheet	template	data compatibility
spreadsheets	analytic graphics packages	concurrency
rows		integrated series
columns	presentation graphics packages	integrated packages
cells		integrated operating environment
values	plotter	
labels	coordinates	

TERMINOLOGY CHECK

For each of these definitions, choose the correct term from the list of Terms for Review:

1. Output device used in computer graphics that moves pens across paper to produce a fine-lined drawing. *plotter*

2. The ability to transport data from one application to another without elaborate translation programs. *data compatibility*

3. Feature of spreadsheet software for copying formulas so that they are adjusted for their new cell positions. *Relative Reference*

4. Devices drawn on with a stylus to create or manipulate an image on the computer screen. *Graphic Tablet*

5. Words entered in the cells of a spreadsheet, whether as titles or item descriptions. *Labels*

6. The ability to run two programs in a computer simultaneously. *Concurrency*

7. Diskette for a spreadsheet program that includes labels and formulas but no data, so that it can immediately be used for a specific application. *Template*

8. Display screens that allow computer users to position the cursor or move through a series of menus by touching the screen with a finger. *Touch Screen*

9. Places on a spreadsheet where a row and a column intersect. *Cell*

10. Technique that enables users to view different parts of a spreadsheet or other document side by side on the same display screen, or that allows two applications to be viewed together. *Windowing*

INFORMATION CHECK

1. Why is a spreadsheet more efficient than a manually prepared worksheet?

2. How are values, labels, and formulas displayed on a spreadsheet?

3. Identify several standard operations that must be performed when using any spreadsheet software.

4. When entering data on a spreadsheet, how do you move from cell to cell?

5. What makes spreadsheet software such a flexible tool?

6. What are templates? Why are they so useful?

7. List several important factors that may vary from one spreadsheet to another.

8. Why are graphics so important to organizations?

9. How have computer graphics eliminated some of the problems associated with traditional methods of preparing graphic presentations?

10. What is the difference between analytic and presentation graphics?

11. What capabilities are provided by typical analytic graphics software?

12. How does such software simplify the process of selecting the most effective graph? What features of computer-generated graphs can be easily modified?

13. Integrated software eliminates several factors that cause inefficient data handling. List them.

14. Which aspect of integrated software do you think is most important—command consistency, data compatibility, or concurrency? Explain your opinion.

15. Describe the major types of integrated software. Discuss the advantages and limitations of each.

PROJECTS AND PROBLEMS

1. Case Study

Suppose you are employed by Major Bank and Trust, Inc., located in Heartland, Nebraska. Its departments include installment loans, mortgage amortization, checking and savings accounts, electronic fund transfers, and selling savings bonds and treasury bills.

All record keeping is handled by using microcomputers with appropriate but separate software programs. Recently, the board of directors told the bank's management team that it must streamline operations. The first area the management team investigated was the vast array of hardware and software used within the bank. It appears that each department was using the hardware and software it liked best, without regard to other departments.

The management team has hired you as a consultant to help them resolve this problem. Make a list of points you think you would include in such a report. What questions would you need to ask about the different types of software in use? What solutions are you likely to suggest?

2. Visit your local computer store or a software trade show. Find out the titles of the most popular integrated software packages. Ask someone to demonstrate how the software operates. Write a report comparing the features of two integrated packages. Be sure to include information describing the ease with which data is transferred from one program to another. Which package is a better buy? What groups of users would be attracted to each? Collect descriptive brochures to share with the class.

3. Suppose you decided to create a spreadsheet template to balance your checkbook. What information should be included on your template? Using paper and pencil, create the skeleton of the template. Include the column and row labels and the formulas you would need.

4. Choose a particular graph or chart shown in this textbook or in another convenient source. Study it, and draw it in another form. For example, convert it from a bar graph to a set of pie charts. Which version illustrates the data more dramatically? Could you draw different conclusions from seeing the data displayed in a different format? Demonstrate to the class the alternatives you explored.

6

Special-purpose software

In Chapters 4 and 5, you learned about the five major types of office applications software for the microcomputer: word processing, database management, communications, spreadsheets, and graphics. In addition, integrated software packages that combine two or more of these applications are available, and are used by businesses in a variety of industries to perform different tasks.

Office workers, managers, and other professionals can use word processing software to create letters, memos, and reports. They can use database management systems to keep track of parts inventories or client records. A controller or a manager can use a spreadsheet to analyze the effects of inflation on business performance. Salespeople can use graphics programs for making presentations to compare the sales of their company's products with those of competitors. And businesses can transmit important information instantly between distant offices by using communications software. Because these programs can be used by managers, lawyers, doctors, office workers, salespeople, accountants, and other professionals in a wide variety of fields to do many jobs, they are often known as **general-purpose software.**

In addition to these types of software packages, which can be turned to many uses, there are applications packages targeted at more specific business problems. These **special-purpose software** packages are the subject of this chapter. They include, first of all, software aimed at specific major tasks that must be accomplished in any organization. Here we will examine accounting, project management, and desktop publishing software. **Accounting software** is used to keep the financial records of an organization. It can track billing, inventory, and accounts receivable and payable as well as prepare payrolls, reports, and financial statements. **Project management software** makes it easier for people to oversee large projects, such as the building of a bridge or the publication of a book. It helps managers to control project schedules and budgets by breaking each project down into individual actions and events. **Desktop publishing software** enables people to combine text and graphics to produce

148

reports and newsletters of nearly the same quality as those from professional print shops.

The chapter also looks at another group of applications software packages that are designed to improve the performance, increase the convenience of operation, and expand the capabilities of the major applications software packages. Because these programs *enhance* the effectiveness of applications software packages, they can be termed **enhancement applications.** They allow users to make their general-purpose programs more specific to their own particular needs. Enhancement applications discussed in this chapter include desktop accessories, outliners, spelling checkers, and printing enhancements.

Finally, this chapter focuses on a type of software that is even more specific in function. Even special-purpose software can be employed by organizations in widely different fields. Programs that are used in much the same way by a broad range of organizations are termed **horizontal applications.** But there are also software packages designed for people working in a particular industry, in a specific job, performing a distinct function. Programs that are intended for the special needs of a particular profession are known as **vertical applications.** They include information programs for doctors' offices, airline reservation systems, real estate management, and many others.

After you have read this chapter, you should be able to:

■ distinguish between general-purpose and special-purpose applications software

■ describe how organizations use accounting software to manage financial information

■ discuss the functions of project management software

■ explain the advantages desktop publishing offers organizations and describe some of the capabilities of desktop publishing software

■ specify the function of several enhancement programs for applications software and describe how desktop accessory, outlining, spelling check, and printing enhancement programs let you use applications software packages more efficiently and productively

■ distinguish between horizontal and vertical applications and list some roles of vertical applications software in medicine, law, engineering, manufacturing, and training

Applications software for specific tasks

Many highly specialized applications programs are used in organizations today. Describing most of them would clearly be of limited helpfulness, as they are often developed by specific organizations for their own purposes, and only a few people will ever use them. However, this chapter examines three software tools that are more specialized than any of the five major types of applications software discussed in the previous chapters but are still widely used. They are aimed at specific tasks, yet they can be employed in many different organizations with varied goals.

ACCOUNTING SOFTWARE

Accounting, the methods by which organizations manage financial information, is a business practice that dates back to ancient times. Now all businesses, large and small, use standardized accounting techniques to track billing, inventory, accounts payable, and accounts receivable as well as to prepare payrolls and financial reports.

In business organizations, computers and data processing were first adopted by accounting departments. Accounting is ideally suited to electronic computing because it involves many precise, detailed calculations and follows strict procedures. Today, computers help businesses by automating a wide variety of accounting functions, speeding and simplifying what were previously complex, time-consuming manual tasks. Modern accounting software can be used not only to keep accurate financial rec-

```
                    Tiffany Tinsel Corporation
                          Balance Sheet
                        December 31, 1987

    Assets
      Cash                                           $ 15,000
      Accounts receivable                             121,000
      Inventory                                       140,000
      Equipment less depreciation                     400,000
         Total assets                                $676,000
    Liabilities and owners' equity
      Accounts payable                               $ 20,000
      Notes payable                                   100,000
      Mortgage                                         18,000
      Federal income tax payable                       82,090
         Total liabilities                           $382,090

      Paid-in capital                                $100,000
      Retained earnings                               193,910
         Total owners' equity                        $293,910
           Total liabilities and owners' equity      $676,000
```

Figure 6-1 A Balance Sheet
Owners, creditors, managers, and government authorities have an interest in the financial position of a firm. Balance sheets give a standard "snapshot" of that position in the form of an equation: assets = liabilities + owners' equity.

ords but also to generate automatically the receipts, invoices, checks, and financial statements that are the lifeblood of a business enterprise.

A typical business accounting system, manual or computerized, includes a number of separate **accounts,** or records of different areas of financial activity. For example, accounts may be set up to keep track of different types of supplies purchased. One account may list all expenditures on computer supplies, another may record purchases of general office supplies, a third may cover duplicating supplies. Another account (called accounts payable) will cover all money owed to, and paid to, outside organizations. And other specific accounts cover many other functions.

These accounts are grouped into three main classes: assets, liabilities, and equity. Assets are the things of value owned by a business: cash, money owed to the business (called accounts receivable), buildings, land, equipment, supplies, and so on. **Liabilities** are amounts owed by the business: accounts payable, loans, and so forth. **Equity** is how much the business is currently worth—in other words, the assets minus the liabilities. There are also accounts to keep track of **revenues,** the money that flows into a business, and **expenses,** the money that flows out.

An important part of accounting is the day-to-day record keeping on all financial transactions. Journals are kept, in which all transactions are listed as they occur. Then these are posted, or written in a **general ledger,** where separate records are maintained for each account that has been set up. Most postings are quite complex. A monthly payment to an office supply house, for example, may require writing entries in accounts payable, in the general office supplies account, in the computer supplies account, and perhaps in an account for furniture or equipment. Such multiple postings involve much careful calculating and record keeping.

In addition, at the end of an accounting period—usually a quarter (three months) but never more than a year—a business must prepare financial statements that summarize activity in the accounts during that period. The two most important financial statements are the balance sheet and the income statement. The **balance sheet** shows the financial position of the company in terms of assets, liabilities, and owner's equity at the end of the period. The **income statement** lists the revenues and expenses of the business and shows whether there was net income, or profit, or whether the business suffered a loss during the accounting period. Examples of computerized financial statements are shown in Figures 6-1 and 6-2.

Accounting software simplifies all of these tasks by automating them. Postings are performed automatically, and summaries can be produced to order. Some packages are quite inexpensive, yet they allow a business to set up accounts relevant to its particular operation, to post transactions appropriately, and to produce financial reports. Many will also automatically prepare invoices, payrolls, receipts, and inventory reports.

As noted in the previous chapter, spreadsheet software can also handle accounting work. This is particularly true if a set of spreadsheet templates is purchased, saving the considerable labor of devising formulas to handle the accounting tasks. But in general, the cost of a spreadsheet plus appropriate templates is considerably higher than that of an ac-

```
                        Tiffany Tinsel Corporation
                           Statement of Income
                    for the year ended December 31, 1987

  Net Sales                                              $700,000
  Cost of sales                       $290,000
  Inventory 12/31/87                   140,000            150,000
       Gross profit                                      $550,000
  Less:
    Selling, general and
      administrative expenses                           $ 50,000
    Depreciation                                         200,000
       Operating income                                 $300,000
  Less:
    Mortgage and note
      interest expenses                                   24,000
       Income before income taxes                       $276,000
  Less:
    Income taxes currently
      payable                                           $ 82,090
       Net income                                       $193,910
```

Figure 6-2   An Income Statement
An income statement is more like a moving picture of a firm's financial position. It shows how money was earned and spent. Accounting software generates financial information quickly and frequently, enabling managers to obtain timely information for decision making.

counting package. Consequently, accounting packages are used by a variety of businesses to perform their accounting functions. Though not as flexible as spreadsheets, accounting packages do have enough built-in flexibility to meet the accounting needs of businesses of varying size in different industries.

PROJECT MANAGEMENT SOFTWARE

Like accounting, project management is a task performed by a broad range of businesses and other organizations. There are, of course, many sorts of projects. In the publishing industry, a project might be the compilation and publication of a new dictionary or encyclopedia. In the automobile industry, it might be the design and production of a new car model. A foundation or government agency might undertake the construction of a hospital or the establishment of a new research institution.

To better understand what project management may involve, imagine for a moment that you are in charge of building a road between your town and a nearby city. Although this project may seem straightforward, try to think of all the steps necessary to complete it on time and without exceeding your budget. You might have to start by ordering a survey of the land on which the road is to be built. You would also need to obtain the required building permits and government approvals. The roadway must be designed, and the building materials needed to complete the project must be ordered and received at the right time. You will need the proper construction equipment, and you will have to hire the right number of people with the proper skills to do each job. Factors such as the changing seasons, labor disputes, and shifts in prices of materials must be taken into account. Finally, to complete the project in the least amount of time, you need to determine which processes can proceed concurrently, or at the same time, and which must occur in a particular sequence, or only after other tasks have been completed. This simple example only touches on the hundreds of tasks and events that make up a typical project.

Project management software makes it easier for people to oversee large projects. It helps project managers control schedules and budgets by breaking down a complex project into individual actions and events. Every project can be broken down into a series of significant interim events, or "milestones," on the way to completing the project. These events are linked by the specific actions or tasks that must be performed to reach successive milestones. Project management software simplifies this task by automating the three traditional methods for managing projects: Gantt charts, PERT charts, and the CPM method.

Gantt chart. A Gantt chart is one of the oldest and simplest project management techniques. As shown in Figure 6-3, a **Gantt chart** is a simple table used for scheduling project activities. The whole project is analyzed into separate tasks, which are generally listed in order of earliest starting time. The time line for completing each task is indicated graph-

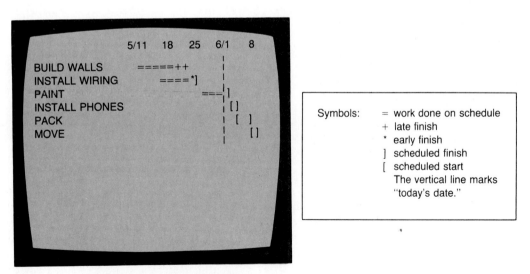

Figure 6-3   A Gantt Chart

An office move, like any other project, can be depicted on a Gantt chart. First, the project is divided into activities, which are listed on the left in order of their start dates. At the top of the chart is a timeline divided into segments—5-day weeks, in this case. Sets of symbols indicate when each activity is scheduled, which tasks are in progress or complete, and whether tasks began and ended on time. The task of building walls, for example, ended two days late.

ically. As you can see, some tasks overlap, and others cannot begin until a previous task has been fully completed. Although a Gantt chart is easy to use, its use is limited to fairly simple projects because it lacks a mechanism to take account of the relationships among project activities. For this reason, project management techniques based on networking of project tasks and events have been developed.

PERT charts and CPM. The **Project Evaluation and Review Technique (PERT)** of project management is based on estimating the resources necessary to complete each task throughout a project. The **Critical Path Method (CPM)** relies on estimating the times needed to complete each project task. In Figure 6-4, the circles represent project tasks, and the lines that connect the circles show the relationships among the tasks. The **critical path** represents the longest path through the network, as well as the shortest possible time required for completion of a project.

These charts by themselves can allow managers to tell whether their project is still on schedule. But if it is not, they may need to prepare a whole new chart to meet their desired end date. Project management software simplifies rescheduling by automating the production of these charts. It also allows managers to ask "what if" questions while planning and controlling large projects. A project manager can use this type of software to see the effect on the critical path, or time needed for completion

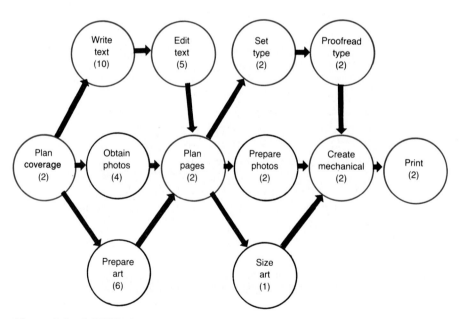

Figure 6-4 A PERT Chart

One way to arrange production of a newsletter is shown here. An arrow from one task to another indicates that the first must be completed before the second can start. Estimated time in days is shown for each task, and colored circles represent the critical path. Other tasks can fall behind—but if critical path tasks take longer than estimated, the newsletter will come out late.

of this project, if certain materials are delivered ahead of schedule, if there are unavoidable delays, or if labor costs increase. Project management software allows a manager to analyze situations automatically and adjust for changes.

THE HUMAN SIDE

A Guide to Buyer's Guides

If you ever need to shop for software, a good way to begin is by consulting one of the buyer's guides that are published periodically in computer magazines such as *Byte* and *Personal Computing*.

Buyer's guides provide information that can save you a lot of time, trouble, and money. They are often set up as tables or grids. Assume, for example, that you intend to buy a project management program. Here is a shortened version of a buyer's guide grid for this type of software. (It is based on real programs, but the names are fictional.)

A typical buyer's guide lists the names of the programs and the price of each one. It also provides information about the hardware requirements of each product. If your computer has only 128K of RAM, you can see from this grid that one project management program, Skedule, will not run on it.

Other listings give you information about each product's capabilities and special features. You can see here that, of the three

products listed, only Dartmouth Tracker generates PERT charts. This product also offers you a choice of scheduling units, whereas tasks must be scheduled in days with the other two. On the other hand, Dartmouth Tracker is the most expensive of the three.

Buyer's guides can also alert you to the amount of help you can expect from the software's producers. As in the example, they generally tell you if a program includes on-line help and if the producer has a hot line you can call for technical support. Buyer's guides frequently offer comments about the quality of the product's documentation as well.

Some of the information in a buyer's guide may be of a technical nature that not all users will understand. If any information in a buyer's guide is unclear to you, take it along to a computer dealer and ask for an explanation. Buyer's guides can help you avoid costly mistakes.

Software	Price	Memory Required	Maximum Tasks Per Project	Generate PERT Chart	Scheduling Units	On-line Help	Support Hot Line
GANTTmaster	$249.00	128K	600	No	Days	Yes, with windowing	Yes
SKEDULE	$149.95	192K	250	No	Days	Yes, context-sensitive	Yes
Dartmouth Tracker	$395.00	128K	200 per subproject	Yes	Variable, from seconds to years	Yes, context-sensitive	Yes

DESKTOP PUBLISHING SOFTWARE

Every business needs to have documents from time to time. Most companies use several printed forms for bills, orders, price lists, bid proposals, memos, and so on. Some firms periodically publish technical reports, newsletters, and catalogs, and many businesses issue quarterly and annual reports. Large companies that generate a high volume of printed materials often maintain their own in-house print shops, whereas a small company typically engages a job printer whenever it has a specific type-setting or copying job to do. In either case, the production of professionally printed material can be laborious, expensive, and time-consuming. **Desktop publishing** has become very popular in the business world in recent years because it takes a lot of the time, cost, and work out of printing documents. Desktop publishing software enables office workers to perform all or most of the steps involved in preparing a document for print right on their computer screens.

Imagine that you have been asked to produce a 16-page annual report. If you were going to have the report published by an in-house or commercial print shop, your first task would be to assemble the text, photographs, and graphics you plan to use. Then you would draw a detailed diagram, or layout, showing how all of these elements would be placed on each page. You would need to make many typographical or production decisions, such as how many columns of type to use on each page, whether

Figure 6-5 The Do-It-Yourself Method

Annual reports, financial forecasts, and corporate restructure plans are typical sensitive documents businesses publish often—and more often with eleventh-hour revisions! Desktop publishing gets the job done fast and well, with guaranteed in-house control as well. (Courtesy of Xerox Corporation)

to justify, or align, the type on one or both sides, and whether to use vertical and horizontal lines to separate items. Another important decision would concern the sizes and fonts of type to use for the text and for the titles or headlines. A font is a set of characters (letters, numbers, and punctuation marks) in the same typeface or style—for instance Roman, italic, or Helvetica. As you planned your report, you might, for example, decide to use one font for titles and another for the text.

Once the production decisions are made, a typesetter would set up all of the typewritten text and titles in the fonts and sizes you have selected, usually on strips of photographic paper that can be cut and pasted to conform to your diagram or layout. At the same time, another organization may reproduce the graphics and photographs you have selected in the correct sizes and in a form that can be printed. Then, following your diagrams, a layout artist would paste the photos, graphics, and type for each page on a layout sheet, called a **mechanical.** The mechanical would then be photographed to produce a plate, from which the printer would produce the finished documents.

This process involves many people, often working for different companies. To produce the same annual report using a desktop publishing program, you instruct the computer to prepare the text in your chosen font. Then you build each page just as the layout artist does, but you compose your pages in soft copy on the computer screen. For this reason, desktop publishing programs are also commonly called **page composition programs.** As you assemble the text, titles, photos, and graphics for each page, you can see exactly how the page will look—or a close approximation of it, depending on the program you are using. If you don't like the page you have designed, desktop publishing programs enable you to alter it quickly and easily. You can change typefaces, enlarge titles, crop illustrations, or widen columns, just by using a few keystrokes. One set of commands will let you move a graphic from the top of a page to the bottom, another will wrap text around it, another will relocate text from one page to another, and so on. Then you simply print your document, usually with a laser printer. If you need only a few dozen copies of a document, you can print them all on your computer printer or copy them on a photocopying machine. If you need hundreds of thousands of copies of the document, you can use the printout as a mechanical, which you can take to a print shop for reproduction.

Although conventional printing still has some advantages—high-quality professional results and a wider choice of colors and bindings—desktop publishing can deliver very good-quality printing suitable for most business uses. It is about half the cost of conventional printing, and you don't have to waste time going back and forth to the typesetter and conferring with the printer. In addition, with conventional printing you can't really tell how a document is going to appear until the mechanical has been composed or the document has been reproduced. Then it can be expensive and difficult to change. Desktop publishing software eliminates this problem. If you want to make any last-minute changes, you can recall the page on your screen, make the alterations, and print out a new version. You can also be as creative as you like. It costs only a little time to change a page design.

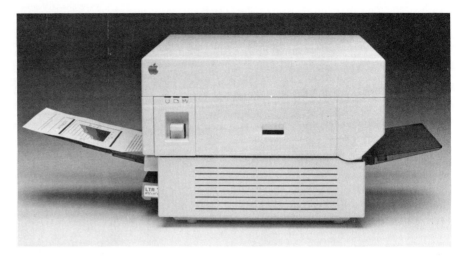

Figure 6-6   Quality, Speed for the Efficient Manager
This laser printer uses a narrow beam of light to form images on paper. High-volume readers like managers prefer GANTT, PERT, and CPM charts as well as other documents produced on a laser printer because of high quality and readability. (Courtesy of Apple Computer, Inc.)

In Chapter 5 you learned that integrated software allows you to perform several tasks at once. You could view desktop publishing programs as a type of integrated software that allows the user to carry out one specific task—combine graphics and text from other software into a single file. You could also view them in another way: as enhancement applications—programs that expand the capabilities and usefulness of word processing software. In the next section we shall discuss other enhancement applications that are commonly used today to help users get more out of their software packages.

Enhancement applications

The applications software packages described in Chapters 4 and 5 are some of the most powerful and popular programs available today. Yet it would be difficult to find anyone who is completely satisfied with any given program. Why is this so? You already know the answer: general-purpose programs are used by a variety of people performing different tasks in various industries. Thus they fulfill the majority of demands of most users but cannot perfectly match everyone's needs and work habits.

Several enhancement applications have been created to improve the performance, convenience, and versatility of popular applications software packages. These enhancements range from programs that allow you to organize your work more productively to software that allows you to format, or structure, a report to your particular needs. Such programs are often called utilities because, like the systems software utilities described in Chapter 7, they provide useful support for other software.

DESKTOP ACCESSORY PROGRAMS

If you are like many people, you feel more comfortable working at a desk— writing notes on a pad, using a typewriter or perhaps a calculator—than sitting at a computer workstation. If this is how you feel, do not be alarmed. Most people have been trained in pencil and paper environments throughout their education and careers.

Programs have been developed to provide people working at micros with computerized versions of tools they commonly use at their desks. Such enhancement applications are known as **desktop accessory programs** because they imitate a desktop featuring a traditional appointment calendar, notepad, calculator, and so on. A desktop accessory program allows you to "call up" a typewriter-like notepad, calculator, appointment calendar, phone number listing, clock, and more, all while working with an applications software package.

As pointed out in the previous chapter, most programs for the microcomputer erase all previous programs when they are loaded into the computer's memory. This problem can be solved by using integrated packages or integrated operating environments, which allow different applications to run concurrently. An alternative approach, used with desktop accessory programs, is to make the software **memory resident,** designing it specially to remain in memory while other programs are loaded. This enables it to remain in the computer's memory while you are using an applications program. Therefore, when you issue an appropriate command, it can immediately appear on your monitor as a window.

Figure 6-7 Using Desktop Accessory Software
Software such as Sidekick (on which this screen is based) enables you to perform a calculation that you may need while writing a wordprocessed letter. For many users, desktop accessory software can be an inexpensive alternative to fully integrated software.

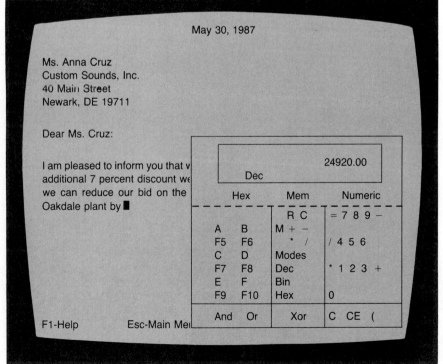

In fact, several desktop accessory functions can be called to the monitor at the same time. For example, while using a spreadsheet, you can call up a calculator in one window to compute a figure before entering it in a given cell. You can use a notepad in another window to jot down notes for a presentation that will be based on the results of your spreadsheet analysis. You can even use a phone dialer feature to call colleagues to set up a meeting for your presentation, and then record the date and time you have arranged in an electronic appointment calendar. You have accomplished all these tasks without ever leaving your micro—and without terminating the spreadsheet program you were using!

Valuable enhancement applications have been created to expand the usefulness of each category of applications software. The rest of this section will discuss how productivity tools and printing enhancements have increased the efficiency of word processing, spreadsheet, and database management programs.

OUTLINERS

Like most students, you have been asked to write reports from the time you were in elementary school. One technique you learned early on was to prepare an outline to help you organize your thoughts before writing.

Today many people create letters, memos, and reports directly at

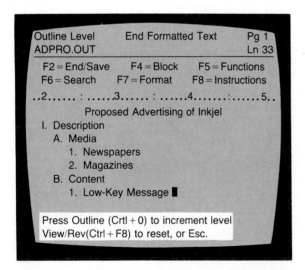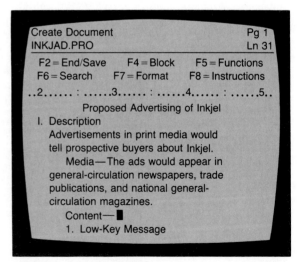

Figure 6-8 Using Outline Software

When you generate an outline like the one on the left, outline software saves you time by automatically indenting each heading and assigning it the correct number or letter and punctuation. Depending on the outline and word processing software you use, you may be able to copy the outline into a document file. Then you can reuse the headings without retyping them. You can delete their numbers or letters, if you wish, and fill in the text that goes under them, as on the screen at right. This outline and document were prepared with IBM DisplayWrite word processing software, which has a built-in outline program.

computer workstations. Outlining programs are designed as companions to word processing software to help people write more effectively. Also known as thought or idea processors, **outliners** help you to organize your thoughts into main topics and subordinate topics.

To use an outlining program, you simply begin by entering the main topics, or headings, that you plan to cover in your writing. Then you enter subtopics, sub-subtopics, and so on. Outliners force you to organize your ideas according to priority. Figure 6-8 shows how an outlining program is used to structure a subject into topics and subtopics. When you have completed your outline structure, you can then insert explanatory paragraphs below each heading. You repeat this process until you are ready to begin writing. When you outline a report in this fashion, the report is only a few steps from being written.

Once you have completed an outline, it is easy to convert the outlining file to a word processing file. You can then use your word processing software to insert additional copy, enhance text with boldface and underscoring, or format it differently to suit your needs. You can also print your outline in a standard structured format. This format is particularly useful for making presentations.

THESAURUSES AND SPELLING CHECKERS

Though outliners were first marketed as systems support software and can still be purchased as separate packages, word processing software developers quickly saw the value of this feature and began to provide outlining as part of their more expensive word processing packages.

This pattern is also taking place with other advanced features for word processing. For example, a thesaurus can often be purchased to work with word processing software that does not include one as part of the basic package. Thesauruses, you may remember from Chapter 4, can help you to find the right word when you are composing or editing a document. And spelling checkers can also usually be found to enhance a document production system. Many word processing programs have built-in spelling checkers. But if your word processing program does not offer such a feature, you can get a separate spelling checker that will work with just about any program.

One note of warning is necessary on spelling checker programs. This enhancement simply compares your text against a dictionary file. It will not find typographical errors that create legitimate English words, nor will it find words that are used incorrectly. For example, a spelling checker will not mark the word *bus* when you meant to type *but,* or *there* when you should have entered *their*. Thus, use of a spelling checker program is no substitute for thorough proofreading and good grammar.

PRINTING ENHANCEMENTS

The nature of computer software is such that it may have to support, or work with, many brands of printers. Different printers need different sets of commands from the computer they are working with if they are to accomplish the formatting you require—for example, line spacing, bold-facing, margins, and similar items. Therefore, the software you use must be set up to produce the appropriate commands to "drive" your particular printer.

When you use an applications program for the first time, you are usually prompted to identify the printer you will be working with. (Questions about other output devices may also be asked—for example, about your monitor.) In response to your answers, the applications software can usually activate a part of itself, called a **driver,** that enables it to work with the peripheral hardware you are using. Software packages today include drivers for most printers that are available on the market. But if you have an unusual printer, you may need to obtain a separate driver program if your applications software is to work with the printer.

One interesting printing enhancement application is used chiefly with spreadsheet files. Complex spreadsheets often have too many columns to fit on standard-width computer paper. There are printer packages that allow you to turn your spreadsheet on its side so that you can print its full width at once.

Vertical applications

The software packages described thus far have been horizontal applications, adaptable to many different situations in many industries. Enhancement applications may make them even more flexible. But some businesses may be unable to adapt horizontal applications software to meet their needs. An airline, for example, may find no horizontal applications package that is able to handle the complex task of making its seat reservations. A medical practice may require some unique features in an accounting system, such as special procedures to handle patients' medical histories, diagnoses, medical insurance forms, and so on. Car dealers, restaurants, clothing stores, and others might also benefit from functions and capabilities that go beyond what is generally available in horizontal packages. Moreover, there are areas within the accounting field, like tax accounting, that require special tools tailored to their particular needs.

For such organizations, vertical applications software, designed to meet the needs of particular types of businesses, is often available. Examples of vertical software include engineering programs used to design cars, airplanes, or computer chips; hotel reservation systems; banking and financial systems; textbook publishing programs; automotive parts inventory tracking systems; real estate management systems; and so forth. This list is far from complete. Vertical software is available for practically every industry, job, or function to help businesses manage information.

This section presents five examples of vertical applications software: computer applications in medicine, law, engineering, manufacturing, and business training.

Figure 6-9 Special Needs, Special Qualifications
Take this travel agency. It makes hotel and airline reservations. It locates competitive tour packages. It subscribes to magazines and even advertises. And don't forget it pays its staff and creditors! This unique organization and others like it turn to vertical software for their computerized operations. (Courtesy of UNISYS)

MEDICINE

Everyone has visited a doctor's office at some point in life. As patients, people are mostly concerned with the healing aspect of medicine. But doctors and their staffs also must be concerned with business. **Office management programs** have been developed for managing the business aspects of a medical practice so that doctors can concentrate on healing their patients. Such programs automate the maintenance of patient histories, keep track of lab reports and prescriptions, process insurance claims, and prepare billing. Office management packages are by no means limited to medical practices but have been designed to suit the needs of a variety of professions, including law, real estate, and architecture. Moreover, individual office management programs are available to help the various specialty fields within medicine, such as neurology, obstetrics, and internal medicine, to manage information.

The medical profession also maintains several specialized on-line databases to provide physicians with the latest information on diseases and treatments. Some examples of databases used by doctors are Medical Research Director, offered on the DATA-STAR database system; Medline, from the National Library of Medicine; and Medis, available from Mead Data Central. A specialized medical database of a different sort, the national organ transplant network, helps match organ donors and potential recipients.

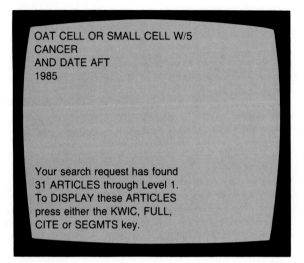

OAT CELL OR SMALL CELL W/5
CANCER
AND DATE AFT
1985

Your search request has found
31 ARTICLES through Level 1.
To DISPLAY these ARTICLES
press either the KWIC, FULL,
CITE or SEGMTS key.

Figure 6-10   Using a Medical Database
Services such as Medis (shown here) can scan journals and textbooks for information relevant to your topic. The computer searches for key words or combinations of words. Here the computer will locate documents published after 1985 in which *oat cell* or *small cell* occurs within five words of *cancer*. You may then view the documents in full or summary format.

Another type of special-purpose software in the medical field is used for diagnosing illnesses. **Diagnostic aids** exploit the power of the computer to manage the large amount of information available on diseases and drugs. One type of diagnostic aid available to doctors is based on expert systems. An **expert system** is a very advanced, sophisticated kind of database that can simulate the judgment and advice of a human expert. (Expert systems are one product of research in the area known as artificial intelligence, which you will learn more about in Chapter 15.) Medical expert systems use the knowledge gained by physicians through years of experience and research, and are increasingly used to help doctors diagnose and treat patients.

An expert system has two parts. The first component, known as the **knowledge base,** is the database that contains the expert knowledge—in this case that of medical specialists. The second part of an expert system is a so-called **inference engine,** which in a medical expert system compares the data entered by the physician about a patient's history and symptoms with its knowledge base and suggests possible diagnoses and treatments. The specialist's knowledge is incorporated into the database in a structured manner so that the computer can evaluate the patient's symptoms.

One medical expert system developed at the University of Pittsburgh is known as **INTERNIST/CADUCEUS.** Its knowledge base covers about 500 diseases and more than 3,500 symptoms of those diseases. INTERNIST/CADUCEUS is expert enough to solve most cases that appear in the *New England Journal of Medicine.*

Another medical expert system is **MYCIN,** developed at Stanford University. MYCIN performs diagnoses on blood and meningitis infections. First the doctor's staff enters data on the patient's history and lab reports. Then the doctor "converses" with MYCIN, responding to MYCIN's questions as well as asking additional questions of his or her own.

MYCIN then advises the doctor on the proper antibiotic for treating the infection.

LAW

The legal profession also takes advantage of specialized office management programs. These programs automate the preparation of client statements, track lawyer time, maintain fee balances, and help in the preparation of client reports. Legal office management programs include functions to simplify real estate closings, estate planning, patent and trademark searches, and business valuations.

One such program lets an attorney's staff track time and expenses for client billing purposes. It allows them to bill clients on an hourly, fixed, contingency, or percent-of-settlement basis. This program also includes an appointment scheduling feature to keep track of court appear-

---

STATE OF THE ART

Profile of a Law Firm's Use of an Office Management System

The law partnership of Muller, Goldstein, and Fitzgerald employs seven attorneys, four secretaries, and two word processing specialists. To increase office productivity, the partners purchased a specialized law office management system.

They bought it from a single-source supplier, which provided not only the software but also the hardware. It also offered training for users as well as service and maintenance for the system.

Every terminal at Muller, Goldstein, and Fitzgerald can use all the functions in the system. The terminals are interconnected so that they form what is called a local area network. This means, for example, that the legal secretaries and word processing specialists can work together to process and proofread a long brief for an upcoming litigation, each working on a portion of the brief at a different terminal, then saving it on a centralized data disk. Each terminal has a modem, which enables the attorneys and their staff to communicate directly with clients, other law firms, and databases such as Lexis.

The system can also keep track of client phone calls for billing purposes. All information about services rendered to clients (for example, consultations, phone calls, court appearances, preparation of papers) is maintained by the computer and fed directly into the firm's accounting system.

Some programs in the office management system were specifically written for Muller, Goldstein, and Fitzgerald. One of these is a conflict of interest check. This scans the firm's records to ensure that, for example, the firm is not representing a prospective client's opponent in a different case.

Another custom feature is the docket and critical dates calendar, which tracks important deadlines and court appearance dates for all the cases the firm is handling. Although it is the responsibility of the attorneys and their assistants to keep track of these dates, one staff member acts as the office manager to prepare a report on critical dates in the near future. With the system, the secretary can carry out this task more thoroughly and in less time than before.

ances, client conferences, and other engagements to make sure that there are no scheduling conflicts.

Law offices also rely heavily on word processing software to prepare briefs, contracts, and other legal documents. The legal system in the United States is based on precedents, or case law. This means that a case being tried today is argued on the basis of similar cases tried in the past. When a lawyer prepares a brief, or a report that cites the points of law to be used in a case, he or she draws on all the legal precedents that might be used to decide the case in the client's favor. Briefs can therefore be the opposite of brief—very long.

Lawyers also prepare contracts for a variety of legal matters, from home purchases to wills to business incorporations. Because each of these involves certain standard provisions, lawyers often save time by beginning with boilerplate contracts. **Boilerplate** means standard documents or portions of documents that can be used repeatedly. The basic contract is then customized to suit the needs of the individual client.

You can see, then, that law offices need powerful word processing

Figure 6-11 DB Law
Organizations need a basis for their decision making. Finding that basis can involve long hours of backbreaking research. Databases like LEXIS allow attorneys and paralegals to complete this research quickly so that their decision making—in a courtroom or in a boardroom—can start. (Courtesy of Mead Data Central)

software. In some cases, they may require specialized word processing packages offering features to facilitate the preparation of legal documents. The advent of word processing has made it possible for attorneys to manage the volume of legal information necessary to compete in today's business world.

There are also a variety of on-line databases to serve the information needs of the legal profession. **Lexis,** from Mead Data Central, is one of the best-known and most popular services. All U.S. Supreme Court decisions dating back to 1925 are accessible through Lexis. Court of Appeals and Federal Circuit Court of Appeals decisions are also stored on Lexis. An attorney can use Lexis to research legal questions relating to patents, trademarks, copyrights, tax information, securities, maritime issues, labor law, and more.

Lexis is a **full-text retrieval** service. This means that a paralegal can search the database using **keywords,** or terms that are most likely to appear in documents on a specific subject. The paralegal can then obtain the complete text of any documents that are indexed under those keywords. With the aid of an on-line legal database, attorneys and paralegals can save an enormous amount of time doing research.

ENGINEERING

Engineers and architects spend long hours drawing and revising blueprints, or plans, for new buildings and machinery. Just as word processing allows writers to create and revise text easily, **computer-aided design** permits engineers to draw complex objects and manipulate the drawings with ease. Computer-aided design (CAD) software allows an engineer to design objects using a mouse and sophisticated graphics on the microcomputer. The engineer can flip or rotate the object for viewing from different angles and zoom in and out for detailed work. Plans for buildings, aircrafts, automobiles, microprocessors, and so on, which used to take months and years to develop, can now be generated and revised in a matter of hours or days. And when a design is complete, the software can calculate how much the finished object will cost to create, using materials and unit costs entered by the designer.

MANUFACTURING

Computerization has arrived on the shop floor in several ways. **Computer-aided manufacturing (CAM)** systems keep track of parts inventories to be used in assembly and regulate the flow of parts to the shop floor. Some CAM systems, which are mechanical in nature, transport parts to appropriate work areas on the shop floor. And in a complex specialized integration called CAD/CAM, a CAD drawing can be developed and then used to help control manufacturing.

Another area of computer-aided manufacturing is robotics. **Robotics** involves the use of computer-aided machines to perform repetitive tasks with precision. Most industrial robots are simply mechanical arms with "gripper" hands that have been programmed to do specific jobs repeatedly.

Some of the latest advances in robotics involve the use of robots with "vision," or TV cameras that serve as eyes and allow them to distinguish between different objects. Robotics has been used extensively in the automotive industry to paint and assemble cars. Robots are being used for jobs that are too dangerous or too boring for humans.

BUSINESS TRAINING

As you well know, your education does not end when you graduate from school. Today's business world is very complex, and employees need a variety of skills to succeed. Thus all businesses continue to educate their employees to increase their skill levels and allow them to perform more productively. This training includes seminars and workshops provided by the employer, videotape courses, and training manuals. One of the most recent trends in business training is computer-based training.

Computer-based training (CBT), also known as computer-assisted instruction (CAI), simply means using a computer to teach and test employees. It may be used as an entire method of instruction, or just to supplement traditional classes. Businesses use CBT to teach management and supervisory skills, sales techniques, and clerical and technical skills. CBT can also, but does not necessarily, include teaching employees how to use computers. It is used for "drill-and-practice" exercises, simulations

Figure 6-12 It Starts With a Picture
Design—it's the basis for your home, the car you buy, and the plane for your flight. The engineers who create them go back to the drawing board a lot—they create, revise, test, and revise again. Special-purpose software like CADCAM has become an engineering "must" in these construction environments. (Courtesy of International Business Machines Corporation)

Figure 6-13   For the Computer, By the Computer

Meet the new instructional assistant—the computer. Computer-assisted instruction has become a valid and cost-effective method of teaching. What is most exciting about CAI is that computer users can work one on one with a software instruction program. That way, they can set the pace for their own progress. (Courtesy of Apple Computer, Inc.)

of live work situations, and training on actual production systems. Software tutorials are one popular way to teach people the applications software packages you studied in Chapters 4 and 5. These tutorials either simulate or run concurrently with the word processing, database, spreadsheet, graphics, or communications packages they teach.

Companies that need to train many people each year sometimes use authoring systems to create their own CBT. **Authoring systems** are special software packages that allow trainers without programming experience to create computerized lessons. Companies use authoring systems to create computer-based training that is customized to their business objectives and the educational needs of their employees.

SUMMARY

- There are two distinct types of applications software. General-purpose software, which includes the five major applications software packages, can be used to do a variety of jobs. Special-purpose software is designed for more specific tasks.

- Accounting software helps businesses to manage financial information. Businesses use accounting software to track billing, purchasing, inventory, and accounts payable and receivable as well as to prepare payrolls, reports, and periodic financial statements.

- Project management software is useful to people who must oversee large projects. It helps managers to control schedules and budgets by breaking down a complex project into individual actions and events. Project management software automates traditional tools such as Gantt charts, Project Evaluation and Review Technique (PERT), and the Critical Path Method (CPM).

- Desktop publishing software reduces the time, cost, and labor required to print newsletters and other types of documents. It enables office workers to prepare a document for printing right on the computer screen. Desktop publishing programs, also known as page composition programs, allow text, titles, photos, and graphics to be assembled for each page of a document and then printed.

- Enhancement applications improve the performance, expand the capabilities, and increase the versatility and convenience of applications software packages. Popular enhancement programs include desktop accessory programs, outliners, spelling checkers, and printing enhancements, which provide drivers for different printers.

- Programs that can be used by many different organizations in various fields are termed horizontal applications. Specialized programs designed to meet the unique needs of particular businesses and professions are known as vertical applications.

- Doctors and lawyers use a variety of software designed for their specific needs. Among them are office management programs, which manage the business aspects of a practice, and on-line databases containing relevant research information. Expert systems are structured databases to help diagnose patients' symptoms and suggest treatments.

- Other specialized vertical applications include computer-aided design (CAD), computer-aided manufacturing (CAM), robotics, and computer-based training (CBT) software.

TERMS FOR REVIEW

general-purpose software
special-purpose software
accounting software
project management software
desktop publishing software
enhancement applications

income statement
Gantt chart
Project Evaluation and Review Technique (PERT)
Critical Path Method (CPM)
critical path
desktop publishing
mechanical

diagnostic aids
expert system
knowledge base
inference engine
INTERNIST/ CADUCEUS
MYCIN
boilerplate
Lexis
full-text retrieval
keywords

horizontal
  applications
vertical applications
accounting
accounts
liabilities
equity
revenues
expenses
general ledger
balance sheet

page composition
  programs
desktop accessory
  programs
memory resident
outliners
spelling checker
driver
office management
  programs

computer-aided
  design (CAD)
computer-aided
  manufacturing
  (CAM)
robotics
computer-based
  training (CBT)
authoring system

TERMINOLOGY CHECK

For each of these definitions, choose the correct term from the list of Terms for Review:

1. Component of an expert system that compares data entered by the user with the knowledge base to suggest a possible solution to a problem. *inference engine*

2. Another name for desktop publishing programs. *Page composition programs*

3. Specialized software package used to track billing, inventory, and accounts receivable and payable, as well as to prepare payrolls. *accounting software*

4. Type of software designed to remain in memory while other programs are loaded. *memory resident*

5. Software packages that are intended for the special needs of a particular profession. *vertical application*

6. Standard word processing document or file that can be used repeatedly. *boilerplate*

7. Software package that enables trainers without programming experience to create customized CBT lessons. *authoring system*

8. Simple table used in project management for scheduling project activities over time. *Gantt chart*

9. Graphics software that enables engineers to create and manipulate designs on a computer, and to perform many related calculations including quantity and cost of materials needed. *CAD computer-aided design*

10. Part of an applications package, or a separate system support program, that enables a computer to work effectively with a printer or other output device. *driver*

INFORMATION CHECK

1. Briefly describe the difference between general-purpose and special-purpose software. Give two examples of each.

2. What features make accounting ideally suited for computer applications?

3. Although spreadsheets are more flexible, many businesses prefer to use accounting packages to handle accounting work. Why?

4. Project management software automates three traditional methods for managing projects. Describe each briefly.

5. Discuss the advantages and disadvantages of desktop publishing for business organizations.

6. Describe some capabilities of desktop publishing software. Why are these programs sometimes called page composition programs?

7. What is the purpose of enhancement applications?

8. Describe briefly four types of enhancement software.

9. What is the difference between horizontal and vertical applications software? What feature makes vertical software so useful to certain industries and professions?

10. What types of vertical applications software are used by doctors, and why are they useful?

11. What is an expert system? What are the components of such a system? How do doctors use expert systems to diagnose and treat illness?

12. What kind of information can you find stored in on-line databases designed for lawyers? How is this information used?

13. How has CAD software changed the way engineers work?

14. How has robotics changed manufacturing?

15. How is computer-based training used in business situations?

PROJECTS AND PROBLEMS

1. Case Study
Peabody, Trumbull, and Adams, a small law corporation, realizes that it must use computers and software to make its operations more efficient. The firm has asked you, a legal secretary with an interest in software and computers, to make some recommendations. Write a memo to the senior partners, outlining the types of programs you feel might be useful, their capabilities, and their potential benefits.

2. Visit a medical office that uses a microcomputer for record keeping. Interview the person responsible for record keeping. Find out how the computer has changed his or her job. What information is recorded? What tasks can now be done that were impossible before? What tasks might be more difficult to perform with the computer? What future changes does the interviewee foresee for this medical office?
   Write up your visit in an interview format.

3. On the basis of your experience as a student, what type of software and hardware do you think your school's accounting department uses?

Write down your guesses; ask your classmates to give you their impressions. Then visit the accounting office and talk to the person responsible for the software it uses. What accounting tasks are performed by computer? What software is used? Does the staff use a microcomputer, a mainframe, or both? Is the software customized, or is it a package or a spreadsheet template? Find out any other pertinent information.

How do your guesses compare with reality?

4. Research how three corporations are using robots. Look for the following information: What task is the robot doing? Were people previously doing that work? Why were the people replaced by the robots? Describe what the robots look like, and compare them with robots described in a science fiction novel that you know.

7

Systems software

So far you have read about the many types of applications software, which enable people using computers to accomplish so many tasks. But there is another important class of software called **systems software.** Systems software itself does not perform specific business operations, rather, it helps the computer system to perform those operations more efficiently.

In this chapter you will first learn about operating systems, which are written for specific computers to allow them to work efficiently with applications software. In fact, without today's operating systems, most applications software could not work at all. Operating systems are usually provided by the computer manufacturer, and they give the computer many abilities that would otherwise have to be provided by each applications program. One example of this is the ability to run the disk drives in a microcomputer.

Operating systems do not, however, provide all the features that a particular organization might want. Many systems software packages are therefore available to supplement the features provided by operating systems. This chapter refers to these packages as *systems support software.* They include the operating environments you read about in Chapter 5 and many other programs, ranging from software that allows you to use different types of printers to programs that can calculate square roots or write out numerical digits as words.

The third type of systems software is computer language programs. Some of these may be provided with your operating system. (BASIC is a language commonly provided with microcomputers, and COBOL is usually one of several languages used with larger computers.) However, many languages need to be purchased separately. Language programs make it possible for programmers to create or customize applications software as well as systems programs.

These three types of systems software—operating systems, systems support programs, and language programs—are the subject of this chapter. When you have read it you will be able to:

- explain in general terms what an operating system does
- describe the idea behind families of operating systems on the microcomputer
- differentiate among several kinds of operating systems, especially those for microcomputers and mainframes
- describe different types of support programs available as systems software for microcomputers
- define programming
- explain the function of a language translator
- list levels and examples of programming languages

Operating systems

Operating systems are a very basic part of computer systems today, but they are not nearly so obvious to users as are applications programs. An **operating system** is software that enables the computer to obey the applications software commands. It therefore usually functions *between* the applications software and the computer hardware itself. Many users are unaware of what operating systems are and of what they can do. However, it is sometimes necessary to issue commands directly to an operating system. Knowledge of these commands allows users to accomplish more with a computer.

WHAT IS AN OPERATING SYSTEM?

A general understanding of how operating systems work can help you to use them, and to understand what they accomplish and how they influence the computer's abilities. Picture an unusual, mechanized office peopled by very efficient but inflexible robots. Try thinking of yourself, the user, as a busy executive and of the applications packages you work with as your robot assistants. These robots take care of the many tasks that you lack the time—and often the skills or knowledge—to perform.

For example, you indicate to one robot that you want to move a paragraph to a new location in a letter and that the paragraph introduction must be changed in a certain way. The robot (your word processing application) can change the sequence and print out the letter with the new sentences in almost no time at all. It can also, at your direction, copy the letter and file it away as a record. Similarly, another robot is an expert at handling figures and producing tabular reports for you to study. This assistant (actually your spreadsheet software) also appears to take care of copying and filing.

From your executive office, you might think that your robots do everything themselves, including the copying and the filing. But when you

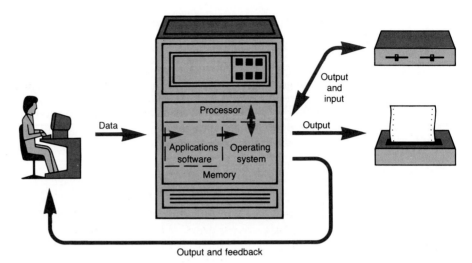

Figure 7-1 An Operating System at Work

Though users are mostly aware of their applications software, it is the operating system that tells the processor how to handle applications software and user input. The OS also regulates the flow of data and instructions within the computer system. For example, it tells the disk drive how to send a program or a data file to memory. It also sends data and program instructions to the processor. And when the processor has generated output, the OS regulates the flow of that output to the monitor, storage disk, and peripherals such as printers.

step out of your office, you see that the real picture is very different. Your robots work hard, but they are aided by a staff of specialized support robots that is normally hidden from view. This hidden staff represents a computer's operating system, or OS.

This staff has an expert at copying. It also might include a filing specialist and other support robots with special expertise in performing certain common tasks. When your "applications" robots need copies, they ask the OS staff specialist for them, because they are not capable of producing copies themselves. And if you issue the right commands, the support robots, each a part of the operating system, will do similar work for you. You can thus bypass your applications assistants and work directly with the computer's operating system. However, even if you have no reason to use the operating system's special capabilities directly, your applications software will certainly employ those capabilities to operate efficiently.

MICROCOMPUTER OPERATING SYSTEMS

A common task of typical microcomputer operating systems is working with the disk drives. They are therefore often called DOS, for **d**isk **o**perating **s**ystems. When you command your applications software to read a file from a disk or to save your work on a disk, the applications program calls on a part of the DOS to perform these tasks. Similarly, if you ask your applications software to delete a disk file, it is the DOS that actually performs the deletion.

In addition to working with the disk drives, a typical microcomputer operating system handles even more basic tasks. When the computer is turned on, the operating system checks all components and attachments to be sure that they are working properly. And it is the operating system that actually reads input from the keyboard and writes it onto the screen or onto a printer.

Typically, some of the operating system instructions may be on a diskette or other storage device. Computers with hard disks load the DOS automatically when you turn them on. With a computer that doesn't have a hard disk, your first step is usually to load the operating system from a diskette, even before loading an applications program. At least part of the DOS, however, is stored permanently in the computer—without this, the computer couldn't get started; it wouldn't even be able to read instructions from the DOS disk.

DOS commands. As suggested, you can directly command the DOS; in fact, this is often essential. When you start many applications, for example, you need to tell the DOS to load the software you are going to use. You may also need to instruct it to delete files you do not want, to copy files, and to help organize files.

One useful DOS command gives you complete information about what is on your disk. For example, keyboarding CATALOG or DIR, depending on the computer, makes the DOS give you both a full list of file names and additional information, such as the amount of free space left on the disk. Other common file handling commands on different microcomputer operating systems are presented in Figure 7-2.

DOS commands are not limited to handling files on the disk drive. Because operating systems also handle input and output, a typical DOS

Figure 7-2 Direct Commands to an Operating System
Microcomputers that use MS-DOS are controlled by keyboarded commands. So is the Apple IIe, if it is running under DOS 3.3, though the commands are different. Another OS for the Apple is PRODOS; this system offers users a set of menus from which to make selections.

FUNCTION	COMMAND		
	MS-DOS-Based Computers	Apple DOS 3.3	Apple ProDOS System Utilities
Lists files on diskette	DIR	CATALOG	L-LIST PRODOS DIR.
Deletes file from diskette	ERASE	DELETE	D-DELETE FILES
Formats new diskette	FORMAT	INIT	F-FORMAT VOLUME
Copies diskette	DISKCOPY	COPYA	C-COPY VOLUME
Changes file name	REN	RENAME	R-RENAME FILES
Compares files	COMP	—	K-COMPARE FILES
Copies files	COPY	—	C-COPY FILES

Figure 7-3 Issuing Commands to an Operating System
Most operating systems require the user to type commands. However, the Wang VS300 supermini-computer is one that provides a menu of operating system commands. The user selects the desired command by pressing a number, such as 8 for "manage communications." (Courtesy of Wang Laboratories, Inc.)

allows you to indicate if you want something unusual in this area too. For example, if you know the correct keyboard commands (which are explained in the documentation for your operating system), you can order your DOS to change some of its printer instructions so you can work with a different printer. A few systems will also let you change the keyboard configuration you are using.

A convenience available in several microcomputer systems is the ability to write strings of DOS commands on the screen, then save them into a file. If you later call on this file by name, the operating system will automatically obey each command in sequence. This type of file is often called a **batch file.** It can be useful if several standard DOS commands must be given before you start a particular applications program or after you finish work with it. An example of a batch file is shown in Figure 7-4. Batch files are simple computer programs, as you will see later in this chapter.

Operating system families. Though microcomputers have different operating systems, these differences are being overcome in many cases. When microcomputers first came out, no two brands had compatible operating systems. Applications that could run on a Radio Shack computer, for example, could not run on an Apple computer, because a Radio Shack applications program could not activate the Apple-DOS functions. The DOS in each computer DOS "understood" a different set of commands. Applications software developers, therefore, had to create different versions of their programs for different computers. This was a considerable expense for them, and it increased the prices of their software.

Though this problem is by no means solved, systems software designers have devised a solution: "families" of operating systems. These families understand the same commands and can therefore operate with the same applications programs even though they work on different types of computer hardware. Thus, the details of copying may be different on an IBM than on a Compaq computer, in that the hardware in each computer requires different specific instructions from the software to do the operation. But the DOS commands expected from the user or applications program are the same for both operating systems; therefore, the same applications software can work on either system.

The first operating system family for microcomputers was, in fact, developed to run not on a particular computer but instead on several types of computers. CP/M (or **C**ontrol **P**rogram for **M**icrocomputers), as it was called, had to compete with already established operating systems for each computer. But it became very successful because it was so versatile and enabled many machines to share the same applications programs.

Other operating system families for the microcomputer include MS-DOS and UNIX. **MS-DOS** (MS stands for Microsoft, the company that sells the system) was originally prepared for the IBM-PC. But because of IBM's reputation, other computer manufacturers quickly saw that software for MS-DOS would become very popular. Therefore, they obtained operating systems of the same family to run with their own machines. Now all of these computers can run the same user software. The applications programs are actually being written for the operating system, not for the computer hardware.

UNIX is unusual because it is a microcomputer operating system that was originally developed as an OS for larger computers. However, it is rapidly becoming important for microcomputers to be able to work directly with larger computers. So versions of this operating system have been developed for several of the more powerful micros. These computers often share characteristics with larger systems—for example, they can serve several users at once. UNIX is an operating system that allows them to do this. (A new system, IBM's OS-2, also designed for many users, will soon rival both UNIX and MS-DOS in popularity.)

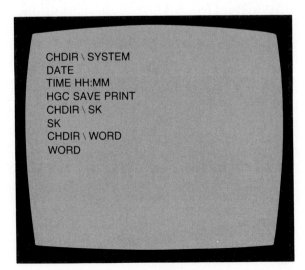

```
CHDIR \ SYSTEM
DATE
TIME HH:MM
HGC SAVE PRINT
CHDIR \ SK
SK
CHDIR \ WORD
WORD
```

Figure 7-4   A Batch File
Batch files automatically execute several DOS commands in a row. This one includes three directory changes, a call for the date and time, activating a graphics card (HGC) and loading two applications programs. Without it, the user would have to keyboard each command separately.

Figure 7-5 UNIX Operating System
UNIX is an operating system ideal for networks of communicating equipment, including mainframes, minicomputers, and microcomputers. Here a worker uses an
AT&T computer that can communicate with up to four microcomputers or terminals. (Courtesy of AT&T)

LARGER COMPUTER OPERATING SYSTEMS

The major difference between microcomputers and larger computers is
their capacity for work—both the amount they can hold in memory and
the speed with which they perform. This means that larger computers
can handle much larger programs as well as input from many people at
the same time.

Multi-user systems. Computer systems that work with many users
are called **multi-user systems.** In addition to requiring great memory
and speed, such systems need an element that is not found in most microcomputer operating systems. That element is a "priority manager."
Comparing the computer to a mechanical office again, robots that do jobs
for several users at once may annoy the users if they do the wrong jobs
first. They need someone to assign priorities to different tasks and to
decide how the full workload can be done most efficiently. A multi-user
computer's OS includes an element that acts as a priority manager, this
element is known as the **executive program.**

In addition to allowing many people to use the system at the same time, an executive program has other important advantages. Large computers can calculate many thousands of times faster than users can enter data. They can also work faster than printers can print and faster than disk drives can enter information. Thus, while the computer is waiting for these input and output operations to be completed, it could spend a lot of time doing nothing. But add more users, together with an operating system that can keep their work apart, and the power of the computer can be used far more effectively. While it waits for input from one user, it can be processing calculations for another.

How It Was

History of Operating Systems

In the early days of electronic computers, each program was developed from scratch. There was no such thing as systems software. Programs were written in machine language, so there was no need for programming language software, and the functions now taken care of by operating systems were built individually into each program. Users soon began to develop their own operating system programs, however, to take care of commonly needed operations like driving the printer or saving material on magnetic tape.

It was not until enough computers of the same kind were sold by computer manufacturers that a demand developed for commercially prepared operating systems. Businesses wanted common OSs to allow programs to be shared by similar machines. The computer manufacturers, who stood to gain by encouraging businesses to use one brand of computer exclusively, created operating systems that worked only with their own models.

Initially, operating systems were small, but they quickly grew larger and more complex. IBM's System 7000 series, introduced in the early 1960s, used a small, simple operating system. For IBM's next generation of computers, the System 360-370 series introduced in the mid-1960s, a new operating system performed many more tasks.

Business soon began to demand operating systems that made computers "upwardly compatible" so that programs developed on a specific computer could be used by later versions of that computer.

CP/M and UNIX represented a new direction in operating systems. They were generic, which means they could be used by different brands of computers. Likewise, applications software written for a generic operating system could be run by many types of computers.

IBM initially approached Digital Research, the developer of CP/M, about using CP/M as the operating system for the IBM PC. Digital Research did not wish to give IBM control of CP/M, so IBM went to Microsoft, a competitor of Digital Research. Microsoft developed MS-DOS, which has become the standard operating system for business micros.

Today, most experts agree that operating systems are lagging behind other computer technology. As they catch up, operating systems will make computers easier to use. Microcomputer operating systems will provide more support for new multi-user microprocessors. Direct links between two operating systems running on the same machine may allow for smoother file transfers. New operating systems for large computers will provide better support for "parallel processing," breaking large tasks into parts to be handled by several processors working simultaneously.

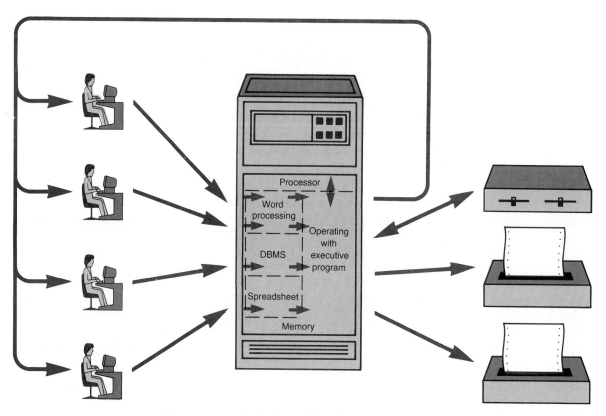

Figure 7-6   A Multi-User System
In a multi-user system, several people may be working with different kinds of applications software. The operating system acts as a traffic director, assigning priorities to input and output tasks, and ensuring word processing files don't get mixed up with each other or with DBMS and spreadsheet files. Users can thus share all the facilities of the computer system.

Even microcomputers, with the appropriate software, can occasionally do more than one task at a time. For example, several word processing programs can print out one file while the user is working on another. This process is known as **spooling.** Spooling on a micro may slow down the computer. But with a larger, faster computer, many users can work at one time, and each user will be unaware that the computer is spending time on other people's work. All this occurs thanks to the executive program in the operating system. More information about this feature of larger computer operating systems is provided in Chapter 9.

Special features.   With several users at work on the same computer, other features become desirable. One of these is **data security.** Nobody wants to feel that confidential files on which they are working might suddenly show up on someone else's screen or, worse still, be called up deliberately by a third party. Most large operating systems, therefore, provide security by allowing the assignment of passwords to individual operators. They can also arrange that certain files may be seen by all users, whereas others are to be viewed only by particular people.

In a large system, keeping a record of "who did what, when" may also be important to help track down any violations of security. Thus, large operating systems frequently provide **automatic logging** of all computer activity. This shows who was on the system, for how long, what files they used, and other important tracking information. Such records can also be used to watch the productivity of individual workers—an incentive to some employees and a concern to others.

Multiple operating systems. Operating systems for large computers, like those for microcomputers, were originally totally incompatible with each other. Applications software therefore had to be created for particular computer models. In fact, applications were often developed for particular machines, because many organizations created or customized their operating systems to perform tasks in a way that best suited their goals. They also hired teams of programmers to write their own applications programs.

The overall effect of this was that many organizations using large computers had unique operating systems, with important programs and data in forms unsuited to any other operating systems. This led to a serious problem. Organizations often wished to update their hardware because of the constant advances in computer technology. Programs and

Figure 7-7   Unique Operating Systems
Very large organizations often built complex systems around the unique operating systems of their large computers. The mainframe shown here was installed to handle many specialized applications for Chase Manhattan Bank's computer operations. (Courtesy of Raymond Juschkus/The Chase Manhattan Bank)

Figure 7-8   Job Control Languages

Some computer systems, such as the IBM 360 shown here, have large vocabularies in their JCLs (job control languages). An operator keys system commands at
a terminal, which can be adjacent to the computer. Users in remote locations may
also benefit from knowing a few JCL commands. (Courtesy of NOAA)

data created for the old system had to be reworked for the new system—
almost always a huge task. Therefore, computer manufacturers began to
create operating systems that remained consistent with their earlier models,
so the old data could still be used.

Thus, the same issues of compatibility that you read about regarding
microcomputers are beginning to concern users of larger computers—and
not just compatibility between different models from the same manufacturer but also between completely different computers. Communications
between computers are greatly helped if operating systems are compatible. The problem, therefore, is to allow a computer to handle the old data
and yet communicate fully with other dissimilar systems.

One solution is operating systems like UNIX. As you read earlier,
UNIX exists in different versions for a variety of machines—mainframes
as well as micros. Another solution involves a system that allows two or
more operating systems to be in effect at one time, so that one user can
work with programs designed for the "traditional" OS while another can
simultaneously work with a different OS.

Command languages for larger systems.   Just as a DOS for microcomputers provides a way for the user to instruct the operating system
directly, larger operating systems also allow you to talk directly to them.

These **command languages** (sometimes called **JCL,** or **Job Control Languages**) are sets of commands similar to the DOS commands available on microcomputers, though they usually do more.

Command languages allow you to call files, request priorities, specify which printers you want to use, address messages, and give other similar instructions. They also require you to identify yourself when you sign on. One of your early tasks when you join a new organization is to learn what is required to enable you to deal with the operating systems of its computers.

Systems support software

What is provided in operating systems varies from one manufacturer to another. For example, one operating system may allow you several formats in which to view a disk directory; another may give you only one. Or one may offer you the ability to create automatic chains of DOS commands, whereas another allows you to enter the commands only one at a time. Fortunately, operating systems can be supplemented with additional features, similar to the ways in which applications software can be enhanced.

Such additional features can often be purchased as **systems support software,** or skilled programmers may be able to create them. One way of looking at these support programs is to remember that an operating system is like a hidden staff of specialist robots who help the user and applications programs. Buying a new systems support program is like buying a new robot for the hidden staff, with different specialized skills.

This support software can be thought of as falling into several groups,

Figure 7-9 Creating Systems Support Software

Although some systems support software can be purchased "off the shelf," changes in existing programs must often be made to suit the users' special needs. Systems programmers may also be required to write such software from the ground up. (Courtesy of Bell Labs)

corresponding to the different types of services that operating systems provide. One group has to do with basic OS functions like handling printers and disk drives. These parts of an operating system are called **utilities.** Additional utilities may be available, especially if you purchase new pieces of hardware that need special software support. Another group consists of programs to provide working help to applications programs, not by doing basic tasks but by providing special "expert" help. Such programs are called **libraries.**

UTILITIES

Every operating system includes certain "housekeeping" functions, or utilities, that make computing easier. Some of the common utilities allow users to back up disks; to copy disks and files; and to open, close, rename, print, edit, sort, and merge files. However, there may be useful types of utilities that do not come as part of your operating system. In such cases it is advisable to see if they can be bought independently.

For example, there is a set of programs created to supplement MS-DOS that includes a data recovery program, which can often re-create a file that was accidentally erased from a disk. It also provides programs that let you search the disk directories in various ways, allow you to provide for data security, and perform various other services, like allowing you to choose screen colors.

You may also come across utilities that are essential with particular hardware. For example, your organization may purchase an **expanded memory card** for the microcomputer you are using. This card adds more memory space to the computer, which is useful for handling large databases. The card will probably come with a diskette to be read into the computer so that it can use the new hardware efficiently. The program on the diskette is a support utility—a new hidden specialist added to the operating system team.

LIBRARIES

In addition to utilities, operating systems frequently contain libraries. These are sets of files that can be used as part of applications programs. Library files are particularly useful to programmers because they can save a lot of work. For example, if a library has a program on file to calculate square roots, programmers don't have to write that part of a larger program; they can just call the square root routine into action out of the library.

Similarly, when an organization creates a set of boilerplate paragraphs for standard letters, it is setting up a library that can be used by the word processing program. Many other types of libraries are possible— a library of graphics, a library of command language routines, and a library of macros are just a few examples. As indicated in the chapter on word processing, these may sometimes be called glossaries instead of libraries; they may also be considered a part of the applications programs, rather than being viewed as systems software.

Figure 7-10 Operating System and Other Libraries
Operating system library files are often stored on on-line disk packs, such as those in the lower left of this picture, so they are immediately available to users. In contrast, other library files that supplement applications programs are often stored off-line on magnetic tape. (Courtesy of International Business Machines Corporation)

Computer language programs

A third type of systems software, which is frequently included in operating systems but can be added later, is computer language software. This software allows programmers to develop special applications for the computer and to customize both applications software and operating systems for a particular business.

As you learned earlier, software packages are actually sets of instructions to a computer, telling it exactly what to do and the order in which to do it. Computer languages are used to develop and sequence these instructions.

However, the computer doesn't understand words like *CATALOG* or *SAVE*. These words need to be translated into the electronic code that your computer responds to. **Computer language software** translates the instructions that a programmer writes into that code.

Language software also checks the work of programmers for logical errors and other mistakes. Programmers may make careless errors—for example, mistyping a command as CATALG instead of CATALOG. Or they may make a logical mistake, thus spoiling a set of instructions that looks correct in all other ways. Most language programs will alert programmers to errors of both kinds.

Three basic elements, called command structures, typically make up a computer program. The following section explains the type of code that a computer is able to understand but that also happens to be very difficult for programmers to write. Finally, it looks at several languages that have been developed so that programmers can create programs more easily.

COMMAND STRUCTURES

A good computer program is carefully planned. Computers need very accurate, very specific directions. It is not enough to say, in a general way, "Copy this text from one disk to another." There has to be a specific instruction for each character: copy the first letter; then copy the second; then the third; and so on until the whole text has been copied. Nothing can be left to the imagination; every detail must be covered, in precisely the right sequence.

To write a successful program, programmers therefore need to plan the steps it will follow in great detail. What will the program do first? What comes next? Under what conditions must it follow one course? What

Figure 7-11   Flowchart Illustrating Sequence
This diagram shows how the computer is to perform a simple sequence of operations. First, it calculates gross pay. Then, it calculates net pay. Finally, it prints the check. One step depends on the other. The computer must perform the operations in order.

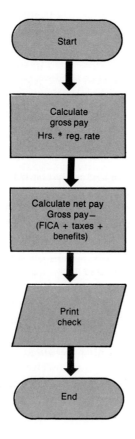

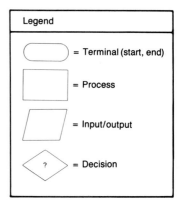

should it do otherwise? How many times should it repeat this procedure?

Computer programs are often planned using techniques like **flow-charting** (see Appendix). These techniques allow the programmer to see how all the elements and steps fit together and whether they will in fact lead to the desired results. As you see, several types of steps are possible. One is a straight sequence of commands, such as the one you saw in the MS-DOS batch program. But a program can follow two other simple structures, which require the computer to make decisions based on information you give to it. These structures are called selection and repetition.

In fact, programmers have found that, if they allow for just these three types of structures—sequence, selection, and repetition—they can accomplish all the programming that they need. Programming that uses only these three structures is called **structured programming** and has been found to be the most efficient way of producing software. It is also most easily understood and amended if organizational needs change.

Sequence.   The idea of sequence is very familiar to every human being. For example, if you drive into a gas station, a predictable sequence of events occurs. The cap on the car's gas tank is removed, a gas hose is placed in the tank, gas is pumped into the tank, the hose is removed, and the gas tank cap is replaced. You can easily imagine what would happen if the sequence was out of order and the gasoline cap was replaced before the gas was pumped.

Of course, an intelligent person would figure out that there was something wrong with any procedures manual that advised replacing the gas tank cap first. But computers are not like people, able to guess what the other person means. They cannot do what is wanted unless the directions are absolutely clear. If any steps are missing, expressed confusingly, or given in the wrong order, the task will come out wrong.

Selection.   Computers can, however, do more than merely follow a sequence of orders. A batch program such as that shown earlier could not handle the types of operations that you have seen applications software perform.

For example, to respond to a menu choice, a program needs to consist of more than a simple sequence. It must provide at least two alternative directions to follow and a reason for selecting one or the other. At the gas station, one instance of selection occurs when the attendant asks if the oil needs to be checked. If the answer is *yes*, the attendant selects one response (opening the hood and so on); for a *no* answer, the response will be different. Similarly, computer programs can be constructed to respond to different features of their input—either to a direct command (as in a menu choice) or to the result of some internal calculation (such as, "Is the number of letters keyed into the computer equal to the memory capacity?" In this case, a computer might be instructed to say: "No more memory available. Please save your work.").

Repetition.   A series of identical operations, such as looking for an occurrence of a word in a document, would also be difficult to set in motion if straight sequence was the only option. Either the computer will search

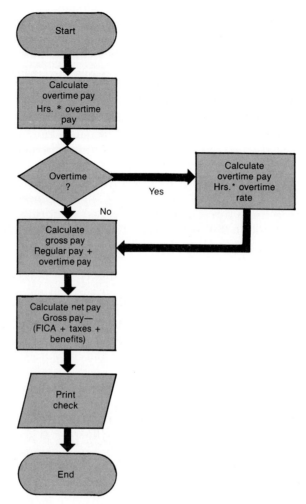

Figure 7-12 Flowchart Illustrating Selection
The diamond in this flow-chart shows where the program *selects* employees who have worked overtime. If an employee has worked overtime, the program calculates the additional pay due. If an employee has not worked overtime, the program by-passes this step, and moves through its regular sequence. Many techniques can be used to assess overtime—another is shown in the Appendix to this book.

too few times, or it will continue to try searching after the search is over, depending on how many times the search procedure is repeated in the program sequence. But a gas station attendant, while repeating the process of filling gas tanks, knows when to stop. Computer programs can also count how many times they have done something and stop doing it if the repetitions exceed a certain amount or if other conditions are met.

MACHINE CODE

It is one thing to know what to say to the computer and the order in which to say it. It is quite another to be able to say it so that the computer can understand. Computers do not understand the 26 letters of the alphabet. They do not even understand the 10 digits of our number system. All they can respond to are two states, usually symbolized by zero and one. Everything that is said to a computer must at some point be expressed with these two symbols only.

However, it is possible to express all our letters, and all our numbers, using these two symbols. Specific instructions to the computer about what is to be done with these letters and numbers can also be expressed using only zeros and ones. For example, the sequence of symbols 0100 0111 means the letter G in a code understood by some computers; 0000 0110 means the number six; and 1100 1001 can tell the computer to perform a comparison. Programs written with only zeros and ones are said to be in **machine code** or **machine language.**

Different computers use different machine codes. All machine codes use just two symbols, but a second machine might perform a comparison only in response to the instruction 1101 1100. And others might not understand a direct command to compare at all but might accomplish comparisons in a more roundabout way. As you can imagine, this makes it very difficult for a programmer to write a program that will work on several kinds of computers.

Even a simple set of instructions in a machine code looks long and incomprehensible (see Figure 7-14). As you can imagine, composing commands in machine code is very painstaking work, and composing sequences of instructions takes intense concentration. The fact is, in the

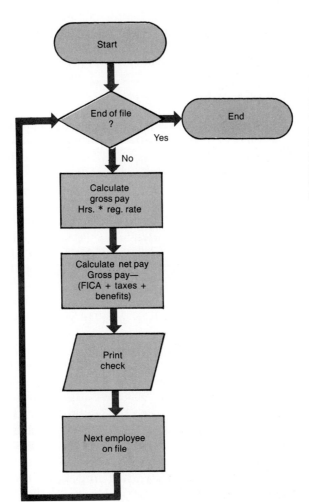

Figure 7-13 Flowchart Illustrating Repetition
This program calculates and prints a paycheck for each employee in a business. Rather than end the program when just one check is printed, the program moves to the next employee on file and begins calculating that employee's pay. The program ends only when there are no more checks to print.

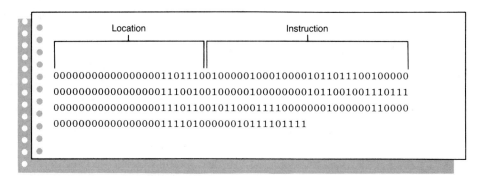

Figure 7-14 Using Machine Code
These binary code statements are from a program to process payroll. The digits to the left on each line show the computer the exact memory location the instruction is to occupy. To calculate this, early programmers had to keep track of how much memory space each instruction would occupy.

earliest days of computers, when programs themselves were simpler, programming was actually accomplished with the zeros and ones of machine language. But programmers soon developed an easier way of creating software. That way involved using the computer to help write its own programs.

ASSEMBLY LANGUAGES

The first languages that programmers developed to help them write programs were called **assembly languages,** because they help to assemble the complex sequences of zeros and ones needed to instruct the computer. In one sense, these languages are very simple—they are a one-to-one code. This means that every highly specific machine language instruction—get the first letter, copy it, and so on—has to be expressed in the assembly language version. However, these instructions are expressed in letters and numbers rather than in zeros and ones; for example, the character "7" is used to represent the number seven, and "CMP" could be used for the operation compare. To make their task easier, programmers made the sets of symbols into **mnemonics,** shortened or abbreviated words like *CMP* that would be simple for them to remember. You will notice that this principle is used in applications programs too—menu selections are often made with initial letters, for example.

A program written in assembly language cannot be understood directly by the computer. Instead, with assembly language, as well as with all higher-level computer languages, there are two versions of any program: the **source code,** which is written by the programmer, and the **object code,** translated by the computer into its familiar strings of zeros and ones. To translate source code to object code, early programmers developed assembly language programs, or **assemblers.** Although they are the oldest language translation software, assemblers are often referred to as **second-generation languages,** because machine languages came even earlier.

With assembly languages, it became more possible for expert programmers to look at a program and quickly understand what it would accomplish. It also became easier to find and correct errors. However, assembly languages didn't make programming easy by any means. Machine codes are all different, and because they are one-to-one codes, so are assembly languages. Also, the basic machine language instructions to computers are very detailed and precise—"get this piece of data from the memory"; "place it in this spot"; "compare it with another number"; "make this value equal to 15"; and so on. It is still a painstaking job to write assembly language. Assembly language is still used today, however, when a programmer wants to create the most economical code possible—in certain graphics routines, for example, which could otherwise take up too much computer memory.

THIRD-GENERATION LANGUAGES

The success of assembly languages, coupled with the difficulty of using them, has led to the creation of many other computer languages and computer language software. These languages share many characteristics, but each one is different and appropriate to various kinds of tasks.

STATEMENT NUMBER	SOURCE STATEMENT		
58	GETNEXT	DS	OH
59		GET	PAYCARD, CARDIN
60 +		LA	1, PAYCARD
61 +		LA	0, CARDIN
62 +		L	15, 48 (0, 1)
63 +		BALR	14, 15
64		BAL	R7, EDIT
65		CLI	ERRSW, C'1'
66		BE	GETNEXT
67		PACK	WKHOURS, HOURSIN
68		PACK	WKRATE, RATEIN
69		BAL	R7, FORMAT
70		CP	WKHOURS, =P'40'
71		BH	OVERTIME
72		MP	WKRATE, WKHOURS
73		BAL	R7, PRINT
74		B	GETNEXT

Figure 7-15 Using Assembly Language
This portion of a payroll program calculates and prints a record of wages earned by each employee. (Figure 7-14 showed lines 60 through 63 expressed in machine code.) Note the use of mnemonics: Line 70 instructs the computer to compare the number of hours worked against a 40-hour standard.

The next type of languages programmers developed are called **third-generation languages.** Most of these can also be called **procedural languages**, meaning that they allow the programmer to tell the computer what procedures it must follow to achieve their objectives. Procedural languages are still widely used; in fact, most of the computer languages you have heard of are probably procedural languages.

Like assembly languages, third-generation languages allow programs to be written in one form (also called a source code), then translated by their software into an object code. However, third-generation languages all differ from assembly languages in several important ways. First, they are not one-to-one code. This means that a single line in the source code can become many instructions in the object code. For example, this instruction:

IF RESPONSE = 999, THEN END

might tell the computer to perform all the operations needed to compare a particular response from the keyboard to the value 999, then terminate the program if they are equal.

Second, the symbols in third-generation languages are usually closer to English words than are the mnemonics used in assembly languages. In fact, it is the goal of some program developers to create language software that can translate English itself into object code. This has, however, proved to be far more difficult than people expected.

Third, most higher-level language software is available for many computers. If a programmer knows COBOL and creates source code using this language, that source code can be translated for many different computer systems, using various versions of COBOL language software. In effect, there are "families" of language software, similar to the families of operating systems mentioned earlier. Each version can read the same source code, but each translates it into object code for a different computer.

Interpreters and compilers.

The process of translating a complete program from a third-generation language into object code is called compiling, and the programming tools that do this are called **compilers.** Software written in a language that uses a compiler can run very fast, because all the required translation takes place before it runs. But because no part of the program can be run until the entire program is compiled, writing and perfecting such software can take a long time.

Several languages, however, create their object code in a different way. These languages, which include the common microcomputer language called BASIC, translate their instructions one at a time, while a program is running and the computer follows each instruction as soon as it is translated. This process, called interpreting, is similar to the work of a diplomatic interpreter at the United Nations who translates each statement as it is spoken. The software that performs this kind of translation is called an **interpreter.**

Most commercially available applications programs are already compiled into machine language, because if they are already in object code, they will run faster. However, some translation must take place even in

```
                              FORTRAN
        INTEGER Cust_no, Item_no(10), Qty_Sold(10), Tot_Qty Sold

        Tot_Qty = 0
        Retry = 'y'
        DOWHILE (Retry.EQ.'y')
        WRITE(5,2)
        READ(5,3) Cust_no
      2 FORMAT(22H ENTER Customer number:)
        DO 120 1ctr = 1,5,1
        WRITE(5,4)
        READ(5,3) Item_no(Ictr)
      4 FORMAT(19H ENTER Item number:)
        WRITE(5,6)
        READ(5,3) Qty_Sold(Ictr)
      6 FORMAT(21H ENTER Quantity sold:)
        Tot_Qty_Sold = Tot_Qty_Sold + Qty_Sold(Ictr)
    120 CONTINUE
        WRITE(5,7)
        READ(5,3) Retry
      7 FORMAT(11H MORE Data y/n?)
        ENDDO
        END
```

```
                              PASCAL
    VAR
        Cust_no                   : INTEGER;
        Item_no, Qty_Sold         : ARRAY[1..10] OF INTEGER;
        Tot_Qty_Sold, Counter     : INTEGER;
        Retry                     : CHAR;

    BEGIN
        Tot_Qty_Sold := 0;
        REPEAT
           WRITELN('ENTER Customer number: ');
           READLN(Cust_no);
           FOR (Counter = 1 TO 5) DO
             Begin
               WRITELN( 'ENTER Item_no and quantity sold: ');
               READLN(Item_no[counter], Qty_sold[counter]);
               Tot_Qty_Sold = Tot_Qty_Sold + Qty_Sold[counter]
             End; {for loop}
           Writeln('MORE Data y/n? ');
           READLN(Retry);
         UNTIL (Retry = 'n');
        END. {main}
```

Figure 7-16   A Program in Two Third-Generation Languages
Both these programs tell the computer to do the same things: accept customer order data input from a terminal and calculate a new sales total for each item ordered. You can see several shared elements; however, the Pascal version is structured, even in its appearance on the page.

these programs, if only to translate user commands down to the machine level.

A tour of third-generation languages. Each language differs in the purposes for which it was created and in its particular strengths and weaknesses. Here is a brief roundup of the common procedural languages, starting with the ones that you are most likely to have heard of and that are used extensively in business.

More people are familiar with **BASIC** (which stands for Beginners All-Purpose Symbolic Instruction Code) than with any other programming language because it is included in many popular microcomputer operating systems. However, it was first developed as a mainframe language in the early 1960s by two professors who wanted a programming language that would be easy for their students to learn. BASIC is sometimes used by small businesses that want to develop their own programs, because people without previous training as programmers can learn it easily. However, because it commonly uses an interpreter, BASIC is slow running. And it is in some ways too flexible—programs developed in BASIC tend to be unstructured programs that are difficult to understand or revise.

COBOL is the traditional language for business. In fact, its letters stand for Common Business-Oriented Language. It was designed to be easy for nonprogrammers to understand, so its instructions look very much like English sentences. However, this makes it rather a "long-winded" language. Most other languages are far more economical in the way they express their instructions. And it is a poor language for complex mathematical calculations. COBOL is one of the earliest structured programming languages.

Pascal was developed in the early 1970s after structured programming had become popular. It is thus well suited to structured programming, and it is more concise in its expressions than COBOL. Pascal is suited to mathematical and scientific applications, but it is also frequently used for business programs.

C is another language that embodies structured programming concepts. C was used to create the UNIX operating system and is well suited to both business and scientific applications.

FORTRAN is the earliest third-generation language, designed in the mid-1950s. Standing for Formula Translator, it is to the scientific community what COBOL is to the business community—the time-honored granddaddy of useful languages. In the early years, FORTRAN was used for business programming too, but it is less user friendly than many other languages.

RPG is a very early language of a somewhat different type. It was developed in the 1960s specifically to produce business reports and is much easier to handle than the other languages described so far. However, it is of limited use because it is so specifically directed at one type of problem. In fact, it can be considered more of a **problem-oriented language** than a procedural language—an ancestor of many more recent languages of the same type.

Figure 7-17　A Programming Language for Children
LOGO is an interactive programming language designed to get children involved with computers in a creative way. Children use simple LOGO commands based on basic English words such as "right," "left," "forward," and "backward" to get the computer to perform. (Courtesy of BankAmerica Corporation)

Other third-generation languages include **Ada,** a language sponsored by the United States Department of Defense for large-scale projects; **APL** (A Programming Language), which is particularly economical in handling complex instructions; **LOGO,** which uses a graphic "turtle" to teach programming in elementary schools but can also handle complex applications; and **LISP,** one of the earliest languages, which is suited to developing the expert systems described in Chapter 6.

FOURTH-GENERATION LANGUAGES AND BEYOND

In third-generation languages, the programmer usually has to tell the computer the steps needed to solve a problem. But with several more recent languages, called **fourth-generation languages** (**4GL** for short), all the programmer needs to do is explain what the problem is. These language programs have built-in strategies that enable the computer to solve the problem.

One type of fourth-generation language is a group known as **applications development languages,** or **program generators.** You can use these to create your own applications software even if you are not a professional. With program generators you simply answer questions that appear on the screen. For example, one screen prompt might ask how often a report you are working on should be issued. For some uses, however, program generators may be slower than third-generation languages. Some examples of applications development languages are FOCUS, RAMIS II, and NOMAD2.

Figure 7-18 Database Query Languages
Symantec's microcomputer database program features a "special assistant" which allows the user to phrase commands in different grammatical forms of English. The advantage to the user is that less memorizing or looking up commands is necessary. (Courtesy of Symantec Corporation)

Query languages, another type of 4GLs, are used for searching, entering, and manipulating information in a database. They often use commands that sound quite like English. Here is an example of a formal query:

PRINT 1987-JULY-ACT-SALES

WHERE DEPT = ('Toys' OR 'Appliances')

This instruction asks for all actual sales of July 1987 in the toys or appliances department. Two well-known query languages are DATA-TRIEVE and DATAQUERY.

Though they sound like English, such languages, however, do not approach the flexibility of the English that we naturally speak and write. As indicated earlier, programmers are beginning to develop so-called **natural programming languages,** which would allow you to tell the computer what to do in natural sentences. Natural programming languages are another product of the artificial intelligence research first mentioned in Chapter 6. Here is one way that you could ask the preceding question using such a language:

DISPLAY THE ACTUAL SALES FOR JULY 1987

FOR THE TOYS AND APPLIANCES DEPARTMENTS

Unlike earlier computer languages, however, these languages allow the computer to understand the question if you phrase it in another form, such as:

FOR TOYS AND APPLIANCES

GIVE ME JULY 1987 ACTUAL SALES

And they can sometimes interpret your questions with the help of other information in the computer's memory—for example, a knowledge base created by analyzing the types of questions you usually ask.

These natural programming languages, sometimes called **fifth-generation languages,** cannot fully understand human sentences. But if the computer fails to grasp your meaning, it can prompt you to give your command another way. And on occasion it may be able to learn new sentence forms as a result of your response. However, there is still a long way to go before computers will successfully respond to human language.

As you can see, there is a clear trend toward making programming languages easy enough for anyone to use. However, it will probably be some time before a true natural language is developed—one that makes it possible for us to talk to the computer the same way that we talk to each other.

STATE OF THE ART

Trade-Offs in Using Fourth-Generation Languages

It is tempting to think that the latest version of something is the best. Our experience tells us, however, that this is not always true. In some cases, improvements may come at the expense of other desirable attributes. So it is with fourth-generation languages.

The goal of fourth-generation languages is to increase programming productivity. For the most part, they do just that. With a fourth-generation language, a programmer need only describe the desired output of a program, and the language creates a program that will produce it. This characteristic makes it easier for a nonprogrammer to develop software. But it can pose problems too.

For one thing, programs developed with fourth-generation languages are usually slower running than those developed with lower-level languages. For another, some programmers rely on the assistance too much;

consequently, they spend too little time analyzing tasks and designing programs. Also, many fourth-generation languages do a poor job of handling systems tasks, such as error recovery, restarting, and reorganizing.

Thus, fourth-generation languages are appropriate for some systems but not for others. When one state government used a fourth-generation language to computerize its motor vehicle department, the result was disastrous. The computer system's long response time and the difficulty of updating information daily doomed it from the start.

To determine whether a program should be written in a fourth-generation language, a specialist evaluates the information system carefully: the specialist must consider who will be using the system, how much data it must handle, how fast the data must be processed, and many other questions.

SUMMARY

- Systems software is a category of software that does not perform applications directly. Instead, these programs make the computer able to accomplish applications programs. They represent a level of programs between the applications software and the computer hardware. Operating systems are one type of systems software. Other types are support programs and language software.

- The central type of systems software is the operating system. Operating systems are software packages that accomplish standard computer operations like input and output and that may allow software written for one computer to work on another. Commands can be issued by the user directly to operating systems.

- Microcomputer operating systems essentially serve the needs of the user and the applications software, handling basic functions like storing and retrieving disk files, operating the monitor and printers, and organizing the computer's memory.

- Multi-user operating systems enable large computers to balance the needs of different programs and users at the same time and allow more efficient use of the machine's computing power. They also provide for data security and automatic records of computer use.

- Support programs include utilities, which add basic capabilities not provided by the central programs in the operating system, and libraries, which contain commonly used routines for applications programs.

- Programming language software allows the use of programming languages, with which programmers can create customized software if prepackaged software is not available to meet a business's specific needs.

- Programming involves telling the computer, very precisely and in an exact sequence, all the steps that it is to perform. Three basic structures are involved—sequence, selection, and repetition. All programs can be produced using these three structures.

- Each computer responds to only one code—its own particular machine language, which is expressed using two types of symbols only, zeros and ones. Machine languages are very difficult to work with, and different levels of languages have been developed to simplify the task of writing programs.

- The first languages to be developed were assembly languages, which use mnemonics to represent strings of zeros and ones. These languages are translated into machine code by programs called assemblers, which are specific to particular computers.

- Many newer languages have been developed, at increasing levels of sophistication. These, too, need to be translated into codes of zeros and ones to be understood by the computer, but they look far more like English and can be used on a variety of computers.

■ Developments in computer languages are still taking place. The most advanced languages are increasingly like English, able to tolerate ambiguities and mistakes by the programmer and still provide results.

TERMS FOR REVIEW

systems software	flowcharting	FORTRAN
operating system	structured	RPG
batch file	programming	problem-oriented
MS-DOS	machine code	language
UNIX	machine language	Ada
multi-user systems	assembly languages	APL
executive program	mnemonics	LOGO
spooling	source code	LISP
data security	object code	fourth-generation
automatic logging	assemblers	languages
command languages	second-generation	4GL
JCL	languages	applications
Job Control	third-generation	development
Languages	languages	languages
systems support	procedural	program generators
software	languages	query languages
utilities	compilers	natural
libraries	interpreter	programming
expanded memory	BASIC	languages
card	COBOL	fifth-generation
computer language	Pascal	languages
software	C	

TERMINOLOGY CHECK

For each of these definitions, choose the correct term from the list of Terms for Review:

1. Software that translates certain computer language instructions line by line.

2. Central type of systems software that directs software operation.

3. Recent language programs with built-in strategies enabling the computer to solve problems presented by a user.

4. Simple computer program for a micro that allows a sequence of commands to be executed in order by the operating system.

5. Programming that uses only the three structures of sequence, selection, and repetition and is considered the most efficient way of producing software.

6. Traditional computer language used for business, with instructions that resemble English sentences.

7. Sets of commands for communicating directly with large operating systems.

8. First languages developed to write computer programs, which express instructions in sets of letters and numbers rather than zeros and ones.

9. Original version of a program, written by the programmer in assembly language or a higher order language.

10. Language expressed in zeros and ones that is understood by computers.

INFORMATION CHECK

1. List three types of systems software, and explain each briefly.

2. What types of general activities can an operating system perform for you?

3. What common tasks will a typical microcomputer operating system perform.

4. Explain the idea of "families" of operating systems.

5. Identify operating system features usually associated with larger computers.

6. Name some uses for command languages.

7. Describe two types of system support software.

8. What are the three command structures that are used in structured programming? Describe each briefly.

9. What are the two versions of an assembly language program? Describe each.

10. Why are third-generation languages also called procedural languages?

11. How do third-generation languages and assembly languages differ?

12. What is the difference between a compiler and an interpreter?

13. List the most commonly used third-generation languages, and identify the applications they are best suited to handle.

14. What is one major difference between third- and fourth-generation languages?

15. As programming languages have progressed from the first generation to the fourth and even fifth generation, what trend is continuing to develop?

PROJECTS AND PROBLEMS

1. Suppose you've decided that being a programmer for Lakeland Software, Inc., the only software company in the Fortune 50, is not for you. You accept a programming position with Blue Skies Corporation,

a small start-up company specializing in customizing microcomputer software for small local businesses.

Write a description of what your new programming environment will probably be like. Use the following questions to guide you:

- What kinds of systems software are you likely to find in your new job?

- What kinds of system support program features will you probably have to develop on your own?

- What programming language or languages will you be using?

2. Identify and contact a local company that uses mainframe language software. What generations are they using and for what functions? If they aren't using fourth-generation language software, have they investigated using it? Why are they implementing it—or why not? What problems or advantages have they noticed with the transition from one generation to the next? Compile your responses into an oral report. Compare your findings with those of other people in your class who have completed this project. Are most of the companies interviewed using third- or fourth-generation software?

3. As programming languages come to look more like English, programmers will encounter problems that developers of first-, second-, third-, and fourth-generation languages never had to handle.

What are some of these problems? Are they problems only with English? In which other human languages is natural-language software currently available? Why isn't it available in more languages?

4. Several software developers are developing natural-language software for use on microcomputers. Visit your local computer store. Compile a list of natural-language programs available through the store. Select one to study in depth. Contact the developer for brochures describing the software. Prepare a report describing how it operates. Share this information, including the brochures, with the class.

PART THREE

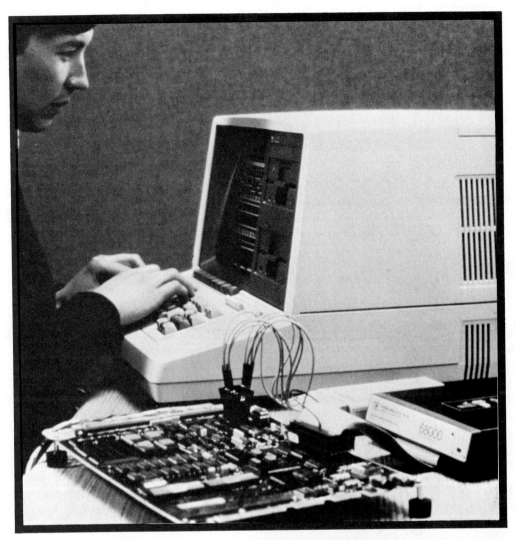

COMPUTER HARDWARE

8

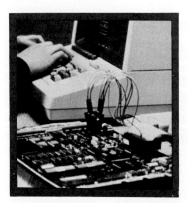

Elements of a computer system

In Part Two of this book you learned about software. Software is the element in a computer system that determines what the system will do. You examined several types of applications software that enable computers to perform specific tasks which are useful to business—for example, word processing and spreadsheet analysis. You also looked at systems software, which allows applications software—and users such as yourself—to have direct control over many computer operations.

Understanding software is a vital part of being able to handle computers. If you have learned how to deal with menus, how to issue commands, and what different applications software programs can do for you, you can probably begin working with them. If you also understand the nature of systems software, you are beginning to develop the ability to troubleshoot problems when something goes wrong. But your picture of computer systems, and your power to deal with them, is not complete unless you have some appreciation of the hardware as well—the computers themselves and the various peripherals (keyboards, printers, and similar devices) that surround them.

Part Three of this book is therefore about hardware. It does not explain the electronics, because these differ from computer to computer. Instead, it presents a broad description of the types of equipment you will encounter in a business office and some facts about how this equipment works. These facts will make it easier for you to understand and remember some of the strengths and weaknesses of computers.

You will begin this part by looking at the microcomputer and its standard peripherals. Then you will learn about some of the capabilities of larger machines that result from their greater power, and about some of the labor-saving peripherals that are becoming more and more popular. Finally, you will be introduced to data communications, in which computers are linked into larger systems called **networks.** Such networks are becoming very common in today's businesses because they offer many advantages in both convenience and cost.

206

Chapter 8 begins the treatment of hardware by presenting some basic facts about computers. Then it looks at a typical microcomputer system and examines how data is input, processed, and then output in a more useful form. The chapter should enable you to:

- identify typical components of a computer system

- explain the relationships among these components in a microcomputer

- show how they contribute to the system as a whole

- describe in general terms how they work

- note important differences among components of various systems

Computer fundamentals

Many types of computers are used in business and other organizations today, but they have several features in common. An important similarity is the way in which they process data. Two key elements of a computer are its memory, which stores both the software instructions and the data that the computer is given, and its **central processing unit (CPU),** which interprets the instructions and does the work. The CPU is the heart of the system, as it controls every operation that takes place inside the computer. Both the memory and the CPU are made up of many tiny electronic circuits that can store and release data signals.

Another similarity shared by most computers used in business is that they are **digital** computers. This means that, rather than work with continuously varying data, like a dial watch (which has hands that keep moving smoothly to indicate the time of day), they work in discrete units, as digital watches do. However, unlike the 10 digits used by digital watches, computers work with only two digits.

CIRCUITS AND BITS

You will remember that before any program can be processed by a digital computer, it must be translated into object code. This code is expressed in machine language, using only zeros and ones. Machine language uses only two symbols because of the nature of computer circuits. Even a microcomputer contains several million electronic circuits working together. Whether these circuits are used for memory or are part of the CPU, they have only two positions: on and off.

The circuits are therefore like switches. In fact, early computers included rows of mechanical switches. To program one of these computers for a new task, operators had to set all the switches by hand, a long, tedious, and usually complicated job. Today, however, the circuits are

Figure 8-1   A Mechanically Programmed Computer
This early IBM computer could be programmed by means of mechanical switches with values from 0 to 9. The computer was capable of converting these decimal values to binary values, the 0s and 1s of machine language. Nevertheless, programming a new task was very laborious. (Courtesy of International Business Machines Corporation)

controlled electronically by the machine language programs, which turn circuits *on* with a one and *off* with a zero.

Because digital computer circuits have only two states—on and off—they are called **binary** computers. (Binary refers to the number two.) It is hardly surprising, then, that the smallest measure of computer memory and activity, the single zero or one, is called a **binary digit,** or **bit** for short.

THE POWER OF THE BIT

A bit has two states only. If this were also true of the computer itself, it would obviously be a useless machine, at best capable of giving simple yes or no answers. However, computer circuits work in endless combinations, giving the computer its power. Perhaps you heard the following problem when you were in grade school. You are sitting at a checkerboard (with 64 squares) and someone offers you a choice. Would you like to be given $1,000 on each square of the board? Or would you prefer a cent on the first square, two cents on the second, twice two on the third, twice that on the fourth—each time doubling the amount on the last square? Which offer would you choose? The answer is surprising to most people. It is better to accept the cents option. If you took the thousand dollars, you would end up with $64,000—not bad for a grade school student. But by choosing the cents, you would earn yourself almost $200 quadrillion!

Though this problem is from a game rather than from a computer, it dramatically shows the power of twos in combination. If 64 circuits are electrically linked in the right way, they can represent any number from zero to a vast amount. And computers have many more than 64 circuits. This is part of the power that underlies the computer.

That power is added to by three important features of computers today. The first has to do with the processing capacity of the machines. Because the switches on early computers had to be set by hand, they were set one at a time. Today, even on the smallest microcomputers, software sets the circuits eight at a time. On some micros, 16 circuits are set simultaneously; on minis and more powerful micros, 32; and on larger machines, 64 or 128. The number of bits that a computer processes together is an important measure of its capacity.

The second feature of computer power is processing speed, and it is dramatic. An expert computer operator in the early days would probably have found it difficult to set more than one switch each second. Modern computers can perform each setting operation (of 8, 16, or more circuits) several million times per second. This processing speed is measured in **megahertz (MHz)**—one megahertz represents one million cycles per second—and is another indicator of computer power. (Larger computers use a related measure, **million instructions per second (MIPS)** to measure their processing speed.)

The third feature is memory capacity. Early computers were limited in the amount they could store because storage was bulky and expensive. One important early model had space for just 18,000 bits of information. This may seem a lot until you compare it with the memory of even a modest microcomputer today. To measure memory, bits are grouped into units of eight called **bytes.** A group of just more than 1,000 bytes—1,024 to be precise—is called a **kilobyte (K).** A typical microcomputer used in business may have upwards of 640K of memory—or more than six million bits. When you consider the power of just 64 circuits, you can imagine what six million can do.

INFORMATION FLOW

Six million circuits may sound very complicated—and it is. The details of how these circuits are linked to each other in different computers are beyond the scope of a nontechnical course for users. In fact, many computer circuit boards are designed and manufactured by computers rather than by people; this means that even an expert computer scientist may not know exactly how information is being processed at a given point in a program. Fortunately such detailed understanding is unnecessary for the average business computer user. But it can help to have a broad picture of the structure, or **architecture,** of a computer system.

Knowing what the main parts of the system are called, and how information is handled by them, provides a basic understanding that can help you to use the computer more intelligently. The overall flow of information through any computer is easy to describe and understand. The first stage, input, may be done from the keyboard, from a disk drive, or from several other devices. These input devices convert the keystrokes and other signals into electronic impulses. The impulses enter the CPU, which sets the different memory circuits on or off as the program requires. Thus, the input stage prepares the computer for action.

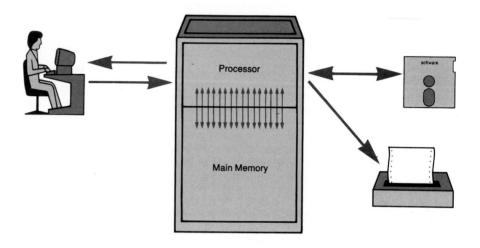

Figure 8-2 Data Flow Through a Computer System

Input from a keyboard or other device goes to the processor, which transfers data to the computer's main memory. The processor then retrieves from memory the data it needs to work on. Many office micros are 16-bit computers, which means they can transfer 16 bits of data at a time between the memory and the processor, as shown above. A 32-bit computer can make the transfers twice as fast, so tasks can be performed in less time. After processing, the changed data is returned to memory displayed on screen, and then sent, perhaps, to a secondary storage device or printer.

The second stage is processing, when the system manipulates words or data according to the instructions in the software and your own commands. You issue a command or make a menu choice and this information goes to the CPU, setting processing in action. The computer is no longer a passive storage device. It acts on the words and data (and pictures) that have been stored in the memory. It moves them around and combines them as the program and your commands dictate, converting them into useful information.

After you have given a command, you may input further data and give additional commands, or you may be content with the output from what you have done. Output is in many ways the opposite of input. When you input, you convert signals (for example, letters on the keyboard) into electronic binary impulses. When you output, you convert electronic impulses into letters or other signals again.

This output may be the continuous, automatic output that many software packages allow you to see on the monitor screen. It may go to a printer, which performs on orders from you. The output may also be routed to a storage device so that you can recall your file for further work at some later time. Or it may be sent to a communications device, which can send it on to a remote printer, to remote storage, or for use as direct input to another computer some distance away.

MICROCOMPUTERS AS MODEL SYSTEMS

Input, processing, and output take place in all computer systems, however different they may look. Large mainframe computers can accept input from hundreds of remote terminals and workstations, and they may be connected to several high-speed printers and other devices for output. Microcomputers usually have a single keyboard and one or two disk drives for input and use one monitor and one printer for output. But in spite of differences in size and capabilities, mainframes and micros have plenty in common. By studying micros, you can learn much about computers in general.

For one thing, even microcomputers show tremendous variety. They differ in external appearance—what are peripheral devices to one computer may be built in on another. They also differ in internal design. If you open a typical microcomputer, you will see that most of the circuits are attached to a flat "motherboard," but there are often other circuit boards (called cards) fitted into slots on the motherboard. The slots are called expansion slots. They allow you to add special-purpose cards if you need additional memory, graphics capabilities, or other enhancements. Some microcomputers rely on external cartridges to provide these extra features or else make no provision at all for expansion.

Figure 8-3   An Expansion Card

The basic circuitry of a microcomputer is contained in the motherboard (lower right). Additional circuitry, or an expansion card, is here being inserted into a slot on that board. It will allow the computer to show more characters at a time on the monitor screen. (Courtesy of Apple Computer, Inc.)

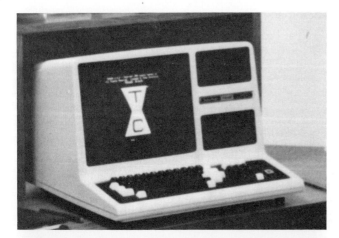

Figure 8-4 Microcomputer "Packaging"
Although the basic components of a microcomputer are the same, they can be packaged in several ways. All the parts can be housed in the same cabinet (left); the monitor can be a separate unit (lower left); or keyboard, monitor, and CPU can all be separate (below). (Courtesy of Tandy Corporation, Apple Computer, Inc., International Business Machines Corporation)

Still other differences are less obvious to the eye or invisible. For example, as you learned earlier, microcomputers differ in the number of bits they can process at one time. Older models handle 8 bits (a byte) at a time, which is adequate for many purposes. Others work with 16-bit words (a **word** in this context means the number of bits that the CPU handles at one time). This makes for faster processing. Several micros process 32-bit words. These bits travel together within the computer, are processed together by the processing circuits, and are stored together in the memory circuits.

As you may have guessed, microcomputers differ not only in capacity but also in the other two features described earlier, processing speed and memory. Their speeds may be as slow as 4 MHz or as fast as 12 MHz. Some even have switchable speeds so that users can select 6, 8, or 10 MHz. The variation in memory is even greater. Some portable computers have only 24K to 32K of memory that cannot be expanded, but micros with 640K or more of memory are commonplace today. In fact, it's not unusual to see micros with expansion cards that bring memory up to 1,280K or more.

The remainder of this chapter looks in more detail at typical components of a microcomputer system, starting with input devices, then examining the memory and processing circuits of the CPU, and finally studying how output devices work. By the end of it you will be much more familiar with the micro, and you will also have mastered several concepts that are useful for understanding larger computers.

Input devices

As you know, the first phase of computer processing is input. All input may take place before the processing starts, or the software (operating system and applications) may be input initially, with words, data, and commands fed in as they are neeeded. But without correct input of programs and data, no computer can perform the tasks people want.

Today's standard input devices for the microcomputer are the disk drive and the keyboard. The disk drive is used for entering most packaged software and for storing work that has been done. The keyboard is the main tool by which users enter the specific data and commands called for by the software.

THE DISK DRIVE—FOR INPUT AND STORAGE

Programs stored on floppy disks are the basis of the whole commercial software industry. Although companies still create and distribute customized software on tapes for mainframe computers, the diskette has revolutionized the lower end of the industry, creating an "off-the-shelf" product that sells itself—and helps to sell microcomputers. Without the ability to input software from diskettes, microcomputers would never have become the powerful business tools that they are today.

Software diskettes come in several sizes, the most common for the microcomputer being 5¼ inches and 3½ inches in diameter. A diskette is a circular piece of Mylar coated with a material that can be magnetized. It is held in a square jacket for protection and used in a disk drive. The diskette is magnetized somewhat like a recording cassette, except that the recording is digital. This means that it holds just two types of signals, corresponding to the ones and zeros of machine code.

The disk drive "reads" these signals, converting them into electronic impulses suitable for the computer. Among other things, it contains a speed-controlled motor, several thousand circuits to help control its operation, and one or two recording heads called **read/write heads.** These

Figure 8-5 Read/Write Heads

Among the few moving parts of a computer are the read/write heads in its disk drives. During the life of a single diskette, the read/write head may pass over its surface more than two million times. Read/write heads are likely to require repair over the life of a computer. (Courtesy of Digital Equipment Corporation)

heads, unlike those in a cassette recorder, are movable. They can be directed to read any part of the diskette without delay. Later you will read that they also record information from the computer to any part of the diskette without delay.

The read/write heads in any disk drive are under control of the computer's operating system; otherwise they would be unable to find the information on the disk. Typically, diskette information is laid down in circular **tracks,** which are divided into several **sectors.** (Figure 8-6 shows what this looks like.) To locate the beginning of a particular information file, the heads need only be "told" which sector of which track to search. Each sector is the **disk address** of the information recorded there.

How does the disk drive "know" where to find a particular piece of information? There is a record of the information files on a diskette, along with their disk addresses, called a **directory** or a **catalog.** This is usually held on a track determined by the computer's operating system. When the user directs a program to call for a file, the DOS finds the file through the directory and then copies it into the computer so the user can work with it.

THE KEYBOARD

Not surprisingly, the typewriter-style keyboard has become the major device by which users enter data and commands into the computer. The typewriter has been used for more than 100 years to transfer peoples' ideas onto paper. It is precise, unlike handwriting, and it has proved to be an easy device to link to other devices. In the early years of computers, the keyboard was joined to a card punching machine so that it punched holes through cards instead of typing letters onto a sheet of paper. These cards were then fed into a computer device designed to turn the punched holes into electronic signals. Now the keyboard has been adapted to create electronic signals itself so that it can be linked directly to the computer. It generates a different signal for each key on the keyboard. In fact, it can create several different signals for each key. For example, the CONTROL key used simultaneously with an alphabetic key creates a different signal for that letter.

INPUT PORTS AND INPUT BUFFERS

The electronic signals from an input device are fed into the computer itself through a connection called an **input port.** Most input ports include

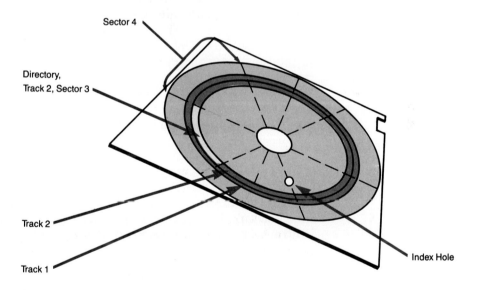

Figure 8-6   Locating a File on a Diskette

When a typical disk operating system formats a diskette, it divides each side into tracks and sectors. Each file stored on the disk has an address consisting of its track and sector numbers. The OS sets aside a predetermined address for a directory of files. When you call for a file, the OS uses the directory to find the file's address. The read/write head then searches for that new location and reads the file into the computer's memory. The index hole in the diskette indicates where the tracks begin.

sockets into which input devices are plugged; though when the device is built into the computer, the input port is totally internal to the system.

An input port, or in some cases the input device itself, usually includes a small "memory" element that keeps a record of the most recent signals generated. This is called an **input buffer:** it means that, for example, even if the computer is busy when a keystroke is made, the keystroke is not "forgotten"—a record of it remains until the CPU is ready to process it. If you make relevant keystrokes while the disk drive is running, you will often find that the computer can process them after the disk drive finishes its work.

Active memory

The memory associated with input devices is very small compared with the memory of the computer itself. A typical input buffer can hold a few dozen characters at most. But even a laptop computer can have a memory of 200K or more, meaning that it can hold upwards of 200,000 characters. And it is usually possible to add "memory chips" to such a machine, bringing its capacity up to 640K or more—the usual basic memory of today's desktop microcomputers.

A microcomputer's **active memory** is where the computer's work is laid out and where results are stored as the work is performed. As you know, its capacity is measured in bytes and kilobytes. It is also arranged in the same way: the memory circuits in a typical micro are organized in groups of eight (remember, 8 bits make 1 byte). As you will realize, a typical microcomputer therefore has thousands of these groups, creating a problem similar to that posed by diskette sectors—how does the computer know where to find the particular information it wants?

MEMORY ADDRESSES

The solution to this problem is similar to the one given for diskettes. In the same way that each sector of a diskette has a disk address, each byte in memory has a **memory address.** Thus, when the computer needs some information from memory, it need only call on the right address to find the information it needs. Relevant memory addresses are an important part of the machine language (object code) for any applications software, and they are a vital ingredient of the systems software.

To help you to picture this, try thinking of the active memory of a computer as a huge table with thousands of banks of switches on it. Each bank includes eight switches, and each switch represents a circuit or bit. Therefore, each bank represents a byte. The computer reads the memory by looking at the pattern of switches on each bank, and it can also change the arrangement of switches to represent new information. But for the picture to be complete, you must imagine that each bank of switches is numbered and that the object code, helped by the operating system, supplies the number or address of the switches that must be read next.

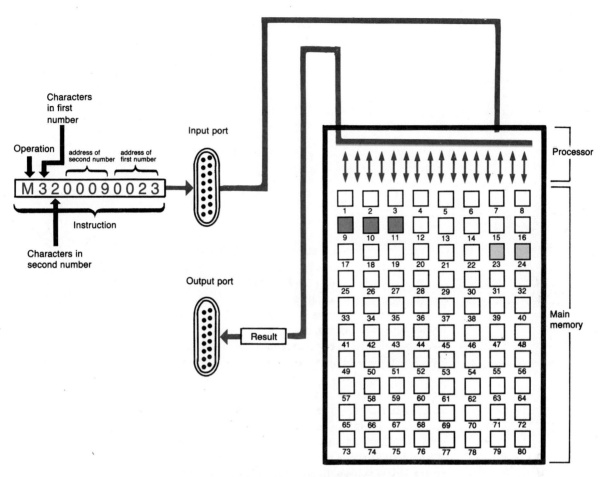

Figure 8-7   Finding Data in Main Memory

Each memory address in this computer's main memory can hold eight bits (one byte) of data, representing a number. The assembly language instruction above tells the processor to multiply the three numbers beginning at address 9 by the two numbers starting at address 23. After receiving the instruction the processor can retrieve the data from memory, perform the calculation, and send the result to a peripheral device.

MEMORY HARDWARE

Of course, the real memory is not housed in banks of switches (though you will find one or two banks of switches in many of today's computers and peripherals—see Figure 8-7). Today's computers use **microchips,** tiny pieces of silicon that each carry many thousands of circuits.

Microchips are a miracle of modern engineering, even though scientists are continually trying to improve on them and will probably succeed in doing so. A typical chip is no larger than a contact lens, yet it may contain upwards of half a million circuits, or 64,000 8-bit bytes (64K). This enormous number of bits is made possible by photography. A huge, highly detailed drawing is made of the desired circuitry. This image is

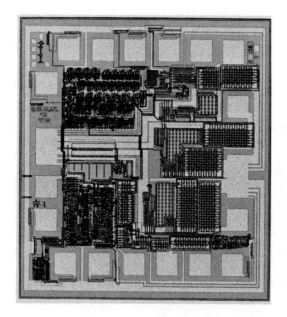

Figure 8-8   Microchips

Microchips, first introduced by Intel in 1971, are what make today's powerful computers possible. Here is a small picture of a detailed circuit drawing, and an actual chip shown to scale. Thirty-five years ago a room full of vacuum tubes would not have had the same power. (Courtesy of Zilog, Inc. and AT&T/Bell Laboratories)

then photoreduced and projected onto a layered silicon chip. Material in some of the layers is etched away to create the tiny circuits. Finally, the chip is placed in a plastic mount with metal legs that connect to the rest of the computer.

In a typical microcomputer, you can see several dozen chips housed in black mounts attached to the motherboard and to the special function cards. These chips are of several types. The two main varieties are **RAM** and **ROM** chips, standing for **r**andom-**a**ccess **m**emory and **r**ead-**o**nly **m**emory, respectively.

RAM.   **Random-access memory** can be continually changed to represent the latest input or the latest calculation. RAM is the computer's logbook, where it writes down the particular instructions it receives from the applications software, notes any results it needs to keep for future reference, and prepares the report that it will output. RAM chips contain banks of switches that can be set up to represent whatever the computer wants them to store. A RAM address will hold data or program instructions until one of two things happens—a new instruction or piece of data is sent to the same location or the computer is turned off. When electrical current ceases to flow through the computer most RAM chips become neutral, and the information stored in them is lost. That is why it's important to save your work on a disk from time to time.

ROM.   The contents of **read-only memory,** on the other hand, cannot be changed. It is as though the switches are locked in place, so they cannot be moved. ROM is more like an instruction manual than a logbook; it is used to carry permanent instructions that are needed for the computer to function or that the manufacturer wants to preserve. It can be read, but it cannot be erased, even by switching off the computer. The early dedicated word processors often carried the main word processing program in ROM; users of these machines did not have to load software from disks before they started work. Many microcomputers carry BASIC language interpreters in ROM, allowing users to write programs in BASIC even though they have not loaded any language software. And any computer needs at least a part of its operating system built into its ROM so that it can accept and interpret the rest of that system from a disk.

Variations.   Although ROM and RAM represent two basic types of memory, there are many variations. For example, there are chips called **PROM** chips, standing for **p**rogrammable **r**ead-**o**nly **m**emory. These chips can be programmed (have their switches set) one time only; after that, they can only be read. As you can imagine, this could lead to frustration if a mistake is made in programming. So another type of chip was invented—the **EPROM** (**e**rasable **p**rogrammable **r**ead-**o**nly **m**emory chip). After EPROM chips are programmed, they cannot be erased by the CPU or by turning off the computer, but the programs can be deleted by special processes. One type of EPROM chip needs to be bathed in ultraviolet light before it can be reprogrammed.

RAM is also available in several forms. One type, called **static RAM,** requires less current than other chips to retain information. Another type, called **bubble memory,** can hold data even when the computer is turned off. Bubble memory uses a different technology than the standard silicon chip. Both bubble memory and static RAM chips are used in portable computers, which may need to hold data for a long time using very little power.

The CPU: the microprocessor

The masterpiece of chip design, however, is not any type of memory chip but the microprocessor itself. Placed on a larger mount to accommodate all the electronic connections needed, the microprocessor does more than store data—it processes the data according to the instructions provided by the applications program and operating system. Different microcomputers use different microprocessors. Two used by the IBM PC are the Intel 8088 and the Intel 80286. The Apple Macintosh uses a Motorola 68000. Despite their unglamorous names, these are the stars of microcomputer circuitry. A microprocessor includes registers, a control unit, and an arithmetic/logic unit.

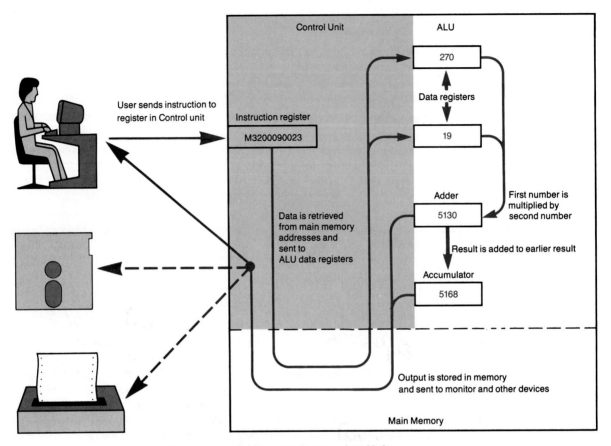

Figure 8-9   The Central Processing Unit
When you run applications software, each instruction is held in a control unit register while the CPU carries it out. The instruction above told the CPU to multiply two
numbers stored at different memory addresses. The control unit finds the numbers
and sends them to data registers in the arithmetic/logic unit, which uses still other
registers—the adder and the accumulator—to reach a final result. This result is
returned to the control unit, stored in memory, and perhaps presented as output.

REGISTERS

To manipulate an instruction or piece of data taken from active memory,
the microprocessor begins by copying it to one of its **registers.** A register
is a memory element that holds data for a short time while the microprocessor does its work. Registers are small; an 8-bit computer will frequently have 8-bit registers, a 16-bit computer 16-bit registers.

The registers carry several kinds of information. One will hold a copy
of the program instruction that the microprocessor is currently working
on—for example, the machine language code for "add." Another will hold
the address from which the next instruction is to be collected. A third
may hold the address of the data being worked on, and a fourth may hold
the data itself. A fifth may hold the result of the last calculation, to which

the data must be added. Processing is completed in the registers before the results are returned to the memory. If RAM chips are like a logbook that the computer keeps to organize its work, registers are the scraps of paper on which it makes notes or the back of the envelope on which it records a result before writing it up in the logbook.

THE CONTROL UNIT

The **control unit** is the part of the microprocessor that manages the processing operation. It responds to commands from the user and copies

---

How It Was

The Birth of the Microcomputer

With more than eight million microcomputers adorning the desks of corporate America, it's hard to believe that the micro is a relatively recent invention. Yet it wasn't so long ago when it would have been difficult to find a businessperson who had ever touched a microcomputer.

The micro, the first computer to place all circuitry on a single motherboard, initially attracted only electronics hobbyists. A kit for building the first true microcomputer, the Altair, was first advertised in *Popular Electronics* in 1974. It sold for $500. Although the Altair had very little memory, it became popular among hobbyists. Soon, other electronics manufacturers were also selling microcomputer kits.

In 1977, working out of a garage, Steven Jobs and Steve Wozniak began producing a kit for a more powerful microcomputer called the Apple I. Jobs and Wozniak soon followed this model with the Apple II, which they sold not as a kit but as a fully assembled computer. The Apple II, which used an 8-bit microprocessor and had a 48K RAM, was the first microcomputer to gain popular acceptance.

Even so, the micro continued to appeal mainly to hobbyists and programmers. Not until the introduction of the Visicalc spreadsheet program did the Apple II capture the interest of the business world.

Soon, other manufacturers entered the competition to produce the standard micro for business use. Each manufacturer contended that its hardware and operating system was the most powerful.

The IBM Personal Computer, introduced in 1981, was the clear victor. The IBM PC was the first microcomputer to be based on a 16-bit microprocessor, which gave it significantly greater processing speed and memory than the Apple II. Its operating system became the accepted standard as programmers created more and more software for this powerful new machine. IBM eclipsed Apple and other brands in the business market within a few months.

Continuing developments in technology have since produced several more powerful versions of the IBM PC, and scores of manufacturers are now selling compatible micros that run the same software. Other companies, too, have vastly improved on their early micros.

However, one thing has remained constant: the cost of microcomputers has come down as their power and usefulness have increased, and this is likely to remain true for the foreseeable future.

program instructions from memory addresses into the registers. Then it sends signals and information to other parts of the computer, causing them to act as the software directs.

For example, when a character is typed on the keyboard, the control unit checks the input port and summons the character into the computer itself. Then it checks the operating system to determine where that character is to be placed in memory and sends it to the appropriate address. It also sends a signal ordering the monitor to display the character where the cursor is currently located. Finally, it directs the cursor to move ahead one space, then checks the input ports to see if there is any new input.

Of course, all of these operations are extremely fast. Speed, too, is related to the control unit. The control unit includes a rapidly vibrating clock element, which determines the speed at which the computer operates. Each vibration causes the computer to take another step. Even on a relatively inexpensive microcomputer, the clock may vibrate more than two million times per second, or at 2 MHz. As you can imagine, this means that a great deal can be accomplished in a short time, even if each step taken is very small.

THE ALU

One thing that the control unit does *not* do is perform computations. This is the function of the **arithmetic/logic unit** or **ALU.** The ALU takes care of two tasks: mathematical calculations and logical comparisons. The data is handed to it by the control unit, which also passes on directions about what operation to perform. But it is the ALU that performs the operation. The result is stored in a register called the **accumulator;** more data is provided; another operation is begun; the number in the accumulator may be changed once again by the new operation. Millions of these steps are taken in a single second, and very complex calculations are thus performed very quickly.

As the caculations are performed, data may need to be sent back to the computer's active memory, either to await output or to allow another set of figures to be handled by the ALU. This is accomplished by the control unit, under the direction of the software. When the program is ready to print output, that material is already organized in a particular set of RAM addresses, which have been defined by the systems software (the operating system) as an output area.

BUSES AND OUTPUT PORTS

For the ALU to accomplish anything, information must reach its registers from the active memory. Carrying the information back and forth is the role of the buses. In a computer **buses** are the connections between the different electronic elements. They usually consist of several wires running parallel to each other or several parallel metal traces on the circuit board that holds the individual microchips. Buses carry several bits at a time; on an 8-bit computer, for example, 8 bits will usually travel side

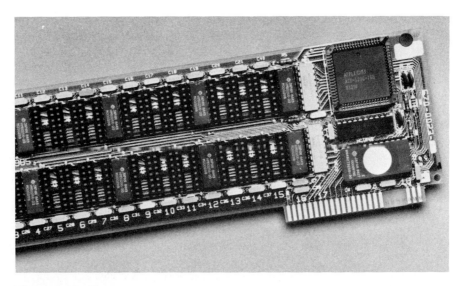

Figure 8-10 Buses
Buses are the parallel sets of wires that carry information from one part of a computer to another. They also connect parts of expansion cards, as shown here. Note that many buses lead to the tab at right, ensuring that proper connections will be made when it is inserted in the motherboard. (Courtesy of Apple Computer, Inc.)

by side. This enables the computer to manipulate each byte instantaneously, without having to wait for the bits to arrive one at a time. From the output area of the computer's active memory, the information must be bused through an **output port** to an output device. In fact, there may be several buses leading to several ports. These ports are attached to output devices, such as monitors and printers.

The flow of output data must be carefully controlled so that the attached devices won't miss important material. A printer can handle only a certain number of characters per second. A monitor needs time to form each letter. Depending on the speed of a particular device, the microprocessor sends data along the output bus, always waiting till the device is ready before it sends further material. A printer typically sends a signal back to the computer indicating that it has printed a character and is ready to handle another. Two types of output ports are commonly found on computers: parallel ports and serial ports.

Parallel ports. Some devices are made to handle information the same way that the computer does—a byte at a time. The output bus can be extended directly from the computer to such devices, continuing the parallel wires outside of the computer. These wires may run side by side in a flat "ribbon" cable, or they may be contained in a standard round cable. Such an output device is said to have a **parallel** connection in which bytes of data travel over 8, 16, 32, or more separate wires at the same time, with each wire carrying a single bit.

Serial ports. Other output devices, however, are made to respond to streams of bits in series. For this reason, a computer may need to be fitted with a **serial** output port to connect it to a serial printer or a modem. A serial port is also needed for any printer farther than six feet from the CPU. This type of connection still needs several wires in the connecting cable. However, the data sent to the output device moves down only one of these wires, so the bits must travel one behind the other, like cars in a train. The other wires in a serial connection are used to carry feedback from the output device to the computer. A common type of serial port is the RS-232C interface.

Output devices

Attached to the output ports of a microcomputer are one or more output devices. **Monitors,** also called VDTs (video display terminals), and printers get the greatest use.

MONITORS

The most commonly used monitor in offices is the **cathode-ray tube,** or **CRT,** which is essentially like a TV picture tube. Most CRTs used in business display 25 lines of text with 80 characters possible per line, although this varies on different monitors. Some CRTs display as much as a full "page" of text—54 lines—whereas others display less than the standard 25 lines at a time.

CRTs also vary in many other ways. The most primitive type is the television itself, which can be linked up to most microcomputers. TVs, however, lack resolution (image sharpness) as monitors. Most businesses purchase dedicated computer monitors, which cannot be tuned to TV stations but provide much sharper images for computer output.

Monochrome monitors. Dedicated monitors may be monochrome (single color) or color. The monochrome variety often displays white characters against a black background. More and more often, however, one sees green on black, amber on black, or black on white—combinations found to be more restful to the eye. Monochrome monitors are usually "character addressable," which means that cursor movement is limited to the screen locations where characters will appear. (Graphics on these monitors are therefore not shown in fine detail.) However, high-resolution monitors are available that can present much more detail and display many typefaces—italic as well as roman, for example.

Color monitors. Color monitors are more often "dot addressable." The inside surface of a CRT is covered with phosphorescent dots, called pixels, which glow when they are struck by a cathode ray. On a color monitor,

Figure 8-11 Monitors
Oversized monitors display whole pages of text, which is especially useful in desktop publishing. But when portability and weight are critical factors, a small monitor displaying fewer lines of text may be used, as on this nine pound, battery operated microcomputer. (Courtesy of Xerox Corporation and Hewlett-Packard Company)

these dots glow three different colors. Many of these dots together make a character. But the dots can also be treated as separate entities, which makes for much more finely drawn graphics. The most advanced type of color monitor available today is the RGB monitor (for red, green, blue), because it addresses the different colors with three different signals from the computer, leading to a greatly enhanced display.

Other monitors. In addition to CRTs, other types of monitors are used with microcomputers. The second most common is the liquid crystal display (**LCD**), used for many portable computers. This type of monitor provides a black image on light gray. LCDs may be familiar because they also appear on many calculators and digital watches. LCD screens may show fewer than 25 lines (eight has been common in the past), but 25 is fast becoming standard with these displays, too.

Another relatively new display technology is the plasma panel, also known as the electro-luminescent or **EL** screen, which consists of a tight grid of electrodes sealed in a flat gas-filled panel. When an intersection on the grid is energized, the gas glows, thus causing an image to appear. Plasma screens take up very little space and can produce bright images with very high resolution.

PRINTERS

The days of the paperless office are not with us yet. Even though many communications are now being sent electronically and are being read only on monitors, paper is still the standard medium for business communications. Printers are therefore vital to the functioning of the modern office. As you may recall, there are impact printers and nonimpact printers, and a printer may produce copies of draft quality, letter quality, or

STATE OF THE ART

Microcomputers: A Second Generation?

Finally, it seems, there is a second generation of office microcomputers. Up until the beginning of 1987, *generation* was used for mainframes and computer languages. Micros were always viewed as a single group.

Of course, new microcomputers had often been introduced to the market before. Back in 1983, Apple Computer Corporation brought out the Lisa, which was hailed as a breakthrough in computing—it was more powerful and easier to use than any micro then in existence. However, it was priced in the $10,000 range.

This was followed by the MacIntosh, offering many of the same features for far less—but even the MacIntosh was slow to gain acceptance in the office; it didn't make a real impression until desktop publishing became popular. Other manufacturers also developed micros that were very different from their earlier models—for example, Commodore, known for its C-64 and C-128, produced the totally new Amiga, and Atari, best known in the early eighties for computerized video games, came out with the sophisticated ST.

Organizations did not buy many of these new wave computers, however, probably because IBM's PC series and similar "clone" micros had gained a firm grasp on the business market. Most business software was written for the PC/MS-DOS operating system, and unless a new machine seemed to have incredible powers, it was unlikely to sell to business.

Therefore the idea of a second generation for business had to come, in the end, from IBM. The Personal System/2 differs greatly from the PC series, and will soon be able to use a new operating system (OS/2). Because it comes from the maker of the series of computers already accepted in the nation's offices, it is, truly, a second generation.

Among other manufacturers, only Apple, whose MacIntosh is also accepted by business, can be said to have a second generation business machine: the MacIntosh II. And in Europe, perhaps, where Commodore's earlier computers are widely accepted in business, the Amiga might merit a 2G label.

These new microcomputers, whether called new wave or second generation, offer business more processing power and greater access to memory. Built around new state-of-the-art microprocessors, they can handle more complex programs without delay. Integrated packages and operating environments can run with ease. Beautiful graphics, too, can be created much faster. And, because large organizations value computers that can share data easily, the Personal System/2 computers are designed to communicate easily, with each other and with larger computers.

One important question remains—will they sell? Only time will tell, and the American marketplace. By the time you read this, you may know the answer.

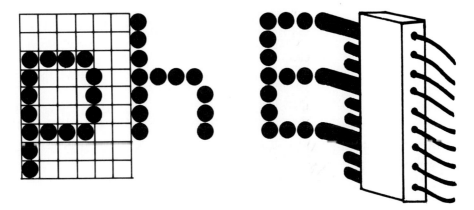

Figure 8-12 How a Impact Dot Matrix Printer Works
The printer head (right) contains a column of movable wires that can print a complete column of dots. Each time the head is activated, a particular set of wires is driven against the ribbon. Characters are formed as a series of columns, so that the dots are arranged within a grid (matrix), as shown on the left. The number of columns and rows in the grid varies, depending on the design of the printer.

both. Microcomputer systems generally include dot-matrix, daisy-wheel, or laser printers.

Dot-matrix printers.   The idea behind the **dot-matrix printer** is the same as that behind the monitor—characters are made up of dots. The term *dot-matrix* is applied almost exclusively to devices that print by impact, even though some nonimpact printers also form characters from dots. The dot-matrix printer has a print head that holds a dense cluster of movable wires. As the print head moves across the page, the printer's own microchip causes some of these wires to be propelled in sequence against a typewriter-style ribbon to create the image of a letter on the paper. For another character, a different grouping of wires is activated. Although the print is not as crisp as that produced by an office typewriter, it can be nearly as good, depending on the quality of the printer. In fact, the better dot-matrix printers are termed *near letter quality*. In addition to numbers, letters, and punctuation marks, a dot-matrix printer can produce graphics, because, like the more expensive monitors, they can be made dot addressable.

Daisy-wheel printers.   Like typewriters, some impact printers have precast type elements. The most common of these is the **daisy-wheel printer.** The type element of this printer is a metal or plastic daisy wheel, on which characters are arranged in a circle at the ends of the wheel's many spokes, or "petals." Close relatives of the daisy-wheel printer use different precast type elements—rotating thimbles or balls like those found on office typewriters. All of these printers produce letter-quality

Figure 8-13 Laser Printers
Laser printers are the most versatile printers used with microcomputers. They can print forms, letterheads, signatures, and other graphics as well as text. Many are capable of combining different color inks and different type styles on a single page. (Courtesy of Hewlett-Packard Company)

copies. Some of them operate at fairly high speeds—up to 60 characters per second—through not nearly as fast as dot-matrix or laser printers.

Laser printers.   The fastest printers used with microcomputers are **laser printers,** which can produce up to 15 pages or more per minute. These nonimpact printers use laser beams and an electrostatic process similar to that used in photocopying. They produce higher-quality copies than daisy-wheel printers, and they can print a wider range of type styles and type sizes than dot-matrix printers. Like other nonimpact devices, laser printers can't produce carbon copies—but at 15 pages per minute, printing extra copies is no problem!

Other printers.   Two other nonimpact printers often used with microcomputers offer similar advantages, though they are less sophisticated than laser printers. One of these is the **ink-jet printer,** which places an electrical charge on paper and then sprays magnetized ink onto the charge to form a character. The other is the **electrothermal printer,** which uses a combination of heat-sensitive paper and a heatable print head to etch characters on pages. Both of these devices can print around 200 characters per second—fast, but not as fast as the laser printer, and the printed images are not as sharp.

DISK DRIVES FOR SECONDARY STORAGE

Disk drives have already been described in this chapter as a major means of input to the microcomputer. As you know, they are also capable of accepting output. In fact, because a disk drive can handle both output and input, it is an ideal vehicle for saving information. It creates a record of your work in a form that can easily be fed back into the computer later on. Thus, you can keep your work on hold if the computer has to be switched off or used for another purpose. In a very real sense, disk drives can supplement the active memory of the computer itself. They are therefore also called **secondary storage** devices.

So far this chapter has described disk drives for diskettes. These can be used to introduce new software and data into the system, as well as for secondary storage. Another type of disk drive is the **hard disk drive,** usually a sealed unit built into the micro itself and containing its own read/write heads. Hard disk drives work much faster than diskettes; you need to wait less long to save files you have created or to load them back into the computer. They can also store up to 40 times as much software or data as a diskette the same size. However, they are for secondary storage only; to use them to run applications software, you must first have installed the software by copying it from a diskette.

Before a new disk can be used, it must be prepared by the disk drive so that the computer can interact with it. The process is called **formatting** or **initializing.** In this process the user gives the DOS a command that makes the disk drive lay out tracks and sectors on the disk in the format required by the computer. As you read earlier in this chapter, different computers' operating systems read disks differently. Therefore, they also format them differently. They may set up more or fewer tracks, divided into different numbers of sectors. They may record the information more or less densely; many require double-density disks to keep the information clear. A disk drive may use both sides of the disk, or it may have only a single read/write head. Single-head systems have less storage capacity, but you can use less expensive single-sided disks with them.

Secondary storage devices not only save data but also enable the computer to handle programs or data files that might otherwise take up too much active memory. Parts of a large program or data file may be kept on the disk during most of a work session, to be brought into active memory only when needed. This creates **virtual memory,** a memory larger than the actual storage capacity of the computer.

Virtual memory is used extensively in larger computer systems, but it is also used with some microcomputer software. You can tell it is operating if the disk drive suddenly starts spinning while you are using an applications program. This and other refinements found on larger computers are discussed further in the next chapter.

SUMMARY

- Though computer performance depends on software, the capabilities of computer systems depend on their hardware.

- Most business computers share these hardware features: they have a single central processing unit (CPU); they are digital computers working with two symbols only; and they consist of memory circuits and processing circuits, each of which can be turned on or off.

- Though circuits have only two states, they can combine to demonstrate incredible power. This power is measured in bits to determine processing power, in MHz (megahertz) to determine processing speed, and in K (kilobytes) to determine memory capacity.

- Computer systems handle data from input (using peripherals or built-in devices to convert signals from the outside into computer-readable impulses) through processing, an interaction of the CPU and memory circuits, to output, which converts the electronic impulses back into appropriate signals for outside use.

- Microcomputers, though the least powerful of computers, demonstrate most of the major features of computer systems. The input devices most commonly used with micros are disk drives, used to input software that is recorded on magnetic diskettes, and the keyboard, used to input commands and new data. These devices send electronic signals to the CPU through the input port, which usually contains a buffer to preserve data that is not immediately read.

- The CPU usually begins by sending instructions and data to the active memory circuits, to be stored at specified addresses. These addresses are contained within RAM (random-access memory) microchips, highly miniaturized circuits that can hold a charge until further instructions or until the computer is turned off. Another type of microchip is ROM (read-only memory). ROM chips have instructions built in, and they hold the instructions permanently.

- The most important chip is the microprocessor, which acts as CPU for a microcomputer. This chip includes registers, which temporarily hold relevant data; a control unit, which interprets the software and determines where different pieces of data and instructions are to be sent; and an ALU (arithmetic/logic unit), which performs calculations and logical comparisons.

- Data and other information move around the microcomputer in parallel strips of wire called buses. These buses continue through a parallel output port for connection to some types of peripherals and may be connected to others through a serial port.

- The most common output devices for micros are monitors, which may be monochrome or color, and printers. (Dot-matrix, daisy-wheel, and laser printers are the most popular.) In addition, disk drives can be used for output, making them convenient secondary storage devices, for both data and for adding virtual memory, during large programs.

TERMS FOR REVIEW

networks
central processing
  unit (CPU)
digital
binary
binary digit
bit
megahertz (MHz)
million instructions
  per second (MIPS)
bytes
kilobyte (K)
architecture
word
read/write heads
tracks
sectors
disk address
directory
catalog

input port
input buffer
active memory
memory address
microchips
RAM
ROM
random-access
  memory
read-only memory
PROM
EPROM
static RAM
bubble memory
registers
control unit
ALU
arithmetic/logic
  unit
accumulator

buses
parallel
serial
monitors
CRT
LCD
EL
dot-matrix printer
daisy-wheel printer
laser printers
ink-jet printer
electrothermal
  printer
secondary storage
hard disk drive
formatting
initializing
virtual memory

TERMINOLOGY CHECK

For each definition below, choose the correct term or terms from the list of Terms for Review.

1. Permanent memory that provides operating instructions to the computer. *Read only memory*

2. A list of files stored on a diskette.

3. The type of monitor most commonly used by businesses. *CRT Cathode-ray tube*

4. The use of disk storage to store parts of a program, thus saving actual memory space.

5. A piece of silicon that holds thousands of circuits. *microchip*

6. Memory that is continually updated by the last activity performed. *RAM*

7. The first stage in the flow of information through a computer; when data is entered into the system. *input*

8. The part of the computer that does mathematical calculations and makes logical comparisons. *ALU arithmetic/logic unit*

9. Preparing the diskette so that the operating system can find and read the directory. *read/write heads*

10. The usual measuring unit for computer memory capacity. *Kilobyte (K)*

INFORMATION CHECK

1. Why are today's business computers called binary computers?

2. List three important measures of computer power. Describe each briefly.

3. Describe the relationship between bits and bytes. What does K mean?

4. What is the function of the read/write head(s) in a disk drive?

5. Describe briefly the physical features of floppy disks. Why do you suppose they come in more than one size?

6. What happens when you try to use a diskette formatted for one system on a different system?

7. How can a key on the computer keyboard create different electronic signals? Why is this useful?

8. What is an input buffer? How does it help the user?

9. Compare a disk address and a memory address.

10. Describe the process used to produce microchips.

11. How do the main varieties of memory chips differ?

12. Describe the main elements of microprocessors.

13. An output port can have either a parallel or a serial connection. How are the two different?

14. List four common types of monitors. How do they differ?

15. List the types of printers most commonly used with microcomputers. Explain how two of them work.

PROJECTS AND PROBLEMS

1. Bourton and Zellers, a supplier of restaurant equipment in a rural area, employs 50 people and earns close to half a million dollars a year. All of its correspondence, inventory record keeping, and order processing is done by hand. But business is booming, and the staff cannot keep up with the paperwork.

   You have been able to convince your bosses, Bourton and Zellers, that a computer system will improve the efficiency of the office staff, speed up collecting receivables, improve office morale, and generally increase profits.

   What computer components would you suggest they buy? What business functions would you suggest be computerized?

2. Select one category of component commonly used with microcomputer systems. Find out which brands are most frequently used by small businesses by browsing through computer magazines or by going to a computer store. Select the three most popular models. Make a chart that includes all of the hardware features available on each model.

Indicate the optional and standard features available with each model, and note the cost. What model do you think is the best buy?

3. Find pictures and descriptions of the early ENIAC and UNIVAC computers in your library. Note similarities to and differences from present-day computers. (Be sure to look for more than the obvious differences of size.) Share your findings with the class.

4. The size, complexity, and sophistication of both hardware and software have changed dramatically in a short time. Choose one example each of both hardware and software changes. Write a brief history of each, giving as many details documenting the changes as you can.

9

Large computers for added capability

The microcomputer is a masterpiece of modern technology that can help with an array of business tasks, from accounting to word processing. But, although it can often handle the computing needs of a small business, the micro alone is usually not adequate to fulfill the high-volume processing demands of medium-sized and large organizations.

When an organization that uses a microcomputer expands or computerizes more of its information systems, it frequently purchases more micros so that many more people can perform different tasks. But this can soon get out of hand: people find themselves working on different versions of the same numerical data or of a given form letter. Such lack of central coordination makes it difficult for people to keep up with each other's work, and this leads to confusion. The need to coordinate work is one reason why larger computers are so widely used in business. This does not mean, however, that the microcomputer is completely replaced by a larger computer. Usually, a large organization finds a place for both types of computers.

Before the 1970s business computers were large; in fact, all computers were large then. As you have read, today's microcomputers can outperform those early machines. However, large computers have also increased greatly in power, and as the technology has developed, organizations have developed with it. Many organizations now depend on the capabilities of large machines; without powerful computers, they would find it extremely difficult to conduct business.

Today's large computers fill organizational needs in a variety of ways, depending on the needs of the people who use them. A single large computer may handle all information processing tasks. The computer may be connected to many terminals at which people work and to many peripheral devices for different kinds of input and output. Or, in addition to controlling an organization's main information tasks, a large computer may coordinate the work of smaller computers that use the same data at different locations. This is often referred to as distributed processing.

In other business situations, a set of small computers may each perform different specialized tasks, using software that allows them to exchange information when the need arises. In all these arrangements and in others, organizations usually depend on computers that are larger than the desktop micros described in the previous chapter.

This chapter begins by taking a closer look at the various large computers that were described in Chapter 1. Then it describes some of the capabilities that their added computing power gives them and some of the different memory devices that further increase their usefulness. Finally, you will learn more about the variety of input and output peripherals that are being used to extend the power of computers and make them more efficient tools.

When you have read this chapter, you should be able to:

- describe some of the major features of minis, mainframes, and supercomputers

- indicate the usefulness of batch processing as compared with transaction processing

- explain in general terms the concepts of multiprocessing, multiprogramming, and multitasking

- identify the data storage hierarchy and the advantages and disadvantages of various types of storage

- list and describe the major input/output devices

Minis to monsters

Before learning the differences among the three general classes of large computers, you should understand some of their common features. As explained earlier, large computers are usually superior to micros in at least three ways—they have larger memories, greater processing capacity, and greater processing speed. The central processing unit (CPU) of a typical large machine consists of not one but several microprocessor chips. In fact, some mainframes and supercomputers operate with two or more separate CPUs. All of these features make large computers better able to meet the complex demands of today's large organizations.

The exact lines of difference among the classes of large computers are far from precise. There is often considerable disagreement as to what label should be attached to a given computer, mainly because there is a great deal of overlap in performance and features. For example, some of the large minicomputers, called superminis, cost more and have greater performance capabilities than some machines that are labeled and marketed as mainframes. There are also microcomputers that cost more and are more powerful than some minis. These computers are often referred

Figure 9-1   A Minicomputer System
All the workstations in this office are run by the minicomputer beside the desk in the foreground. This mini supports its own terminal as well as a word processing station (left), a printer, an executive personal computer, and a graphics station (right). (Courtesy of Hewlett-Packard Company)

to as micro-mainframes. However, it is usual to speak of three classes of large computers—minicomputers, mainframes, and supercomputers.

MINICOMPUTERS

The minicomputer was first built in response to the needs of the user who couldn't afford a mainframe but still required a computer to perform a range of tasks. It has been a workhorse for many businesses since the late 1960s. Technicians in those early years of computer development thought of a computerized system as an array of expensive equipment isolated in a large glass-enclosed, dust-free, air-conditioned room. It was a shock for them to see this new minicomputer, which was a little larger than a dishwasher, placed directly in an office environment.

Today's minis, although still roughly the same size or even smaller, are packed with microchips and have considerably more power than early models. Indeed, they often have more power than the mainframes that the first purchasers of minis could not afford. Some of the current minis are even more powerful than today's smaller mainframes. However, an advantage of these minicomputers is that they can typically run by themselves; they do not require a team of technicians to operate them.

Minicomputers are often used for specialized tasks, such as handling mailing lists and billings, or efficient, centralized word processing. Minis are also used for specialized nonoffice applications, such as monitoring the heating and cooling of large buildings, controlling security systems, or conducting quality control programs on production lines. But, as with microcomputers, the uses to which minis are put are largely controlled by the software. Minicomputers are capable of a wide range of computing tasks and are often used by mid-sized businesses, laboratories, and small colleges to handle all of their computing needs. The main reason minis are not more widely used in large organizations is that, in general, larger computers can still perform more tasks and perform them faster.

MAINFRAMES

Although there is certainly overlap in the cost and processing speed of mainframe and minicomputers, there tends to be a clear division in the way they are used. Whereas minis are often dedicated to a single task or group of related tasks, mainframe computers are most commonly used in environments in which a number of very different tasks are to be performed. The term *environment* is frequently used in information processing to indicate the size and complexity of a system. A "mainframe environment" will definitely include hardware and software to perform a number of relatively complex jobs.

A mainframe computer system includes many types of software that

Figure 9-2 A Mainframe System
This large mainframe computer is surrounded by many secondary storage devices, keeping millions of pages of data on-line to users. The structure in the middle houses the main memory and CPU. For speed, and for economical handling of quantities of data, such systems are hard to equal. (Courtesy of Honeywell Bull, Inc.)

perform widely varying functions. Accounting packages, database management systems, and scientific applications programs might all be installed and running at the same time. The system will usually have a number of computer languages available to it and perhaps more than one operating system. Processing at speeds of 50 MIPS (million instructions per second) and more, which is equivalent to between 300 and 1,000 MHz in a micro, mainframes perform several different functions at once and are the workhorses of the computer industry.

Today's mainframe typically requires a staff of operations personnel to keep it running. This staff includes **computer operators,** who perform many of the manual tasks still necessary for running a mainframe, such as setting up storage tapes and disks and checking and controlling the execution of programs at the main computer **console,** which is the command terminal for the system. The staff also typically includes **program librarians,** who control and catalog the many storage media generated by a day's work, including all the backup tapes. Further, there is often a staff of **programmers,** who develop and maintain specialized software that accomplishes specific needs of the organization. Other related tasks are systems analysis, database administration, and information systems management, all of which will be examined further in Part Four of this book.

As a result of the volume and complexity of the mainframe environment, the technology of peripheral mainframe hardware such as printers, disk drives, and input devices has been one of the fastest growth areas in information processing. Users purchasing machines that cost between $500,000 and several million dollars have created a demand for input and output equipment that complements the speed and flexibility of their computers.

Mainframe software developers are attempting to keep pace with this rapid growth of hardware options. Though the most dramatic advances in software packages have recently been at the microcomputer level, mainframe software is also pushing to anticipate and help define the needs of tomorrow. Ideally suited to such use, the mainframe is no longer just a number-crunching machine. Integrated database management, graphics, and large mathematical modeling packages are among the software offerings available for these powerful computers. In addition, micro-to-mainframe communications devices have allowed mainframe users to take advantage of the array of software developed for the micro-computer. Today's mainframes provide the means for every office to have instant access to highly detailed information.

SUPERCOMPUTERS

Often referred to as "monsters," **supercomputers** are the prodigies, or geniuses, of the computer family. Supercomputers, which are frequently made up of several mainframes designed to work together, are generally used in very special and relatively limited environments. They are employed for such tasks as weather forecasting, monitoring national defense, planning and executing space exploration, and developing weapons. These uses require extremely fast access and processing of vast amounts of data, beyond the capabilities of even a fast mainframe loaded with high-quality peripherals.

Supercomputers operate at speeds approaching one billion instructions per second (BIPS), considerably faster than the typical mainframe. These astronomical processing speeds, however, have price tags to match. The cost of a supercomputer starts around $10 million

Computing options

No large computer, whether a mini, a mainframe, or a supercomputer, is so inexpensive that an organization can afford to use it inefficiently. Therefore, modern computers have been designed with efficiency in mind and can usually accept and process input in several ways. When you consider the speed at which a computer can operate, as compared with

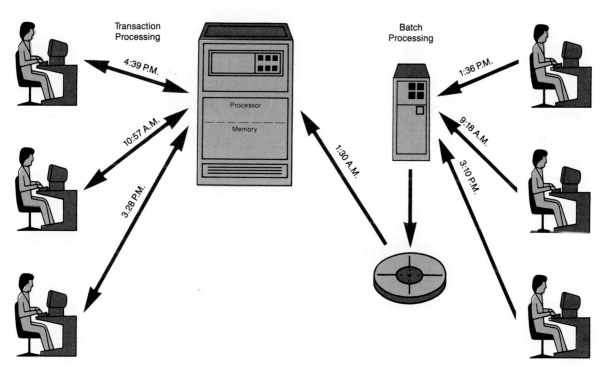

Figure 9-3 Batch vs. Transaction Processing
In transaction processing, depicted on the left, input is processed by the central computer as soon as a user sends it, and output appears on the user's monitor immediately. But in batch processing, shown on the right, input from several sources can be sent to a minicomputer at different times, saved on tape, and later fed to the central computer for processing all at once. The mini may edit the input, ensuring that all required data is present.

the speed with which a typical user can provide input, you can realize that accelerating input is a key to using computers effectively.

INPUT MODES

In your study of microcomputers, you have been introduced to what is called **transaction processing** (or interactive processing), in which a user enters data and commands directly into the computer and the computer instantly responds to each piece of input. But there is another input mode called **batch processing,** which involves collecting all data and specific instructions in a group, or batch, before processing begins.

Transaction processing. If you go to a department store, select an item, hand the salesclerk your credit card, and the clerk keys your account

---

THE HUMAN SIDE
Transaction Processing on the Turnpike

Kim Walton works as a toll collector on the New Jersey Turnpike. When a car pulls up to her tollbooth, the driver hands Walton the toll card received when the car entered the highway. Kim feeds the card into a scanner in her booth, which sends data to a computer to calculate the amount of the toll. The amount instantly appears on a screen in front of Walton so that she can inform the driver and collect the money. With the data input from the cards, the computer can also generate reports on a variety of subjects, including the number of vehicles using the road.

In the early 1980s, the turnpike's toll collection system still used punched cards, and the information they contained was processed in batches. The punched cards have now been replaced by cards with magnetic strips. These have information recorded onto them both when the card is picked up by the motorist and when it is turned in for payment. The information includes where and when each vehicle entered and left the highway. It also includes, for vehicles other than cars, a vehicle identification. Walton must enter this data by hand in the tollbooth.

Should a driver ask Walton for a receipt, she has only to push a button to print one. The computer data is also used to generate reports on a variety of subjects, including the number of different types of vehicles that use the road and peak rush hours on the turnpike. Overall, toll collection is now so automated that Walton has to fill out papers only occasionally—for corporate charge accounts, like those for buses, and vehicles exempt from tolls (such as state vehicles and police cars).

As a check against theft and loss, the amount of money collected can be compared with the information gathered by the computer system. For additional security, toll collectors must log on and off the system when they begin and end their shifts, so the system has a record of the booth in which each collector worked. Accurate records are also needed for projecting the turnpike's future revenues, a crucial task since funds for maintaining the road are allocated on the basis of these projections.

The new system works very well. Even if it breaks down, however, the turnpike can gather and process the information it needs, because the new cards can also be batch processed as a backup.

Computer manufacture

Plate 1

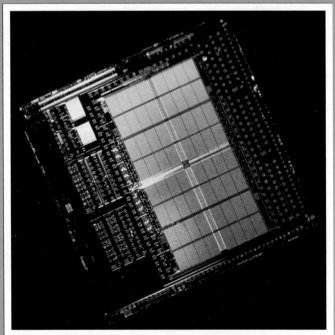

Plate 2

Over 18,000 vacuum tubes were used in the ENIAC, the first general purpose computer constructed in the mid 1940s. Each tube could hold a single bit of information and the computer could make 300 calculations per second.

Today, tiny chips that can store over a million bits of information are being manufactured. Chips with a capacity of between 4 million and 16 million bits are well on their way to production.

Plate 3

Plate 4

Silicon chips have many layers of circuitry that can control the operation of the computer keyboard, CRT, memory, processor, input/output, and power supply.

The complex circuitry on each chip is worked out on computer-aided design (CAD) equipment and meticulously checked. The design is photographically reduced to the size of a single chip. Then it is duplicated many times onto a glass disk called a photomask.

Photomasks are used to imprint the circuitry onto thin wafers sliced from a cylinder of purified silicon. After the wafers have been imprinted, they undergo many chemical and heating processes. These processes fix the circuitry onto the wafers, dissolve the excess silicon, and deposit several layers of chemicals that will function as insulators, conductors, transistors and resistors.

Plate 5

Plate 7

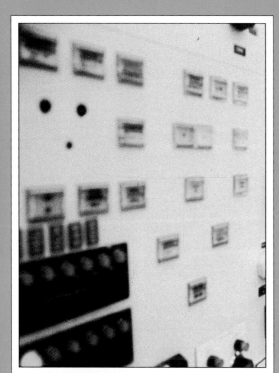

Plate 6

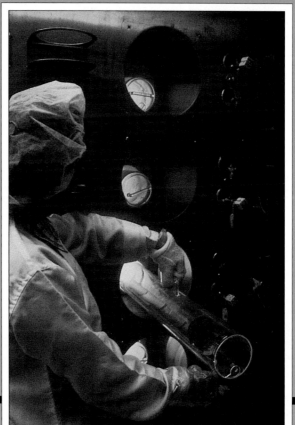

Plate 8

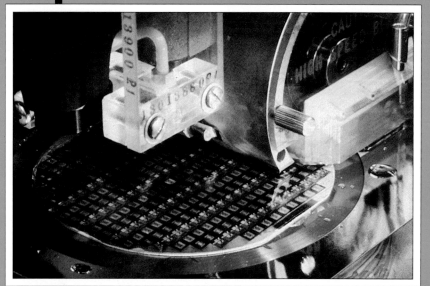

Diamond saws cut up the wafers into chips. Then, each chip is individually checked under a microscope. About 70 percent of the chips survive the 300 to 400 steps in the manufacturing process.

Plate 9

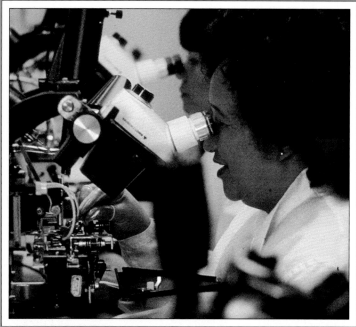

Plate 10

Plate 11

Plate 12

Next, gold wires are bonded to the circuitry and the chips are fitted into individual protective carriers called dual in-line packages. Finally the chips are plugged into printed circuit boards along with other electronic components.

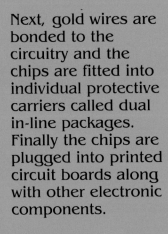

Plate 13

Circuit boards are repeatedly tested before they are assembled into a computer. Depending on the size and function of the computer, anywhere from one to 500 or more circuit boards are used. By the time the computer rolls off the assembly line, it is a highly sophisticated electronic system, needing only software to unlock its vast potential.

Plate 14

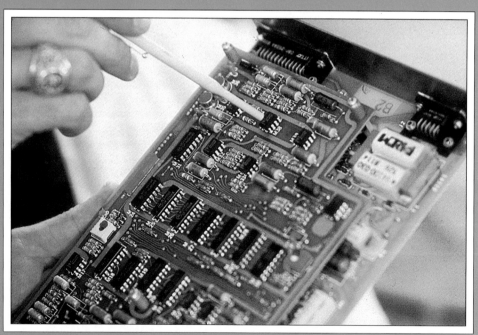

Plate 15

Plate 16

Plate 17

Plate 18

Computers are manufactured in a wide variety of sizes, with many capabilities. They range in size from small-battery-powered computers, primarily used for testing components to enormous supercomputers used for scientific research.

Plate 19

Plate 20

number into a terminal or reads the price tag with some input device, you are participating in transaction processing. If you go to a bank machine, insert your bankcard, press buttons, and withdraw, transfer, or deposit money, you are participating in transaction processing. If you are at work and use a terminal to look up a name, a part number, or any other piece of information, you are participating in transaction processing.

During transaction processing, you are directly in touch with the computer. If you are working with a database, you have immediate access to account records, inventories, and other types of information. If you add, delete, or alter the data, your input, too, is immediately reflected in the database. Thus, transaction processing is highly efficient for the user. There is no need to wait for the computer department to deliver a report—the report is generated as you work. And with transaction processing, the system's database is always up-to-date. However, transaction processing is often costly in terms of computer time—*you* don't have to wait, but unless there are many people recording transactions, the computer may be idle while it is waiting for you.

Batch processing. If transaction processing is thought of as instant processing for the user, batch processing could be characterized as instant input for the computer. In batch processing all the data and programs are prepared beforehand, then fed into the computer as a single stream of input. There is no room for users to change their minds or react to computer prompts, so batch processing cannot be used for many tasks. Word processing, for example, is not possible in this mode. But payroll, billing, mass mailings, and other such high-volume, routine tasks are usually done with batch processing, because the data for each of these activities can be prepared beforehand and input all at once.

The advantages of batch processing will be clear if you consider one typical batch job, the payroll. If the payroll were done by transaction processing, office workers would keyboard data from each employee's time sheet, then the computer would calculate the correct figures and print out a check—one check at a time. But with batch processing, data from all the time sheets is input simultaneously, and the computer and check printer can do the job as a single operation; the check printer doesn't stop until the task is over. And the payroll can be processed after business hours, when the computer is not busy with users who need the instant feedback from transaction processing.

PROCESSING OPTIONS

Even though batch input is fast, it is still not fast enough to keep the average large computer fully occupied. For this reason, techniques have been developed that allow several programs to run at one time. Depending on their complexity, four or more batch programs can be run together on an average mainframe. And mainframes can support several dozen to several hundred users working in the transaction mode.

It is easy to understand how a computer with several CPUs can run several programs. But most computers still work with a single processor.

Figure 9-4 Computer-Generated Payroll Documents

One of the most common examples of a batch processing job is preparing an organization's payroll. In addition to printing payroll checks, the computer can be programmed to produce many other payroll documents, such as the payroll journal, at the same time. (Courtesy of Automatic Data Processing, Inc.)

You may recall reading about spooling, the technique whereby a person using word processing software can work on one document with the keyboard while the computer is printing another. This chapter looks at similar techniques used with large computers, which enable them to work on many jobs at the same time.

Multiprogramming.   The basic technique used to enable one CPU to handle many programs simultaneously is called **multiprogramming.** Multiprogramming is directed by the computer's operating system, which arranges for the active memory to be divided into "partitions." The memory addresses in each partition receive the program instructions and data for one of the programs to be executed.

The operating system directs the CPU to perform a few instructions for one program in one partition, then a few for the next, then a few for the third, and so on. These instructions are performed so fast that, in almost no time, the computer is back processing instructions for the first program again. In fact, it seems as though each program is running continuously, though a little more slowly than if it had the undivided attention of the CPU.

The slightly reduced speed troubles nobody. Even the fastest batch input devices are slower than a large computer's CPU; it can therefore handle input from several devices at once. Users working interactively, as already suggested, leave plenty of time for the CPU to perform other operations too. And the fastest output devices are usually too slow to keep the CPU working full time. Thus, whether the computer is receiving input, processing, or outputting, its CPU is unlikely to be fully occupied by a single program or user. But with an operating system that allows multiprogramming, the CPU can be kept busy. Many users, using several programs, can be served apparently at the same time. To each user, it seems that the computer is working only on his or her task.

Multitasking. A special type of multiprogramming is called multitasking. In **multitasking,** it is the applications program rather than the operating system that partitions the memory. Thus, you as the user are aware of more than one task being performed at once, and both tasks are being accomplished for you. Spooling is an example of multitasking; when you direct the computer to print a document, it stores an electronic version of that document in one partition of the memory and spends some of its

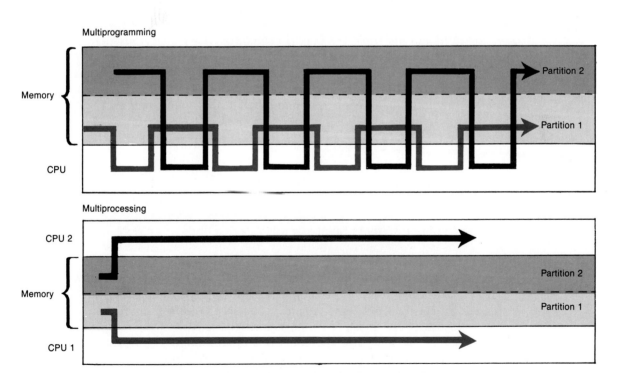

Figure 9-5   Multiprogramming and Multiprocessing
Multiprogramming is like juggling. Though the computer has only one CPU, it is able to handle several programs together, working on one and then another in quick turns. Each program is held in a different memory partition when not being processed. Compare this to multiprocessing, where the computer has two or more CPUs available to work with different programs.

time accomplishing the printing task. However, it also has time to work with you on another document, accepting your input into a new partition of its memory.

Multitasking applications software can be run with multiprogramming operating systems. As you can imagine, this involves some intricate coordination on the part of the CPU. But this is just the type of work that today's large CPUs are built to do.

Multiprocessing. Even though today's state-of-the-art CPUs can perform such complex and speedy work, they are not adequate for some applications. This is particularly true in the field of supercomputing, in which vast amounts of data need to be processed in a hurry—for example, before a missile reaches its target or a hurricane makes a landfall in a populated area. Some complex mathematical operations needed by business organizations also require high-speed results. **Multiprocessing** involves the use of more than one CPU in a single computer. It is a case of two (or more) heads being better than one. If the work of these CPUs is properly coordinated, they can cut processing time greatly, as several instructions can be processed at one time.

Many coordinating techniques are used. In some arrangements, different CPUs take care of different programs. In others, the CPUs are placed in a kind of "production line" and pass the information from one to another until the task is completed.

In some arrangements, one CPU is responsible for coordinating the operation; in others, coordination is handled by operating system instructions. These different arrangements are variously described as vector processing, diatic processing, and parallel processing.

Storage options and the storage hierarchy

As vital to a computer as its processing potential are its storage capabilities. Without an active memory and without storage devices that can save work more permanently, the most advanced CPUs and operating systems would be unable to perform their tasks. Like micros, large computers operate by constant busing of data between the arithmetic/logic unit and areas of memory. The speed with which memory can accept and yield information is crucial to the speed of a computer. For larger computers, the speed of its storage devices is almost as crucial.

You have already read how a microcomputer can occasionally use its disks as **virtual memory,** when the active memory is full. Most large computers also use virtual memory. Program instructions may be kept on a storage device until they are needed, instead of being held in active memory. Or data may be placed in disk addresses to be accessed, rather than in microchip storage. Virtual memory operates somewhat like a "mechanics" toolbox: mechanics don't hold all of their tools in their hands at once; instead the tools shuttle back and forth between the boxes and their hands. See Figure 9-6 for more information on virtual memory.

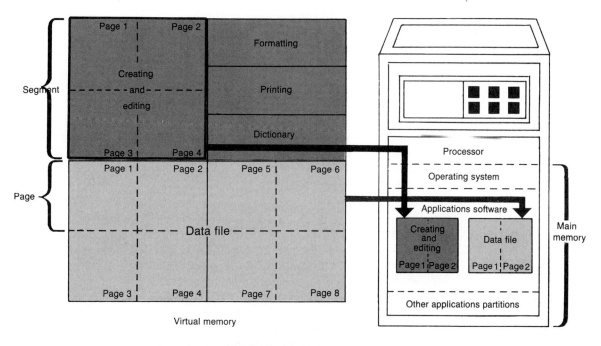

Figure 9-6 Virtual Memory at Work
Applications software is often divided into segments corresponding to the software's logical functions. These are loaded into main memory when the user calls for them. If a segment is too large for allocated memory space, however, it is further subdivided into pages, of a fixed size determined by the computer's hardware. The operating system transfers pages to memory only when they are needed; the user remains unaware that they are not there all the time. Large amounts of data may be handled the same way.

The boundary between active memory and storage is less clear than you might think. Early computers actually used magnetic drums, somewhat like magnetic disks, as their primary memory, and even today, magnetic drums are sometimes used as virtual memory devices. Rather than think of two separate concepts, memory and storage, many computer experts prefer to speak of **storage hierarchy,** a ladder of storage techniques with active memory technologies such as microchips and bubble memory on the top rung and slightly slower but still highly accessible devices such as magnetic drums and hard disks, on the next rung down. Diskettes, which can be accessed randomly, are on a lower rung still, with tapes and cassettes, which can only be read sequentially, at the bottom of the hierarchy.

ACTIVE MEMORY

Though several types of memory have been used during the 35 or so years that computers have been commercially available, almost all of today's machines, from micros to supercomputers, use the microchip technology described in Chapter 8. Silicon microchips have a great many features that make them suited to the task—they are highly reliable; they are very small; they use little electricity; the circuits on them can be switched on and off very fast; and although not simple to manufacture, chips can be produced in quantity at very low cost. In fact, their only disadvantage is that they cannot remember data through a power failure. Many computers compensate for this with battery backup systems to preserve power in case of a blackout.

Other technologies exist, of course. You learned in the last chapter about bubble memory, which keeps its charge even when the computer is turned off and is thus useful for portable computers. There are other technologies, too, that could become very important in the future, as Chapter 15 will discuss.

RESIDENT STORAGE DEVICES

Microcomputers typically use three types of storage devices—floppy disk drives, hard disk drives, and occasionally cassette recorders for backup. The hard disks are often built into the computer. The data stored on them is continually on-line, accessible so long as the computer is operating. They are therefore called **resident storage devices.** Diskettes and cassettes, by contrast, can be taken off-line; they are loaded and brought on-line only when needed.

Large computers make considerable use of resident storage devices.

STATE OF THE ART

Computers More Powerful Than the Human Brain?

Although no one has yet devised a machine that can handle the many subtleties of human thought, parallel processing has brought computers closer to that standard. Parallel processing is a type of multiprocessing in which several CPUs are coordinated to work together on a number of tasks at once. Many scientists believe the neuron centers of the human brain act together in much the same way.

Some parallel processing computers have a few powerful CPUs, and others have many less powerful ones. What makes parallel processing revolutionary, however, is not just the number and size of the CPUs but the interconnections among them. The workings of any one CPU may be relatively simple, but the pattern of activity in the network is very complex.

So far, parallel processing has been used mostly for sophisticated applications such as weather forecasting, speech recognition, and expert systems. Many organizations that could use parallel processing computers are reluctant to purchase them because they are expensive. Besides buying the hardware, purchasers must pay to have their software rewritten for parallel processing. For organizations that have purchased parallel processing systems, however, the cost has often been justified by the increases in processing power.

Eventually, as microprocessors become less expensive, most parallel processing computers will probably include a great many CPUs, all very powerful, and the interconnections will be all the more complex. By the year 2000, experts say, computers with a billion processors will be technologically feasible. Those machines may well have more processing power than the human brain!

These provide virtual memory, as explained earlier, and store commonly used software and data that must be kept accessible. The word processing program used by an organization will usually be kept resident so that it is available whenever an office worker needs to use it. Commonly used language compilers may also be kept on-line for the convenience of the programming staff. The organization's main databases, which are continually updated and must be available for many different applications, are also likely to be kept on a resident storage device.

Resident storage devices must be able to access information fast. This need has already been explained in connection with virtual memory. But programs and data must also be read quickly into a particular user's memory partition, or other users may be kept waiting for information from the same device.

As with microcomputers, hard disks are the standard on-line storage medium for larger computers. They combine rapid access to data and high-storage volume. The primary differences between the disk drives in a large computer and a hard disk drive used with a microcomputer are size, storage, and data transfer rate. Instead of a single hard disk, or two disks mounted one above the other, a large computer uses **disk packs,** each of which might include six disks or more in a single airtight container. The disks are spun together at high speeds—3,600 revolutions per minute is common—and can store billions of bytes of data.

Depending on the design of the disk drive, data is read at speeds ranging from a few hundred kilobytes per second to several megabytes (more than one million characters) per second. These disk drives work somewhat differently from those in micros. As with diskettes, a microcomputer hard disk has a read/write head that moves across the disk, reads information in a selected sector of a particular track, then moves to the next sector for more information.

The fastest type of disk drive for a large computer has one head for each track of each disk, fixed in position so that it can read data almost instantly. These **fixed-head disk drives** locate data by activating the appropriate head rather than by moving it   a very fast technique.

A slower type of disk drive for large computers has a set of heads that move together on a device called a **comb,** with one read/write head for each disk surface. Instead of storing data on consecutive tracks on one disk, as a microcomputer does, these drives store it in cylinders. A **cylinder** is the set of tracks with which the heads are in contact at any one time. Thus, a six-disk package might have 12 read/write heads and would therefore have 12-track cylinders. This means that at any one time, the disk drive can read any of the 12 tracks of information without moving the heads. To picture this, see Figure 9-7.

Both of these types of disk drives are classified as **direct access storage devices,** or **DASDs.** This means that they can go quickly to any file or piece of data, even if it is in the middle of the disk.

MOVABLE STORAGE MEDIA

Resident storage devices are not the only DASDs. You already know that diskette drives allow equally direct access to all files that they carry. But

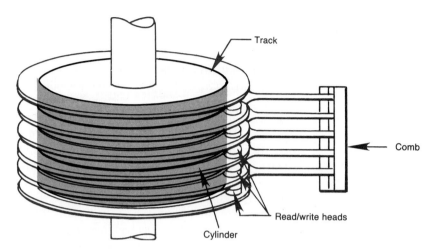

Figure 9-7 Disk Packs and Cylinders
This disk pack has 10 working surfaces—the top and bottom are not used. Each working surface is divided into tracks, which can be used when the comb's heads are appropriately placed. At any one time the comb covers 10 tracks of information. These can together be visualized as a cylinder.

diskettes can be removed—they are **movable storage media.** When new applications or data are needed, such media are replaced, allowing one device to handle an almost unlimited amount of information. In addition to diskettes, which are widely used with minicomputers as well as with micros, many disk packs are replaceable, allowing direct access to vast quantities of data. But one of the most commonly used movable storage media for large computers is magnetic tape, and this is a sequential access medium. The tape drive must search the tape from the beginning until it locates the file or data that it is looking for.

Tape drives. Half-inch Mylar tape, similar to the tape used in audio- and videocassettes, has long been a standby for computers. The standard storage formats for magnetic tape are 800, 1,600, and 6,250 characters per inch, and the tape frequently comes in reels of 2,400 feet. This means that well over 120 million characters can be stored on a single tape, making it a very inexpensive storage medium.

Computer tape drives, like disk drives, have read/write heads that record data on the tape and read it back into the computer system. These heads typically place eight or nine tracks side by side on the tape: each bit of information in a byte goes onto a separate track.

Tape drives move the tape extremely fast. This leads to one problem: they take a certain amount of time to stop. For this reason, gaps between entries must be left on the tape so that the machine doesn't overrun the data to be read. Though these gaps may take up a considerable amount of the tape, they are not a major disadvantage because tape is so inexpensive.

The main disadvantage of tapes is that they can only be read sequentially. This makes them inefficient for everyday use in most applications. But because of its low cost, tape is the ideal medium for backing up a day's work, and, as mentioned earlier, it is the usual medium on which mainframe software is delivered.

Other movable storage. Movable storage media also include microforms (microfilm and microfiche). Computer output microfilm (COM) and computer input microfilm (CIM), described in Chapter 2, are methods that allow microforms to store and input information originally generated by a computer. In addition, the emerging technology of **optical disks** presents interesting possibilities for movable storage. Today they are used largely as input media, because recording information on them is currently expensive—laser beams are used to cut holes in the disk surface that are one micron (one millionth of an inch) in diameter. However, when the recording process becomes commercially feasible, the optical disk could well become an ideal medium for storage. Optical disks have a vast capacity: a disk the size of an audio compact disk can store an entire encyclopedia, with room to spare. And optical disks are difficult to damage—they would be excellent for an organization's permanent records.

STORAGE HIERARCHY

Given the storage options that are available and the needs that must be met, decisions are required about what information should be kept

Figure 9-8 Tape Backup Systems
This small computer has a tape backup system, which enables the user to duplicate data onto a second tape to ensure that information is not accidentally lost. Some tape backup systems can be set to copy all the day's work automatically, in a matter of minutes. (Courtesy of Hewlett-Packard Company)

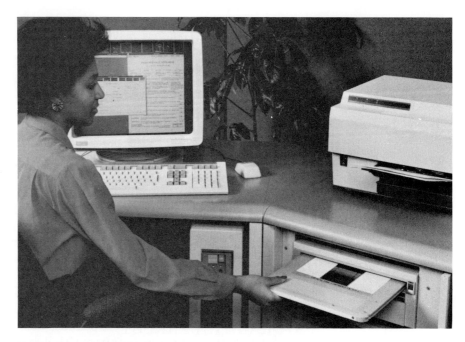

Figure 9-9   Optical Disks

The computer system shown here provides data storage through two 12-inch optical disk drives which can store about 120,000 document images. This system can present images of handwritten documents windowed with computer-generated material. (Courtesy of Eastman Kodak)

on-line (resident) and what should be stored off-line on movable media. These decisions are made easier by the concept of a storage hierarchy, which involves ranking the available media in terms of speed, capacity, and cost (see Figure 9-10). Because slower media are less expensive, organizations try to use them when speed is not crucial. Movable storage on tape, for example, requires only a tape drive and a librarian to manage and load the tapes when needed. This method makes a vast amount of data accessible inexpensively.

Clearly, it is desirable to use tape storage whenever possible, because of its low cost. But this advantage must be balanced against the time likely to be lost in using the slower medium. If 12 office workers lose 10 minutes each day waiting for their word processing program to come up on the screen, the decision to use tape storage was probably wrong. A resident disk, higher in the storage hierarchy, would in the end have saved money for the organization.

Input options

No matter how advanced the technology is, storage or processing speed is of little help if a user can't enter data into the system. Earlier in this chapter you learned of the input modes that can be used—batch or transaction. But the input hardware involved is also important. As with microcomputers, storage media for large computers—disk packs and tapes, for example—can be used as very effective input devices; keyboards, too, are widely used with large computers. The computer industry has also produced a wide variety of other input options: mark and character readers, graphics tools called digitizers, and voice recognition devices.

STORAGE MEDIA FOR INPUT

Software for large systems is commonly delivered on tapes. These tapes are kept for backup purposes as a master copy outside the computer system, and a working copy is created for everyday use. This working copy may be placed on a hard disk if it is used frequently or on a removable tape if it will be needed only occasionally. Floppy disks are also used for entering software into some large systems.

KEYBOARD DEVICES

Entering data directly from a workstation, as you would do if you were working with a microcomputer, is possible with a large computer. But it isn't a practical option when dealing with large amounts of data because

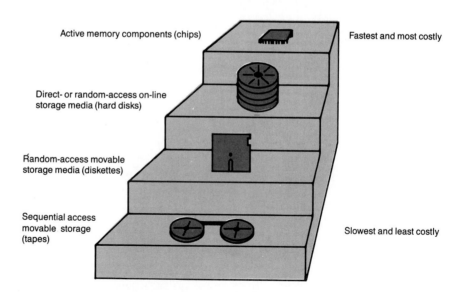

Figure 9-10   The Storage Hierarchy
Computer storage techniques can be ranked as if on a stairway. At the top are microchips and other active memory components—fastest for storing and retrieving information, but usually only good for temporary storage. At the bottom is magnetic tape, the slowest and least expensive permanent storage medium. These rankings help systems planners determine the least costly way to meet an organization's storage needs.

it would tie up too much valuable CPU time. One alternative is for a pool of data entry clerks to key in the data using devices that don't immediately access the main computer. Instead, these devices create a tape or disk that is used later for batch mode entry or simultaneous transfer of data.

Key to tape. Key-to-tape devices are similar to some electronic typewriters. They "remember" the sequence of characters keyed by an operator and record it as magnetized bits on a computer tape. Some systems record the keystrokes of just one keyboard operator, and others can combine the work of several operators on a single tape. Like electronic typewriters, most of these systems have limited editing capability so that errors can be found and changed before the main computer's time is wasted.

Key to disk. Key-to-disk devices are similar, but their editing capabilities are often greater—they commonly use a separate minicomputer to enter data onto a hard disk. Besides allowing more complex editing of the entries, this computer can double check that the formats are correct— that letters, for example, are used where appropriate and that no essential commas are missing. Once the data has been entered, by one or several operators, it can be transferred to a tape and entered into the mainframe that will process it.

MARK AND CHARACTER READERS

In addition to devices that can speed up standard keyboard input, there are many peripherals that can convert symbols on paper directly into computer input. These readers use several technologies. Ordinary light, laser, and magnetic sensing are among those employed.

Optical mark readers. If you've ever taken a test for which you used a No. 2 pencil to fill in numbered boxes, you've been involved with an **optical mark reader (OMR).** The marked sheets are fed into a scanner that reads the answers directly into a computer, where a program can read and score them. OMRs are also used for many organizational purposes, ranging from recording hospital lab results to making advertising bookings.

Bar code scanners. Long before stores were fully equipped to take advantage of them, bar codes or Universal Product Codes (UPC) were being printed on manufacturers' labels to identify each of their products. Today these codes are frequently seen in grocery stores. A checker can pass an item over a **bar code scanner** that reads its code and transmits it to a computer. The computer can then check its database to determine the item's price, tax status, sale or nonsale status and other critical data. Each pass over the scanner causes a customer's bill to be adjusted and the store's inventory report to be updated. Some stores also incorporate voice synthesizers to report to the customers each item and its price.

Figure 9-11   Bar Code Scanning with a Wand
Bar codes are also used in computerized manufacturing systems to summarize data about production processes. This plant operator is using a wand to provide the computer system with information about a manufacturing operation on the part he is holding. (Courtesy of UNISYS)

Wands.   More recent adaptations of UPC coding are being seen in inventory applications. Codes on shelved products can be scanned with a portable reader, or **wand.** Similar wands are used for a number of other applications: they can read characters from the backs of credit cards, from an inventory slip, from price tags in a store. Connected to a terminal, they can also read from a monitor, relay data to the computer, and adjust inventory and billing.

Magnetic ink.   If you've ever made a deposit and written a check on the same day only to find that the bank subtracted the check from your account before it added the deposit, you know how fast checks can be processed. Bank checks use another input technology, **magnetic ink character recognition,** or **MICR** (rhymes with *hiker*). The bank number and your account number are printed across the bottom of every check with a special magnetic ink. At the end of each day, the checks are passed along a conveyer station, the characters are read with a magnetic ink character reader, the check amount is added from a keyboard, and the transaction is immediately charged to your account.

Optical character readers.   Commonly referred to as OCR, **optical character readers** are becoming more and more widely used. Originally, OCRs could interpret only special computer-readable characters, so documents fed into them had to be typed in one particular typeface. Using a computer technique called character recognition, OCRs can now read more and more typefaces so that typed and printed documents from a variety of sources can be entered into a computer without repetitive keyboarding. OCRs can also read careful hand-lettering, and advanced systems are being developed that can learn to read handwriting.

DIGITIZERS

Characters are, of course, not the only type of input that a computer system must process. Many types of software, especially graphics programs, require the use of **digitizers.** These devices can keep track of physical movement and convert it to digital input that a computer can understand. One digitizer that has already been described is the mouse, which can be moved around on a flat surface and causes the cursor to move similarly on the monitor screen.

A mouse can be used not only for drawing freehand graphics but also for making menu choices and for other tasks that can be performed by using the cursor as a pointer. Other devices that act as digitizers include pressure-sensitive pads, light pens, and touch screens.

Graphics tablet. A **graphics tablet** is a notepad-like soft plastic case with internal wiring that serves as an electronic grid. When pressure is applied to the surface of the tablet, electrical contacts are made in the grid, sending signals to the computer. If a stylus or finger is moved across the tablet, the cursor on the computer's screen follows a similar path. At the same time, the coordinates, or identifying sets of numbers, of touched locations are stored in the computer's memory for later use.

Like the mouse, these tablets have buttons that can be used to convey

Figure 9-12 Graphics Tablet and Stylus
Digitizers come in many forms. The graphics tablet and electronic stylus shown here are especially useful to technical illustrators, engineers, architects, and others whose work involves technical drawings and blueprints that are prepared on CAD systems. (Courtesy of George Omura)

Figure 9-13 Touch Screens
Touch screen techniques can be adapted to many applications. With appropriate software and hardware, a block move in word processing can be accomplished with one fingertip. Tap some menu choices at the screen bottom—touch the two ends of the block—and then, point the sentences to their new location. (Courtesy of Hewlett-Packard Company)

additional information. By pressing one button, you may make a menu choice or, with different software, draw a line. You can also use graphics tablets to enter characters or other readable marks. By pressing in the appropriate place, or even writing the appropriate letters, a user can input verbal messages from a remote location.

Light pens.   Although it might seem that **light pens** would shine a light on the screen, they actually work in just the opposite way. The pen contains a light-sensitive tip that, when placed against the screen, transmits the coordinates of the tip's location to the computer. In engineering applications, the light pen is widely used to change or test diagrams that are displayed on the screen.

Touch screens.   The use of **touch screens** is growing rapidly. With touch screen technology, the user can move through a series of menus by touching designated spots on the computer's screen. One typical application of touch screens is in libraries. Instead of using the familiar card catalog, you can locate a book by pressing points on a computer monitor in response to a set of questions. Similarly, workers and managers who lack keyboarding skills can make menu choices very simply and quickly using touch screen technology.

VOICE RECOGNITION MODULES

In addition to interpreting handwriting, computers are becoming able to recognize the spoken word. Although developing software that recognizes grammar has proved very difficult, the sounds of human language are easier. Even though people's voices differ, voice recognition devices can "learn" to interpret different individuals' commands. This is useful when a job calls for the simultaneous use of both hands but requires the employee to enter data into the computer—for example, when performing an inventory check. Although the use of voice recognition requires careful tuning to ensure that the computer doesn't misunderstand what is said, the technology also offers significant promise as an aid to the handicapped.

Output options

The output devices described in the discussion of microcomputers are all available to large computers. The additional capabilities of large computers, however, mean that other devices can also be used. A fast computer should not be delayed by a slow printer—that is a waste of the computer's potential. But speed is not the only feature of large computers that makes demands on output devices. The variety of applications that large computers can perform leads to a variety of peripherals to produce different kinds of output.

IMPACT PRINTERS

As explained earlier, an **impact printer** strikes a ribbon to transfer ink to a page. Impact printers function in different ways: some, called **character printers,** print one character at a time; others, **line printers,** print many characters together. One advantage of impact printers is that they can make carbon copies.

Character printers. For applications for which high speed is not important, the **dot-matrix** and **daisy-wheel** printers described earlier are as useful with large computers as they are with micros. In fact, they are standard with minicomputers. They may be linked to mainframes, too, if short documents with quality printing are needed. However, for volume work in which speed is important—for example, printing out accounting information—line printers are traditionally used.

Line printers. Line printers operate at higher speeds than character printers because they print many letters at the same time. The operation of the most popular type of line printer, the **chain printer,** is typical of the way these machines work. The characters of a chain printer are mounted on an endless chain loop. Each character is repeated several times on the chain—some more than others because they are more commonly encountered in writing. The chain spins above an inked ribbon over the paper. When any character reaches the place where it is to be printed, the back of the paper is struck by one of a full line of hammers, and the character is printed on the paper. At the same time, other hammers are striking the paper against other characters.

Another form of line printer, the **drum printer,** uses a similar principle, except that the characters are on a drum that rotates vertically behind the paper. Both chain and drum printers are well suited to high-volume use, printing at the rate of 200 to 3,000 lines per minute. Their disadvantage is that they are extremely complex mechanical devices. They need considerable maintenance and are very noisy.

NONIMPACT PRINTERS

Nonimpact printers, such as ink-jet and laser printers, are used with large computer systems as well as with micros. They are quieter than impact printers, and they produce high-quality copies very fast, as discussed in Chapter 8. However, though simple mechanically, they tend to be expensive because of their advanced electronics. They also cannot be used with carbon paper. Those disadvantages aside, nonimpact devices have made significant inroads into the printer market. In fact, laser printers are often described as **page printers,** because they print full pages at once. One of the fastest laser printers available for mainframes can print 120 pages per minute—two pages each second.

PLOTTERS

Another type of output device, the **plotter,** is used to print copies of drawings and other graphic output. A **table plotter** uses pens that move over the surface of a page. With a **drum plotter,** the paper moves under the pens. Because the pens can be either drawn across the page or lifted from the page, drawings of high quality, even those containing broken lines, can be easily produced.

Figure 9-14 Page Printers
Many high speed laser printers look like photocopying machines and share some of the same technology. But there is no "original" copy, and documents are produced as fast as or faster than photocopies. This photo shows documents in the sorting bins of a laser printer. (Courtesy of Xerox Corporation)

Special-purpose input/output devices

Some peripherals of large computers are so specialized that they don't fit into a neat category. One example is the **automated teller machine** at a bank, which allows you to make deposits and withdrawals. This machine performs both input and output functions. The **point-of-sale terminal** in a store also performs both input and output functions, accepting data about a transaction and then printing a sales slip. Another example can be seen in **reservation ticket terminals** used by travel agencies that tell the computer a ticket has been sold and then print the ticket. Most of these machines, and others like them, are specially manufactured for particular applications.

One other input/output device of great importance is the modem. As you read earlier, this device allows computer-readable signals to travel on telephone lines intended to carry the human voice. Modems vary in size; some, a little larger than a paperback book, are used with micros, but others, for use with large computer installations, can be the size of a microwave oven. Without modems, much of the data communication described in the next chapter would be impossible.

SUMMARY

- Large computers are useful to organizations because they can aid, and help to coordinate, the work of many employees. They are now essential tools for most large organizations.

- The three main groups of large computers—minicomputers, mainframes, and supercomputers—are all usually superior to micros in processing capacity, speed, and memory size. However, the dividing lines between these groups are somewhat arbitrary because of the remarkable development of additional power for computers of all sizes.

- Minicomputers are frequently used for specialized tasks and seldom use an operations staff. By contrast, mainframes usually have large teams of operators and quantities of software for different applications. Supercomputers are huge installations, usually put together to work on particular problems.

- Organizations benefit when their large computers are used most efficiently so that they can take full advantage of their speed and size. One way that this is done is by selecting the appropriate input mode—transaction processing or batch processing.

■ Other techniques for maximizing the use of a computer include multiprogramming, in which the CPU partitions the active memory among the various applications it is running and divides its work among them; multitasking, which is similar but usually within a single application; and multiprocessing, in which the computer actually has more than one CPU.

■ To make more efficient use of active memory, the technique called virtual memory is commonly used on large machines. This technique involves the use of disk drives to hold information until it is needed; at any one time, only parts of the program or data being used are located in active memory.

■ Large computers have many more secondary storage devices than do standard microcomputers, ranging from high-speed memory drums to tape backup devices. These can be classified into resident storage devices, such as fixed-head disk drives, and movable media such as diskettes, tapes, microforms, and optical disks.

■ Large computers also support a much wider range of input and output devices than do micros. Input devices include key-to-tape and key-to-disk equipment, optical and magnetic character recognition devices, voice recognition modules, point-of-sale terminal devices such as bar code scanners, and graphics devices like pressure-sensitive pens, light pens, and touch screens. Output devices include high-speed printers of the impact and nonimpact types, plotters, and high-speed modems.

TERMS FOR REVIEW

computer operators	cylinder	light pens
console	direct access storage	touch screens
program librarians	devices	impact printer
programmers	DASDs	character printers
supercomputers	movable storage	line printers
transaction	media	dot-matrix
processing	optical disks	daisy-wheel
batch processing	optical mark reader	chain printer
multiprogramming	(OMR)	drum printer
multitasking	bar code scanner	page printers
multiprocessing	wand	plotter
virtual memory	magnetic ink	table plotters
storage hierarchy	character	drum plotter
resident storage	recognition	automated teller
devices	MICR	machine
disk packs	optical character	point-of-sale
fixed-head disk	readers	terminal
drives	digitizers	reservation ticket
comb	graphics tablet	terminals

TERMINOLOGY CHECK

For each definition below, choose the correct term or terms from the list of Terms for Review.

1. Person who controls and catalogs the daily work of a mainframe computer. *computer operator*

2. Fastest type of disk drive for a large computer, with one head for each track on each disk. *Tape drives*

3. Devices of several types that allow physical movement to be converted to matching digital input, usually used for creating graphics. *digitizers*

4. Most popular type of high-speed line printer. *chain printer*

5. Set of tracks with which the heads on the comb for a disk pack are in contact at any one time.

6. Scale of storage techniques that enables speed on the one hand to be balanced against cost on the other.

7. Input technology used by banks for the numbers printed at the bottom of a bank check.

8. Processing technique that inputs data as one continuous stream, all preparations having been made beforehand. *batch processing*

9. Pressure-sensitive pad that enables users to create graphics and to respond to menus. *graphics tablet*

10. Technique that allows computers with a single CPU to handle many programs simultaneously.

INFORMATION CHECK

1. Name three advantages that the minicomputer had over computers developed earlier.

2. What are some tasks for which minis are used?

3. What features characterize a mainframe "environment"?

4. List and briefly describe three major categories of staff typically required to operate a mainframe.

5. Why is user input a key to efficient use of the computer?

6. What are the advantages and disadvantages of transaction processing and batch processing?

7. List and briefly describe several processing options available on larger computers.

8. What is the difference in function between active memory and storage devices?

9. Describe virtual memory. Why is it useful?

10. Name and briefly describe two active memory options.

11. What are some of the features and requirements of resident storage devices?

12. What is the major difference between the types of hard disk drives commonly used as resident storage devices?

13. Describe the two major types of movable storage devices for large computers, and give one example of each.

14. What criteria must a business consider when setting up its storage hierarchy?

15. Describe briefly the major types of hardware used to input data into large computers.

PROJECTS AND PROBLEMS

1. A small wholesale company that sells shoes to small independent shoe stores has just been contracted by a chain of 25 regional department stores to set up and supply shoe salons in each of the stores.

   Until now, the wholesaler's order entry and other bookkeeping functions were adequately handled by one person using a microcomputer with a hard disk drive and a daisy-wheel printer. To service the new accounts, the president of the wholesale company realizes he must expand his computing capabilities. He will now have to process the following information from the 25 stores:

   - daily sales figures

   - inventory control and ordering

   - weekly status reports to management

   Suppose you were asked to identify how to expand the computing facilities. Write a memo advising, among other things:

   - whether to purchase additional micros, a mini, or a mainframe

   - what method to use for data entry

   - how to store the accumulated data

2. What kind of computer system does your school or college use? Interview the person in charge of the computer center. Write up your interview in an article format. Include information about the hardware currently in use and some details about the hardware used in the past. (If your school doesn't have a computer center, contact a local business.)

3. Browse through computer magazines. Respond to three ads that offer free information about resident storage devices and movable media devices. Write a summary describing the major features of the products available.

4. Gather information regarding three different printers, and write a report comparing their features.

10

Data communications networks

You have seen how a business can take care of several jobs at once by using large computers linked to many terminals. Few big organizations today, however, rely entirely on one computer—or on one kind of computer. Instead, they depend on many computers of different types to process their business information.

Increasingly, organizations are linking their computers in **data communications networks**—often called **datacom networks**—that enable the computers to exchange information. With these networks, organizations of all kinds can collect input from multiple sources and send output to multiple destinations with greater speed, accuracy, and efficiency.

Datacom networks deliver answers to customer's inquiries, and they give employees instant access to information they need for their jobs. When you check your bank account balance at an automated teller machine, for example, you are using data communications. So is the store clerk who pushes a few buttons on a terminal to record a sale or inquire about the validity of your credit card or your check. Any exchange of information between two computers, or between a computer and a terminal in different locations, involves some type of datacom network.

A simple data communications network may consist of two or three computers in a single office sharing a central processing unit and a printer. Most networks, however, are much more complex. An organization may use a large central mainframe computer as its chief processing unit, linked by a network to many terminals. Also common today are **shared systems,** in which the mainframe is linked to several micros and mini-computers as well. In such systems, authorized users of smaller computers can **download,** or retrieve information from the central computer and then, at their own workstations, process it independently or save it on diskettes. Distributing computer power in this way reduces the processing demands on the large computers, and it gives users faster access to the information they need.

A large multinational corporation's datacom network may involve interconnections among many types of computers and a variety of input, output, storage, and distribution devices that are scattered around the world. In addition to transferring data among computers, parts of a large network may handle the exchange of voice, graphics, and video communications. For this reason, the terms **telecommunications** and **telecom** are often used instead of **data communications.**

The signals involved in different types of telecommunications are often standardized so that they can travel over the same transmission media. Frequently, computer signals are converted to resemble voice signals; the trend today, however, is toward converting other signals, including voice signals, to the digital form used by computers.

This chapter explores how datacom networks connect computers and permit users to share information and increase their productivity. The discussion ranges from simple systems to complex networks in which different types of computers at distant locations can exchange many forms of information simultaneously.

After studying this chapter, you will be able to:

■ list several transmission media and methods and discuss their advantages and disadvantages

■ identify and describe five protocol decisions on which agreement must be reached for successful data communications

■ describe several types of network topologies and discuss their advantages and drawbacks

■ discuss efficiency and data security in complex datacom systems

Transmission media

Data communications are generally transmitted over telephone lines or microwave frequencies. In fact, the signals for a single communication, such as an electronic mail message from St. Louis to London, may travel part of the distance over several kinds of wire and part of it through the air, with help from satellites and other devices. The wires, frequencies, and devices that transmit data are called **transmission media.**

TWISTED PAIRS

Early telephone lines were not insulated. They were strung in **open pairs** over telephone poles. The signals on different pairs were apt to interfere with each other. As a result of such interference, people talking to each other on the telephone could often hear another conversation in the background. In data communications, such electrical interference is called **noise.**

Noise is significantly reduced through the use of **twisted pairs,** which are pairs of thinner, insulated wires twisted together. This is the most common wiring arrangement for local telephone lines today. A standard telephone is served by two twisted pairs, and several pairs are bundled together to make heavier telephone cables. Twisted-pair wiring can handle data transmission more quickly than open pairs, because the twisting and insulating reduce the noise level between the pairs. This results in more accurate signals and permits faster transmission speeds.

COAXIAL CABLE

Still further improvements have come with the development and use of **coaxial cable,** in which a wire mesh tube made from an electrical conductor, such as copper, encloses a single insulated, high-capacity wire. The cable is also insulated on the outside. Microcomputers and printers are generally connected by coaxial cables.

Coaxial cables can handle very rapid transmissions of data, as well as complex signals like video messages. They are often packed together with twisted-pair cables to form large trunk lines that can carry up to 108,000 two-way telephone transmissions at a time.

MICROWAVE FREQUENCIES

You have no doubt seen dish-shaped antennas next to houses, on the roofs of tall buildings, or on towers at the tops of hills. These antennas are

Figure 10-1   Coaxial Cables
Coaxial cables have been used to transmit data for many years. This cross-section of a telephone trunk line shows 22 coaxial cables, each of which can carry more than 5,000 conversations at once. Relays are spaced at mile intervals to amplify the signals. (Courtesy of AT&T/ Bell Laboratories)

used in the transmission of **microwaves,** communications signals or frequencies that travel through the air without wires. Dish antennas exchange microwave frequencies with each other or with similar antennas attached to satellites orbiting above the earth. The microwave frequencies can carry larger amounts of data than most kinds of wiring. Telephone calls and video transmissions are also frequently carried by microwaves.

Though microwave frequency transmissions are still subject to interference from each other and are also prone to interference from weather, they offer significant improvements in both cost and accuracy over the

---

STATE OF THE ART
Digital Transmissions, From Telegraphy to Fiber Optics

The telegraph was the very first means of transmitting messages electrically over long distances. When it was introduced in the 1840s, pioneers were still crossing the country by wagon train. Telegraphy must have seemed like a miracle then, but by today's standards it is crude. To send a message, a telegraph operator used Morse code to transform it into dots and dashes, then transmitted them as electrical impulses by opening and closing an electrical circuit. Because it used discrete on and off signals, the telegraph was a digital transmitting system. Morse code was a precursor to the binary system used to encode computer data today.

When Alexander Graham Bell invented the telephone in 1876, he found a way to transmit voices electrically by transforming sound waves into analog or similar waves of electrical current. These waves were carried over copper wires to the receiving end, where they would be converted back into sound waves.

The analog transmission system used by telephones (and later television) prevailed until recently. Even telegraph signals were translated to an analog form so that they could travel down telephone wires. But now the growth of data communications has created the need to transmit messages digitally once again. And the volume of messages today is greater than anything the inventors of the telegraph could have envisioned. As a result, the communications industry is now in the process of changing over to a third transmission system that will result in the combining of telephone, TV, and computer signals onto rapid and efficient digital channels.

The technology that has made this new communications revolution possible is fiber optics. Fiber optics works in a similar fashion to the telegraph; each pulse of light is an on and off signal that represents a piece of data, much as a dot or dash once did. One fundamental difference between fiber optics of the 1980s and telegraphy of the 1880s is their transmission speeds. The average telegraph operator of 100 years ago could send two signals per second. A commercial laser today can pulse 400 million times a second, fast enough to transmit about 6,000 telephone calls simultaneously over a single fiber!

Within a few years, fiber optics will allow you to talk on the telephone even when your computer is communicating with another computer over the same telephone line. In addition, some experts believe fiber optics will replace copper telephone wiring by the end of the century. It may even replace communications satellites, because ground communications will be just as efficient but much less expensive.

use of cables. Many large organizations lease microwave channels and equipment for their data communications, and some have complete microwave transmission systems of their own.

FIBER OPTICS

A more recent development in cable technology is the use of **fiber optics,** in which pulses of light flow through extremely long and thin glass filaments that are sheathed in plastic. Because the fibers carry light pulses rather than electrical signals, the transmissions are noiseless. A laser is frequently used as the light source. This generates ultrapure light pulses according to the sending computer's digital on and off signals. There is virtually no deterioration in the strength of laser pulses as they travel along the fibers.

Fiber optics gives new meaning to the concept of high-speed datacom transmissions. The capacity of a transmission medium can be measured in bits per second (bps), which means the number of information bits (zeros and ones) it can carry each second. This measure is often called the **baud rate.** A baud rate of 2,400 (2,400 bits per second) is considered fast for a microcomputer connection today; at that rate, text to your terminal comes in at 300 characters per second—it scrolls off the screen too quickly for you to read it without printing it or storing it on a disk. With fiber optics, baud rates of one billion bits per second may soon be common.

Fiber optics also provides more security than other datacom media. In other words, it is more difficult for unauthorized people or organizations to intercept signals that are traveling over optical fibers. So, even though installation is expensive, telephone companies are using more and more fiber optics connections because of the advantages they offer.

Transmission hardware

In addition to the wires and other hardware needed as transmission media, other hardware devices may be required to enable computers and users to communicate effectively over long distance. These devices include relays, modems, multiplexors, and front-end processors.

RELAYS FOR VOICE AND DATA

A general problem with transmission media is that the strength of the signals fades as the signals travel. Therefore, **relays** are needed along the way that amplify (strengthen) signals or repeat them. Telephone lines include relay boxes to strengthen signals, and microwave dish antennas have similar devices built in for the same purpose. However, relays that are commonly used for voice transmission are not effective for strengthening digital computer signals and vice versa.

Remember that in many networks computers communicate over telephone channels. Telephone relays are generally designed to amplify voices and other **analog** signals, which are continuous wave-like signals as

Figure 10-2   Modems

An acoustic coupler (left) creates sounds which are picked up by a telephone handset that is placed directly on top. An external modem (right) makes no sound—it sends electronic signals directly into the telephone system, usually through a telephone jack in the wall. (Courtesy of AT&T and Tandy Corporation)

opposed to the separate and distinct digital on and off pulse signals that computers generate. Signal-converting devices are therefore needed to enable computer communications to travel on standard telephone lines.

MODEMS

Modems, which were briefly described in Chapter 4, are the devices that perform this signal conversion. They take their name from the first two letters of the word *modulate* and the first three letters of *demodulate*. A modem connected to a sending computer modulates the digital signals for transmission over analog lines. Another modem, connected to the receiving computer, demodulates the signals, or converts them back to digital signals so that the receiving computer can process them.

Several types of modems are commonly used today. One type, called an **acoustic coupler,** actually generates an audible signal that is fed into the telephone receiver; it can also "listen" to a similar signal from the handset and convert it to digital pulses. Other types bypass the telephone handset and yet create (and interpret) an electronic analog signal that can be faster than that from the telephone mouthpiece. These include **external modems,** standalone pieces of equipment attached to an output port of the computer as well as to a phone line and **internal modems,** which are installed inside the computer housing.

Modems are usually set to operate at particular transmission speeds, as you will read in the section on communications protocols later in this chapter.

MULTIPLEXORS

Just as the CPU of a large computer can process data considerably faster than a typical user can produce it, so too can many communications media transmit more signals in a given second than are needed for a particular

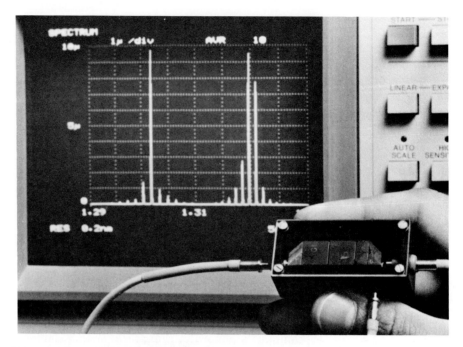

Figure 10-3   A Fiber Optic Multiplexor
The multiplexor being held here is a recent development. It allows two signals to
be transmitted in the same fiber optic communication channel by dividing the signal wavelength. The screen in back shows a graphic representation of signals the
device is carrying. (Courtesy of GTE Stanford, Conn.)

message. Therefore, it is desirable to have one medium carry many transmissions at the same time. This can be accomplished through a technique
called **multiplexing.**

Devices that divide a medium so that it can carry several channels
at once are called **multiplexors.** An important concept related to multiplexors is **bandwidth,** the range of frequencies that are available for
transmission through a particular medium. Bandwidth can be broad or
narrow. Just as a broad highway can carry more traffic than a narrow
street, a **broadband** medium can carry more communications channels
than a narrowband medium. Microwaves and coaxial cables are broadband media; they carry many more channels and thus more data, video,
voice, and graphics than do twisted pairs. A twisted pair can carry only
one set of signals at a time; it is categorized as a **baseband** medium.

Multiplexing can be used with both broadband and baseband media,
but each requires a different technique. Broadband media use **frequency-
division multiplexing.** Because coaxial cables can carry a broad range
of frequencies, they can carry many channels, with each channel on its
own frequency. In an example not related to computers, think of how a
single cable can bring 30 television channels or more to your TV set.
Baseband media must use **time-division multiplexing,** in which a narrowband wire carries signals first from one message, then from another.

This technique bears a resemblance to multiprogramming (described in Chapter 9), in which the computer handles several programs at one time by working briefly on one program, then on another.

FRONT-END PROCESSORS

In a large system, a special-purpose computer called a **front-end processor** may be set aside to handle communications tasks. This leaves the central computer free to work on basic information processing. A front-end processor, sometimes confusingly called a communications channel, typically includes a multiplexor. It also includes many output ports

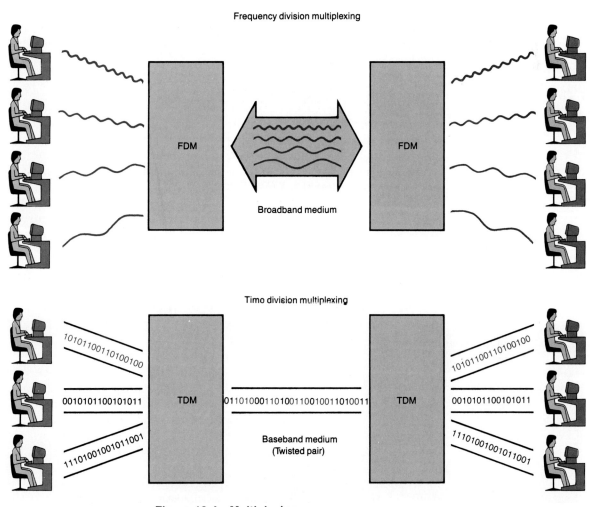

Figure 10-4 Multiplexing

A frequency division multiplexor (FDM) takes signals input from different sources and allocates a different communications frequency to each one, so that they can be transmitted together. A time division multiplexor (TDM) interleaves the different inputs. Both types must send control data to the destination multiplexor, so that it can correctly separate out the signals again.

connecting with different communications lines. And it usually has a sizable memory, where it can assemble groups of messages before sending them at high speed or where it can sort them out before sending them on to the central computer itself.

Communications protocols

In addition to appropriate equipment and communications media, another requirement for successful exchange of information in a datacom network is an established **communications protocol.** A protocol is a set of decisions about different aspects of the exchange so that all users involved in it are working by the same rules. In Chapter 4, you read about the importance of agreeing on a speed for the data transmission. Many other decisions are needed; among the most important are mode of transmission, code used for transmission, how to handle any interchange of messages, and how to check for errors.

TRANSMISSION SPEED

Just as some computers can process data much faster than others, transmission media and communications devices differ in the speeds at which they can send and receive information. An acoustic coupler, for example, is limited by the capacity of the telephone mouthpiece, which is likely to produce noise (distort the signal), at speeds above 300 bits or 37 characters per second. But an internal or external modem can work closer to the limits of twisted-pair wiring—1,200 bps is a comfortable baud rate for these devices. And if the network does not include twisted pair wiring, far higher baud rates are possible.

All equipment involved in the information exchange must be sending

Figure 10-5   Faster Transmission Rates
The faster information can be transmitted, the lower the telephone bills. This internal modem is an expansion card that fits into a micro, with a port that connects to the phone system. Its complex circuitry can transmit accurately at a rate of 2,400 bits per second. (Courtesy of Hayes Microcomputer Products, Inc.)

or receiving at the same baud rate. Sophisticated front-end processors can usually detect the baud rate automatically and set themselves to receive. Otherwise, users must be aware of this element of the protocol so that they can set up their hardware and software correctly. For microcomputer communications, 300 and 1,200 bps are most common, and most modems are built to work at one or both of these transmission speeds, although faster speeds are possible with micros.

TRANSMISSION MODE

The speed at which computers can communicate may depend not only on the media and equipment being used but also on the mode in which data is transmitted. Computers communicate primarily in one of two modes: asynchronous or synchronous.

Asynchronous communications. In **asynchronous** communication, characters are transmitted as you type them. After each character, the receiving computer must stop to wait for the next one. The top speed for asynchronous data communication is about 1,800 baud. When a user at a remote workstation is connected to a computer by asynchronous communication, this is sometimes called **real-time computing,** because each piece of data is sent immediately to be processed by the receiving computer.

Synchronous communications. **Synchronous** communication is somewhat like batch processing. Characters are stored and then sent together, so the receiving computer can process them together without delay. Synchronous data communication is more efficient than asynchronous communication. It is also very fast, because the receiving computer doesn't have to stop and wait after each character. Instead, the internal clocks of the computers are synchronized so that the machines send and receive data at the same pace.

CHARACTER CODES

As you know, different CPUs use different machine languages. Shared **character codes** allow these different processors to communicate with each other. Several character codes have been developed by interest groups within the computer industry.

ASCII. One of the most frequently used data transmission codes is **ASCII** (pronounced AS-kee), which stands for American Standard Code for Information Interchange. ASCII was developed by the American Standards Organization. It assigns a 7-bit binary sequence to represent each of 128 numerals, letters, and other symbols. A capital T, for example, is assigned the binary sequence 1010100; a capital K is represented as 1001011. Other characters in ASCII are shown in Figure 10-6.

Baudot. The **Baudot code,** also known as the international alphabet, was developed by the International Consultative Committee on Inter-

Character	Code		
	ASCII	Baudot	EBCDIC
A	1000001	10000	1100 0001
B	1000010	00110	1100 0010
C	1000011	10110	1100 0011
D	1000100	11110	1100 0100
0	0110000	11110	1111 0000
9	0111001	10110	1111 1001
8	0111000	00110	1111 1000
7	0110111	01010	1111 0111
?	0111111	01101	0110 1111
=	0111101	11011	0111 1110
%	0100101	11111	0110 1100
Return	0001101	11000	0000 1101
Space	0000010	00001	0100 0000

Figure 10-6   Binary Character Codes

The codes used in datacom networks are all made up of binary digits or bits. The more bits used per character, the more characters can be represented. ASCII and EBCDIC both represent all required characters and control codes (such as the carriage return). But Baudot code only gives capital letters—and must use a shift signal to change from letters to numbers and back.

national Telephone and Telegraph, which is affiliated with the United Nations. Baudot code, which represents each of its characters with 5 data bits, is used primarily for telex transmissions, most of which now pass through computers. This code was named after French telegraphy pioneer J.M.E. Baudot, the same person commemorated in the term **baud.**

EBCDIC.   Another data transmission code used by many computer systems is **EBCDIC** (pronounced ebb-SEE-dick), which is short for Extended Binary Coded Decimal Interchange Code. Developed by IBM, EBCDIC uses 8 bits to represent each symbol. Because it uses more bits, EBCDIC can represent more characters than ASCII. The ability to represent extra characters is important for international communication using several alphabets.

INTERCHANGE RULES

Data transmissions can be either one way or two way, regardless of the media being used. Radio and television broadcasts use **simplex** transmissions, which carry signals only one way—from sender to receiver. Simplex transmission is inadequate for most datacom applications, however. The reason is that, at the least, sending devices need feedback from the receiving devices in order to check for errors, as will be described later in this section. Therefore, data communications generally use **duplex,** or two-way, transmissions. This two-way flow of data can be either full-duplex or half-duplex.

Half-duplex.   In **half-duplex** transmissions, data travels in both directions, but in only one direction at a time. A citizen's band radio, on which you push a button to talk and release it to listen, is half-duplex equipment. Ask-and-wait data communications, such as credit card checks, also use half-duplex transmissions. As you can see in Figure 10-7, they make use of less wire or a narrower microwave band than do full-duplex transmissions.

Full-duplex. **Full-duplex** transmissions carry signals in both directions simultaneously. Telephone service on twisted pairs is an example of full-duplex transmission: you and the person you have called can both talk at once. Most datacom systems use this more expensive but faster method.

ERROR DETECTION

Even when agreement between the sending and receiving computers has been achieved in all the ways described so far—on the speed, the mode, the code, and the type of information flow—errors can creep in. One reason already mentioned is transmission noise. The relays on analog lines strengthen the signal, but if distortion has occurred, they will strengthen the distortion. Therefore, in most datacom applications, sending devices need feedback from receivers to identify where there have been transmission errors. If the receiver signals an error, the sender

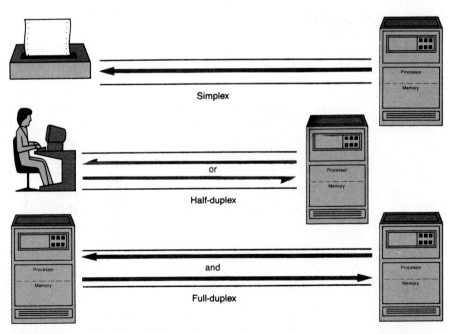

Figure 10-7 Data Interchange

Simplex transmissions are used when information needs to travel in one direction only. For communications between terminals and computers, half-duplex transmissions may be adequate. For large volumes of data, however, such as might be exchanged between mainframe computers, full-duplex transmissions are almost essential.

automatically retransmits the garbled portion of the message until the receiver has the correct version.

One of the most common error detection and correction techniques is the **parity check,** which is used with ASCII code transmissions. The seven bits that ASCII uses to represent a character may add up to an even number: the digits in 1001101 equal the number 4, for example. Or they may total an odd number, as in the binary number 1101110, in which the five ones make a total of five. To make a parity check possible, the sending computer adds an eighth "parity" bit to each character. This bit is selected to make the totals for all characters consistently even (or, in some systems, consistently odd). Thus, an extra zero would be added to 1001101, so that the total remains an even four; but an extra one would be added to 1101110 to make that total an even six. If interference in the

THE HUMAN SIDE

Sending Instructions to Outer Space

When something goes wrong with your office microcomputer, you can either call in a technician or send it to a repair shop. But what happens when equipment goes haywire more than one billion miles away, in the farthest reaches of space? This question has plagued the engineers at the National Aeronautics and Space Administration (NASA) who monitor the Voyager I and II satellites on their 38-year journey through the solar system.

Before the satellites were launched, NASA engineers tried to anticipate as many potential problems as possible. They installed onboard computers that could be programmed from Earth to fix those problems if they arose. The engineers also included redundant, or duplicate, electronics equipment so that if one component failed its twin could take over. When a radio receiver failed on Voyager II just eight months after it was launched, NASA engineers reprogrammed the satellite's computer to switch to a backup receiver.

The Voyager satellites were launched in 1977, equipped with what were then the most sophisticated computers available. In addition to controlling the movements and functions of the satellites, these computers are still gathering and transmitting data. They can detect problems and make corrections on their own, or they can stand by while Earthbound scientists work out a solution. Sometimes correcting a problem takes months or years. NASA engineers once spent three and a half years finding a way to unstick a jammed scanning platform!

If the Voyagers were being built today, their computers would make the 1977 models look primitive. Nevertheless, these computers have performed astonishingly well. For instance, when the satellites flew by Uranus in 1986, NASA reprogrammed the computers to compress their data so that the images transmitted to Earth—through more than 1.8 billion miles of empty space—would be sharper. The reprogramming worked so well that the pictures of Uranus the Voyagers sent back were clearer than those they had transmitted years earlier of the closer planets of Saturn and Jupiter.

In their first 10 years of operation, the computers transmitted four trillion bits of information back to Earth. They are expected to keep up the good work until about 2015, when they will pass out of the solar system and head for the stars.

transmission changes a digit in any byte of data, the total of its digits will no longer be even. The receiving computer sends an error signal to the sending computer, and the byte is retransmitted until it reaches the receiver correctly.

Parity checking isn't foolproof, because it is possible that interference could change *two* digits in a character code. However, that is less likely than a change of only one digit, so parity checking is reasonably reliable.

Another error checking technique, used by the Voyager satellites (see the box on page 274), involved sending each bit three times in a row; if a set of these was not identical, the bit would be retransmitted. This technique is more reliable, but it triples the communication time.

Computers carry out parity checks and other error correction techniques automatically. Your only involvement might be to set your micro system for an odd or even parity check by responding to a prompt from its communications software.

Network topology

Most of this chapter has dealt with communications networks as if they linked only two computer systems. Such networks do exist and are called **point-to-point links.** However, most networks contain many computers, all joined by communications equipment and software. Protocols need to be agreed on for the whole system. The protocol rules must fit the **network topology,** which is the specific arrangement of the computers, terminals, and other elements of a data communications network.

A network's topology determines the flow of data and information within the system. It is affected by many factors: the kinds of equipment the network includes, the nature of the organization and the arrangement of its business systems, and the distance data has to travel within the network. The following sections discuss several types of network topologies along with their advantages and disadvantages.

STAR

A **star network** has lines leading from a central **host computer** to other equipment, which may include only terminals and peripherals such as printers or may include smaller computers as well. Any signal from one piece of equipment to another within a star network must pass through the host computer. The host **polls** the other equipment; that is, it checks to see which equipment is ready to transmit data and to determine the order in which the signals are transmitted.

One kind of information processing system in which star networks are used is **time-sharing,** in which a mainframe host computer allocates time to many users at terminals in different locations. Time-sharing dates back to the early days of computing, when smaller computers were not yet available and few organizations could justify the expense of purchasing their own mainframes. Through time-sharing, even the small

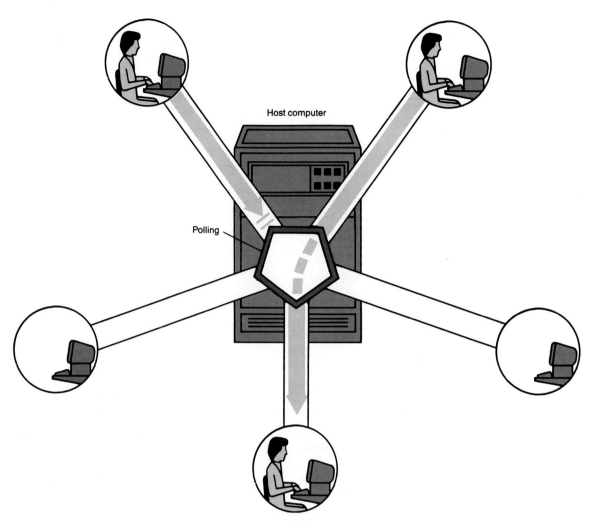

Figure 10-8   A Star Network
Star networks have terminals linked to a host computer. The host polls the terminals one at a time to see which one is ready to transmit a message. No messages, even those to other terminals, can get through without the host's assent.
This topology can provide efficient use of a mainframe computer in a network
where each terminal transmits a low volume of data.

companies could computerize specific business operations, such as payroll
and billing. Time-sharing is still being used today.

One advantage of arranging a computer system in a star network is
that **private branch exchanges (PBXs),** the telephone switching systems used internally by most organizations, are also arranged in this
way. Thus, organizations that configure their computer systems in a star
network may be able to transmit data over their existing telephone wires.

Star networks also have disadvantages, however. Even very large
computers slow down if they have to run several highly complex programs
together, so computer users in star networks sometimes encounter processing delays. Another problem with star networks is that if the host

computer breaks down, the whole system is disabled. You may have had the experience of trying to get information from an organization only to be told, "The computer is down."

BUS

A **bus network** uses a single line of cable or some other transmission medium. This has several **nodes,** or junction units, attached to it. The nodes monitor traffic along the network. Several input and output devices (for example, computers, terminals, printers) may be connected to each node.

When a user sends data by generating a signal in a bus network, only the nodes to which the signal is addressed can receive it. The signal pauses for a tiny fraction of a second in front of each node. A node intercepts those signals that are addressed to it; other signals bypass that node.

One advantage of a bus network is that if one node fails, the other nodes and the users whose terminals are linked to them are not affected.

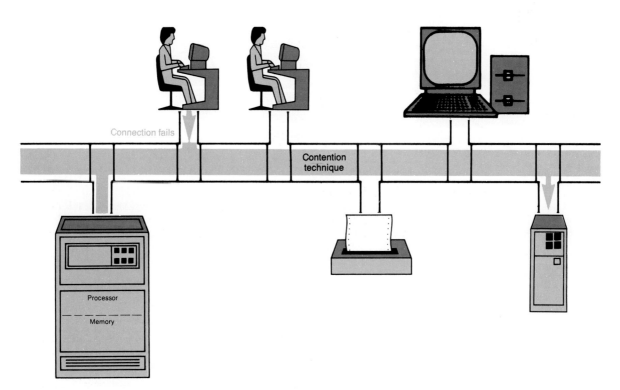

Figure 10-9   A Bus Network
Many bus networks use a system known as contention to prevent messages from clashing. If the line is busy, stations are programmed to wait and try again later. If two stations try simultaneously, they wait for different amounts of time, so the clash will not occur again. Bus networks, also known as multidrop lines, are often used to link several terminals to a mainframe.

Another advantage to this type of interconnection is that expansion of the network is usually easier than with the other topologies.

RING

In a **ring network,** the nodes are linked to each other in a circle instead of individually to a line. If one node fails, the entire network may shut down, although the newest ring networks are designed to avoid this problem.

As in a bus network, signals generated in a ring network are addressed to specific nodes. Rather than pause in front of nodes, however, the signals in a ring network are received by each node. A node holds and processes only those signals that are addressed to it; it retransmits the others to the next node.

A **network controller** monitors traffic on a ring network by polling the nodes to determine if one is ready to transmit. One type of ring network passes an electronic **token,** or distinctive pattern of bits, around

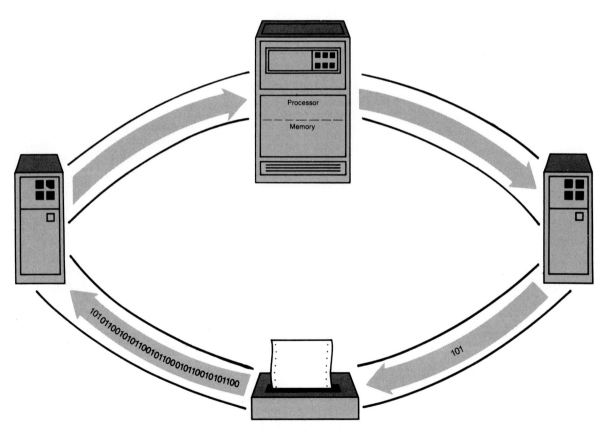

Figure 10-10   A Ring Network
In a ring network, messages pass through each piece of hardware, or station, in turn. The token-passing protocol allows a station to put a message on the network only when it receives the special bit pattern token generated by the central computer. When there are no messages being exchanged, the token is passed around the ring by itself.

Figure 10-11   Bridges
This little device looks very much like an external modem for a computer. But unlike modems, which are used to connect two or more computers, bridges are used to connect two or more *networks* of computers. The networks may be in the same building, or in different states. (Courtesy of Hayes Microcomputer Products, Inc.)

the system with the messages being sent. There is only one token in the network; thus at any one time only one computer can actually use the network. The token is passed so quickly, however, that many messages seem to be sent at once.

BRIDGES, GATEWAYS, AND COMPLEX NETWORKS

Networks can be joined in very complex systems. Ring networks may be connected to each other by high-speed switches called **bridges.** Bridges are used to connect similar networks so that data can pass directly out of one and into another. A network may also be linked to a **gateway,** a computer that can connect it with outside networks of different types, even those using different protocols and incompatible operating systems.

In fact, a complex network may include several kinds of topologies. It could, for example, consist of a host mainframe computer with several rings of minicomputers linked to it in a star pattern as well as minicomputers on a bus network. Just as advances in computer technology have blurred the distinctions between different types of computers, the increasing sophistication of data communications has often made networks difficult to categorize.

Local area and wide area networks

In addition to being described as star, bus, or ring networks, datacom systems are also commonly categorized as either local area networks (LANs) or wide area networks (WANs). LANs and WANs differ in the size of the territory they cover and, consequently, in the transmission media and equipment they use. They also differ in the way that messages are routed from one point to another.

LOCAL AREA NETWORKS

A **local-area network** connects computers and terminals over short distances, usually within a single building. A very simple LAN may use software and ordinary computer cables to link several micros with one printer in a small office. In a more sophisticated LAN, a permanent coaxial cable may be wired into the building walls, and relays may be involved to strengthen the signals.

LANs may be configured as star networks so that they can send and receive data over PBX systems. Or they may be arranged in bus or ring patterns, transmitting data over their own cables. Separate LANs within a building or cluster of buildings may be connected to each other with electronic bridges. Or they may use gateways and modems to connect them to outside telephone lines and larger, external networks.

Over the years, even a small office may have acquired several computers with different operating systems, each of which excels at a particular application. A major advantage of some LANs is their ability to integrate computers that use different operating systems. This allows the use of the most suitable computer for each job without inhibiting the sharing of data.

WIDE AREA NETWORKS

Wide area networks are used for sending data over long distances. The sending and receiving computers in a WAN may be just a few miles apart, or they may be on different continents. External transmission media and equipment for a WAN are frequently provided by a **common carrier,** a telephone company or other organization that provides public communications service. Thus, WANs may send signals on microwave frequencies or cables, depending on the distances the signals must travel. However, large corporations often build their own microwave networks and may even rent or own relay facilities on a communications satellite.

Wide area networks may be used not only for messages among computers but also for teleconferences. In a **teleconference,** several people or groups of people at scattered locations hold a long-distance meeting. A simple teleconference may be nothing more than a conference telephone call involving three or more people. An elaborate teleconference may include video presentations as well as audio, and the participants may use microcomputers, facsimile transmitters, and other electronic equipment to exchange written and graphic information.

ROUTING METHODS

Complex networks, especially wide area networks, carry many different signals and types of messages. Depending partly on the configuration of the network and on the equipment incorporated into it, these signals may reach their destination in several ways.

Nonswitched messages. The simplest method of routing information from one station to another is a point-to-point connection. Point-to-

**Figure 10-12
Teleconferences**
Video teleconferences are becoming more common-place as large businesses recognize the savings in travel time and expenses that they represent. Em-ployees at scattered locations can "meet" electronically without disrupting their regular work routines. (Courtesy of GTE Stanford, Conn.)

point connections are frequently used in small offices to connect computers directly to peripherals. They are also used over long distances when a high volume of information must continually travel between two locations; in this case a line will commonly be leased from the telephone company, or a channel will be dedicated or reserved in a microwave system. Such reservation is expensive, however, and is only efficient if there will be a lot of traffic on the line.

More complex nonswitched connections are made on bus and ring networks, where messages from different stations travel on the same channel, but there is still only a single route that they can follow.

Circuit switching. The nation's telephone system works with a complex system of switching. Switching occurs whenever selections must be made about what route a call is to take. Telephone calls involve switching. When you dial a phone number, the telephone companies' computers determine which wires or microwave links your call should follow, balancing the need for a direct route against the need for connections that are not busy. Thus, a call from Chicago to Washington, D.C., might travel direct, but if lines are busy, it could be switched to travel via St. Louis.

The first and last parts of a call's journey will be on private lines, used only for the callers' and receivers' telephones, respectively. These lines, and the links selected between them, make up a communications circuit that is kept open until the caller hangs up, regardless of whether any signals are being transmitted. Such an arrangement, called **circuit switching,** is expensive, as anyone who has been put on hold during a long-distance call knows only too well.

Message switching. For many computer transmissions, message switching is more economical. **Message switching** is frequently used for one-way transmission of written records; an entire message is stored in a computer's memory and then forwarded as a single block. For this reason message switching systems are also called store and forward systems. Message switching is economical because the lines are never idle. However, it doesn't allow asynchronous, or real time, transmissions, so message switching is not appropriate for interactive uses.

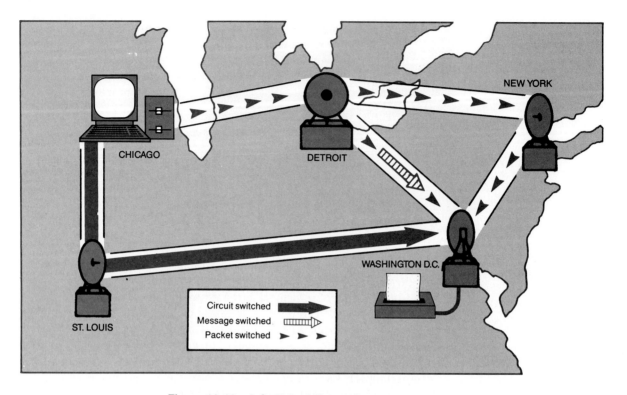

Figure 10-13   A Switched Network
The nation's telephone system is a switched network. It can handle circuit switched
calls, which tie up a whole channel for the duration of a call. It can also carry message switched data, clearing a channel for other calls far more quickly. And the
phone network also carries packet switched calls, with messages broken into many
pieces, perhaps sent by different routes. Packet switching is used by database access services like TYMNET and Telenet, providing very economical use of the
phone system.

Message switching can work reliably in poor conditions and offers
secure communications, so it is often used in military and diplomatic
communications.

Packet switching.   A variant of message switching that works with
interactive data transmission, **packet switching** is superior to both circuit switching and message switching. This procedure stores a complete
message, then breaks it into small packets of data: a new route may be
specified for any packet at any time during a transmission. Packet switching is used by companies that provide access to large information services.
These companies allow consumers to place a local call and then handle
the long-distance information exchange with the database computers by
means of packet switching. This keeps costs as low as possible.

The challenge of network design is to plan datacom systems that are
as economical and error free as possible. The user organization's priorities
must be taken into account because there is such a wide variety of switching methods, network topologies, and datacom system components.

SUMMARY

■ Few large organizations today use only one computer. Most have several computers of varying types to handle their information processing needs. These computers are usually linked in data communications networks, through which data flows from one machine to another.

■ Datacom signals can travel along cables or through the air. Media include twisted-pair wiring, coaxial cable, microwave frequencies, and fiber optics.

■ On all transmission media, data signals deteriorate to some extent over distances. Networks, therefore, include relays that amplify or repeat signals along the way. Telephone relays are intended for voice transmission; therefore, computer signals may need to be changed to analog form using different types of modems.

■ Multiplexing allows one medium to carry many transmissions at the same time. Broadband media, such as coaxial cables, use frequency-division multiplexing. Baseband media must use time-division multiplexing. Multiplexors may be included in larger computer devices called front-end processors.

■ A protocol, or set of communication rules, must be agreed on before computers can communicate. Protocols govern many variables, including transmission speed, transmission mode, character code, information flow, and error checking.

■ The topology of a network depends on many factors, including the types of computers involved and the distances data must travel. Networks may use star configurations, bus configurations, ring configurations, or combinations of those arrangements.

■ Networks are generally categorized as either local area networks (LANs), for data communications within a building or cluster of buildings, or wide area networks (WANs), for longer-distance data communications. Through gateways and other devices, LANs can be connected to a WAN.

■ Data messages are routed in several ways in order to reach their destinations. The methods include nonswitched techniques as well as circuit switching, message switching, and packet switching.

TERMS FOR REVIEW

data communications networks	multiplexors	point-to-point links
	bandwidth	network topology
	broadband	star network
datacom networks	baseband	host computer
shared systems	frequency-division multiplexing	polls
download		time-sharing
telecommunications	time-division multiplexing	private branch exchanges (PBXs)
telecom		
transmission media	front-end processor	bus network

open pairs	communications	nodes
noise	protocol	ring network
twisted pairs	asynchronous	network controller
coaxial cable	real-time computing	token
microwaves	synchronous	bridges
fiber optics	character codes	gateway
baud rate	ASCII	local area network
relays	Baudot code	wide area network
analog	EBCDIC	common carrier
modems	simplex	teleconference
acoustic coupler	duplex	circuit switching
external modems	half-duplex	message switching
internal modems	full-duplex	packet switching
multiplexing	parity check	

TERMINOLOGY CHECK

For each definition below, choose the correct term or terms from the list of Terms for Review.

1. Standard transmission code for communications that assigns a 7-bit binary sequence to represent 128 different letter, numeral, and other symbols. *ASC II*

2. Type of wiring commonly used for local telephone service, able to carry digital signals with the help of a modem. ~~Coaxial cable~~ *Twisted pairs*

3. Variant of message switching that stores a complete message, but breaks it into separate parts for transmission. *Packet switching*

4. Description of transmission speed, usually given in bits per second. *buad rate*

5. Group of computers and terminals linked together over a short distance, usually within a single building. *Local area network*

6. Computer that connects a network with outside networks and devices of different types. *gate way*

7. Describes wires and other media that can carry many message-carrying channels simultaneously. *board band*

8. Why are error detection protocols important? *protocol*

9. Describe three types of network topologies.

10. What are the advantages and disadvantages of each type of network?

11. What criteria are used to differentiate LANs and WANs?

12. What features and advantages characterize a LAN?

13. What features and advantages characterize a WAN?

14. Identify network types that are not likely to involve switching techniques.

15. What types of switching are used in datacom? Explain them.

**INFORMATION
CHECK**

1. List several transmission media. Discuss the advantages and disadvantages of each.

2. Why are modems necessary for data communications by telephone?

3. Identify two methods of multiplexing, and explain why multiplexing is an efficient technique for data communications.

4. In larger systems, what equipment usually prepares signals for data communications?

5. Identify five protocol decisions that must be coordinated in order to accomplish successful data communications.

6. What feature makes synchronous communications similar in style to batch processing?

7. Data transmissions can be one-way or two-way. Identify and describe two types of two-way transmissions frequently used.

8. Set of decisions that must be agreed upon if a data exchange is to take place successfully.

9. Type of modem that generates an audible signal that feeds into a standard phone receiver.

10. Network configuration that connects computers and other units together in a single line.

**PROJECTS AND
PROBLEMS**

1. Suppose you are a sales representative for a national paper manufacturer headquartered in another part of the country. You must travel to five customers daily, taking new orders and checking on inventory. In addition, you successfully open at least 10 new customer accounts each week. By the end of the week, you've accumulated lots of information that must get to the national accounting and shipping departments immediately. In the past, you've had to telephone or mail in the information. Neither method has been satisfactory—too many inaccuracies and too slow.

   You want to convince the regional sales manager that a data communications network would improve accuracy, speed up order processing, and shorten the billing cycle. Write a memo to the manager explaining how you would collect, transmit, and store the data for orders, new account information, and shipping.

2. Visit a business in your town that routinely transmits data to other offices. Write a report that describes its data communications network.

3. Visit a computer store or a computer trade show. Find out what technological advances have been made in improving the reliability of data communications. Prepare an oral report for your class. Use brochures and pamphlets to illustrate your report.

PART FOUR

DESIGNING SYSTEMS FOR MANAGING INFORMATION

11

Information systems and information centers

Parts Two and Three of this book have discussed the software and hardware that make up computer systems. However, as you learned in Part One, organizations consist not just of computer systems but of information systems. A computer system is but one part of an information system, which also includes people.

Hardware and software are valuable to an organization only when they do something worthwhile for a user. They must perform functions that help the people within the organization to accomplish their goals. Spreadsheet software in a microcomputer is useless by itself. But add a set of templates specifically designed for the organization's financial reporting procedures and a team of people who know how to use the software, and you have a financial reporting system for the organization.

This financial reporting system could be improved in several ways—by purchasing a faster computer that will run the same software, by developing a new set of templates, or by purchasing new and more sophisticated software. The system could also be improved by hiring more data entry personnel or new accounting professionals with technical training. But if any of the three key elements—software, hardware, or people—is missing, the system cannot function. These three elements constitute the basis of a computerized information system, as described in Chapter 2.

Part Four of this book continues and expands the discussion of information systems. Chapter 11 examines some information systems in depth, exploring how they work together and how they are managed and maintained. Chapter 12 presents the process of systems analysis and design and explains how feedback is used to adjust systems so that they better fulfill their goals, including cost-effectiveness. Finally, Chapter 13 investigates the important question of how to ensure the best fit between the machines and their human users—a subject called ergonomics.

This chapter begins a detailed study of information systems. In general, the word *system* will be used to refer to computerized information systems unless otherwise specified. You will examine how general-purpose software and special-purpose packages fit together with varying types of computers into an overall organizational environment. What kinds of information systems exist in an organization? How do computers support these systems? Who makes sure that they are running correctly? Who helps users when they need advice? Who identifies weaknesses in systems or recognizes when they can be improved? What criteria can be used in judging a system's effectiveness?

After you have completed this chapter, you should be able to:

- describe how information systems work together to fulfill the multiple needs of an organization

- list and explain some concerns of managers about the systems for which they are responsible

- outline three approaches to information management

- describe the purpose and typical functions of an information center

- list and explain major criteria for evaluating information systems

The importance of information systems

Information has always been an important resource for organizations. Even the most primitive operations keep records, such as data on the money they spend and the money they receive from sales. The Internal Revenue Service (IRS) requires that every business keep records, and you still hear stories about small entrepreneurs who visit the IRS with their papers in old shoe boxes. Most organizations, of course, maintain records in a more systematic way—in file cabinets, file rooms, and fireproof vaults—and have done so for many years. These records include copies of correspondence, contracts, bills of sale, purchase orders, and many other important pieces of information that are valuable to the organization—application forms, time sheets, and more.

People in an organization regularly need to consult the information in such records. A purchasing agent may need to check specific facts, such as how much was paid for a particular item when it was last ordered. A manager may need to identify recent trends—has employee overtime increased during the past six months? The company president may need to make predictions about the future based on what has happened in the past; for example, at current prices, will the company still make enough profit if demand drops off as it did three years ago?

Information about the past helps an organization answer many questions. But storing and using this information cause problems. The longer a company is in business, the more information it accumulates. The more

Figure 11-1   Executive Level Information Systems
Use of information systems is not confined to office workers and their supervisors. Today's systems provide a wide range of data at all levels of an organization. Here a high level executive and his assistant are using a computer for forecasting sales trends. (Courtesy of International Business Machines Corporation)

information is on file, the longer it takes to find specific information. There is also a greater chance for confusion caused by misfiling. And there is always the need for more space to store information.

A computer system provides some solutions to these problems. As you have seen, a computer system can store huge amounts of information in a small amount of space, and it enables people to find specific information quickly and manipulate it accurately.

Information systems at work

To understand in more detail how information systems work, consider the operation of a modern mail-order company—Executive Look. This company buys a variety of clothes and accessories and keeps them as inventory in a central warehouse. It informs the public of its offerings by direct mail, sending out fliers and catalogs; then it processes the orders it receives and sends merchandise to customers all over the country and abroad.

The company relies on accurate and up-to-date information, and it uses computers to store and access this information. Two important records are a list of all items in inventory and a mailing list of people who receive catalogs. Both of these lists are stored as databases, which are used continuously by people working in several parts of the company. The inventory list must be adjusted whenever a new shipment of goods arrives and whenever items are sold. The mailing list must also be adjusted repeatedly, both in response to address changes and as a result of actual orders.

The remainder of this section describes three important information systems at Executive Look and explains how they use these databases. The first is the catalog production system, which produces the selling documents for mailing to customers. The second is the mailing system,

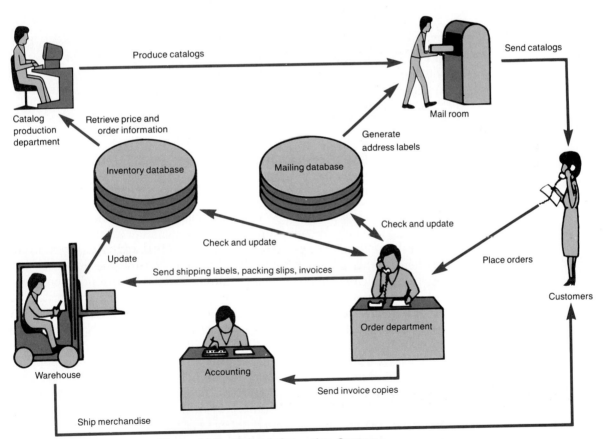

Figure 11-2 Using Information Systems
This diagram shows how information workers in different departments use Executive Look's inventory and mailing databases. The DBs help them to get product information to customers and to take and fill the customers' orders.

which handles the mailings themselves. And the third is the order processing and fulfillment system, which receives orders by mail and phone and makes sure that the merchandise is sent. Clearly, there are many other systems at Executive Look—purchasing and accounting, for example. But for now the focus will be on just these three.

THE CATALOG PRODUCTION SYSTEM

Preparing a catalog—or even a flier—involves a great deal of work. At Executive Look, the office workers, writers, editors, designers, and managers in the catalog production system use several types of software on a variety of computers and peripherals to publish their documents. They use the inventory database to get information about order numbers and prices and word processing software to prepare the catalog text. In addition, the designers create page layouts with desktop publishing software, deciding how the text and pictures will be arranged on each page.

THE MAILING SYSTEM

The mailing system is simpler. The mailing list database is used to generate mailing labels, which are sorted by zip code and sometimes by addressee type (such as only those who have ordered previously). Mail room workers attach the labels to catalogs and put the catalogs in the mail. The mailing list is updated by data entry clerks in the order processing and fulfillment system as they process orders.

THE ORDER PROCESSING AND FULFILLMENT SYSTEM

Order processing and fulfillment is one of the largest systems at Executive Look. It involves many steps and cross-checks. First, a clerk working at a terminal receives an order and checks the customer's name and address by accessing the mailing database. He or she makes additions, corrections, or deletions as appropriate. If this is the first time the customer has ordered, the clerk adds a customer number to the mailing database.

Next, the inventory database is consulted to make sure the order can be filled. If a product is not available, the clerk begins a back-order procedure to notify the customer that the order will be shipped as soon as possible. If the product *is* available, the clerk uses the computer system to generate a shipping label, an invoice, and warehouse packing slips. At the warehouse, workers locate the product (using a computer system), pack it, and mail it. The inventory database is automatically updated to reflect the shipment. And appropriate entries are made into a customer database, using the customer number recorded on the mailing list.

OTHER SYSTEMS

Data about orders is shared with other systems as well. For example, a record of each sale is passed from the order processing system to the

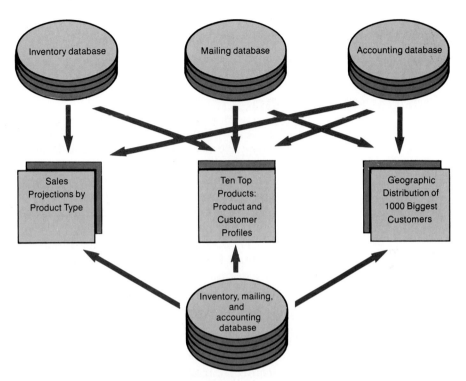

Figure 11-3 Single and Multiple Systems
Executive Look managers who need to prepare reports can draw information from the three databases shown at the top of the diagram. Their tasks would be simplified if Executive Look had a single comprehensive database, as shown at the bottom.

accounting system. The accounting system monitors the cost of purchasing more products for inventory. It also keeps track of payments received from customers, payments that are due and overdue, and other important financial data, including the payroll and the "bottom line," the company's net profit or loss.

To keep the same up-to-date information available throughout the company, a communications network is used to transmit information among the various databases and the information systems in different departments. Thus, accounting's record of sales will match inventory's record of products shipped, and the addresses on the mailing list will match those in the customer database.

The individual departments work together as a unified, overall system so that the company functions profitably and grows. At Executive Look, the various information systems have been integrated into one computerized system. This overall system is complex; it includes minicomputers, microcomputers, terminals, and other peripherals in different locations, all linked in a communications network. The same computer may be used by several departments; one worker may use several computers; one piece of software may be used for a variety of tasks. To understand fully how computers help the organization to accomplish its goals, you need to view the organization as one large, complicated system, comprising various related subsystems.

The tasks of management

Ensuring that the subsystems of an organization work well—and work well with each other—is the responsibility of management. Management tasks are distributed throughout an organization. Top management monitors the performance of the organization as a whole, making decisions that shape its overall policies. Responsibility for the different parts of the organization lies with middle managers, who oversee groups of departments or information systems, and with the managers of the individual information systems. These department managers have four major tasks: maintaining the information systems, ensuring that they operate effectively, coordinating the systems, and looking for ways to improve them.

MAINTAINING THE SYSTEM

An important part of a department manager's job is to supervise the workers in the system for which he or she is responsible. Are employees performing their work, are they doing it correctly, and are they satisfied with their responsibilities? A satisfied worker is usually a more productive worker. A good manager realizes that the human factor is the most critical component of any system. Without it, the system will fail.

If an employee is out sick or has left for some reason, it is the manager who ensures that the necessary work continues. Someone else must take over the job—someone who may need to be trained. Assigning people to jobs and seeing that they are trained are important parts of keeping a system functioning.

The manager of an information system also makes sure that equipment remains operational. Schedules for routine service on equipment must be observed to minimize the risks of a breakdown. If a component does fail, repair technicians must be called in quickly and alternative arrangements made until the equipment works again.

A lack of supplies could also cause a system to stop working. A printer may run out of paper, or it may need a new ribbon. There must be an adequate supply of diskettes. Though a manager may delegate the task of keeping supplies on hand, the task is ultimately his or her responsibility—one that is crucial to running and maintaining the system.

CONTROLLING THE SYSTEM

A manager also needs to control the system's effectiveness. Is time being used productively? Is the quality of work adequate? How can effectiveness be measured? At Executive Look, for example, the mailing list manager knows how many catalogs are returned undelivered, as a check on the procedure for keeping the list up-to-date. A supervisor of word processing might want to know the speed and error rates of a group of operators. Is

Figures 11-4   Using Computers to Manage Work

Managers use computer information systems in many ways. They use the system to control workflow and perform administrative tasks (top left). They work with other managers to ensure cooperation among departments (above). Managers also train and assist their staffs in the use of the system (left). (Courtesy of TWA, Tom Hollyman/J. P. Morgan & Company, and Xerox Corporation)

their productivity improving? Are there problem areas? A manager needs this kind of information to keep a system productive and to deliver the best possible results for the money being spent.

ENSURING COOPERATION BETWEEN SYSTEMS

Another major concern of management is to make sure that systems work together efficiently. Are different systems sharing resources well? For example, if the monthly accounting and mailing list updates each need the full power of a central computer for two hours, a manager must coordinate the schedules of the accounting department and the mailing list group and determine who goes first. A job that will tie up a major computer for several hours can be scheduled to run overnight, when there is less demand for computer time.

UPDATING AND IMPROVING THE SYSTEM

A fourth area that a manager must consider is how an information system can be improved. Would changes in the system add to the overall productivity of the organization? This is part of the systems analysis and design process, which is the focus of the next chapter, but improvements are a concern of managers as well as systems analysts. Clerical workers, too, should be concerned about improvements; they will gain job satisfaction and sometimes bonuses if they suggest improvements that are actually made in a system.

The structure of information management

The aforementioned tasks are part of the management of any system; their application to information systems is relatively recent. The importance of information as a resource began to be recognized in the early 1970s, and since then methods of managing it have been revolutionized by changes in technology. As a result, there is no standard way of structuring the management of information. Organizations usually develop their own information management structures, based partly on their needs, partly on their history, and partly on the advice of management experts.

To provide some idea of the range of approaches used, here are three typical structures—an informal management approach that might be adopted by a small company new to computers; a centralized approach that might exist in a traditional organization that began to use computers in the early 1960s; and an integrated approach that reflects more recent management theory.

SMALL BUSINESS—AN INFORMAL APPROACH

In a small business that is planning to use computers, top management may ask an employee with some knowledge of computers to research the purchase of the company's first computer system for word processing. In fact, the employee, who may not have had previous management experience, may even be given a budget and the authority to buy a system. If this happened to you, you would be taking on a major management responsibility—deciding how best to spend the organization's money. And your responsibility would probably not stop there. You might also be put in charge of installing the system, mastering its operation, and using it for tasks such as generating form letters and envelopes for mass mailing. You would probably be asked to train fellow workers so that, if you call in sick, need help with a heavy workload, or get a promotion, someone will be able to take your place.

When the company's demands on the system are not excessive, this informal approach, relying on a single computer "expert," may work suc-

Figure 11-5 Informal Information Systems
Small businesses and small offices within larger organizations may take an informal approach toward information management. Employees with a special interest in computer systems often take on the roles of trainer, coach, and problem-solver in relation to their fellow workers. (Courtesy of International Business Machines Corporation)

cessfully for a time. However, requiring a nonmanagement worker to make many management decisions is usually a mistake, because either the work or the management will suffer. Typically, the worker does not have the same understanding of an organization's structure and goals that a manager has. And having the worker gather the information needed to make a decision takes time away from the worker's primary tasks. Also, if the organization continues to grow, more computer expertise will be needed than can be provided by a self-taught office worker, or even an office worker with a few courses in managing information. Thus it is preferable that upper executives take responsibility for understanding a system, directing its use, and planning its growth.

A LARGE TRADITIONAL COMPANY— CENTRALIZED DP AND MIS

Until the microcomputer put computing power on office desks, most large companies used only centralized mainframe computers for their data processing. These computers were often a part of the accounting operation. Centralized mainframes were very successful in the 1970s. Though other departments invested in smaller, specialized systems such as dedicated word processors, the major numerical analyses that managers needed— financial reports, sales reports, inventory reports, and the like—were all produced by the centralized data processing (DP) system. The system was

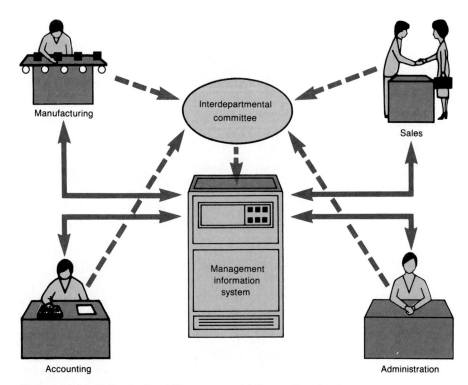

Figure 11-6 A Centralized Management Information System

A centralized MIS controls the flow of information among departments, each of which also has its own internal information systems. The solid lines show the flow of information in such an arrangement—the broken lines indicate feedback from the departments.

run by a department known as DP or MIS (for management information systems). Information produced was consistent and reliable, because it came from a single source. This approach is sometimes referred to as the **corporate solution.**

The disadvantage was that some aspects of the system were very slow. Though the computers themselves were fast, the printing and distribution of reports took time. It also took a long time for programmers to develop the specialized software that would produce the reports. There could easily be a delay of a year or more between a request for a particular type of report and the first issue of that report.

This time frame was tolerable as long as there were no alternatives. However, as managers at all levels realized how quickly microcomputers could provide reports, they began to expect similar capabilities from their mainframe departments. Many managers have bought micros and can now process their own data. As a result, there is often friction between traditional MIS/DP departments and microcomputer users: the mainframe specialists feel that microcomputers allow information to be used or altered carelessly, and the microcomputer users look at MIS/DP controls as a straightjacket on their activities.

In organizations that maintain this traditional MIS/DP structure, each department is commonly responsible for managing its own internal information systems, but the MIS/DP group sees to processing and regulating information that must move from department to department. Frequently, a committee of representatives from each department works out information resource problems for the company as a whole. Training is handled within each department, as is the acquisition of software and hardware. This approach is often called the **departmental solution.**

IRM—AN INTEGRATED APPROACH

A third approach to information management is gaining support from forward-looking organizations and management experts: the integrated or **information resource management (IRM)** approach. With IRM, responsibility for management of all information resources is centralized in one department—usually MIS—but the resources themselves are dis-

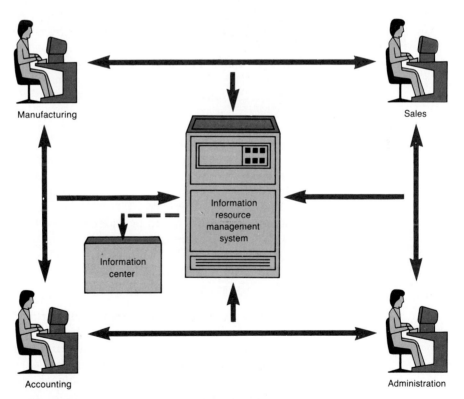

Figure 11-7   An Information Resource Management System
In an IRM system, the MIS group is responsible for effective use of information processing resources in all departments. An information center operated by MIS can provide all workers with help in using or purchasing computer resources. No longer dependent on MIS for all information, department managers can gain immediate access to many kinds of data for developing their reports.

tributed throughout the organization. Information resources include the telecommunications system, the records management system, the reproduction, graphics, and publishing systems, and all computer systems: end user, departmental, and corporate. The major function of IRM specialists is to ensure the most effective use of these resources by the employees.

In the days of mainframe dominance, the only way for employees to use the computer for solving problems was through the DP department. Software development was a specialized task, requiring highly skilled programmers. But recent advances in software have placed more power in the hands of the users. Users can now either buy software for a particular task or develop a software tool, such as a spreadsheet, without specialized programming help. The result is usually a great saving in time and money and more productive use of information resources.

Of course, giving computing power to users throughout the organization could confuse the lines of communication. What if the legal department needs to use the customer service department's mailing list? Who makes sure that the computer systems that handle the catalog mailing list can communicate with the systems that handle order processing? Standards for compatibility of software and hardware, including communications between systems, are necessary for any organization to function smoothly. Developing standards is one task of the information resource management team, which may be headed by a **chief information officer (CIO).** The CIO is usually a member of top management with a place on the executive board, which determines overall company policy.

The IRM staff is more often responsible for making recommendations about equipment purchases than for buying and running systems. It researches what software and hardware are compatible and provides the individual departments with lists of recommended products. The departments then take the step of actually selecting computers appropriate to their needs, choosing software that fits their particular tasks, and processing their own data. The IRM group also frequently runs an **information center,** which provides many other services on a centralized basis—including training and systems analysis and development.

The information center

The information center is an important part of the IRM approach. Information centers are not limited to companies that adopt IRM: they are occasionally set up in organizations that use more traditional approaches to information management. However, the goal of any information center is to maximize the effective use of people who use computing facilities in an organization.

The rapid pace of developments in computer system design—both hardware and software—puts considerable pressure on managers and office workers alike. Managers must stay informed about current system capabilities in case new products could be used in their departments. Workers need to master current systems quickly and explore the full capabilities of the software they use.

Figure 11-8 Formal Training on Information Systems

Employees often undergo formal training in the use of computer systems, especially after the introduction of a new system or application. Here an instructor is helping employees master a new software application in a specially equipped classroom. (Courtesy of International Business Machines Corporation)

In an information center, people and resources are available to make training and research as painless, and efficient, as possible. The center may include classrooms and a library; often there are facilities for testing and trying out new equipment. A variety of experts are based in the information center to help employees use existing systems and develop new systems.

CLASSROOMS

A well-equipped information center will feature one or more classrooms, which often resemble school language labs. Each classroom has several computer workstations for training employees on the hardware and software they'll use on the job. The information center employs experts in the use of each of the organization's computer systems. These experts lead classes that cover the skills needed to use the systems successfully.

LIBRARY FACILITIES

The information center will often maintain a library of computer-related magazines and books, along with manuals for the software used by the company. Here employees can look up details about software they use infrequently or learn about new techniques or tools that might improve productivity. An employee who wants a new, more responsible job might take out a book to learn some of the needed skills before applying for the new assignment, to demonstrate serious interest. And managers can quickly find out about the latest developments in software and hardware that might be useful to their own departments.

A TESTING CENTER

Another part of an information center may be a testing lab, for evaluating new hardware and software as well as troubleshooting existing systems. Before a new system is installed in the organization, it is often assembled and tested by the information center to make sure it works as expected. If problems occur, it is better to solve them during testing in the information center than to risk losing information or business through faulty systems on the actual job.

The testing lab also checks for compatibility, or whether that particular hardware and software can work and communicate with the systems already in use. Hardware and software that prove compatible with existing systems are put on an approved list. In many organizations, the proposed purchase of new hardware or software must be reviewed by the information center to head off compatibility problems in the future.

EXPERT ADVICE

The experts who work in the information center are often drawn from throughout the organization. The most efficient word processing operator in the organization might be asked to join the information center to share his or her expertise with other word processing users. Someone who is very proficient in using a spreadsheet might be asked to join the staff and help others understand this tool. Professional trainers might be hired to explain organizational policies and procedures. Data processing and office automation technicians and professionals, often with a strong managerial background, would likely be hired to staff the testing laboratory.

Information center staff members provide expertise for a whole range of problems and needs. When a department wants to change the way it handles information, the department manager will meet with the information center's professionals, outline the department's needs, and discuss how the problem can be solved most effectively. When a new employee needs to learn how to use a particular workstation, he or she will be told to sign up for the appropriate course at the information center. When an existing system has to be upgraded to meet increasing demand on its resources, the information center will offer help.

Aside from teaching classes, testing systems, and offering consulting help, members of the information center staff must devote time to continuing their own education. They must keep up with new products and technological advances in both the computer field and the management field to make sure their company is purchasing high-quality hardware and software and using it effectively and productively.

Figure 11-9 Consulting the Experts
Information centers often provide one-on-one coaching for employees with specific needs. Here a middle-level manager, who already has considerable computer expertise, is updating his skills with the assistance of an information center staff member. (Courtesy of Xerox Corporation)

What makes a good system?

Because of the importance of information systems to an organization, the ability to judge their effectiveness is vital. How can an information manager, or an information worker, know when a system is failing to perform adequately? There is a constant pressure to upgrade, to improve, to be up-to-date. But changes cost money. Organizations need specific points on which to evaluate their systems and determine what changes, if any, are needed.

Systems can be measured on several points, beyond whether or not they perform the required tasks. Speed is a consideration, as is accuracy. Flexibility and expandability may be important. Compatibility with other systems could be crucial. Convenience to the user is usually desirable, as is security. And probably more influential than all the others is cost-effectiveness—is the system paying for itself in money saved or money earned?

SPEED

Perhaps the most obvious consideration when looking at a system is the speed with which information can be made available to the overall organization. In general, computers are valued because they are fast. An order processing system that takes a half-hour to confirm a telephone order is not going to help business, especially if the customer needs to stay on the phone the entire time. A mailing list system that takes two months to update will mean wasted effort if a catalog comes out every month. A customer service department that takes six months to reply to a complaint isn't going to make customers eager to do more business with the company.

Speed is more important to some applications than to others, of course. Having air-traffic-control computers get five minutes behind on tracking planes is far worse than having the monthly report on consumption of

THE HUMAN SIDE
Going to Work in an Information Center

As he drove to work, Glen Fairley thought about his upcoming day. Like every other day since he had become director of the Information Resource Center (IRC) at Manstrom-Pfieffer, Inc., it would be busy.

As soon as he got into the office, he had to meet with his boss, Maureen Stevenson, chief information officer at Manstrom-Pfieffer, to go over his plans for a new addition to the IRC's Training Center. The center already had three classrooms, each with 10 workstations, but there was no place for training many employees. Next year the Agricultural Products Division (Ag) would begin using a new inventory system. Hundreds of people would need to be trained for the Ag system as soon as it was ready.

This made him think about Joe Danielson. Joe headed the IRC team of system analysts who were designing the new Ag system. Joe had asked Glen to hire some outside consultants. Joe and his group were working as hard as they could, and the budget for the project could probably be stretched to accommodate two consultants. Glen would talk to Joe this afternoon and authorize the consultants.

It would not be as easy to solve Mary Snowden's problem, however. Mary managed the software training classes in the IRC, and she had just been asked to train seven new product managers from the chemical products division in the use of Lotus 1-2-3 software. But she did not have any additional trainers for this three-day project, and Glen knew he could not hire any outside help for her. Mary would just have to conduct the sessions herself.

Perhaps when Mary conducted the sessions on Lotus she could also include one of the new software packages that allows notes to be incorporated into Lotus spreadsheets. Four competitive packages of this type were being evaluated in the testing center; if one of them was approved for use, it would make sense for Mary to start including it in her training procedures.

The testing center was also evaluating a new workstation that was advertised as being completely compatible with the workstations currently in use. Glen recalled seeing a magazine article about the workstation. He made a mental note that before he went home he would ask Bob Ralston, manager of the IRC's library, to find the article for him.

As he pulled into the parking lot, Glen realized that he had just reviewed each of his departments. Each was contributing to the IRC's overall job of helping Manstrom-Pfieffer maximize its use of computer facilities. Yes, Glen thought, it would be busy today—but it would be productive.

Figure 11-10   Productivity Through System Speed
Applications such as graphics and word processing make particular demands on a computer system's speed. When you are creating a diagram, or a written document, it is very important that you see the effects of your work immediately. Even small delays could destroy your concentration. (Courtesy of International Business Machines Corporation)

coffee, tea, and milk delayed an hour. For many applications, in fact, additional speed may be totally unnecessary.

ACCURACY

Another important criterion is the accuracy of the information. Having inaccurate information is usually worse than having no information at all; with no information at all, you are likely to ask questions that can help you. Inaccurate information may result when data from different systems is inconsistent. It might also result from errors during data entry.

Inconsistent data.   If the inventory and order processing systems at Executive Look don't have the same up-to-date information, order clerks will be telling customers that products are out of stock when they are not or in stock when they are out of stock. If the accounting, ordering processing, and inventory systems don't adequately communicate with each other, the company may lose track of whether or not it is making a profit, which gets managers very nervous very quickly. Therefore, information systems must be coordinated. Controls are needed to prevent systems from using different versions of the data they share.

Preventing errors at data entry.   A set of controls to keep information accurate and up-to-date is also needed. Suppose an order clerk makes an error, like typing a quantity of 1,000 instead of 100 or billing an order to the account of James T. Smith rather than James R. Smith. If not caught in time, these keyboarding mistakes will create errors in the order processing, accounting, inventory, and mailing list systems. A set of controls is needed to record each transaction, check it for obvious errors, and keep track of its possible impact. For many systems, these controls can be built into the software they use, providing what is called error trapping for data entry. **Error trapping** can alert a user to an obvious mistake, such as entering a number where a word is required.

FLEXIBILITY AND EXPANDABILITY

In time, the needs of an organization change. Imagine that Executive Look decides to hold a holiday sale, with an automatic 10 percent discount

Figure 11-11   Systems Designed for Future Expansion
A good design alllows for flexible use and future expansion. Many systems today include hardware modules that can be rearranged and added to in order to increase the system's capabilities. A business can start out with one or two modules and add to them as necessary. (Courtesy of NCR Corporation)

on all orders received between Thanksgiving and New Year's. One way to effect this change would be to give every clerk a calculator and let the clerk calculate the discount for each order. But this procedure would take a lot of time. And one wrong key press could have surprising results for both the customer and the company. Another way would be to change the program, making the system automatically discount all orders received during this period. An even better way, however, would be to design the software from the very start with the flexibility to create or change a discount by a single menu choice. Flexibility is also valuable in generating reports, where the information or format needed may change because of the company's growth, new tax laws, and the like.

Related to flexibility is expandability. If the organization outgrows its system, will it have to install a new one? Or can faster hardware, more capable software, or additional users be added to the existing system? Sometimes needs change so drastically—going from a system shared by eight people to one shared by 100—that starting from scratch may be the only sensible decision. At other times, especially when a substantial investment has already been made in the existing system, it may make sense to improve it rather than replace it.

COMPATIBILITY

You are already aware that compatibility between systems is a critical need in information resource management. Suppose that the word processing software best suited to sending form letters for the customer service department is not well suited to preparing the legal department's contracts. Ideally, each department should be free to choose the software best suited to its needs. The increased efficiency in using the best tool for the job gives greater cost efficiency overall.

However, there may be times when the two departments wish to share information. For example, a section of a contract may be an important part of customer negotiations. In this case, it would be helpful to communicate the relevant parts of the contract directly from the legal department's computer into the letter being composed, rather than rekeyboard the paragraphs. This can be achieved only if the two word processing packages are compatible.

CONVENIENCE

Another important consideration is how easy or convenient the overall system is to use. An order processing system won't work very well if a clerk has to run down the hall to the computer room to check inventory for each order as it arrives. Nor will a system based on software that requires six months of intensive study before you can use it comfortably. A user-friendly program should be easy both to learn and to use. Note that "easy to learn" and "easy to use" are two different things. Word processing software that gives you many messages about what to do next will be very easy to learn, but the messages may slow down a user who can keyboard 85 words per minute.

SECURITY

A major criterion in evaluating systems is their security—both from accidents and from criminal tampering.

Guarding against accidents. Accidents can occur for many reasons. You have already learned about the dangers of power outages, the importance of saving information regularly, and the need to make backup copies in case a disk is lost or damaged. Many organizations require that data be backed up daily, with the duplicate copy stored in a vault or other safe place. Then, the worst that can happen in case of a power failure is that a day's work may be lost.

STATE OF THE ART

Controlling Productivity and Quality in the Office

Dinah Gelton is the manager of document production at SLF, Inc. With SLF's current word processing software, Dinah is able to get a report of the number of keystrokes entered by each of the specialists. However, this report does not make an allowance for the difficulty of the material to be typed, the condition of the manuscript, or the specialist's accuracy. She is looking for a system that can provide more information—for example, the number of corrections needed per document.

Charles Fried uses computers in a different way to increase the quality of the output of the word processing specialists who work for him. He asks them to keyboard as quickly as they possibly can. He has two specialists type the same document. Then he uses the computer to compare one document with the other. Because it is unlikely that the specialists would make exactly the same mistake in exactly the same place, any mistake would immediately be recognized by the computer. A specialist can then correct the error.

Paula Wagner is a word processing specialist for a large law firm. Because it is very important to keyboard the firm's complicated legal papers correctly, the law firm installed a system that provides an audit trail of its documents. As you learned in the chapter, an audit trail shows exactly what was done to a file, when it was done, and who did it. Using this system, Paula's manager evaluates the job performance of each of the word processing specialists.

There are also programs that provide an audit trail for a spreadsheet. These programs increase the quality of the spreadsheet by producing easy-to-read reports on the contents of all the spreadsheet's cells (including variables, functions, and formulas).

Roger Williams is one of three associate analysts at the First National Bank of Connecticut who uses an audit program to maintain and update spreadsheets containing mortgage information for the bank. Without an audit report, it would be much more difficult for three people to work on the same spreadsheet. Every analyst would tend to do things just a little differently, and before long, the spreadsheet would contain many small inconsistencies and errors that could cost the bank millions of dollars.

Although computers do increase office productivity and quality, they can also cause managers to lose sight of things that cannot be measured quantitatively. Ultimately, a computer is only one management tool among many, to be used humanely and professionally by managers.

Other accidents may be caused by user error or by user ignorance. Instead of pressing the keys that save data on a disk, an operator may press the keys to delete the data. To prevent this kind of error, some software displays prompts asking users for confirmation of such commands. Other software may go ahead and perform the deletion but will hold a temporary copy in a memory buffer, ready to be brought back by a special command if the deletion was not intended. Both these types of software packages are preferable to one that deletes without safeguards.

User ignorance can cause problems if a worker does not fully understand procedures. Several users might need to work with the company's sales figures for forecasting future sales. In the course of their work, it's possible that one user might change the data, then save it in place of the original file. Some safeguard is needed against having altered data saved as the master record of sales. One method is to provide **read-only access** to central data so that users can see and work with information on their micros but cannot change the central record.

Guarding against crime.

Guarding against crime. Innocent mistakes and accidents are one thing, but a well-managed system must also be designed to defeat intentional attempts to defraud the organization or damage its information resources. Occasionally disgruntled or dishonest employees or mischievous computer hobbyists will try to tamper with information either to commit or conceal a crime or to create havoc for the company. One way of protecting the information is with passwords and other security codes built into the software. With this technique, users are assigned individual passwords. They are required to **log on,** or follow a special start-up procedure that includes entering their password.

A related security technique is **encryption,** in which data is scrambled by a special program and then unscrambled only for users who enter

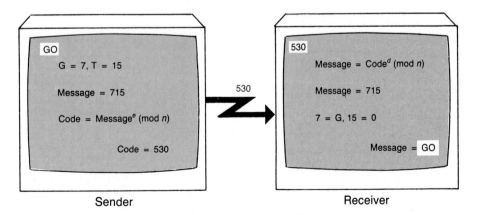

Sender   Receiver

Figure 11-12   Data Encryption
The word *go* is encrypted on the sending computer's monitor screen (left), then decoded by the receiving computer (right). The sending computer applies a secret variable number to each character in the message. These variables are part of a complex mathematical formula that scrambles the message. The receiving computer must apply another, related set of secret variables to unscramble the message.

the required codes. This is particularly effective for protecting transmitted data from wiretapping or other forms of eavesdropping.

As an additional measure, many applications programs provide audit trails. An **audit trail** is a report that shows exactly what was done to a file, when it was done, and which password was used to gain access to the file. Then, if errors or sabotage do occur, management can at least trace the origin of the errors and take steps to prevent recurrences.

COST-EFFECTIVENESS

Finally, of course, a system must be evaluated by the bottom line—is the system worth its cost? Organizations always need to consider costs. A beautifully engineered system that costs more than it's worth isn't very practical. Therefore, the **cost-effectiveness** of the system becomes another important criterion. To keep costs down, an organization may do without some optional features in a system. The function of the system is crucial in determining what features are important. For example, consider speed. An ideal system would respond instantly to any user request. For tasks heavily involving the user (such as word processing), a noticeable delay between the time you press a key and the time the letter shows up on the screen would be unacceptable. But for reporting sales, which requires less keyboarding, a slower response time might be acceptable. When judging a system—and when comparing systems with a view to replacing one with another—speed is a very important factor, but it must be viewed in the context of the system's overall function and cost.

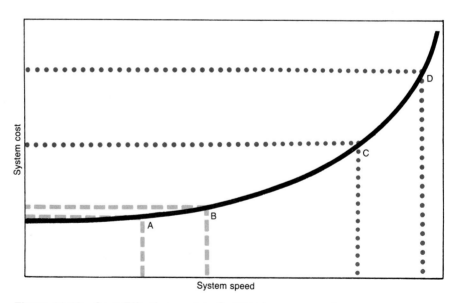

Figure 11-13   Cost-Effectiveness or System Improvements
Managers use graphs such as this one to assess the cost-effectiveness of system improvements. Notice that the speed increase between A and B is relatively inexpensive, but increase in speed between C and D is more costly.

SUMMARY

- As indicated in the introductory chapters of this book, information is an extremely valuable resource to any organization, and computers are the state-of-the-art technology for handling and analyzing it.

- Organizations may differ in the precise details of how they set up and integrate the different information systems that they use. However, the ideal is always to integrate the operation of different systems in order to accomplish the organization's goals in an economical and effective way.

- Managers of information systems are responsible for a wide range of tasks: they must maintain their systems, ensure that the systems are productive, make sure that related systems work well together, and look for ways of improving their systems.

- The importance of information management is increasingly being recognized, but there are a variety of approaches to this task. Small businesses new to computers may leave much decision making to system users. Some larger, traditional organizations adopt a departmental solution, with each department largely taking care of its own needs, and the MIS/DP department controlling systems that must cross departmental lines. The most modern approach is information resource management, which centralizes management of all information resources while the resources themselves are distributed throughout the organization.

- Many key functions of information resource management are performed in the information center, where employees throughout the company can learn to use organizational systems efficiently. The information center also helps different departments to meet their computing needs by evaluating existing systems and developing new ones.

- Effective systems can be identified by their performance on several points. These include speed, accuracy, flexibility, expandability, compatibility with other systems, convenience to the user, security, and cost-effectiveness.

TERMS FOR REVIEW

corporate solution
departmental
    solution
information resource
    management
    (IRM)

chief information
    officer (CIO)
information center
error trapping
read-only access
log on

encryption
audit trail
cost-effectiveness

TERMINOLOGY CHECK

For each definition below, choose the correct term or terms from the list of Terms for Review.

1. A member of top management who heads the information resource team.

2. A safeguard that allows users to see and work with information on their micros but prevents them from changing the central record.

3. A report that shows exactly what was done to a file, when it was done, and which password was used to gain access to the file as a means of tracing the origin of errors or sabotage.

4. The quality of producing enough benefits to justify cost.

5. A place in an organization where employees can go for help in using computers in their jobs, which also provides such services as training and systems analysis and development.

6. An approach to information management in which each of an organization's departments is responsible for managing its own internal information systems and a central MIS/DP staff processes and regulates information that moves from department to department.

7. A built-in control in a computer system that alerts a user to mistakes made in data entry.

8. A security technique that involves scrambling of data by a special program and unscrambling of it only for users who enter the required codes.

9. To follow a special start-up procedure that includes entering a password as a security measure.

10. An approach to information management in which responsibility for management of all information resources is centralized in one department but the resources are distributed throughout the organization.

INFORMATION CHECK

1. In what ways might an information system be improved rather than replaced?

2. What is management's overall responsibility with respect to information systems?

3. What are the four major tasks of information systems managers?

4. What activities are performed to maintain the system?

5. How can managers control an information system?

6. Why is there no one standard structure for organizing information management?

7. How does an organization determine which information management structure it should adopt?

8. What are three typical approaches to organizing information management? What types of organizations are likely to use each of them?

9. Discuss some of the problems a small business may encounter in managing information informally.

10. Describe some of the advantages and limitations of centralized data processing.

11. How did microcomputers affect the relationship between central MIS/DP and other managers?

12. What is the overall function of an IRM team?

13. What are some dangers of putting computing power in the hands of users, and how does the IRM approach handle these problems?

14. Describe several typical activities and features of an information center.

15. List and describe the criteria used to judge the effectiveness of an information system.

PROJECTS AND PROBLEMS

1. Last year, Executive Look realized a substantial profit from its mail order operation. But top management wants to make sure that the company's integrated information system is working as efficiently as possible. Pretend you are a consultant who will be evaluating the system to suggest any areas that might be improved. Use the information about Executive Look and the criteria for what makes a good system. Let your imagination supply any missing details.

   Write a memo to the company president outlining your findings and recommendations.

2. Visit a small company in your area. What kinds of systems does it use to manage information? Write a brief description of your findings.

3. Read a recently published book about managing information systems. How does the author describe the tasks and responsibilities of managers of information systems? Compare that description with the information in Chapter 11. Write a paper outlining the author's views.

4. Visit a company with an information center. Find out the following: What categories of employees run the information center? What is the role of the information center within the organization? What activities are performed by the information center staff? What training and experience did the information center staff members have?

   Share findings with your class. Try to compile profiles of the information centers in your area.

12

The systems development cycle

In the previous chapter, you learned how organizations use and manage computerized information systems to help them accomplish their goals. This chapter discusses how such systems are established and then continually evaluated and developed to reflect the changing needs of organizations.

As organizations change, so do their information system needs. Suppose that an attorney takes in a partner; over the years they expand their practice to include many lawyers. As the firm grows, it gets more bills—from stationers, legal research services, couriers, court reporters, and so on. Before long, the firm is likely to replace its manual bill-paying system with a system better suited to a large volume of transactions—probably a system that uses a microcomputer or minicomputer. As the firm continues to expand, it may eventually outgrow the new system too. For a 50-lawyer firm, it would be inefficient and possibly disastrous to use a bill-paying system designed for a 10-lawyer firm or for one lawyer working alone.

Even if an organization doesn't grow, its systems may change for other reasons. Developments in office technology frequently provide more economical means of accomplishing a business function. Computerized word processing is a good example of this phenomenon. In the 1970s, dedicated word processors cost many thousands of dollars, so most small offices held onto their typewriters. Today, microcomputers and word processing software are much less expensive, and a computerized document processing system is economical for almost any organization that produces more than a few documents a day. An office may be wasting vast amounts of secretarial time, and therefore money, if it has failed to keep its document processing system up-to-date.

Major computerized information systems are established and maintained through what is called the **systems development cycle.** This cycle can be viewed in phases: analyzing the existing system and its problems; defining alternatives for a new system; selecting and refining

314

the new system; getting the new system working; and maintaining and updating the new system. Each of these phases may include several steps, especially for complex systems in large organizations. And because organizations and their systems requirements change, the systems development cycle is continuous. Its phases are repeated over time so that organizations can keep their systems up-to-date and meet their goals as efficiently as possible.

This chapter will discuss systems development in small and large organizations and will detail the phases of the systems development cycle. Note once again that, unless described otherwise, "system" means "computerized information system," which includes hardware, software, and people.

When you have completed this chapter, you should be able to:

- discuss the forces that motivate changes in a system

- discuss how systems evolve in small and large organizations

- describe different options for changing a system

- name and describe the five phases of the systems development cycle

- identify the steps involved in starting the systems development cycle

- list and describe the steps involved in each phase of the systems development cycle

- discuss the roles of computer users in systems development

How systems evolve

Organizations develop information systems, computerized or not, to address needs. The need to pay bills on time is one example. Other needs include the requirement that invoices are sent promptly, that the production department doesn't run out of raw materials, and that managers can get important information when they want it. Of the many kinds of information systems found in organizations today, all were developed after someone identified or anticipated a need.

WHO INITIATES SYSTEMS CHANGES?

Some systems changes originate with employees who believe that new equipment and procedures could help them to do their jobs more effectively. An overburdened project manager may request a microcomputer system that automates tasks such as developing schedules and preparing status reports. Or an administrative assistant might suggest using a mini connected to a remote banking system for transferring funds between accounts and paying bills automatically. In these examples, systems users create pressure for change.

In other cases, pressure comes from an organization's top management. Changes initiated by management are usually part of a long-range plan. For example, the owners of a department store may plan to open branch stores someday. So they decide to install a computerized inventory system that can be expanded to include new stores. Top managers often suggest systems changes as part of an overall effort to expand product lines or services, keep down operating costs, or generally help their organizations to operate more profitably or effectively.

SYSTEMS DEVELOPMENT OPTIONS

Information systems can be changed or brought up-to-date in several ways, whether or not these systems are computerized. As an example, let's take the law firm discussed in the chapter introduction. As the firm expands from 1 lawyer to 10 lawyers and eventually to 50, management can choose from several options in developing an accounting system that keeps up with its needs.

Expanding a manual system. When a manual system is no longer adequate for an organization's needs, one option is to expand the manual system rather than replace it with one that includes computers. The bookkeeper may no longer be able to handle paying the bills along with other duties, but that doesn't mean that the firm must computerize this system. Instead, it could hire an additional bookkeeper, or an administrative assistant to pay the bills and handle other accounting functions.

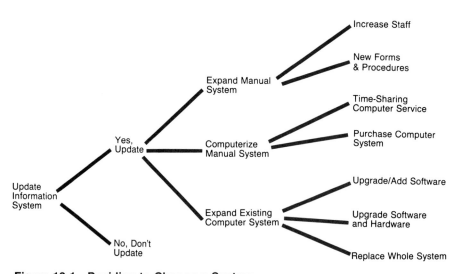

Figure 12-1   Deciding to Change a System
The middle decision, to computerize a manual system, is in many ways the most crucial one for an organization, and many still face it. Increasingly, however, companies are involved in the bottom option—they have already purchased a computer system, but wish to take advantage of new capabilities developed since that time.

Expanding a manual system may also involve new forms and procedures. Perhaps the bookkeeper prepared clients' invoices based on lawyers' haphazard notes, for example. If so, a great deal of time might be saved by developing standard weekly time sheets. These allow the attorneys to indicate quickly and clearly the number of hours they spent on individual clients' cases. It may also be necessary to develop procedures to ensure that attorneys submit the completed time sheets promptly.

Computerizing a manual system. Instead of expanding the manual accounting system, the firm's partners may decide to computerize the system. Purchasing a computer system is only one of several options. Rather than go into debt or reduce its capital, the firm could lease a computer system. Alternatively, it could arrange for a time-sharing computer service to install terminals in the office; accounts could then be processed on a mainframe that also handles jobs for other companies. Selecting from these alternatives requires careful decision making, with sound advice and good research to back it up.

Expanding an existing computer system. Suppose the firm decided to purchase a microcomputer and an accounting software package. This system may be adequate for only a few years. As the firm continues to grow, its computer system will need to be expanded. Expansion may consist of adding software, such as spreadsheet and word processing programs, so the computer can be used for more than one purpose. The firm could also replace its general-purpose accounting software with a program specifically designed for law firms. Finally, the firm might develop or purchase templates for its software. As you have learned, templates are auxiliary programs that make a general-purpose software product such as a spreadsheet usable for specific tasks—for example, cash flow analysis. Modern software packages are in fact beginning to revolutionize systems development, as discussed in the box on the next page.

The firm may add hardware to its computer system, too. New chips or boards could expand the computer's memory and enable it to run more powerful software. A hard disk may also be added to the system, and perhaps a modem and a laser printer. Each of these additions would expand the capabilities of the existing computer system or make it easier to use. The firm's partners might decide that the firm needs more than one computer; they might then purchase or lease additional micros and link them in a network.

By the time the firm has grown to 50 lawyers, a network of micros may no longer be adequate. Once again, the partners must decide whether to replace the system with new equipment and procedures and, if so, whether to lease or purchase new hardware and software.

GUIDING THE CHANGE

When the firm was planning to buy its first microcomputer, the partners may have assigned part of the selection process to one of their office assistants, as suggested in the previous chapter. However, by the time the firm is considering creating links between several microcomputers, it would be wise to hire a consultant. A **consultant** is a person or company outside an organization that provides, for a fee, expertise on a specific subject. The consultant will analyze the existing systems and suggest or design new ones that will better meet the present and future needs of the organization. And soon the partners would do well to hire their own technical staff, perhaps even setting up an information center.

Regardless of whether systems changes are planned by staff members or consultants, the planners must consider the effects that any proposed change would have on the organization as a whole. Some of the questions they must consider are: Do the advantages of a new system justify its cost to the organization? Can the new system be expanded easily as the organization grows, or will it soon need to be replaced? Is the proposed system compatible with other systems that are already in place within the organization? While solving a problem in one department, will the

STATE OF THE ART

The Microcomputer and Systems Development

When microcomputers set the mainframe world in turmoil by speeding up the demand for information and information systems in an organization, it may not have seemed that they could also provide a solution to the problem. But system experts today think this may be happening.

From early on, microcomputer programs emphasized ease of use. Software was designed so that inexperienced operators could get results without being technical wizards or logical geniuses. Early spreadsheets may have seemed complex, but they permitted the development of accounting templates far more easily than mainframes, which called for programs written in COBOL or Pascal. A new standard of user friendliness was being set, which included relative ease for creating specific applications.

Microcomputer database management software has shown a similar concern for the user. Database retrieval programs can be developed by inexperienced users, who can specify just what information they want to see and how they want it formatted on the printed page (or on the monitor).

Today many users, with the help of a knowledgeable assistant or an information center consultant, can create a working information tool themselves. They do not need to wait for a DP programming department to catch up on their backlog and rewrite the program for them. Not only that, they can also perform instant modifications when they realize their original scheme was less than perfect—a problem that has frequently soured relations between programmers and users.

Many experts believe that larger and larger systems will soon be created in this informal manner, using the new fourth-generation languages described in Chapter 7 of this book. And, in fact, this is happening already. Some major new computerized systems have been developed by users while their programming departments have been delayed by massive backlogs. For example, four users employing a fourth-generation programming tool developed a freight-tracking system for a major U.S. railroad in a fraction of the time that it would have taken by traditional means.

Figure 12-2   Consultants Assist the Organization
When major changes or improvements to computer systems are being considered, many organizations hire experts to advise them. Here a consultant presents an analysis of a company's systems to the people responsible for improving them. (Courtesy of International Business Machines Corporation)

proposed system create problems for others? The planners must guide systems changes with the needs of the overall organization in mind, not just the person or department whose problem they are trying to solve.

SYSTEMS CHANGES IN LARGE ORGANIZATIONS

In small organizations, where computer systems tend to be simple and relatively inexpensive, systems development does not need to be a very formal process. Large organizations, however, may spend millions of dollars on hardware and software for some of their information systems, which may be linked to each other in complex ways. In large organizations, therefore, systems development is often a much more demanding process than in smaller offices, and it tends to be rigidly structured. Each phase of the systems development cycle—analyzing the problem, planning alternatives, system selection, implementation, and maintenance—includes its own set of standard procedures. The remainder of this chapter will look at the formal processes of systems development in large organizations.

Starting the cycle

Systems develop in response to current or anticipated needs. An organization's top managers may anticipate a problem themselves as part of

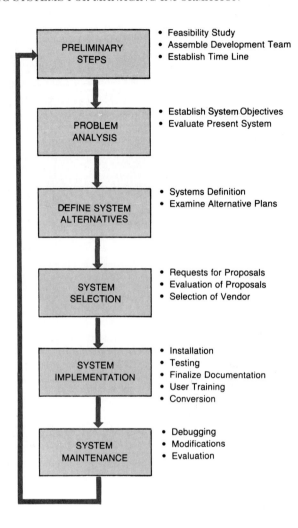

Figure 12-3 The Systems Development Cycle

In the real world, some of these steps may overlap. For example, when alternative plans are examined, more system objectives may need to be defined. And feasibility studies may have to be performed again if new information is uncovered during system selection.

their strategic planning, or a need may be pointed out to them by computer technicians or other employees. Either way, several steps precede the development of a system to solve the problem.

THE FEASIBILITY STUDY

Before committing to the expense of choosing or designing a major new system, management generally assigns systems specialists to perform a **feasibility study.** In a feasibility study, the specialists take a close look at the problem to get a preliminary idea of the size, scope, and likely cost of developing a new system to resolve it. They interview key employees involved with the problem and look at important memos, reports, or documents concerning it. Sometimes the problem may at first appear small but in fact be only one aspect of other, less obvious problems that could change the nature of the study. Large organizations often assign systems analysts from their own staffs to perform feasibility studies, but in some cases they may call in consultants.

When the study is completed, management receives a written report, which discusses the probable benefits as well as the estimated costs of changing the existing system. Using the information in the report, management decides whether or not the project is feasible—that is, whether the benefits are likely to justify the cost and whether the organization can afford it.

INTEROFFICE MEMO

To: Corporate Staff   **From:** MIS Director

Subject: PRELIMINARY FEASIBILITY STUDY:
SYSTEM QXR-360(S) WITH IMS-360 (INVENTORY MANAGEMENT SYSTEM)

EXECUTIVE SUMMARY

RECOMMENDATION:
Proceed with a full-system investigation.

RATIONALE

1. Operational Feasibility
   - System used in Whittenburg plant. Service report excellent.
   - Current inventory system fits well with IMS-360. However, all products inventoried in IMS must have product code number.
   - Good match with system requirements developed by inventory staff.
   - Increases data accessibility and control, allowing increased responsiveness to customers.
   - Requires increased user training, long learning curve.

2. Technical Feasibility
   - Up to 36 work stations.
   - Adequate memory, can be upgraded.
   - Supports all required peripheral devices.
   - Upgradeable to the QXR-540(S); IMS data files are transportable (and can be converted easily).
   - Life-time guarantee against system defects; excellent technical support.

3. Financial and Economic Feasibility
   - Payback period: 13 months

After tax startup costs (including software and training)	$135,000
Monthly after-tax savings over present cost (including labor and equipment leases)	$ 10,500

Figure 12-4   Feasibility Report
This "Executive Summary" is a very brief summary for executives—the first page of a much longer report. Each numbered item would be backed up by several pages of more detailed argument, and there could be several technical appendices. Note that, even in this early planning stage, consideration is given to training, maintenance, and upgrading.

Figure 12-5   A Team Guides Systems Development
The impact of a major new system is often felt throughout the organization, so a large, diverse team may be assembled to oversee its development. This team met regularly among themselves—they were also linked by telecommunications with team members elsewhere. (Courtesy of Hewlett-Packard Company)

ASSEMBLING A DEVELOPMENT TEAM

If top management agrees to the project, its next step is to assemble a team of people to carry it out. Teamwork can ensure that the needs of all groups affected by the system are considered, as well as the needs of the overall organization.

Top management.   Systems development teams generally include representatives of top management. Top managers can provide information about the organization's long-term goals. In addition, their participation ensures management's continuing support for the project. This is important for funding the project, and it also brings other benefits. For example, management can use its authority to gain the cooperation of employees from whom the systems analysts must gather crucial information. Also, top management's participation in negotiations with vendors of software and hardware can result in more favorable prices and services for the organization.

Technicians.   Because of the complex technical nature of a large computer system, the team needs some members with technical expertise. These people include systems analysts, who are specially trained in asking questions about systems and how they work and who are skilled in designing systems. Technically trained team members may also include one or more programmers, who may write or customize the software for the new system.

In addition to technicians from inside the organization, the team may include an outside consultant. Though a consulting firm may charge the organization up to 10 percent of the cost of the new system, its fee may be justified by the expertise a consultant adds to the team. Also, a consultant, as an outsider, may view the organization's overall requirements more objectively than a staff member.

Especially if an existing system will continue to be used, representatives of **systems vendors** may also be consulted by the team on occasion. The vendor that sold the existing system can provide important information about compatibility with the system being proposed. Once the organization has decided which vendor will install the new system, a representative of that vendor may also be consulted by the team.

Systems users.   The team should also include some of the people who will be most directly affected by the new system: users who will work with the system's input and rely on its output. A department manager, for example, probably knows more than anyone else about his or her department's word processing requirements. A data entry supervisor might provide an important perspective on the kinds of input that clerks need to do their jobs effectively. Users can often provide more specific information than upper management or technicians.

ESTABLISHING A TIME LINE

The team's first task is to establish a **time line,** which defines time limits for each of the steps the project will include. A typical time line would show a systems development cycle of 6 to 16 months, depending on the size of the system. The time line breaks the development process into tasks and establishes how long each task is likely to take. It indicates the appropriate time to decide major issues, such as the logical structure of the system, and noncritical issues, such as what types of monitors to use. The time line also specifies when each team member makes his or her contributions to the project.

The team is likely to use project scheduling tools such as PERT and Gantt charts, described in Chapter 6. They may use project management software to generate the charts automatically and to give them better control over the whole development process.

Analyzing the present system

The first phase of developing a new system is to gain a clear picture of the present system and how it is working. Even if there are problems, the present system forms a basis on which to build. People are used to working with the present system, so if many of its features are included in the new system, users will be able to adapt to the new system more easily. For example, if the old system was based on paper forms, the design of those forms could be used for the new system's data entry screens, which would make them easier to work with than a totally new format.

However, the present system's problems must be identified and corrected. The first step in this process is to establish exactly what the system is supposed to do—the **system objectives.** Without these, the team cannot identify just where the present system is adequate and where it fails; nor can it direct the design of the new system.

ESTABLISHING SYSTEM OBJECTIVES

System objectives include both **operational objectives**—what the new system is supposed to accomplish in the daily work of the organization— and **management objectives**—what management hopes to achieve by

```
                        OBJECTIVES DOCUMENT

SYSTEM:
     QXR-360(S)
     IMS-360(S) Inventory Management System

OBJECTIVES:

1    Reduce inventory costs 7% by reducing stock outages and
     surpluses.

     1.1  Ensure that adequate quantities of materials are on hand.
          1.1.1   Determine requirements based on historical analysis.
          1.1.2   Provide for inventory-analyst override in exceptions.
          1.1.3   Provide weekly materials-on-hand (M-O-H) report.
          1.1.4   Determine appropriate reorder points.
          1.1.5   Determine appropriate reorder quantities.
          1.1.6   Prepare order sheets for inventory-analyst.
          1.1.7   Upon approval, place orders directly with vendors.
          1.1.8   Provide on-line exceptions warning report.
          1.1.9   Limit access to inventory-analysts and controllers.
          1.1.10  Allow for easy changing of security codes.
          1.1.11  .
                  .
                  .

     1.2  Ensure that adequate quantities of finished products are on
          hand.
          1.2.1   Determine requirements based on historical analysis.
          1.2.2   .
                  .
                  .
```

Figure 12-6   Objectives Document

Often, objectives documents present a management objective followed by several operational objectives that are required to achieve it. This ensures that the management objectives are carefully examined, and that plans to achieve them are based on concrete strategies. In the document shown above, two levels of operational objectives are shown, but there are often many more.

changing the system. If the present system is well documented, there will already be a record of its own objectives. These need to be examined; many, perhaps all, are still valid. Then the new objectives must be considered—greater speed, perhaps; greater accuracy; or lower cost. Once objectives are established, more information about the present system can be gathered and studied. The results of this study will then be seen more clearly because the objectives are clear.

GATHERING DATA ABOUT THE PRESENT SYSTEM

Systems analysts gather information about the present system from several sources. Each source contributes a different perspective on how the system works and where its problems originate. These sources were consulted during the preliminary feasibility study. Now they are reviewed in depth.

Documentation. One important source of information for analysts is the **systems documentation,** also called **programmer documentation:** the plans, forms, manuals and other printed materials that relate to the existing system. Notes made by programmers about the workings of the software are part of the systems documentation. So are the input and output forms used with the system. Ideally, systems documentation tells the analyst what goes into the system, how the system processes the input, and what the system produces.

Another source for analysts is **user documentation,** which differs from systems documentation because it is written specifically for nontechnical end users. In addition to procedures manuals, user documentation may include a user's handwritten notes on how a specific task is performed step by step.

Documents, however, seldom describe a system completely. People who design and use systems don't always write down everything they know. Even when they do, documents can be lost or destroyed. In addition, users sometimes develop shortcuts that were never thought of when the system was designed. Therefore, systems analysts seek information from other sources as well.

Questionnaires. Questionnaires provide a fast, inexpensive way to collect data from many people. Systems analysts can develop questions about the workings of a large system: Where do its users get their input? How do they process it? How do they think the system could be made more efficient? The analysts compile these questions into questionnaire forms, which they distribute to everyone who works with the system.

Questionnaires have their drawbacks. Busy employees may give questionnaires low priority and fail to answer them promptly. Some users, even when promised anonymity, are reluctant to complete written forms. Others may fill them out too hastily for the data to be meaningful, or their answers to the questions may be biased.

Figure 12-7 Systems Analysts Query Users
In gathering information about the present computer system, systems analysts use many tools. An interview may involve programmed questions asked in sequence— or it may require the analyst to follow up the user's ideas in depth, and to explore the user's feelings about the system and its features. (Courtesy of Wang Laboratories, Inc.)

Interviews. Personal interviews often yield more information than questionnaires. By scheduling appointments with users and questioning them in person, systems analysts can at least be assured that their questions will be answered promptly. Also, an interviewer can pay attention to a user's facial expression and tone of voice. These may suggest information that isn't conveyed on written questionnaires.

Observation. A systems analyst can also learn a great deal about how a system works by watching it in action. By observing people and machines as they do their jobs, the analyst can gain a different perspective on the steps involved in input, processing, and output. To get a better understanding of how a user interacts with the system, the analyst may even step into the user's role for a short time. Observation provides the analyst with information the users may not have thought to mention. It can also create a closer working relationship between the users and the analyst and gives the users more opportunity to express their views of the system.

STUDYING THE DATA

Once systems analysts have gathered as much data as possible about how the system works, they must study it to identify the system's working structure. What exactly happens in the system? And where does it fail to meet the new objectives? How can it be improved? Useful tools for this task include organization charts and data flow diagrams.

Organization charts. An **organization chart** depicts the formal lines of authority within the organization. It shows who reports to whom, and it specifies who is in charge of what functions. Organization charts are issued and revised by top management.

Data flow diagrams. Using the information they have gathered, systems analysts prepare **data flow diagrams,** which are also called **flow charts.** Like programming flow charts, a data flow diagram uses standard symbols to represent input, output, documents, and procedures. The diagram illustrates the flow of data through an information system. It depicts the entire path the data follows and what happens to the data at different points along that path. An example of data flow diagram is shown in Figure 12-8.

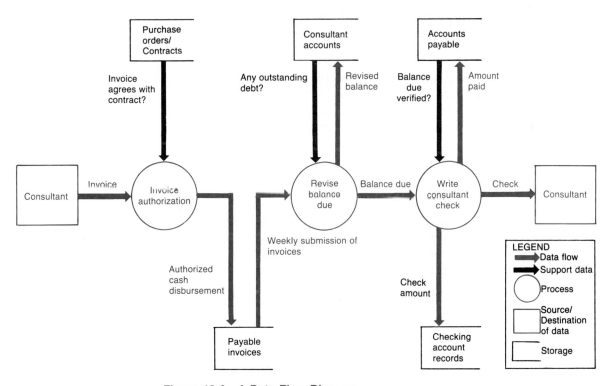

Figure 12-8   A Data Flow Diagram
This diagram explores what happens to a specific piece of data—the amount on an invoice—as it is processed and readied for payment. Other data, shown here by black arrows, is needed along the way. In an information system, making sure that the right pieces of information are on hand when and where they are needed is critical.

Defining alternatives for a new system

The systems development team's detailed study of the existing system should indicate how a new system can carry out the system objectives more efficiently. Team members can then begin the next phase of the development cycle, a detailed definition of the new system. In this defining phase, the development team describes the new system, presents alternatives for new hardware and software, and tells where it can be acquired.

SYSTEMS DEFINITION

The first step in the defining phase is to detail the requirements of the new system. This systems definition step, which is sometimes referred to as **high-level design,** is based on the system objectives. It may include additional requirements, however, that were suggested by the study of the present system. And it provides considerably greater detail than the objectives. Systems definition results in a written document that programmers and other technicians can use to design or modify the system itself.

Systems definition is generally performed by the systems analysts, with approval from the other team members. In defining the system, the analysts must specify the output that will be required, the input the system will need, how the system will process the input, and how the system will communicate with users. The definition must also provide security specifications for the system's data.

Output.　Output definition is usually specified first, because the output represents the needed information—the whole point of the system. Output definition includes not only the final output of the overall system but also the output produced by each of its subsystems. (Remember, output from one system or subsystem often serves as input for another.) Consider a system for managing payroll information. If the output of the system is to include paychecks and stubs, what information must the checks and stubs include, and how should it be arranged on the paper? In addition to the employee's name and the amount being paid, will the checks include the recipient's address, an identification number, or other information? What withholding taxes and other deductions must be itemized on the pay stubs? Most computer systems produce reports about the data they have processed; the content and formats of these reports must also be clearly defined in this phase.

The medium on which the output appears must also be specified. Will the output be on paper, microfilm, or a monitor? Will it be saved on a disk? The content of the output generally determines the medium on which it appears. A payroll system's output, for example, includes W-2 forms, which are income and tax-withholding reports that must be sent to the Internal Revenue Service. This output must therefore appear on paper. Paychecks and pay stubs will also be printed on paper for most employees. However, instead of generating checks, the system may produce records on a disk showing that pay was transferred electronically to employee bank accounts.

Input. Next, the development team must define what input is needed to produce the required output and how the input will be entered into the system. As with output, the analysts must consider both the content of the input and the media on which it is delivered. What data must the input include? Will the system receive the input electronically from another computer system, or will it be presented orally or on paper? In defining input, systems analysts may be greatly influenced by the users who work with the input. These users are likely to have strong feelings about how the input is documented, how easy it is to understand, and how they can verify its accuracy.

User interface. Many computer systems are **interactive,** which means that their communication with users is two way. The system presents prompts or questions to the users, the users respond by inputting data or commands, and the system displays its output.

Figure 12-9 Systems Analysts Check User Interfaces
From the user's point of view, the most important part of a computer system is the interface. Here a systems analyst discusses the features of a newly designed interface with a manager whose staff will use the system. (Courtesy of UNISYS)

This exchange of information between the computer system and the user is part of the user interface described in Chapter 4. For interactive systems, the definition step must describe input and output at the user interface.

For example, will users issue their commands by selecting items from menus, typing command codes, or both? Will the system include a help feature, and if so, how should that help feature work? As with input definition, users' opinions usually play a major role in defining user interface.

Processing. Once output and input have been specified, processing procedures can be described. What operations are necessary to convert the input into the output? What logic and what mathematics, for example, are needed to convert time card data into correctly printed checks? Is other input data needed (for instance, the employee's union status) to produce the complete output that the objectives require? Any new input must be added to the input requirements.

Security. Because information is vital to organizations, the security of this information is a crucial consideration in systems planning. Unauthorized people must be barred from access to the organization's data. Backup procedures must therefore be included in a system to prevent loss of data, and so must safeguards against the introduction of errors into

Figure 12-10 Making the System Secure
Systems designers try to ensure that information is safe from unauthorized use. An automatic bank teller only works if the user inserts a special card *and* keys an identification number. Both elements are needed to gain access to the system—and the money. (Courtesy of International Business Machines Corporation)

the data. Security is particularly important when long distance data communications are involved.

EXAMINING ALTERNATIVE PLANS

Systems definition specifies what the new system is to do; the next step involves determining how to put together a system that meets these requirements. The team must examine and present alternative plans. These plans may involve adapting the present system, customizing a new ready-made software package, or designing a new system. The plans will probably call for the purchase of new software and hardware or an intensive in-house programming effort.

Adapting the present system. One option may be to alter the existing system so that it can better meet the organization's current and future needs. A company that started out with a simple database program, for example, may require a more sophisticated one as it accumulates more data on customers, employees, and so forth. It may also need a more efficient storage method. Systems analysts could instruct programmers to modify the database software. They may select upgrade programs that are available from commercial software producers. They might also consider high-capacity disks or other storage hardware that would fit in with the current system while more adequately meeting the organization's requirements.

Purchasing and customizing a ready-made system. A more radical alternative would be to purchase a new software package from outside sources. The drawback of this alternative is that such ready-made systems are designed for sale to many customers, not just one organization. They therefore rarely meet the needs of any one organization exactly, so they often need to be customized, either by the vendor or by the organization's staff programmers.

Many of these ready-made systems require alterations to the computer's operating system and the addition of new hardware. Even when these elements are sold together with the software in a package deal, the cost is often considerable. However, ready-made systems and software are still less costly than those designed for one organization alone.

Designing a new system. The final option is to design a new system. This may be necessary if the system objectives are unusual or unique to the organization. In this case, new software would need to be written, using appropriate programming languages. And purchase of new hardware may also be necessary if the new system would overload existing facilities.

Presenting the alternatives to management. At this point, the team has identified alternative systems that would fulfill the requirements it defined earlier. The next step is to inform top management of these alternatives so that it can decide the team's next move. A final choice will usually not be made at this point—the prices of the alternative systems have not been settled, and these are usually negotiable. At management's direction, therefore, the team will start negotiating with vendors before making a final selection based on price as well as capabilities.

Selecting and refining the new system

Negotiations involve give and take on both sides. Even if the most expensive option—designing a new system—is chosen, some compromises are likely to be made for the sake of price. When the team approaches vendors with its systems requirements, it must recognize that some requirements are more essential than others. In a payroll system, speed may be essential, and the exact layout of the check stub may be less important. The team will often construct an **evaluation grid** (see Figure 12-11), indicating all the needs specified and allowing the team to record which vendors can meet which requirements. Then the members will launch the bidding process.

REQUESTS FOR PROPOSALS

The first step in acquiring major hardware and software is preparation of a **request for proposals (RFP)**. This is a formal document that defines the system's requirements and invites vendors to submit bids. The RFP reduces the chance that a vendor will misunderstand the organization's needs and supply an inadequate system.

The RFP is usually sent to a group of vendors selected by the systems analysts and top management. It asks the vendors to submit their bids in a standard format for easy comparison. Team members review the bids for the best prices, service agreements, and other terms. During this review, they can reject any vendors whose prices are too high or whose proposals fail to meet the key requirements.

VENDORS' CONFERENCES

The remaining vendors may be invited to a **vendors' conference**. Here, the development team can clear up any misunderstandings about the system definition, question vendors closely about their proposals, and answer questions. The conference also gives vendors an opportunity to see what other vendors are offering, which may increase the competition and lead to a better deal for the organization. For example, a vendor could offer to customize its system at a nominal cost to make it more attractive financially.

EVALUATION GRID

Ev. Grd. Rev. 4/23/8-

Section 25.01
Communication Adaptor (with Processor)
Page 1.0

FEATURES	VENDOR 1	VENDOR 2	VENDOR 3
1. Separate Communications Processor	X	X	X
2. Independent processor operation	X	X	X
3. 16-line communication adaptor (SLCA)	X	X	X
4. Aggregate line speed > 150,000 bps	X		X
5. Individual line speed > 55,000 bps	X	X	X
6. Supports EIA RS232 interface	X	X	X
7. Supports DDSA interface	X	X	X
8. Supports X.21 interface (sw & unsw)		X	X
9. Supports V.35 interface		X	X
10. Supports V.25 interface	X	X	X
11. Supports Autocall	X	X	X
12. Allows auto-answer	X	X	
13. Allows manual answer		X	X
14. Allows use of up to 3 lines with X.25		X	X
15. Full duplex capability		X	X
16. Allows local attachment to QXR-180(s)	X	X	
17. Allows switched/nonswitched BSC	X	X	X
18. Allows switched/nonswitched ASYNCH	X		
19. Allows switched/nonswitched SDLC	X	X	X
20. Allows multipoint tributary operation with SDLC protocols	X	X	X
21. Provides necessary modules to communicate with the following attached devices:			

    21.1 System QXR-180(s)
    21.2 Model 18(s) Remote Display Station
    21.3

Figure 12-11   Information System Evaluation Grid

An information systems evaluation grid can be detailed. This is only a part of an Evaluation Grid that focuses on the communication capabilities of the system's hardware. One thing that is not apparent from this grid is the *relative* importance of the various features. For example, it may matter little if the system does not support the DDSA interface; but it could be critical for it to support the X.21 interface.

EVALUATING THE PROPOSED SYSTEMS

Vendors' bids, and their statements at vendors' conferences, are intended to make their companies' products as appealing as possible. The development team, however, must evaluate the products by more objective criteria. Before deciding on a vendor, for example, the team may study publications issued by independent research organizations that test computer products. The selection process should also include **hands-on evaluation** by people who will be using the new system. Skipping this step is like buying a car without a test drive, but with even more expensive consequences. Ideally, both technicians and nontechnical users are given the opportunity to test proposed systems for qualities such as speed, flexibility, reliability, capacity, and security.

As evaluation proceeds, the evaluation grid is filled out for each vendor. The team, and top management, can see which vendors meet the key requirements and, of these, which have the most attractive prices.

SELECTING A VENDOR

Following evaluation, the systems development team again reports to top management. This time, it presents its opinion of the vendors' proposals and makes a final recommendation on which proposal the organization should accept. Top management makes the final decision. It may at this time, as at any point in the development cycle, either delay the project or cancel it. Usually, however, it follows the team's recommendations and gives the go-ahead for implementing a system.

Implementing the system

Selection of a vendor starts the next phase of the systems development cycle—implementation. **Systems implementation** includes installing the new system, testing it, documenting its operations, training people to use it, and converting from the old system to the new one. The system may be implemented in **modules,** which are small sections dealing with specific functions, or it may be implemented all at once.

INSTALLATION

The first task on the implementation schedule is generally the installation of the system. Hardware and software are delivered, and the hardware components are connected to each other. The hardware may come with the software already installed, or the software may need to be installed after delivery. Software installation generally involves inserting the software disks or tapes into appropriate drives and running a special installation program included with the software. This procedure prepares the software to run on a specific kind of hardware. Software may also need to be installed onto appropriate hard disks within the system. The original disks or tapes are kept for backup purposes.

TESTING

The installed system must then be tested. First, testers run normal, complete, and accurate data through the system to check the system's ability to perform its intended functions. Next, they use unusual data to see how the system handles exceptional conditions, such as the omission of a nonessential entry that is generally filled in on a form.

Finally, they intentionally give the system data that contains errors. For example, a tester may enter a G in a field where users are supposed

Figure 12-12   Installing a New System
Installation of a new system is often a difficult process because it disrupts the normal routine of an organization. Here a vendor's representative and an employee discuss how to handle the various installation tasks with minimum interruption to other workers. (Courtesy of Data General)

to enter *M* for male or *F* for female. From this, the testers learn whether the system detects such errors and how it responds to them. If the system displays an error message that isn't very helpful, such as "Nonmatch code in field 4," the testers may suggest that it be changed to something like, "Error in sex field. Acceptable entries are M or F."

If the software is found to have problems, the next step is to discover what is causing the problems and to fix them. This process is called **debugging;** the details of the program code are studied to find **bugs,** or mistakes in the software. Debugging is usually performed by the software vendor or by the organization's programming staff. It may be required long after the testing phase if an unusual problem occurs that the testing procedures failed to uncover.

FINALIZING THE DOCUMENTATION

Systems documentation and user documentation are as important to the new system as they were to the previous one. Systems analysts and programmers begin preparing systems documentation at the outset of the project, starting with a copy of the system objectives. They then keep it up-to-date as the system develops. User documentation, on the other hand, is often not written until the system itself has been installed and tested and all modifications and corrections have been made. It is very important that both types of documentation reflect the final version of the system.

USER TRAINING

Although users can sometimes learn to operate a system just by studying the user documentation, it's generally more efficient to give them practice and instruction before they actually begin working with the system. This training reduces users' anxiety and shortens the time it will take for them to begin using the system efficiently. Training is generally the final step before converting to a new system, although it can start much earlier if the system is standard and classes are offered elsewhere.

Training can be done in classes or individually. Classes may be held in the employer's offices, for example, at the information center; at the vendor's offices; or at some other location. Some users, especially high-ranking executives who don't want to appear vulnerable in classrooms, may get individual training from instructors. Training tools include printed tutorials (step-by-step operations guides) and computer-based training (CBT) programs. CBT programs allow users to practice at their own pace. A CBT program may present realistic work situations and use the same screen displays and keyboard commands that trainees will encounter on the job.

Figure 12-13 Levels of Learning
The hardest part of user training is usually explaining the software. Not only must learners master the different commands needed; they must also understand the functions of which the system is capable, and how to access those functions. In other words, they must master the structure of the package. (Courtesy of International Business Machines Corporation)

Figure 12-14 Parallel Conversion
Even in a small business, keeping the old system working for a while after the installation of a new system can make for an easy changeover. This farmer is double-checking her paper records before inputting the same data into the new computer system. (Courtesy of USDA)

CONVERSION

Once the new system has been tested, user documentation has been written, and users have been trained, the organization is ready to convert its operations from the old system to the new. Conversion may take any of several approaches.

Crash conversion. In a **crash conversion,** the organization abruptly stops using the old system and begins using the new one. If all goes well, crash conversions are faster and more economical than other methods. The drawback is that some software bugs may survive the testing process and surface only after the conversion. If these bugs are major, a crash conversion can be disastrous.

Parallel conversion. The safest but most costly approach is **parallel conversion,** in which the organization runs both systems at once until management is sure the new system is running smoothly. If the new system fails for any reason during a parallel conversion, the organization can still rely on the old system. The trouble with parallel conversion is that it practically doubles the workload of the users, who have to perform tasks with both systems. The organization may need to pay for overtime work and extra employees during the test period.

Pilot conversion. As a compromise between the extremes of crash and parallel conversions, some organizations use the pilot conversion approach. In a **pilot conversion,** one pilot or trial division of an organization uses the new system, while other divisions continue to use the old one. When the new system is running smoothly at the pilot division, the other divisions convert to it.

THE HUMAN SIDE

Systems Against Drought

The Walnut Grove, California, Water Authority wants to be able to predict floods and water shortages. To do so, it has embarked on a systems development project to computerize the gathering and analysis of data about water flow through its system. The project will take nine months and cost nearly $250,000. The six-person systems development team includes two people from management, two from plant operations, and two from the data processing department. Here are the team members:

William Pelton, assistant to the vice president for financial planning, is project manager, overseeing the day-to-day functioning of the team. Pelton will be responsible for administering the budget and for making sure the project stays on schedule.

George Winkleman is the assistant project manager. It is his responsibility to oversee creation of specifications for the project. Both of these managers serve as a bridge between the data processing experts and the operations personnel on the team.

Richard Stein is an assistant director for operations. Stein's job is to explain to the data processing experts how the Water Authority functions. He knows where the water meters are, what sizes the valves and pipes are, what routes meter readers take when they go out to gather data, how often they

take readings, and so on.

Virginia Tey is an employee supervisor. She will be responsible for training the meter readers and office personnel to use the new system once it is in place. She will supervise preparation of software documentation and users' manuals.

Margaret Freeling is manager of systems and programming in the data processing department. Her role on the team is to determine what new equipment the project requires and how the computers can be programmed to carry out the tasks the project has identified.

Peter Iorio, a systems analyst, will draw up detailed specifications of hardware and software requirements for the new system. They will describe what forms to develop, how reports will look, how data will be entered, how the hardware will be integrated, and so on. The software specifications will be used by the programmers to write the required programs.

For this project, the programmers will need to write 16 new programs and enter data collected over 20 years as a resource database. Once the project is complete, the Water Authority's computers will be able to analyze water flow data in June and determine the danger of having a drought in August or September.

Phased conversion. Another compromise is offered by the **phased conversion,** in which the entire organization converts to the new system one portion at a time. Instead of some users trying out the whole system, as in a pilot conversion, all users try out some of the system. Once any bugs are worked out of that one part of the system, the organization converts to the next part, and so on until the implementation is complete.

Maintaining and evaluating the system

The end of the implementation phase does not mark the end of the systems development cycle. Technicians begin to perform **systems maintenance.** This work may include further debugging and modifications for user convenience or in response to changed conditions. Modifications may be done by vendors' technicians, by programmers on the organization's staff, or both. Maintenance also includes the ongoing process of evaluating the system to make sure that it is still meeting the organization's needs.

DEBUGGING

You might think that the testing and conversion processes would provide ample opportunity for discovering all the bugs in a system, but often that isn't the case. Some bugs don't show up for months, or even years, after a system has been in use. Fixing them can be an extremely difficult and frustrating task, especially when the programmers working on the problems are not the ones who wrote the software. The task is somewhat easier if the programmers have thorough systems documentation to guide them.

MODIFICATIONS

Maintenance may include modifications that are needed for reasons other than correcting system flaws. For example, software used by the payroll department may need to be modified to reflect tax law changes or new organizational policies. Systems may also be modified by adding new features that make them more powerful or easier to use. Modifications, of course, can introduce new bugs into the system. Thus, the steps of modification and debugging may continue throughout the life of the system.

EVALUATION

Throughout the life of any system, management is constantly evaluating it. Most of the time, this evaluation is informal. Eventually, however, a department or organization may outgrow the system, or it may consider replacing it with one that uses newer, more sophisticated technology.

Figure 12-15   Debugging a New System
Only through actual use do all the problems of a new system come to the surface. Users of a new system can call on the developer for help via a hotline. Often the developer can actually work with the user's system via telecommunications to investigate and solve the problem. (Courtesy of Data General)

Then the organization embarks on a new round of study, planning, design, and implementation, thus beginning the system development cycle once again.

SUMMARY

- Information systems develop according to an organization's needs. Well-managed organizations constantly evaluate their systems to ensure that those needs are being met. As needs change, or as new technology becomes available, an organization modifies or replaces its information systems.

- Systems development follows a continuous cycle. Five overall phases in this cycle are analysis, definition of alternatives, selection, implementation, and maintenance.

- Pressure for systems change may come from one part of an organization that is having difficulty accomplishing its goals, or management may initiate a change as part of a long-range plan.

- Systems can be changed in many ways, whether or not they are computerized. They can be expanded by adding employees or modifying procedures. They can be computerized with new hardware and software. Or they can expand an existing computerized system.

- In a large organization, a feasibility study generally precedes a systems development project. This helps management to determine the probable benefits and costs of a systems change and whether the organization can afford it.

- If management decides to go ahead with a project, a development team is assembled. The team includes technicians, users, top managers, and sometimes consultants. The team's first task is to establish a time line for the project.

- During the analysis phase of the systems development cycle, the team conducts a detailed study of the existing system. This study includes the establishment of system objectives and a review of the systems documentation. The team also studies information provided by users and the systems analysts' own observations.

- During definition of alternatives, the team defines what the new system must do. This systems definition includes specifications for the system's output, input, user interface, processing, and security features. Using these specifications, technicians explore and describe alternative plans that would enable the system to accomplish its goals.

- A system is selected after the team solicits competitive bids from vendors, so the organization can acquire the most suitable system at the least possible cost.

- Implementation starts with installing and testing the system. It may also include preparation of user documentation as well as training sessions for users. Finally, the organization converts from the old system to the new one, either abruptly or gradually.

- The final phase, maintenance, continues throughout the life of the system. It includes continued debugging of the system as well as modifications to keep up with changing conditions. During the maintenance phase, the organization conducts an ongoing evaluation. It may consider replacing the system, and a new development cycle would then begin.

TERMS FOR REVIEW

systems
   development cycle
consultant
feasibility study
systems vendors
time line
system objectives
operational
   objectives
management
   objectives
systems
   documentation

programmer
   documentation
user documentation
organization chart
data flow diagrams
flow charts
high-level design
interactive
evaluation grid
request for
   proposals (RFP)
vendors' conference
hands-on evaluation

systems
   implementation
modules
debugging
bugs
crash conversion
parallel conversion
pilot conversion
phased conversion
systems
   maintenance

■■■■■■■■
TERMINOLOGY CHECK

For each definition below, choose the correct term or terms from the list of Terms for Review.

1. Finding and removing the flaws in software.

2. A formal document used by an organization to define its systems needs and invite vendors to submit bids.

3. A chart that depicts input, output, documents, and procedures to illustrate the flow of data through an information system.

4. An approach to converting from an old system to a new one in which a designated division of an organization begins using the new system while other divisions continue to use the old one.

5. An examination of the problems with an existing system and the probable cost of resolving them.

6. Forms, charts, and other documents pertaining to a system's design and function.

7. Small sections of a system, dealing with specific functions.

8. An abrupt switch throughout an organization from an old system to an entirely new one.

9. A chart depicting the formal lines of authority within an organization.

10. What management requires from a system.

■■■■■■■■
INFORMATION CHECK

1. What are the five phases in the systems development cycle?

2. What groups or individuals are likely to suggest that a system be changed, and what are their usual reasons?

3. Describe several ways that computerized information systems can be changed or brought up-to-date.

4. Identify different personnel on whom small, medium, and large organizations might rely to change their information systems.

5. List and describe steps that may be involved in getting a major systems development project started.

6. Why is expressing systems objectives essential for developing new systems?

7. What are four ways in which a systems analyst might gather data about an existing system? Discuss advantages of each method.

8. Briefly describe two tools used to describe and help study a system's working structure.

9. Who usually prepares the document defining the system specifications?

10. What features of a system are usually described in a systems definition document?

11. Name some alternative options that systems analysts may consider before making their recommendations.

12. Describe the procedure followed when an organization decides to purchase software or hardware.

13. List and define key phases during the implementation phase of systems development.

14. Identify alternative strategies for converting from an old system to a new one.

15. Why is the system development cycle continuous?

PROJECTS AND PROBLEMS

1. You are a consultant who has been hired by Aberdeen Power and Light Company to analyze its existing information systems and to recommend any needed changes. Aberdeen has used the same software for more than three years, and top management feels that a change may boost productivity and increase profits. Aberdeen's MIS department has requested the services of an outside consultant to provide a fresh view of the situation.

   Using the information provided in this chapter, outline the steps you would take to find out how productivity and profits could be improved.

2. Contact a company in your area that has converted its operation from one system to another. What conversion strategy did it use? What were the advantages and limitations? Would it use the same or a different approach the next time such a conversion was needed? Write a short report describing your findings.

3. Call the training department of a large organization or a software developer. Ask the department to describe the procedures it uses to train new or experienced software users. Does it use classrooms, tutorials, computer-based training, or a combination? How much time is spent on directed hands-on activities and on lectures? Ask the department to send you any materials it has that describe the training it provides.

   Write a report that describes the training program. Share the report and the materials with the class.

13

Ergonomics— designing the environment

As you have learned in this book, computerized information systems include people as well as hardware and software. An important part of systems design is therefore ensuring that the equipment is convenient and usable and that people can easily interact with it. If office workers have to waste time obtaining the information they must key in to the computer, this is expensive to the organization. If they are uncomfortable or frequently distracted, time may also be wasted. Worse, employees may become restless and disaffected. This could lead to an office with low morale and low productivity, or it could mean that people leave the organization, requiring new workers to be hired and trained. Both these outcomes are bad for the organization as well as for its employees.

In the previous chapter, you learned that a key element in systems design is creating a workable user interface. This interface is largely a function of the software—what kinds of prompts or menus are supplied to the user, what keystrokes are required for different operations. Well-designed, user-friendly software provides an interface that is easy to use and that helps to prevent annoying mistakes; for example, the keys needed for saving are far from the delete key, so there won't be any disastrous mishaps.

However, the right hardware is equally important for your convenience. How user friendly is the equipment itself? Does the keyboard feel crisp to your fingers? How easy is it to read the monitor display? How is your workstation situated relative to the workstations of other people with whom you must work? Is there excessive noise from the printers, distracting you and fellow workers? All of these questions are important. The answers can spell the difference between a smoothly functioning system and one that never works at peak efficiency. They can also spell the difference between a satisfying day in which much was accomplished and a tiring day that leaves you with tasks still unfinished.

All of these concerns are the subject of **ergonomics,** the study of the worker and the work environment. A principal focus of ergonomics is

344

optimizing the design of work space and equipment so that they can be used as effectively as possible. Ergonomics is important to systems designers, to equipment manufacturers, and to workers. As you will learn, ergonomics covers many factors, from overall office layout to the design of chairs to the shape and touch of each key on a computer keyboard.

When you have completed this chapter, you should be able to:

■ define ergonomics, and explain its purposes

■ identify five key ergonomic elements that affect the efficiency and comfort of office workers

■ describe specific features that are desirable in connection with each of these elements

■ explain the use of a systems approach in designing the office environment

■ list typical steps in an ergonomic study

■ suggest some accommodating techniques that can be used when an ergonomically designed environment is not feasible

Organizational needs, human needs, and ergonomics

The main goal of ergonomics is to enhance the work life of employees and the productivity of a system. Organizations must ensure that their equipment and procedures are working as well as possible and that the people can contribute as fully as possible to their smooth operation. Therefore, ergonomics looks at the needs of business in terms of work flow, communications flow, and personal productivity. However, to recommend how productivity can be improved, ergonomics also examines the overall needs of people at work—what makes them comfortable and what improves their morale.

ORGANIZATIONAL NEEDS

Needs vary with different types of organizations. For example, a law firm deals with confidential matters, so it may need more private offices than an architectural firm or an insurance company. Those companies may benefit instead from an open plan, where workers are in the same room and communication is easier. But, whatever their needs, all organizations can profit from analyzing the flow of work and the flow of communications and interaction between people.

Figure 13-1 Office Layout—the Big Picture

Workflow affects individual workers—it also affects how whole buildings are used. On the left is an arrangement for the Executive Look catalog company which is far less than perfect. On the right is an arrangement which seems to suit the workflow better.

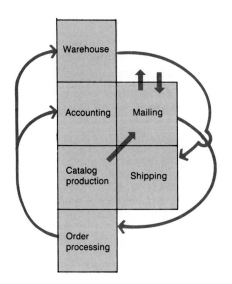

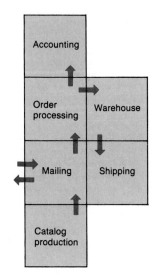

Work flow. Work flow is a key element in efficient systems. It includes how people receive their work, how they perform it, and where the work goes after being completed. Work flow may be affected by characteristics of the individual worker, as well as of the job itself. For example, consider a data entry operator who is keyboarding data from paper forms at a computer terminal. The forms are delivered to him by his supervisor and placed in a bin to his right. He takes the forms one at a time, enters the data, and puts the finished forms in another bin to his right, ready for collection. This could be a very efficient procedure, unless the operator is left-handed. Then he would have to make many awkward movements to perform his job, and this might affect his efficiency.

Communications flow. Whereas work flow usually depends on the movement of papers and materials, the flow of communications depends on the ability of people to talk, as well as on the exchange of written documents. Communications flow covers how information gets from one level of management to another, and then to each employee. It also covers how employees can get help from each other and from their supervisors.

Think, for example, of how an office staff might be informed that the last mail pickup before a holiday will be 3 p.m. There would be plenty of warning time. Probably a memo would be sent to supervisors; the supervisors in turn might use memos to notify individual workers. Or, in a fully computerized office, an electronic message might be sent to every workstation.

The communications flow would be different, however, if a worker needed to get help because she had encountered a problem with the applications software she was using. The sooner she could find the appropriate person to help her, the sooner she could return to her task. Most likely she would leave her desk, find her supervisor, and then call a consultant from the information center. The closer she is to her supervisor's workstation and the information center, the faster she can solve the problem and finish her work.

Communication also occurs in regular staff meetings, in one-to-one conferences with a supervisor, or through informal and frequent exchanges with fellow workers.

HUMAN NEEDS

The needs of people in the office environment are very important in looking at how to improve productivity. People are creative, original thinkers, and they can make experienced judgments that computers are unlikely to duplicate in the near future, and perhaps never will. Therefore, people are vital to a productive system. Though their needs are more complex than those of an organization or of a computer, they must be considered when creating an effective system.

Psychologist Abraham Maslow has been an influential thinker on this subject. He described human needs as falling into five levels, from the most basic to the most complex. This is illustrated in Figure 13-2, which shows Maslow's so-called **hierarchy of needs.** Beginning with the most basic, the five levels of needs and some of the environmental factors associated with each are:

1. Physiological needs—The basic physical needs for comfort and health, including the needs for light, air, warmth, sound, and space.

2. Safety and security needs—These relate to privacy or crowding and to feelings of safety from unexpected interruptions.

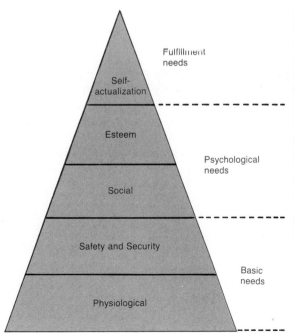

Figure 13-2   Maslow's Hierarchy of Needs

Since Abraham Maslow proposed the theory of a hierarchy of needs in the early 1940s, many in business have adapted it for use in motivating employees. Maslow's theory is often taken into account in planning work environments. (After Abraham H. Maslow, *Motivation and Personality,* New York: 1970. Used by permission of Harper & Row, Publishers.)

3. Social needs—These include the need to see other people, to have the opportunity for conversation, and to gain a feeling of trust and appreciation from fellow workers and supervisors.

4. Esteem needs—These cover people's desire to have some control over their work and environment and to feel that their contributions are valued and respected.

5. Self-actualization needs—These involve workers' creativity and their need to develop their own ideas and see them as being useful on the job.

Maslow argued that when a lower-level need is not satisfied, it diverts a person's energies from working toward a higher need. For example, if a worker feels insecure because his desk is in a busy area, he is unlikely to exhibit much creativity. Similarly, if the office area is too dark, people will have difficulty working efficiently and their feelings of self-worth may suffer, along with their job performance.

WHAT ERGONOMICS DOES

An ergonomically designed office environment strives to satisfy as many organizational and human needs as possible. Sometimes this is quite simple: principles of effective design are understood and can be applied straightforwardly. In many situations, however, compromises must be made. Perhaps the space available is not ideal—there are too many small rooms, and the walls cannot be removed. Or one set of needs may conflict with another. For example, the need for individual privacy may be at variance with the need for open communication. The need for a darkened room to read monitors may conflict with the need for bright lighting to

Figure 13-3   Simple Office Improvements
Not only is the office on the left old-fashioned in appearance and crowded, but its arrangement—with desks facing one another—is distracting to the employees. Even a simple change like modern desks that do not face one another can improve an office environment. (Courtesy of Haworth, Inc.)

read paper documents. The need to accommodate human behavior and preferences may clash with the requirement for cool, clean, and smokeless air in the vicinity of a large computer.

Yet another area of compromise is caused by the fact that people differ. Some are tall, others are short, yet they may need to work at the same terminals. Some like to spread out their papers, and others like to keep their work area tightly organized. Some have intense powers of concentration; others are easily distracted. Because both tasks and the people assigned to those tasks can change, flexibility is a hallmark of sound ergonomic design. Chairs, for example, should be adjustable and work area dividers movable.

Because both organizational needs and individuals are different, there is no single office design that works for everyone. Ergonomic principles can help planners determine how to meet the needs of each individual and the needs of the particular organization in a structured and effective way.

Ergonomic elements

Efficient design is made up of many elements. Think, for example, of a well-designed kitchen. Work areas are located near appliances to save steps for the cook. A counter next to the refrigerator makes it easier to put items away or take them out. Lighting is brighter where chopping is done than where people eat. Not just one factor but many interrelated factors make a kitchen work well. The same is true in the office, where many elements contribute to an efficient workplace.

The ergonomic elements discussed in this section are:

- layout

- workstations

- lighting

- acoustics

- climate control

LAYOUT

The layout of an office is the arrangement of its people, equipment, and furniture. Layout vitally affects efficient work flow and communications flow. Layout is important even when the office area consists of many small permanent rooms; work efficiency can be greatly influenced by appropriate room assignments. But layout is more of an issue in today's open office environments.

An **open office** has few floor-to-ceiling walls. Instead, partitions, often fabric covered and sound absorbing, define work areas. The openness of the space invites a flow of ideas and information that might be hindered by the physical barriers of walls and doors.

Figure 13-4 Open Office

The modern open office layout gives a feeling of spaciousness to the office. Its partitions offer employees some privacy and quiet in which to do their work while the absence of doors prevents people from closing themselves off from communication with fellow workers. (Courtesy of Steelcase, Inc.)

An open office also is very flexible. Because the walls are not permanent and can be moved rather easily, changes can be made quickly and inexpensively. However, although this type of arrangement may be ideal for an organization, it does lessen individual privacy.

Location of people. In an open office, as indeed in any office, where people work can greatly affect productivity. For example, suppose that your department routinely has to enter data from seven-page handwritten forms into its computer system. The task is split among seven workers so that each handles one of the seven pages, and the forms are sent from worker to worker. Clearly, it is most efficient if the workers are placed close together so that they can pass the forms from one person to the next by hand. If they were seated far apart, much more time and effort would be required to move the forms from one location to another.

Physical movement isn't the only consideration in locating people in an office layout, of course. Electronic communication has added a whole new dimension to planning, especially in organizations that work with local area networks or use mainframe computers with remote terminals. The location of cables and wires in floors, walls, and ceilings needs to be carefully planned; it can be difficult to relocate wires once they are in place.

Location of shared equipment. Another important concern in office design is how to position shared equipment. File cabinets are central resources, as are copying machines and computer printers. So too, frequently, are computer terminals. Each of these resources may have several users during a given day.

Whereas file cabinets are relatively noiseless and do not generally disturb other workers, copying machines and printers can both cause considerable distraction. File cabinets can therefore usually be positioned most conveniently for their users, but printers and copying machines often need to be placed in areas where their noise can be muted. The people who work with them most frequently should obviously be located close to these areas, though this should be balanced against their other working needs.

Microcomputers and terminals are sometimes shared because of the cost of placing a computer workstation on every desk. In an open office, a bank of workstations may be arranged along the walls. Alternatively, there may be a cluster of desks with computer terminals. If these will be used by several people, the best strategy is to have chairs, keyboards, and monitors that are easily adjustable. There should also be adequate space for setting up different kinds of work.

No one arrangement of furniture and equipment is better than another. The best layout for an office is the one that is most comfortable for the workers and allows efficiency, thereby promoting productivity.

WORKSTATIONS

Whether a computer workstation is shared or is intended for the use of

Figure 13-5 Arrangements of Shared Equipment
The spare, functional furniture in this cluster of shared computer equipment is ideal for the use to which this area is put. These are not permanently assigned workstations; employees move in and out as necessary to use the equipment, taking their work with them. (Courtesy of Acco International Inc.)

one person only, the user's comfort is a primary concern. At a **dedicated workstation,** where one person works all day, comfort is especially important. An awkwardly positioned screen may cause no trouble if you are at a computer for only 20 minutes, but after several hours the crick in your neck may make productive work difficult for the rest of the day— to say nothing of ruining your evening.

To understand how important the workstation is, compare the processing of a letter on a computer with writing one by hand. When writing a letter, you can constantly make adjustments for comfort. You can shift the position of the paper. You can sit formally at a desk or lean back and place your notepad on your knees. And you can also hold the pen in various ways so that your hand doesn't get tired. But to create the same letter with word processing, you must sit in a chair in front of a monitor and type out the words on the keyboard. If your position at the computer is uncomfortable, you might make more mistakes than if you are at ease. And if you worked in an awkward position for any length of time, you might find that your eyes felt strained, that your back ached, or that you had a headache.

Therefore, the more adjustable the various parts of your workstation are, the better you are likely to feel. It is important that you learn to use any adjustments that are provided; otherwise their benefit is wasted.

The computer. Ideally, a computer workstation or terminal should have as many controls as necessary so that each individual can achieve the greatest degree of comfort. The monitor should have adjustments for brightness and contrast. The angle of the screen should easily tilt to minimize glare. And the keyboard too should be adjustable; ideally, you should be able to detach it from the main unit and arrange it comfortably

Figure 13-6   Flexible Workstations
The modular style of most modern office equipment has contributed greatly to the comfort and ease of its users. Parts of a computer workstation can be moved and adjusted to suit the individual employee and the particular task being performed. (Courtesy of Control Data, Inc.)

Offices and computers

Plate 1

Plate 2

Plate 3

Computers have transformed offices all over the world. Before the computer, organizations relied on typewriters, mechanical calculators, and telephones to transact business. Records of each transaction were stored in ledgers and files located as close as possible to where people worked with them. Each worker usually performed one function, passing the work on when a different skill was needed.

With computers, many functions, including word processing, duplication, calculation, and filing are performed at a single work station. Files can be accessed and modified at any terminal. They can also be sent electronically to remote locations for storage or further work.

Plate 4

Plate 5

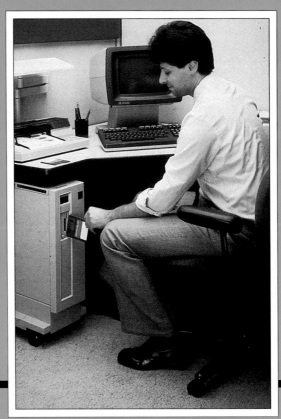

Plate 6

Plate 7

Office computers come in many sizes and have varying capabilities. Portable lap-tops, the smallest, allow you to carry your work wherever you go; yet by using a modem you can share data and information with the central office. Standard microcomputers provide computing power right on the desk in front of you, and can be linked as workstations to larger computers. Minicomputers fit in easily with office furniture, yet can run several workstations at one time. Mainframes provide central computing facilities for large organizations. And supercomputers are used for their speed in performing complex calculations, especially for scientific research.

Plate 8

Plate 9

For organizations, storage of data and documents is often as important as computing speed and power. Like the computers themselves, storage facilities and storage media vary greatly. Even the familiar floppy disk, which you may use at your desk, can store many pages of keyed information in a small space. Other storage systems like the microfilm and optical disk can provide economical storage for diagrams and handwritten documents as well. And in large computer installations, the amount of data that can be stored is enormous, whether on diskpacks that are kept on-line to the computer, or in vast libraries of movable magnetic tapes.

Plate 10

Plate 11

Plate 12

Plate 13

Plate 14

The flexibility and variety of computer equipment is making a new freedom possible in office design. While many organizations have stayed with traditional arrangements, more emphasis can now be placed on the needs of workers and managers, and less on the requirements of workflow.

Plate 15

Plate 16

Plate 17

This is leading to offices that allow open communication and offices that provide privacy and yet a sense of space. Increasing importance is attached to worker ease and comfort, following the principles of ergonomics—the study of workers, work equipment, and how to optimize the design of work space.

Plate 18

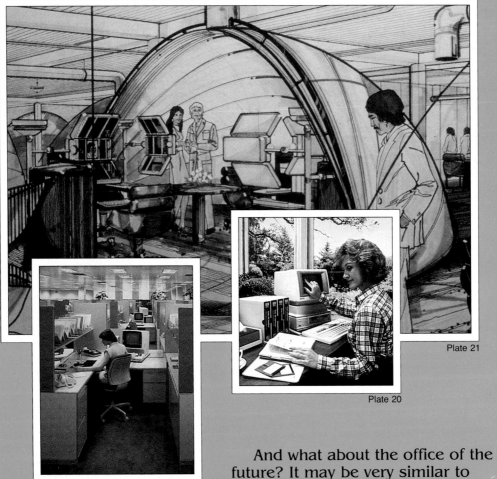

Plate 21

Plate 20

Plate 19

And what about the office of the future? It may be very similar to today's best. It could be far less common, because most office workers will work in their homes and communicate with supervisors and coworkers by modem. Or perhaps the visions of futuristic thinkers are closer to the mark—collapsible "igloos" to provide convertible privacy or openness with individual climate control, a full range of electronic equipment to minimize the use of paper, and multiple panel screens that allow electronic conferencing at the same time as the study and creation of documents.

for yourself. Positioning your equipment carefully can help you avoid fatigue, eyestrain, and other physical problems.

There has been considerable controversy over the safety of video display terminals. Recent findings by some scientists indicate that the monitor itself is not a hazard to workers. Workers' groups, however, assert that radiation from monitors may threaten fertility in both men and women and may pose a danger to the unborn children of pregnant women. Manufacturers have responded to such concerns by producing monitors that emit levels of radiation that are lower than those of many television sets. They have also responded to research showing that the color of the display seems to affect the comfort of people who work at monitors for long hours. In general, workers find green or amber displays most restful to the eyes.

STATE OF THE ART

Ergonomics and the Keyboard

When IBM created the IBM PCjr a few years ago, it equipped the home computer with what quickly became known as the "Chiclets" keyboard. It had fat, widely spaced white keys, resembling pieces of Chiclets chewing gum, which were very awkward for touch typists to use. The PCjr was a commercial failure; IBM took it off the market in less than two years. The PCjr had several problems, but critics agree that the keyboard design was one of the biggest. Despite that false step, however, IBM has set the industry standard for microcomputer keyboards.

IBM was the first major company to offer a detachable keyboard, now a common feature on micros. The IBM PC keyboard also provides an angle adjustment and a ledge across the top to prop up books. Other manufacturers are now building these features into their keyboards.

Most people stick with the keyboards that come with their computers, but you can replace a keyboard with one of a different design. Several companies produce alternatives to the IBM keyboard, with different arrangements of function and cursor keys. Choosing a keyboard is largely a matter of personal preference, but IBM retains one advantage over its competitors: many software packages include cardboard or plastic templates that fit over keyboards to identify software command keys, and most of these templates fit only IBM keyboards.

Most people are accustomed to the standard typewriter keyboard, with the QWERTY arrangement that has been around since 1868. The Dvorak keyboard, which was developed in 1912 but never caught on with typewriter manufacturers, uses a different arrangement: it places the most frequently used keys in the middle row so the fingers do much less work. The Dvorak keyboard has been gaining new popularity in recent years, particularly among executives who never learned to touch type. You can purchase software or chips to convert a QWERTY keyboard to a Dvorak keyboard.

A more popular type of labor-saving software is the "keyboard enhancer" or "macro processor." With one of these programs, you can customize function keys so that one stroke produces a result that would otherwise require a whole series of strokes. This can save time in entering complex commands and repeating text phrases.

Desk. A conventional desk, which is largely used for writing, is too high for a terminal and keyboard. Operators are most comfortable if the height of the keyboard allows for their upper arms to hang loosely from the shoulder, with the elbows bent to form a right angle so that the forearms are horizontal. The top of the computer screen should be approximately at eye level (see Figure 13-7). To achieve this, a desk with adjustable height or a specially designed computer table is best.

The color of the desk is also a factor. Dark work surfaces are known to contribute to eyestrain. Users often have to shift their eyes between their monitors and the papers on their desks. Your eyes constantly adjust to changes in light intensity. Because most papers are white, the eyes have too much adjusting to do if you are repeatedly looking from the paper to a dark surrounding desk surface and then to a computer screen. For workers who must input from paper drafts or forms, a document holder is an important desk accessory. A document holder can keep the papers upright next to the screen, thus minimizing your need to turn your head and adjust your eyes as you work.

Chair. Perhaps the most critical element in the workstation is the chair. An improperly designed chair, or one that was not intended for use in an automated office, can contribute to problems such as fatigue, muscle strain, and backaches. An ergonomically designed chair promotes good posture and thereby reduces stress on the lower back, legs, and arms.

The ideal office chair has several important features. Its backrest can be adjusted to allow maximum support for the lumbar, or lower, back.

Figure 13-7 The Ideal Workstation

This diagram of a workstation shows ideal measurements for such a unit. Notice that the chair is adjustable, allowing users to position the backrest and their arms in the optimum position for themselves. Such a workstation can minimize backaches, neck pains, and general fatigue.

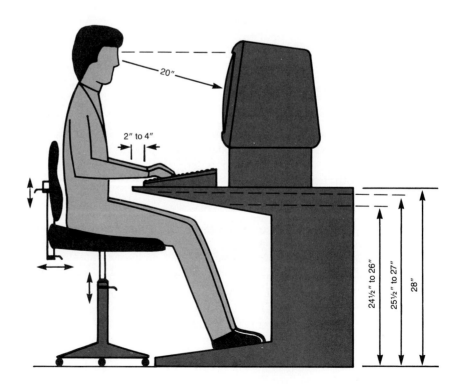

Figure 13-8 Office Chairs
Not only is a well-designed office chair comfortable to sit on, it allows the employee to work with a minimum of stress to the body. Some chairs have no armrests in order to allow free movement when an operator is keyboarding; all have easy-to-reach levers to adjust their positions. (Courtesy of Herman Miller, Inc.)

The front edge of the seat is rounded to reduce pressure on the back of the legs. Its base has five casters instead of the traditional four to provide maximum stability while permitting mobility. And finally, it has a lever that enables the user to adjust the height of the chair while setting in it. The best height allows the user's thighs to be horizontal and the knees bent at a right angle while the feet rest flat on the floor (see Figure 13-8). If the chair cannot be lowered sufficiently, short workers may find that they are more comfortable using a footrest.

LIGHTING

Many problems in lighting a computerized office stem from glare. **Glare** is produced when bright light is reflected from the surface of a computer screen, preventing the user from seeing the display. You have probably had similar experiences at home when trying to watch television in a sunny room: you cannot see the whole picture if sunlight shining through a window is hitting the glass on the TV screen. In the office, glare can be a major problem. Although you can install an antiglare filter on a monitor, proper lighting may offer a better solution.

Low levels of light produce less glare than high levels, but workers need sufficient light to read input papers and other documents. A balance must be achieved, therefore, between two different kinds of light—overall lighting and task lighting.

Overall lighting.   Overhead fluorescent tubes are frequently used in offices to provide overall lighting. Fluorescent lights are preferable to traditional incandescent bulbs because they use less electricity, create less heat, and produce less glare. Baffles or louvers diffuse the light from ceiling fixtures and help minimize glare even further. New office designs often call for **ambient lighting,** which is indirect overall lighting from fixtures built into furnishings. Ambient lighting is generally focused upward and reflected from ceilings. Ambient lighting creates less glare than overhead lamps. Artificial lighting in general causes less glare than sunlight entering through windows. Louvered shades, especially vertical ones, can allow some sunlight into the room while directing it away from computer screens. In addition, many modern office complexes have sunny atriums and common areas where people passing through are exposed to healthful natural light.

Task lighting.   Tasks that involve reading, sorting paper documents, or writing by hand call for brighter light than is desirable for working at a monitor. Illumination for such tasks is provided by **task lighting,** which focuses bright light on a small area where a task is performed.

Often, task lighting is built into office furniture, under overhead cabinets or bookshelves. The best task lighting has brightness controls that allow users to adjust the amount of light that is focused on the work surface.

Task/ambient lighting.   In ergonomically designed open offices, lamps built into the furnishings may produce **task/ambient lighting.** Each

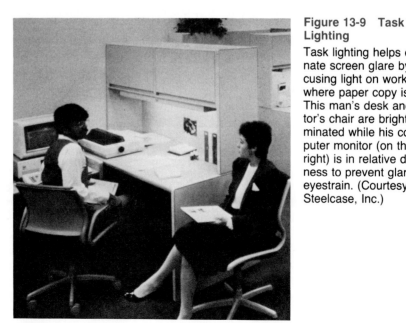

Figure 13-9   Task Lighting

Task lighting helps eliminate screen glare by focusing light on work areas where paper copy is used. This man's desk and visitor's chair are brightly illuminated while his computer monitor (on the right) is in relative darkness to prevent glare and eyestrain. (Courtesy of Steelcase, Inc.)

workstation may include a fixture that focuses light downward, onto the task area, as well as upward, so it can be reflected off the ceiling. Task/ambient lighting sometimes eliminates the need for direct overhead lighting, but it is often used in combination with overhead lights.

ACOUSTICS

The term *acoustics* refers to the qualities of a room that influence how clearly sounds can be heard or transmitted. Unlike the eye, the ear does not adjust to changes in the environment; its opening cannot narrow in response to increased noise. Because the brain associates loud sounds with stress, these can raise blood pressure, increase heart rate, and cause irritability. Sound can also provide annoying distractions. A conversation nearby can break a worker's concentration—quite apart from the fact that it may be about confidential matters. An ergonomically designed office must minimize unwanted sound to prevent these problems of health, morale, and productivity.

Controlling noise does not mean insisting on total quiet, but rather keeping sound at a level that is comfortable to people. In fact, no sound at all is undesirable; it is a form of sensory deprivation. But too much sound, or excessive variations in sound, can have very negative effects.

Modular **acoustic panels** reduce sound inside and outside the workstation. These panels and their fabric coverings absorb sound. Ceiling tiles act in the same way. Office carpeting reduces the noise from footsteps as well as reflected sounds. Noise-reducing covers are available for printers and other equipment. In addition, **white sound,** which is steady, low-level noise like the hum of an air-conditioning system, or other background sounds such as music can be used to mask individual voices and machine noises.

CLIMATE CONTROL

In discussions of office design, one often encounters the initials **HVAC.** They stand for **h**eating, **v**entilation, and **a**ir **c**onditioning and are used by engineers to describe the complete indoor climate. This includes not just the temperature but also humidity, air circulation, and air purity.

A room that is properly balanced for HVAC is a comfortable place to work. The air smells clean and free of cigarette smoke. It is neither too hot nor too stuffy nor too cold, so you can wear clothing that allows for both comfort and easy movement.

People tend to notice HVAC not when it's well balanced but when it is not. In a room that is too hot, cold, dry, humid, stale, or stuffy, they may become annoyed, irritable, restless, or sleepy. Office workers who are uncomfortable are not productive. Poor HVAC may even increase the spread of sickness during flu season.

Each person has an individual level of comfort, depending on such factors as age, sex, size, ethnic background, clothing worn, and level of work activity. But in general, office temperature should be kept around 68 °F, with a relative humidity range of 40 to 60 percent and good circulation of clean air.

Figure 13-10   Climate Control
Proper heating, ventilation, and air conditioning contribute to the comfort of office workers and the efficient operation of their machines. The HVAC system is not always hidden; here the office designers have chosen to leave the ducts exposed for a "high tech" look. (Courtesy of Steelcase, Inc.)

Air quality affects computer equipment as well as people. Sensitive disk drives can be damaged by cigarette smoke and other airborne pollutants. Electronic data can be destroyed by static electricity that results from too little humidity in the air. To avoid these hazards, organizations often use electrostatic carpeting to reduce static electricity, electronic filters to control air purity, and other devices to control humidity.

A systems approach to ergonomics

Ergonomic elements do not exist in isolation. An office chair must be viewed in relationship to a work surface and perhaps to a monitor and a keyboard. Glare is partly a function of lighting, but it is also influenced by the location of a workstation and the position of a monitor. Noise is affected by equipment, layout and the materials used for wall panels, ceilings, and floor covering. Because ergonomic elements work together, they must be viewed as part of a system.

Office design therefore benefits from a systems approach. The elements that make up the office environment can be studied as related parts of a whole. Designing an office can therefore involve steps and procedures similar to those outlined in the previous chapter on systems analysis and design.

A systems approach is ongoing and cyclical. As new work is taken on by an organization or as new or upgraded equipment becomes available, the work flow and communications flow in an office change. The design of the office environment must therefore be an ongoing process parallel to the development of information systems. Like these, the office environment needs regular reevaluation.

As you learned in Chapter 12, systems analysis involves defining the needs of the organization and studying the hardware and software requirements of its users. A systems approach to ergonomics involves similar steps. In fact, effective office design involves the same phases that were identified in the previous chapter. An ergonomics team will:

1. conduct a feasibility study

2. analyze the present design

3. develop alternative strategies for a new design

4. select the best design and equipment

5. implement the chosen design

6. maintain and continually evaluate the design

Of course, this assumes that office design itself is dealt with separately from the design of the computerized systems in the office. Some organizations include ergonomics as one element in overall systems design, with optimal layout and lighting among the goals of that design.

PRELIMINARY WORK

Determining the feasibility of an office redesign is just as important as doing a feasibility study for a proposed computer system. New office furnishings can be very costly, and other expenses are involved in implementing a change: regular work is usually interrupted as people move their belongings to new workstations and as crews install new cables or position new room dividers. Top management needs to know in advance if the change is likely to produce benefits that will justify the costs.

As in a regular systems design project, a team is assembled to plan and implement the change. The team should include representatives of top management, ergonomics experts and designers, and office workers— those who supervise tasks as well as those who perform them. The team's first step is to decide on the goals of the office redesign. What problems

Figure 13-11 Ideas for Office Design
Office designers get fresh ideas from many sources, including magazines, catalogs, and conventions. Office furniture and equipment conventions are an especially good source of ideas, since most vendors set up equipment and furniture
displays for convention-goers to try out. (Courtesy of NOPA)

do they hope to solve? How can the new design increase productivity?
And how long will the changeover take?

ANALYZING THE PRESENT DESIGN

A major part of new office design is an ergonomic analysis of the present
office. What tasks precisely are performed there? How does the present
design help or hinder these tasks? These basic questions are answered
in several ways: by studying job descriptions of workers in the office, by
discussing the office tasks with managers and supervisors, by interviewing and observing the workers themselves, and by analyzing the present
ergonomic elements, including workstation design, layout, and other environmental conditions. The result of these steps in the analysis is an
overall understanding of the work that takes place in the office and how
the ergonomic elements could be improved to increase productivity.

DEVELOPING STRATEGIES FOR A NEW DESIGN

The next phase of ergonomic redesign is to determine what changes need
to be made. At this stage, planning can be quite flexible; several alter-

natives can be considered. A noise problem from a printer could be solved by moving the printer into another room or by purchasing a sound-absorbing cover for it. Similarly, an ambient light problem could be handled by installing dimmer switches on existing lights or by replacing the lights themselves.

Each decision may affect other parts of the system. For example, the printer cover might cost more than moving the printer, but it would save workers from having to walk so far to obtain printouts. After weighing the alternatives, the planning team presents a report to management that defines the office needs, lists the possible design solutions, and recommends one or two of them as the most appropriate. The designs must specify work flow, workstation designs, lighting levels, HVAC specifications, and many other details.

SELECTING THE DESIGN AND EQUIPMENT

As for any systems development project, the bottom line for an office redesign is cost. Therefore, most organizations invite competitive bids from different vendors. These bids may in fact influence which design is selected; usually, though, the design is chosen before bids are solicited.

Figure 13-12 Redoing the Office

The modular design of modern office equipment and furniture makes the installation task relatively easy. Since parts and sizes are standardized, experienced installers can quickly assemble a new office over a weekend or even after office hours to minimize disruption. (Courtesy of Haworth, Inc.)

A scale model of the new office may be constructed at this stage to help guide implementation.

IMPLEMENTING THE DESIGN

The new design must be implemented with the least possible disruption. Several strategies are **crash conversion,** with all changes being made at once during a short time period; an **area-by-area conversion,** with different areas converted at different times; or a **phased conversion,** in which wiring may be laid one week, workstations and dividers moved the next, lighting installed in the third week, and so on. The manager in charge of the conversion may also decide to have equipment installed and structural work done on weekends.

MAINTENANCE AND EVALUATION

At the end of the implementation phase, the new office is essentially in place. The development team can be disbanded. However, a committee may remain on the project to evaluate the changeover and deal with any unforeseen problems. The committee's work includes weighing what workers have to say about the new environment. A few modifications may be necessary. The design may also need to be reevaluated as the office staff grows or new tasks are assigned to the office.

The economic benefits of ergonomics

Ergonomic elements produce numerous measurable long-term benefits for organizations. Office costs often account for well over half of all operating expenses. Increasing administrative productivity, which includes reducing employee turnover, absenteeism, and tardiness, has a tremendous impact on the effectiveness of an entire organization.

However, many organizations cling to the traditional idea that office design should be considered a part of corporate image only. Whereas computer hardware and software actually perform measurable work, the contributions of design to productivity are not so easy to prove. A part of this problem is related to a phenomenon known as the Hawthorne Effect (see the box on the opposite page), which was discovered in a celebrated productivity study which showed that employees respond positively to any kind of attention. Many managers believe that this effect contaminates environmental productivity studies.

Yet today's studies make necessary allowances. For example, in a recent study, data processing workers were divided into two groups. Both groups were encouraged to work harder by being offered incentives for accuracy and speed. One group worked at well-designed workstations with adjustable furniture and proper lighting. The other group worked at traditional desks that were not designed for data processing. The productivity increase for those at the ergonomic workstations was more than 20 percent greater than for the other group. In addition, those at the ergonomic workstation had fewer complaints about physical ailments and discomforts.

Alternatives to ideal ergonomics

Even when organizations recognize the value of ergonomics, they can't always take the steps needed to improve their working environments. Economic constraints on a small business may not allow for investment in new equipment. Workstations, chairs, lighting, and acoustic panels are expensive. Ergonomic design brings many benefits over the long term, but short-term expenses such as payroll and rent must take priority. For various reasons, changes are not always cost-effective for large businesses, either. For example, if a company is moving to new quarters in two years, changes to the current offices probably would not pay.

THE HUMAN SIDE

The Hawthorne Effect: Are All Changes for the Better?

The Western Electric Company conducted a series of tests in the 1920s at its Hawthorne, Illinois, plant to determine how changes in lighting would affect workers' speed in assembling small electrical parts. The company naturally assumed that if it improved the lighting, productivity would increase. The test results, however, were totally unexpected. Productivity did rise when the lighting was improved, but it also increased when lighting was reduced, even when the reduction was severe. Productivity rose even for a control group whose lighting had not been changed at all!

Puzzled by these results, the company's management called in a team of researchers from the Harvard Business School, who then performed more extensive tests among the Hawthorne employees over several years. The researchers varied not only lighting but also room temperature, pay rates, holidays, rest periods, and any other factors that they believed might affect productivity.

The Harvard investigators found that the productivity and morale of the employees continued to rise steadily as the investigators made changes, regardless of whether the changes themselves were positive or negative. Eventually, they concluded that merely paying attention to the workers had a much greater positive effect on their productivity than any particular change in working conditions.

Being part of the study made the workers feel important and special, and it had motivated them to overcome adverse working conditions. This phenomenon is now widely known as the Hawthorne Effect. Today, industrial psychologists and ergonomists take the Hawthorne Effect into account when they investigate working conditions, and they try to identify the factors that continue to improve productivity after the Hawthorne Effect wears off.

Figure 13-13   Personal Ergonomics
No matter how well designed an office is, it is impossible to make everyone completely comfortable at all times. In addition to standard office equipment many organizations allow workers to select personal items, such as this foot-warmer, to make their work areas more comfortable. (Courtesy of Acco International Inc.)

Organizations may try to compensate in various ways for shortcomings in their office environments. Some offer their workers monetary incentives for increased productivity. If an organization has long-range plans to incorporate ergonomic principles, managers can let employees know that they recognize problems in the office design and are planning to correct them.

Some organizations also permit workers to come up with their own ergonomic strategies, such as bringing in fans to cool and circulate the air or desk lamps to improve task lighting. Books can be used to elevate monitors. An added cushion can make your chair more comfortable. And when equipment is adjustable, you should definitely learn to use the controls to improve your working position.

Ergonomics is a field of study that can benefit all workers. Whether provided by your employer or by your own ingenuity, ergonomic improvements can make your work life more pleasant and increase your contribution to the organization.

SUMMARY

- Managers and systems analysts need to ensure that computer systems can be used efficiently by the personnel assigned to them. This involves making the software as user friendly as possible and ensuring that the hardware provided conforms as well as possible to principles of ergonomics: the study of the worker and the workplace environment.

- Ergonomics helps to optimize the design of offices and equipment. It looks at the needs of business in terms of work flow and communications flow. It also looks at the physical and psychological needs of individuals, which must be met if people are to work productively. In an office setting, ergonomics includes the design of the whole office layout, of workstations, of lighting, of acoustics, and of heat and air conditioning.

- Important considerations in office layout include where individual workers perform their tasks and where shared equipment is to be placed. An efficient layout is particularly important in the open office, where many people must work in a common area.

- Workstation design includes design of the computer or terminal itself, of the desk or computer table, and of the chair. Easy adjustability is desirable for all three components so that they can be adapted to the needs of individual workers.

- Lighting should be appropriate to the types of work being done in the office. Ergonomic office design achieves a compromise between ambient lighting and task lighting, to illuminate paperwork and other noncomputer tasks without creating glare on monitors.

- Noise control techniques include the use of sound-absorbing acoustic panels, ceiling tiles and carpeting, covers for printers and other noisy equipment, and neutral or pleasant sounds to mask distracting ones.

- HVAC, which stands for heating, ventilation, and air conditioning, is another concern of ergonomics. It covers not only temperature but also humidity, air circulation, and air purity. Poor air quality can harm computer equipment as well as people.

- A business seeking to improve its work environment generally begins by doing an ergonomic study. The study pinpoints the major sources of worker discomfort and inefficiency and lets managers consider the costs and benefits of making various changes in the office. This approach acknowledges that the office environment is a part of an overall system and that different ergonomic elements interact with one another.

- An ergonomic study is like any systems study in that it involves workers and managers, designers, and analysts. Ergonomic studies may involve interviews and observation.

- The conversion to a new office design may be done all at once, or it may be done one work area at a time. A third approach is to phase in layout changes, then lighting changes, and so on.

- Although ergonomic standards represent an ideal, many businesses cannot meet those standards because of cost or other reasons. Such businesses may try to compensate for ergonomic shortcomings, perhaps by offering financial incentives for increased productivity. In some organizations, individuals can take various measures to improve their work environments. Whatever their origin, ergonomic improvements can make your job more pleasant and increase your effectiveness.

TERMS FOR REVIEW

ergonomics
hierarchy of needs
open office
dedicated
   workstation
glare

ambient lighting
task lighting
task/ambient
   lighting
acoustics
acoustic panels

white sound
HVAC
crash conversion
area-by-area
   conversion
phased conversion

TERMINOLOGY CHECK

For each definition below, choose the correct term or terms from the list of Terms for Review.

1. Indirect overall lighting from fixtures built into office furnishings.

2. Modular units that help reduce sound inside and outside a workstation.

3. Steady, low-level noise like the hum of an air conditioning system.

4. The study of the worker and the work environment.

5. The five levels of human needs as described by psychologist Abraham Maslow.

6. Bright lighting focused on paperwork or other noncomputer tasks.

7. A work area where one person works all day.

8. An office with work areas defined by partitions rather than walls.

9. The qualities of a room that influence how clearly sounds can be heard or transmitted.

10. Heating, ventilating, and air conditioning.

INFORMATION CHECK

1. What is a major goal of ergonomics?

2. Briefly describe the two broad categories of needs that are addressed by ergonomics.

3. List and describe Maslow's hierarchy of human needs, from the most basic to the most complex.

4. Why do organizations often compromise on ergonomic design? List and discuss several reasons.

5. Identify five key elements of ergonomic design.

6. Discuss three major components of a workstation in terms of ergonomics.

7. In what ways can lighting be made ergonomic?

8. What techniques can be used to control noise?

9. What can happen if noise is not controlled?

10. How can you tell if a room is properly balanced for HVAC?

11. What are the effects of an improperly balanced HVAC?

12. Identify the phases of a systems approach to ergonomics.

13. What is the purpose of an office redesign feasibility study?

14. What is the major consideration in planning to implement a new design?

15. Discuss some ways in which companies can compensate for the lack of an overall ergonomic office design.

PROJECTS AND PROBLEMS

1. Pretend you are the director of purchasing for a computer software company that is about to move into a very modern office building. You will need furnishings for dividing a large open room into smaller work areas. On the basis of information supplied in Chapter 13, describe the type of furnishings you would buy. Write a memo to the employees who will be using the work area. Convince them that your selections are appropriate.

2. Visit an office in your school or at a local company, and look at it in terms of ergonomics. What ergonomic principles have been applied? What ergonomic principles haven't been implemented but should be? Talk to some of the people who work in the office. Write a report that describes your findings and recommends improvements.

3. Browse through some catalogs featuring ergonomic office furniture and accessories. Select a piece of furniture, and compare it with its nonergonomic counterpart. Report to your class on the differences and similarities between the two. Which costs more? Which is a better buy? Show pictures that illustrate the differences.

PART FIVE

COMPUTERS AND THE GENERAL PUBLIC

14

Computers and your personal life

Up to now, this book has focused primarily on the great benefits, along with a few problems, that computers have brought to organizations and their employees. You've read how word processing speeds the production of documents. You've also learned how electronic spreadsheets help with financial analysis, how graphics software can clarify complex numerical relationships in an instant, and how computerized database software enables organizations to quickly store, retrieve, and analyze many kinds of information.

This chapter will take a different point of view and look at the benefits and problems that computers bring to people in general. You will examine the computer's impact, for example, on the bank customer rather than the teller and on the private citizen rather than the government clerk who processes data. In other words, you'll be seeing how computers affect individuals as members of the wider public that is served by organizations.

Regardless of whether people use computers in their jobs, computers affect them as consumers and private citizens. Increasing numbers of people use microcomputers for writing term papers, playing games, managing finances, and many other purposes. And for people who don't use computers at home, computers still play a major role in their private business dealings. Computers process driver licenses, car registrations, and tax bills. Bills from businesses are generally processed by computers, too. Travel reservations and credit card purchases depend on computer systems. These are only a very few of the ways in which the information revolution is affecting personal lives.

Computers create challenges as well as advantages for the general public, just as they do for organizations. The use of computers has simplified private business affairs in some ways but has complicated them in others. It has helped organizations to serve the public more efficiently, but these organizations may also give less personal attention than they once did. As the general public continues to enjoy the benefits offered by computers, it may need to find ways of avoiding or coping with the accompanying drawbacks.

The increasing reliance on computer technology has raised serious legal and ethical questions. Some of these questions concern the rights of the computer industry versus the rights of consumers, as you will see. Others involve the security of computer systems that directly affect the physical well-being of individuals, such as those used by the military and the medical profession. Still another issue of growing concern to society is the threat that computer technology may pose to privacy. This chapter will discuss these and other questions. It will also examine some of the laws that have been enacted to protect society against the misuse of computers.

When you have studied this chapter, you should be able to:

- describe the advantages and drawbacks that word processing has brought to the personal lives of individuals

- explain how the use of computerized databases affects private citizens

- discuss the pros and cons of computerized information analysis for the general public

- list and describe several laws intended to lessen the hazards that computers pose to individual privacy and data security

- discuss the role of personal ethics in decisions about the use of computers and software

Word processing

If you have received a business letter in the mail recently, there's a good chance that it was produced with word processing software. Word processing is already among the most widespread applications of computer technology, and more organizations are purchasing word processing software all the time. You learned in earlier chapters how word processing helps organizations save time and money: it enables office workers to personalize form letters, to use boilerplate paragraphs, to make corrections without retyping documents, and more. These savings may allow businesses to keep down the prices of their products and services, thus benefiting consumers. But word processing also affects the general public in several other ways.

WORD PROCESSING AND THE MAIL

Because word processing has made letter writing so easy, some organizations are sending more letters than ever. Like other results of computer technology, this has both advantages and disadvantages for the general public.

Figure 14-1   Desktop Publishing
Desktop publishing software makes professional-looking publications economical
for organizations that might not afford them otherwise. With so much printed material competing for the reader's attention, such publications are more likely to be
read than typewritten brochures and newsletters. (Courtesy of The Aldus
Corporation)

Timely information.   Because of word processing, people now receive
more timely information in the mail. Businesses and other organizations
can respond more quickly—and sometimes more thoroughly—to individuals' inquiries. Word processing has made it easier and less costly for
social, charitable, and religious organizations to send information bulletins to their members. With desktop publishing, which combines advanced word processing capabilities with graphics software and laser
printing technology, even special-interest groups with very small budgets
can afford to prepare attractive and informative newsletters for their
members.

Junk mail.   What some people regard as timely information, however,
others view as **junk mail.** The increasing use of word processing has
added to the tons of unwanted mail that daily stuffs mailboxes, burdens
the U.S. Postal Service, and slows down the deliveries people do want.

In addition to making frequent mailings themselves, many organizations sell their mailing lists to other organizations with overlapping
interests. The publisher of a gardening magazine, for example, may sell
its subscription list to seed companies, nurseries, hardware store chains,
and environmental protection societies, among other organizations. These
transactions earn money for the publisher, so they may benefit readers
by helping to keep down the price of the magazine. On the other hand,
the people on the mailing list then receive catalogs from the seed companies, advertisements from the stores, and fund-raising appeals from
environmentalists, many of which they will not want. Some of this mail

is welcome, but much of it causes irritation and adds to community trash disposal problems.

Impersonal communications. Another by-product of the use of word processing and mailing lists has to do with the quality of communication between organizations and individuals. Correspondence prepared automatically often lacks the personal touch that makes people feel important to the businesses they patronize and the organizations they support. Ironically, this is often a direct result of word processing software's ability to create individualized form letters. In an automated mass mailing, for example, a long-time acquaintance of a small-business owner may receive a cold, formal letter with the owner's signature on it.

Sometimes it's not the tone of a form letter but a mistaken assumption that causes offense. Women often get "personalized" letters addressed to "Mr.," for example, and single people may receive mail addressed to families. These mistakes cause no great harm, but they do detract from the human element of business communications.

Organizations are starting to become aware that impersonal communications to clients and customers can produce negative feelings. They try to restore the personal touch in various ways. For instance, a product you ordered from a mail-order merchandising company may be accompanied by a note saying, "If you have trouble with your bill, write to Sue Jones in our Adjustments Department." Or there may even be a toll-free number at which to call "Sue Jones." However, it could be that no person named Sue Jones actually works for the company—instead, the name is a code word to route your complaint to the department for that particular product!

PERSONAL USE OF WORD PROCESSING

Many people now use computers with word processing software to write letters and produce other documents at home. Some focus mainly on office work, either accomplishing their day's work at home or doing extra work after regular business hours. Others have word processing software strictly for personal use. Word processing offers many of the same benefits to home users that it provides for business.

School papers. Students with access to computers and word processing programs often use them for preparing reports, term papers, and homework assignments. With these computer systems, they can compose and edit their papers faster. They can save several formats if different instructors have different requirements. Because these students can correct what they've written before printing hard copies, their papers may look neater than those prepared on typewriters. Students who use word processing may even use related software to correct their spelling and grammar automatically.

Some people are concerned that students won't learn to spell and write grammatically if they can rely on software to catch their errors.

```
                    Ann DiAngelo
                  324 Fairfield Road
                  Stamford, CT 06901
                    (203) 555-8293


CAREER OBJECTIVE:  Marketing Manager


EMPLOYMENT HISTORY:

1986--(now)  Product Manager, XYZ Publishing
             Company.  Developed marketing
             program for growing product line,
             creating promotion and
             advertising campaigns in close
             association with sales and
             technical product development
             groups.

1984-1986    Administrative Assistant, XYZ
             Publishing Company.  Aided
             Product Manager in creating
             promotional and advertising
             campaigns; handled mailing list
             updates, budget spreadsheets, and
             similar tasks.


EDUCATION:

1982-1984    La Quinta College, Stamford, CT.
             A.S. in Business.

1978-1982    Hudson High School, Bronx, NY.


      (References available on request)
```

```
                    Ann DiAngelo
                  324 Fairfield Road
                  Stamford, CT 06901
                    (203) 555-8293


CAREER OBJECTIVE:  Software Marketing Manager


EMPLOYMENT HISTORY:

1986--(now)  Software Product Manager, XYZ
             Publishing Company.  Developed
             marketing program for growing
             applications software line,
             creating promotion and advertis-
             ing campaigns in close associ-
             ation with sales, programming,
             and instructional design groups.

1984-1986    Administrative Assistant, XYZ
             Publishing Company.  Aided
             Software Product Manager in
             creating promotional and
             advertising campaigns; handled
             mailing list updates, budget
             spreadsheets, and similar tasks.


EDUCATION:

1982-1984    La Quinta College, Stamford, CT.
             A.S. in Business

1978-1982    Hudson High School, Bronx, NY.


      (References available on request)
```

Figure 14-2   A Job Application
With word processing software, you can customize your resume for
each application. The resume on the left is ready to go to any company for a marketing position. The resume on the right shows specific relevance for a marketing position in a software company.
Either can be generated simply and quickly as the need warrants.

On the other hand, many educators feel that students write better when
they use word processing. Knowing that revisions are easy to make, they
are less inhibited and more willing to take chances with their work,
experimenting with different choices of word, phrase, and organization.
Word processing can give the student more time to think, more incentive
to be creative, and more opportunity to polish the final product.

More and more students are using word processing along with other
computer technology in their schoolwork. In fact, some colleges require
that students use computers to assist them with their work in certain
courses. Others have even made it an entrance requirement that the
student own or have access to a computer.

Correspondence. Few people buy computers solely for handling correspondence, but those who buy them for other reasons often use them

for their business and personal letters. The advantages are the same for individuals as for organizations. Writing and revising letters take less time with computers, and storing the copies electronically saves space.

Databases

The mailing lists that organizations use for distributing junk mail and other information are actually simple databases. Databases are also used in more sophisticated ways, and they probably play a bigger part in your personal life than word processing does. You may use them in your personal research or business dealings now and then, even retrieving the data yourself with a home computer. More important to your private life, however, may be the information about you that is stored in databases.

OBTAINING INFORMATION FROM DATABASES

Nearly all of us obtain information from databases on occasion, often without even realizing it. When you call directory information, the operator retrieves the phone number you want from a computerized database, and the system may even output the number to you directly, using a computer-synthesized voice.

Speed and convenience. Directory information is not the only computerized database that you can access by telephone. When you call a ticket agency for theater or concert tickets, a computerized database often informs the reservation clerk what seats are available for various shows on particular dates. The computer will also print out the tickets that you order and automatically charge your credit card account. In this way you are spared the time and trouble of a trip to the box office—or perhaps to several box offices. You also find out whether you can have the seats you want much more quickly than you would if you sent for tickets by mail.

Many retail stores use computerized databases in a similar way. If you go to a showroom to order a chair, there are several choices: for example, the style, the wood, and the type and color of fabric. After you have made your decisions, the salesperson can use a terminal to check whether your selection is currently in stock or, if it isn't, how long it will take to make a delivery.

Computer failures. On the negative side, computers don't always work. And when they break down, you may not be able to obtain the information you need immediately. An electronic database may be inaccessible during a computer failure. If a travel agency's computer is down, you may be kept in suspense for hours before you are sure your vacation is arranged. To avoid (or at least minimize) such delays and inconveniences, more and more organizations are providing themselves with backup systems for their computerized databases.

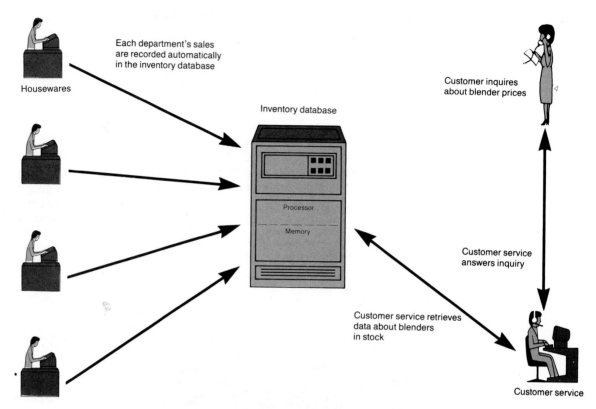

Each department's sales are recorded automatically in the inventory database

Housewares

Inventory database

Processor

Memory

Customer inquires about blender prices

Customer service answers inquiry

Customer service retrieves data about blenders in stock

Customer service

Figure 14-3 Databases Can Benefit Consumers
A department store's inventory database can be convenient for customers. Here, a customer calls Customer Service for blender prices before making a trip there to purchase one. The customer service representative checks the database, which continually receives input from Housewares and other departments. The representative can immediately answer the customer's inquiry, and can also reserve a blender if the customer wishes.

PERSONAL DATABASES

In addition to organizational databases that can make your life arrangements more convenient, many microcomputer database programs are available for home computers. These can give you electronic help for such tasks as keeping track of grocery coupons, planning your garden, preparing monthly checks, devising a customized exercise and fitness program, designing quilt patterns, and composing your own music. Other programs can help you plan dinner menus and prepare recipes. Such packages may inform you when you last served a particular dish (and to whom), tell you how much of each ingredient you need if you're cooking for seven people instead of four, calculate the number of calories in each portion, and even print out your shopping list. Some can also make suggestions, such as what vegetables go well with chicken or how to plan a meal for a diabetic.

DATABASE INFORMATION ABOUT YOU

In addition to providing you with information, databases may record information about you. The U.S. Department of Health and Human Services has well over a million personal records relating to social security alone and maintains hundreds of other databases on other kinds of welfare payments, health programs, and social services. The U.S. Treasury Department keeps records on everyone who pays federal taxes. The U.S. Justice Department maintains data on all people connected in any way with FBI investigations, regardless of whether they were accused of crimes.

The federal government's databases of personal information are among the largest, but other organizations maintain them, too. If your school uses computers to keep track of grades and schedules, its databases are almost certain to include additional information about you. Likewise, data about you can probably be found in your bank's databases, your insurance company's, and those of the publishers of any magazines you receive in the mail. Being included in these databases may offer you several advantages as well as some serious drawbacks.

Figure 14-4 Using a Database at a Convention
The task of registering delegates at a covention can be speeded up by the use of a computerized database. Here convention registrars are checking credentials and printing name badges for a few of the two thousand delegates to this convention. (Courtesy of UNISYS)

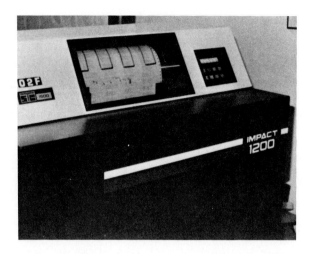

Figure 14-5 Databases and Privacy
This printer for a mailing list database is deliberately shown in a size too small to read the mailing labels. Many people are disturbed by the availability of information about them that is contained in various types of databases, including simple ones like mailing lists. (Courtesy of the College Marketing Group)

Lower costs.   One advantage of electronic databases is that, like word processing, they can save money for organizations and help to keep down their costs. These savings may be passed on to you in the form of lower tuition, smaller insurance premiums, and so forth.

Less paperwork.   Being listed in a database may also reduce the amount of time and effort required for filling out forms. Most states maintain computerized databases about the registered owners of motor vehicles, for example. When you first register a car in one of these states, you fill out a form with your name, address, birth date, insurance company, and other data. The following year, the same information is already filled in on your renewal card by the computer system. This time, you need only note changes, such as a new address or insurance company. Without the electronic database, you would have to complete the full form each time you renew.

Inaccurate entries.   One problem with databases occurs when information is entered incorrectly. The errors can lead to inconveniences or worse, especially because the information in a database may be used for several purposes. Suppose an employee at the state motor vehicle bureau enters the wrong middle initial when keying in your automobile registration data. The mistake is likely to show up not only on your car registration but also on your ownership certificate. You might not even notice the error at first. If the ownership certificate isn't corrected by the time you sell the car, however, you could have difficulty proving that you are the car's legal owner and therefore authorized to sell it. Even if you notice the error immediately, it may take several weeks to obtain the corrected papers.

SECURITY AND PRIVACY

Most computer systems in large organizations have safeguards against unauthorized use of the information in their databases. Still, data can be tampered with illegally or even stolen. Even if no one violates the law, database records can be used in ways that embarrass people or cause them greater problems.

Some organizations sell their databases, including their mailing lists, as discussed earlier in this chapter. Or they may share the data with organizations that have similar purposes. Although the organizations may mean no harm in selling or sharing their databases, such transactions can threaten privacy. Suppose you once belonged to a political organization but you resigned from it because your ideas changed. Perhaps you are embarrassed about your onetime membership, or you don't wish prospective employers to find out about it. Even after your resignation, your membership record would probably stay in the organization's database, and you might be upset if the organization shared this data with other groups. Later in this chapter you will encounter other aspects of the privacy issue.

Data communications and information distribution

Databases can become even more powerful forces in people's lives when they're part of electronic communications networks. By linking their databases to computer terminals in distant locations, organizations can now instantly gather and organize information from nationwide or even international sources. Regardless of whether databases are involved, data communications affect your personal life in a variety of ways. As with other effects of computer technology, the power that results from high-speed data communications is sometimes welcome and sometimes not.

HOUSEHOLD COMMUNICATIONS

Increasing numbers of people are buying personal computers and modems specifically to exchange data with others electronically. However, you've probably sent data from your home even if you don't have a computer.

Telephones and data communications. Because telephone companies are highly computerized, everyone who makes a telephone call is transmitting data to a phone company. When you use a push-button phone or a direct dialing system to place a long-distance call, information about your call goes directly into the phone company's record-keeping and billing systems. The phone company's computers time the call, calculate its cost, and add the cost automatically to your monthly bill. Because of the efficiency such a system provides, your bills are lower than they otherwise would be.

Some businesses have set up automated systems for taking customer orders over push-button phones. If you call such a company, a recorded message tells you which telephone buttons you must press to specify what you want to purchase. Then the recording may ask you to enter your

Figure 14-6 Computerized Operator Services
Today's telephone operator works at a Traffic Service Position System console rather than a switchboard. This computerized system, designed to handle routine functions such as credit card and coin calls, allows operators more time to serve callers with special needs. (Courtesy of AT&T/Bell Laboratories)

credit card number in the same way. This method of placing orders is faster than visiting stores or filling out order forms and mailing them. Your data is transmitted instantly to the shipping department, so you don't have to wait long for the merchandise you are purchasing. Similar systems have been set up by banks, enabling customers to pay their bills by phone. Because these systems don't require human workers to take details on the telephone, considerable cost savings may be passed along to consumers.

Communicating with home computers. Home computers, too, can often be used to place home shopping orders and make payments. People with microcomputers and modems can use their equipment to order merchandise from electronic shopping services. Merchandise may be described on your monitor or even displayed on your TV screen via cable channels. If you see something that you want, you can place your order directly from the computer keyboard. Many observers feel that such systems will be a major force in retailing in the years ahead.

Some computing enthusiasts make a hobby of data communications. They make social connections through electronic bulletin boards or they "converse" on-line with other enthusiasts through information services such as CompuServe. Using communications equipment and software, you can also retrieve information instantly from commercial databases, about everything from historic events to current stock prices, without ever leaving your home.

ORGANIZATIONAL COMMUNICATIONS AND CONSUMERS

This section of the chapter has so far focused on data communications from one individual to another or between individuals and organizations. Personal lives are also affected, however, by data communications within or between organizations.

Improved service. Like databases and other features of electronic technology, high-speed communications often result in better service for the public. Data communications help police departments trace stolen cars and return them to their legal owners, for example. As soon as a car is reported stolen, a local police department transmits a description and the car's serial and registration numbers to the **National Crime Information Center (NCIC)** computer. Meanwhile, police officers routinely check the NCIC computer for information on any cars they stop. In less

Figure 14-7 Shopping at Home
Computerized shopping services are becoming more widespread. After a long day at the office, consumers can order merchandise from the comfort of their homes, often saving themselves the time, money, and aggravation it would take to drive to a shopping center. (Courtesy of Apple Computer, Inc.)

time than it takes to write a speeding ticket, an officer can find out if a car has been reported stolen from anywhere in the country. Similarly, datacom systems enable merchants to detect stolen credit cards, thereby protecting cardholders from unauthorized charges.

Computerized data communications between organizations also speed business transactions for consumers. For example, by using a datacom network, a car rental agent in a Chicago airport can assure a hurried customer dropping off one car that another car will be waiting for her in New York in a couple of hours. Businesses could not provide this level of service and convenience for customers without electronic data communications.

Keeping pace with datacom.

The speed of data communications among organizations sometimes catches people off guard, however. An example is the reduction in the time it takes banks to process checks. At one time, it took several days to process a check that was drawn on one bank and deposited in another. This provided a **float,** or a time lag between when a check was written and when it cleared and payment was actually made. Consequently, people often wrote checks *before* making deposits to cover them, confident that they had a few days' grace. Today's datacom networks allow a check to clear much more quickly. If it is written before a deposit to cover it is made, the check is much more likely to be returned as unpayable.

Datacom security.

Some datacom networks are vulnerable to security problems, causing trouble for consumers and for society in general. Occasionally news reports tell of computer hobbyists who use their micros and modems to access, and sometimes to tamper with, databases of the government, businesses, and research organizations. Transmissions of government and military data are prone to interception by hostile nations. And criminals have used data communications systems to steal from individuals' bank accounts. Most organizations have extensive security systems to protect their data from interception or tampering, but few of these systems, if any, are foolproof.

Law enforcement agencies have applied colorful names to many of the techniques criminals have developed for stealing through the use of computers. In a technique known as the **Trojan horse,** illegal functions are added to a program that otherwise acts normally. Thus, a thief might instruct the computer to add extra zeros to a particular bank account balance. In a **salami crime,** the criminal collects money in an account by instructing a computer to slice very small amounts from many other accounts. A technique known as **data diddling** modifies data as it enters or leaves a computer system; however, the internal processing is not affected, so many systems cannot detect the change.

The potential for the criminal use of data communications is enormous. Stories range from a case in which a programmer designed a bank's security system so that he could later bypass it, and then stole $500,000,

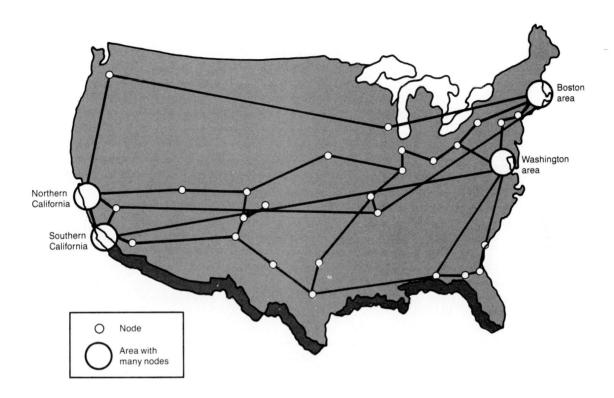

Figure 14-8   A National Datacom Network
In 1968, the Defense Advanced Research Projects Agency started a major re-
source-sharing network of computer systems around the U.S. Arpanet, as it is
called, is a complex web of 94 nodes in 88 locations. Arpanet passes messages
by packet-switching; the exact paths a message takes are decided by interface
message processors (IMPS) along the line. This is done for speed, reliability, and
security. As a further safeguard, each connecting path has at least one alternative.

to one in which a New York bank's computer was persuaded by a bogus
telex message to send more than $20 million out of the country. The FBI
has estimated that bank robbers take about $3,000 in the average holdup—
the average computer bank theft is worth half a million dollars.

Data and information analysis

The effects of computers on people's personal lives are magnified even
further because data stored and transmitted electronically can also be
analyzed with computers.

ANALYZING DATA AT HOME

As more and more households acquire data communications equipment, increasing numbers of people can retrieve institutional data and do their own analyses at home. So far, the primary use of data analysis at home has been for financial management.

Maintaining bank accounts. If your bank offers home banking services, you can use your computer to pay bills, transfer funds between accounts, and verify your account balances at any time. The monitor

How It Was

Profile of a Computer Crime

In early 1973, the nation's attention was focused on Vietnam and the Watergate scandal. In California, New York, and Washington, D.C., however, investigators were beginning to piece together evidence on what was to become the biggest computer crime on record. The investigators discovered that an organization called the Equity Funding Corporation had used a computer to create 56,000 insurance policies for fictitious policyholders. The fictitious policies were entered in Equity Funding's books along with its real insurance policies. Equity sold the policies for cash to other insurance companies, which took over collecting the premiums and responding to any claims.

Small insurance organizations often sell their policies for cash to larger companies. The small company sends out the bills, but the new policy owner collects the premiums and responds to any claims. Equity sold its policies, both real and fictitious, to other groups. The fictitious policies were valued at more than $2 billion.

When Equity sent out the bills, it needed to know which policies were real, so it set up a computer system using secret code numbers (a type of Trojan horse technique). Only real policyholders were sent bills. Equity Funding itself paid the premiums on its fictitious policies.

However, to raise the money to pay for the fictitious policies, Equity had to create even more of them. It was an ever-increasing spiral—and eventually it had to stop.

On March 6, 1973, after the fraud had gone on for more than three years, a disgruntled employee blew the whistle. The Security and Exchange Commission, the New York Stock Exchange, and various other regulatory bodies began their investigations. Soon Equity was in bankruptcy proceedings, and its executives faced criminal charges and were forced to resign.

One question the investigators faced was, "How could this have happened?" The answer is that auditors had not yet adjusted their methods to doing business by computer. Using the old methods of keeping insurance records on paper, it would not have been possible to create so many fraudulent policies in so short a time. Fraud on this scale required a computer, and auditors were not equipped to check a computer run for authenticity.

Auditors, and auditing methods, have come a long way since 1973. Specific methods for auditing computer systems (often referred to as electronic data processing (EDP) auditing) have been developed, and most auditors are trained in these methods as part of their professional studies. Today, it is unlikely that the Equity Funding scandal could be repeated.

Figure 14-9   Bringing the Market Home
Individual investors with microcomputers and modems can access the vast amount of financial data produced by the New York Stock Exchange. Small investors can "read the ticker" through their local brokers or through home services which are on-line to the exchange. (Courtesy of New York Stock Exchange)

displays a running total of available funds in your account, and the computer can deduct the amount of each payment you make. Thus, you know when your deposits have cleared, and you don't run the risk of returned checks. Even a simple data analysis tool like this can help you to manage your finances.

Managing investments.   Increasingly, the tools that institutional investors use are also available to individuals at home. Anyone with a micro, a modem, and a spreadsheet can download stock prices, then use a spreadsheet to analyze the figures. Specialized software packages for financial analysis and investment management are also available. With these tools, even a small-time investor may be able to forecast the best times for trading stocks or other financial holdings. At least one major bank offers a cash management service that lets individuals monitor and analyze financial market data and then buy and sell securities on-line. Users of this service can shift their cash instantly between savings accounts and money market funds, for example, to take advantage of changing market conditions.

The ability to retrieve and analyze information from a database gives an investor an advantage over other individuals in the financial markets. Brokerages and other financial organizations have a greater advantage, of course, because their systems for retrieving and analyzing data are more sophisticated.

INSTITUTIONAL DATA ANALYSIS

Financial organizations aren't the only ones that analyze data in sophisticated ways. Businesses do, too, and so do government agencies. For individuals, these analyses by organizations can bring both benefits and headaches.

Cost cutting. In addition to helping organizations manage their investments, the instant ability to retrieve and analyze data can help keep down business costs. A textile company that uses computers to analyze data on raw materials can respond more quickly to a sudden drop in the price of a fiber it uses. This may result in lower wholesale prices for garment manufacturers and, in turn, lower prices for consumers. The greater a company's capacity for analyzing business data, the more it can maintain profits while keeping its prices competitive.

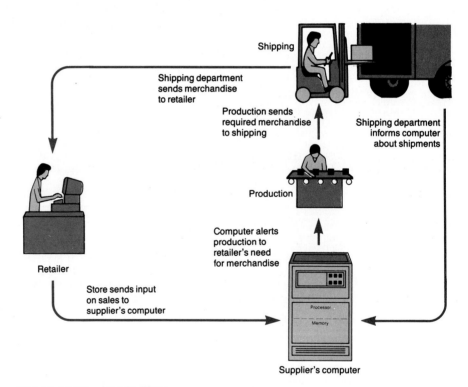

Shipping

Shipping department sends merchandise to retailer

Production sends required merchandise to shipping

Shipping department informs computer about shipments

Production

Retailer

Computer alerts production to retailer's need for merchandise

Store sends input on sales to supplier's computer

Processor

Memory

Supplier's computer

Figure 14-10 Just In Time
Electronic data analysis lets businesses use just-in-time (JIT) inventory control. A retailer's cash register is linked directly to the supplier's computer, sending data each time a sale occurs. Because the computer also receives information about shipments, it calculates when the retailer's stock is running low, and arranges for more merchandise to be sent—and, in some systems, to be manufactured—just in time. This enables the retailer—and the supplier—to work with far smaller inventories than they used to, lessening both cost and risk.

Revenue collections. Data analysis can also help organizations, including governments, to collect money they might not receive otherwise. New York City, for example, began analyzing various kinds of tax data a few years ago in an effort to increase its revenues. Officials found that some residents were deducting housing costs as business expenses on their income tax returns but were not filing business tax returns for the business work that they did at home. The resulting crackdown added quite a bit of money to the city treasury. New Yorkers who had to pay additional taxes were not pleased, of course. But for most of the city's taxpayers, this use of data analysis helped keep tax bills down.

PERSONAL DATA

Although they don't dispute a government's right to analyze its own tax records, some people worry that organizations could use similar techniques to deduce more private information about individuals. Various government agencies have data about people's medical histories, incomes, bank accounts, stock holdings, military records, marriages, and political affiliations. Other government databases may have information about other household members and about any encounters people have had with law enforcement agencies. If the agencies pooled all of their data and analyzed it, they might end up with information that most people would regard as extremely private.

Computers, ethics, and the law

Concerns about individual privacy and data security have already been mentioned in this chapter. Legislators and the court system have been addressing these concerns as well as others that arise from the spread of computer technology. In addition to creating legal issues, the use of computers has raised questions of personal ethics, or of right and wrong, among computer users. Some of these questions involve **intellectual property,** or the ownership of the ideas and logic on which particular computer programs are based. Other questions involve unauthorized use of computers by individuals.

RECENT LEGISLATION PROTECTING PRIVACY

As computers have been used to collect, store, analyze, and distribute more and more information about individuals, lawmakers have started acting to protect individual privacy. One law has established limits on the personal information that's kept in government files. Other laws have

Figure 14-11 Computers and Lawmaking
Lawmakers not only legislate about computers, but also use computers to legislate. Lengthy roll-call votes have been largely abandoned in favor of electronic vote
tallying. The computer in the lower left is part of the electronic voting system in the
U.S. House of Representatives. (Courtesy of U.S. House of Representatives)

given people the right to see data that government agencies and businesses are keeping about them. Another gives individuals control over
the distribution of data about themselves.

The freedom of information act. In 1966, Congress passed the
Freedom of Information Act, which allows individuals to examine the
information that federal agencies have gathered about them. During the
late 1960s and early 1970s, many political activists used this law to
determine whether the Federal Bureau of Investigation had kept files on
them and, if so, to obtain copies of those files.

The fair credit reporting act. Congress enacted the **Fair Credit
Reporting Act** in 1970. This law allows people to see the credit records
that businesses keep about them. Using this law, people sometimes discover credit information about themselves that is inaccurate or out of
date and that may prevent them from obtaining new credit. Before the
law was signed, people had no sure way of knowing about—and therefore
correcting—errors in their records. If they were refused credit, they couldn't
be sure of the reasons.

The federal privacy act. Made law in 1974, the **Federal Privacy
Act** is intended to prevent any misuse of information about individuals

that is kept in federal government files. This law is based on the **CARTS principle,** which states that personal information in federal files must be complete, accurate, relevant, timely, and secure. This act also established a Privacy Commission, which recommended extending the law to cover the personal data files maintained by businesses. So far, Congress has not followed this recommendation. The Federal Privacy Act and the Freedom of Information Act are widely regarded as the two most important laws relating to individual privacy.

The education privacy act. Also enacted in 1974, the **Education Privacy Act** ensures the privacy of student records kept by schools that receive federal funds. Before the law was enacted, such schools (and most schools do receive money from the federal government) could send copies of your academic and behavioral records to anyone who requested them. Now, they can do so only with your consent.

Right to financial privacy act. The 1978 **Right to Financial Privacy Act** gives individuals the right to review information about themselves that is maintained by financial institutions such as banks and credit bureaus.

State laws. In addition to federal legislation that covers computers and information, several states have made laws regarding the use of computers. Some of these state laws concern privacy, the theft of computer time, or the unauthorized use of computers owned by organizations. New laws against the manipulation or alteration of data provide added protection against computer crimes such as illegal funds transfers. States have also enacted new laws against the destruction of data or of data-gathering devices.

INTELLECTUAL PROPERTY, PERSONAL ETHICS, AND SECURITY

Computer and software companies, as well as individual programmers, are protected by other new legislation or new interpretations of existing laws. Legislators and the courts have also acted to combat the use of computers for crimes against both individuals and organizations. Police departments and other law enforcement agencies are learning more about computer technology so that they're better able to detect computer crimes and apprehend the people who commit them.

Federal copyright law of 1976. Among the legal protections for individuals and corporations is the **Federal Copyright Law,** which prohibits the copying or sale of written materials without consent from their authors, publishers, or other copyright owners. Congress revised the Federal Copyright Law in 1976, specifying that the law applies to computer programs and related materials. Duplicating a commercial software disk without permission of its publisher is against the law, just as it is illegal to make and distribute photocopies of a best-selling novel.

Necessary as laws may be, they are not always obeyed or enforced. People sometimes respond to unpopular laws by deliberately trying to evade them, and it may be practically impossible to prove that laws are being broken; or else the cost of enforcement in any given instance may

---

STATE OF THE ART

Copy Protection Schemes

Imagine you have spent months or even years inventing and developing a product. You hope it will sell and provide you with a steady income. Now imagine that someone can copy your invention in two minutes without paying you anything. Software developers are confronted with this plight all the time. In an effort to safeguard their products and their incomes against pirates, they have devised a variety of copy protection schemes. Needless to say, the exact details of these schemes are trade secrets, even though they can often be figured out by determined programmers.

Perhaps the simplest scheme is the use of serial numbers: each copy of a software product is assigned its own number. The number is usually printed on a registration card and on the label of the original software diskette; it is also often coded into the actual program. The developer provides upgrades and technical support only for users who have sent in their registration cards and who can provide serial numbers to match. This copy protection scheme, however, inconveniences only software pirates who need these services from the developer.

Another copy protection scheme places some physical defect (often a tiny laser-burned hole) at a precise location on the disk. The software won't run unless it finds this defect. This technique is expensive, however, because it requires custom-made diskettes.

A third antipiracy technique is achieved by programming only. It involves changing the format of the disk itself from the usual nine sectors to a nonstandard ten perhaps. The software enables the computer to read the nonstandard format, but the DOS copy program cannot create another disk of the same type.

Copy-protected disks obviously create problems for users who wish to make legitimate backup copies or who wish to install their programs on hard disks. So developers have devised methods that allow backups. The software disks contain their own special copying and installation procedures, which permit only a certain number of copies.

Some antipiracy schemes produce dramatic effects when users try to copy software. For example, software can be designed to erase itself in response to a COPY command. Another dramatic copy protection scheme uses a "worm," which is a program that alters or damages a pirate's software or data without warning. One type of worm disables the software after a certain amount of usage, leaving only a phone number displayed on the monitor. If a user calls the phone number, the developer will provide a special code to unlock the software—after the user has paid for it.

Even the most drastic copy protection schemes are foiled by clever pirates sooner or later. And copy protection often inconveniences and annoys legitimate customers. Because of this, many software companies are moving away from copy protection, especially for big corporate customers. Instead, they are selling site licenses, which grant customers the right to make specified numbers of copies. The higher the license fee, the more copies the customer can make. Site licensing represents an attempt by developers to balance the needs of their customers against their own right to profit from their inventions.

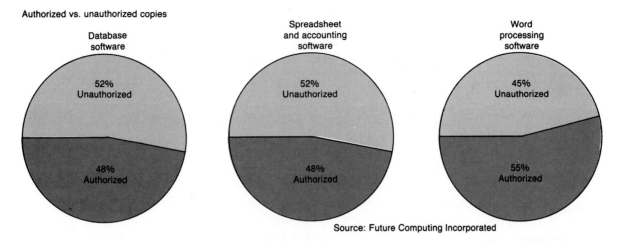

Authorized vs. unauthorized copies

Source: Future Computing Incorporated

Figure 14-12   Illegal Copying
Many people who would never shoplift software think nothing of copying it illegally. Software industry groups call software piracy a violation of U.S. Copyright Law. A 1985 study estimated that almost half of all copies made from microcomputer business software are unauthorized.

outweigh the benefits. Therefore, the safeguarding of individual privacy, the protection of intellectual property rights, and the security of important data often depend as much on the ethics of individuals as on legislation.

Software piracy.   Unauthorized copying of computer programs is called **software piracy.** An organization that buys one copy of a program and then makes illegal copies for several of its employees is committing software piracy. This practice is widespread among individuals as well as organizations, for obvious reasons. Software is often expensive: many popular word processing programs cost $300 to $600. A blank disk, on the other hand, may cost less than a dollar. Using a blank disk, one can copy a program in about two minutes.

Many popular software products are **copy protected,** however. This means that the publishers have included special programming codes or used other technical means to prevent people from copying the software. (See the Box opposite.) Other programmers, however, have built profitable businesses by writing software to foil these copy protection schemes. In many magazines for computer users, you'll see advertisements for software that enables you to duplicate copy-protected programs.

Piracy probably costs software publishers millions of dollars each year in lost sales. Increasingly, companies are tracking down reports of illegal copying and filing lawsuits to recover the money the copying has cost them. However, only a small fraction of the money lost to piracy is recovered. Such losses have forced some companies to stop producing software, whereas others have had to raise their prices still further in order to stay in business. In the long run, piracy harms consumers by making software less available to them.

Security breaches. Just as some people view new copy protection schemes as a challenge, others take pride in evading security measures that limit access to data. Many news stories in recent years have focused on people who gain access to data maintained by business and government organizations. Mixed with the public's general disapproval of their illegal activities is some admiration for their intelligence and technical skill. People may have similar mixed reactions if a student breaks into a school's computer files, looks at other students' personal and academic records, and perhaps changes a few grades.

Many people who engage in such activities do not feel that they are doing anything seriously wrong. Often they are very surprised to be considered criminals when they are finally caught and (in many cases) prosecuted. However, the confidential data accessed by a hobbyist could be about you, and the difference between someone who alters data for fun and someone who does it for criminal purposes is small.

Occasionally, people break into protected systems by accident. For example, you might suddenly find confidential payroll information on your computer screen that you aren't authorized to see. The temptation to check your co-workers' salaries could be enormous. The ethical response, however, would be to report the accident to the technical staff so that the flaws in the system's security can be corrected.

If you violate security measures in a computer system—or if you stay quiet while someone else does so—you cannot expect others to respect the security of data about you. Insecure data can jeopardize not only business operations but also individual finances, privacy, and even physical safety and well-being.

SUMMARY

■ Today's widespread use of computers creates problems as well as benefits for the general public, just as it does for organizations.

■ Word processing software enables organizations to keep down document production costs and send consumers more timely information. It has also led to an increase in junk mail. Because documents produced with word processing can be impersonal, it can also impair the relations between individuals and organizations.

■ Word processing can save students time in preparing term papers and other school reports. However, some people are concerned that the use of software to check spelling and grammar will keep students from learning to write and spell correctly.

■ Most individuals use information from computerized databases from time to time. These databases help organizations to keep down costs while providing better service. Because of their heavy reliance on databases, however, organizations can be greatly inconvenienced by computer failures.

■ The benefits provided by computerized databases must be weighed against threats they pose to privacy and data security. Government agencies and other organizations have enormous banks of information about virtually all U.S. residents. This data may contain inaccuracies, and even if accurate, the information in computerized databases is vulnerable to misuse.

- Data communications technology enables organizations to transmit information quickly and thus provide better service while keeping down costs. However, it is often through datacom networks that criminals obtain database information illegally or commit other computer crimes. Most organizations have extensive security systems for protecting their data, but these systems are not foolproof.

- By analyzing up-to-the-minute data obtained from databases or other sources, individuals and organizations can make speedy and informed decisions that keep down costs and increase revenues. However, organizations may also be able to combine database files to deduce private information about individuals.

- Legislators have enacted several laws to protect individual privacy. Courts and lawmakers have also acted to prevent and punish computer crimes and to protect the intellecutal property rights of software publishers.

- Laws aren't always adequate to counter computer crime or the misuse of software and data. Illegal copying of software is so widespread that it costs software publishers millions of dollars each year. Computer security violations are sometimes greeted with admiration as well as disapproval. The protection of privacy, property, and safety against the misuse of computer technology depends not only on laws but also on ethical behavior by individuals and organizations.

TERMS FOR REVIEW

junk mail	intellectual property	Education Privacy Act
National Crime Information Center (NCIC)	Freedom of Information Act	Right to Financial Privacy Act
float	Fair Credit Reporting Act	Federal Copyright Law
Trojan horse	Federal Privacy Act	software piracy
salami crime	CARTS principle	copy protected
data diddling		

TERMINOLOGY CHECK

For each of these definitions, choose the correct term from the list of Terms for Review:

1. Unauthorized copying of computer programs.

2. Use of a computer to accumulate money in an account illegally by diverting small amounts from other accounts.

3. Law intended to prevent the misuse of information about individuals that is kept in government files.

4. Use of special programming codes or other techniques to prevent software disks from being duplicated.

5. Ideas on which computer software and other products are based.

6. Law that gives individuals the right to see information about themselves that is contained in government files.

7. Organization that maintains a database of information about property that has been reported stolen.

8. Requirement that personal data in federal files be complete, accurate, relevant, timely, and secure.

9. Time lag between when a check is deposited in a bank and when the funds it represents are available for spending.

10. Law that prevents schools from distributing data about students without the student's consent.

INFORMATION CHECK

1. How might the use of word processing affect relations between individuals and organizations? Discuss pros and cons, and be specific.

2. What disadvantages, if any, might there be in using word processing software for schoolwork?

3. What organizations are likely to have information about you in their databases? What potential problems does this pose for you?

4. As a rule, are mistakes in computerized database records more serious or less serious than errors in records that aren't computerized? Why is this so?

5. How are the effects of computerized databases magnified when they're combined with data communications?

6. Can you participate in data communications at home if you don't have a computer? If so, how?

7. Give an example of how data communications can speed business transactions for consumers.

8. Explain how data communications affects the clearance of checks by banks. What problems can this cause for bank customers?

9. How can computerized data analysis help individual investors?

10. Discuss how data analysis by government can help to keep down tax rates.

11. Do you have the right to see the records your bank maintains about you and your accounts? Why?

12. What does intellectual property have to do with computers?

13. If a prospective employer asks your high school for a transcript of your grades, what must the school do, if anything, before sending the transcript?

14. If you wrote a computer program, is there any law that would prohibit other people or organizations from selling your program as their own? If so, what is the name of the law?

15. Why do software companies sometimes attempt to prevent people from making copies of their program disks?

PROJECTS AND PROBLEMS

1. Jeffrey Roberts has maintained checking and savings accounts at the same bank for several years. He always pays his bills on time, he earns a good salary, and he isn't heavily in debt. However, the bank recently turned down his application for a loan to purchase a car. The bank employee who dealt with Roberts said she didn't know the reason for the refusal, but she gave him the name and address of the credit bureau from which the bank obtains credit checks on all loan applicants. Does Roberts have any way of determining why his loan request was rejected? If so, how should he go about it? What advice would you give him, if any?

2. Write or phone an organization that is likely to have information about you in its database, and ask for a copy of that information. If you can obtain the copy without delay, report to your class on the information you obtain. Is it accurate and timely? Is it relevant to the organization's purposes? Could it be used against you in any way? How difficult was it to obtain the information? If you encounter delays or refusals, report to the class on your experience.

15

Computers, information, society, and the future

This book has shown you how organizations are using computer systems and has suggested how these applications might affect you as an individual. You have read throughout about how computers enable businesses, government agencies, and other organizations to store, retrieve, analyze, and distribute information, from financial and personnel records to form letters to long-range business forecasts. And you have just seen how people throughout society benefit from the speed, efficiency, and thoroughness offered by this new technology. You also looked at some of the dangers presented by computers, such as threats to privacy.

As computer technology develops and its use continues to spread, the computer's influence on society is likely to increase even more. Computers offer great hope for helping to relieve some of the world's most pressing problems, such as hunger, natural disasters, and environmental pollution, as well as more local problems like crime and traffic control. In your work, you may someday be using computer technology to deal with some of these problems in ways that are now only being imagined.

However, change rarely happens exactly as people predict. For example, when microcomputers were first developed, few people anticipated that they would have such a startling impact on the world of business. They were primarily sold as household devices, useful for learning about programming, for handling home finances and perhaps writing letters, and for playing computer games. The microcomputer was supposed to join the TV as a great household success story of the twentieth century. After all, what would organizations want with micros? Organizations needed—and many already used—larger computing machines.

You already know the story of Visicalc—how a Harvard business student thought of using a micro to automate the use of accounting worksheets. Suddenly, the micro was vital to business managers, and even more so when they found that spreadsheets could do something that was impossible before: supply virtually instant "what if" projections into the future. Organizations bought micros by the thousands. Home computers have had a comparatively calm history by comparison; they are still nowhere near being the success story that television was. In fact, home videocassette recorders have consistently surpassed micros in consumer electronics sales.

The future remains a mystery. Even if you know the likely developments in the technology of computing—and unlikely breakthroughs can also occur—how those developments will be applied is often unexpected. Nobody should sit back and wait for today's predictions to come true. Instead, you should stay informed about the changes that are already occurring in the field and learn to think about their potential effects on people. This will enable you to steer your own life to fit in with those effects. It will also give you the knowledge and power to express our opinions and influence those effects.

This chapter begins by reviewing some of the new techniques that developers of software and hardware are exploring—techniques that would vastly increase the power and capacity of computers. It then examines ways in which people think this power might affect the world of the future—*if* enough people feel the need and the price can be made attractive. Finally, the chapter encourages you, as a future worker in a rapidly changing world, to keep aware of changes in this field and to think about how future developments are going to affect your life and what you can do about them.

When you have completed this chapter, you should be able to:

- describe ways in which computers and information systems are likely to change in the next decade or two

- discuss possible effects of these technological changes on society

- discuss what's involved in preparing for technological change and adapting to it

- define technology assessment and discuss its importance to society

- discuss how private citizens can influence the development and use of computer technology and its effects on society

Changes in computer systems

How are computers and information systems likely to change the world? That depends partly on how the technology progresses. Suppose that ultimately computers are developed that can truly understand human speech and can respond to different people, with their different voices and different dialects of different languages. Input at the keyboard might become a thing of the past. Computers might be able to take over as interpreters at the United Nations. And if they were also adequately

Figure 15-1 Automated Daylighting System
This building has a sophisticated electronic daylighting system that adjusts the window louvers as the sun moves during the day. Controls can be set to maintain a chosen light level, or to allow for maximum direct or indirect sunlight. This can lessen both lighting and temperature control costs. (The Moore Company)

miniaturized, such computers might be incorporated within true science fiction robots, as easy to speak to as your family and friends.

Or suppose computer systems can be created that predict weather accurately throughout the world—not merely large weather patterns, but local variations too. This would be an incredibly complex task. The forecast would no longer deal with percent probabilities of precipitation; instead, people could have absolute certainty about what the weather would be like in their own backyards. They could plan their activities days, even weeks, ahead. They could program home heating and ventilation systems to take advantage of warm days by automatically adjusting shades and windows and even to close them to avoid summer rain showers.

However, these possibilities seem far away. Software and hardware developers are working toward more immediate goals. This book has examined a few of these areas of exploration. Here we will review some of these and then discuss possible applications.

SOFTWARE ADVANCES

The details of what a computer does are governed by its software. A system may be less effective if the computer hardware operates slowly, less convenient if the computer is heavy and immovable, and less valuable if the computer cannot communicate in a variety of ways. But without specific applications software it could not perform specific tasks. And until appropriate systems software has been developed, powerful new computer hardware cannot realize its full potential. This is a frequent occurrence today.

The software development industry is growing at a phenomenal rate, and this growth is expected to continue. In fact, business analysts predict a 75 percent increase in the size of this industry between 1986 and 1990. Besides designing software packages for particular applications and for particular pieces of hardware, software developers are also pursuing some overall goals that may change the face of computing in the next decade.

One important overall goal is applications software integration, allowing different tasks to be performed together on the computer, often using the same data. Another is to simplify programming, thus simplifying software development itself. A third goal is to extend the range of artificial intelligence, enabling the computer to show some characteristics of human thought, including the ability to adapt to unusual situations and learn from experience.

Applications software integration. In the early days of computers, and even the early days of micros, many software products were used for one specific application only. Users often had to acquire large and expensive software libraries to meet their everyday needs. Lately, as you read in Part Two, software companies have tended to integrate several generic applications into single products or sets of products. The

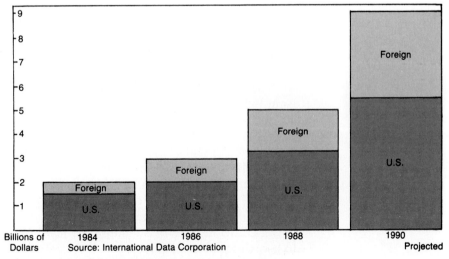

Figure 15-2 Worldwide Demand for PC Software
The worldwide market for personal computer software from U.S. software companies is growing at an average annual rate of 28%. Foreign sales are increasing nearly 50% faster than domestic sales.

popular Lotus 1-2-3 software, which combines a flexible spreadsheet with graphics and database management, is among the earliest examples of integrated software. Desktop publishing software, which combines word processing and graphics to facilitate the designing of printed pages, is another example.

Today's users of integrated programs must often sacrifice some software features for the convenience offered by integration. A word processing program in an integrated package, for example, is rarely as capable as most products designed exclusively for word processing. But, as hardware becomes more powerful, the components of integrated products may soon have just as many features as single-application programs.

Integration can extend far beyond desktop publishing. Particularly on systems with large computers, operations can be integrated from point of sale, to inventory management, to accounting, to billing, to purchasing. As hardware capacity increases, still greater breadths of integration will be achieved.

Automated programming tools.

Among the newest software products on the market are programming tools. Software is being used to help produce other software. Many of the programming tools on the market today are used for debugging programs. However, software today can contribute considerably more to the development of effective computer programs.

Different types of fourth-generation languages, as you read in Chapter 7, are greatly simplifying programming for specific tasks. No longer must line after line of program be written, detailing the exact logic that the computer is to follow. Instead, a programmer can use menu choices or unstructured commands to indicate the general tasks the new software is to perform, and the computer language compiler does the rest. In fact, tools exist that can allow a nonprogrammer to create specific applications. Authoring systems for training software are an example. And more and more software is becoming available that allows users to develop their own systems.

The automation of programming is likely to continue. Programming is an intense and demanding task, requiring careful logic and great accuracy. Both program developers and users stand to benefit from advances in this area.

Artificial intelligence.

A major field of development today is **artificial intelligence,** which has been mentioned several times in this text. Artificial intelligence is a complex concept, but two aspects of it are natural language programs and expert systems. Both are beginning to play significant roles in computer applications software and are expected to become even more important in the future.

Until now, most applications programs have required users to learn many commands or negotiate several layers of menus. A few powerful database management programs even require users to learn special programming languages. Thanks to progress in artificial intelligence, soft-

Figure 15-3   Artificial Intelligence
Computers and robots have difficulty with many tasks that people find very simple—recognizing faces, for example, or catching ping-pong balls. But as research
in artificial intelligence progresses, computers should become able to handle many
more complex "human" tasks. (Courtesy of AT&T/Bell Laboratories)

ware that uses **natural language** commands is now being developed.
Such software comes close to communicating with human beings in the
same language they use to talk to each other. This natural language is
not only used in business applications, needless to say. Software novels
have begun to appear in which the reader can influence the action by
making choices in natural language. This means that the novel can be
different each time that you read it.

Another outcome of artificial intelligence research, as you saw in
Chapter 6, has been the development of **expert systems,** which can use
human-like reasoning skills to solve problems. So far, expert systems
work only with highly specific bodies of information. An expert system
used by a major computer manufacturer, for example, can advise exactly
what combination of memory, cables, storage mechanisms, and other
parts must go into a minicomputer system to meet a customer's expressed
needs. The expert system performs this task much more efficiently and
more accurately than most human beings can. When it comes to other
subjects, however, this system is utterly ignorant. It couldn't produce a

list of other customers with similar needs, for example, or suggest arguments that would help sell the new configuration to these customers.

However, as scientists gain further insight into human learning processes, expert systems will probably become more versatile. Future expert systems will also be designed for users with different levels of skill. An expert system for use in medical practices, for example, may use nonscientific words for soliciting information from patients, a different vocabulary for communicating with nurses, and highly technical terminology for physicians.

Firmware program chips. A different aspect of software that may be important in the future is how it is stored. Some software manufac-

---

STATE OF THE ART
The Printed Word

It's the year 2088. A group of school children are being ushered through a museum. They stop to study an exhibit of objects once used in communication—papyrus rolls, quill pens, and printed books, magazines, and newspapers. Will this really happen? Will books and periodicals become useless, unfamiliar artifacts just as papyrus and quill pens are to us today? It could happen. In fact, the decline of the printed word my already have begun.

Check out your local library and bookstore. You may find that they have become information and entertainment centers no longer devoted exclusively to books. Most libraries now offer a variety of microfilmed periodicals, videotapes, audiotapes, and records. Some even provide microcomputers and software for use on the premises or at home. Bookstores still sell books, of course, but they also sell software, games, videotaped movies, and audiotapes of best-selling novels and literary classics.

Technology is beginning to change the way magazines and newspapers come into our homes. A few entrepreneurs are experimenting with magazines on videotape or disk. Cable television allows people to shop at home and to receive much information that

used to be found primarily in newspapers and magazines. The same compact disk that plays your favorite record album can hold the contents of an entire encyclopedia, for display on a microcomputer monitor. In the future, this may enable you to look up Elvis Presley in a computerized encyclopedia and not only read about him but also see and hear him perform.

Commercial electronic databases can already deliver reams of information to your computer printer on nearly any subject you choose. Someday you may be able to retrieve best-selling novels from a database or purchase them on disks or ROM chips. In five or ten years, you may even be invited to join the ROM-Chip-of-the-Month Club! You can't curl up in bed on a cold night with a computer and a good ROM chip, of course. Soon, though, you may be able to "play" books on computers as small as today's paperbacks.

Despite these possibilities, printed books and periodicals will probably be around for many years to come because the printed word is still a tremendously convenient way for most people to store and distribute information. If that weren't true, computers wouldn't have printers.

turers have begun to produce their programs on read-only memory (ROM) chips rather than on disks. A major motive behind this development is that it may help to counteract software piracy, because users can't copy ROM chips as they can floppy disks. But, as you may remember from Chapter 9, silicon chips are higher on the storage hierarchy than floppy disks, meaning that programs stored there can be accessed faster; the computer doesn't have to spend time transferring instructions to and from disk drives. ROM chips are generally built into computers as firmware. Microcomputers of the future, however, may be designed so that users can insert and remove ROM chips as easily as they now do floppy disks.

The use of firmware chips instead of magnetic disks for storing and selling applications programs is clearly as much a matter of hardware as it is of software. Like other hardware developments, it affects the way that software does its jobs. And other hardware developments also increase the possibilities and performance of software.

HARDWARE ADVANCES

Today, great strides are being made in increasing the capacities of computer hardware. In fact, as noted earlier, much new hardware is not yet

Figure 15-4   Massive Parallelism
Limited parallel processing has been used for years, but some recent computers have taken the idea further. The "Connection Machine" shown here has 64,000 small processors: it can rapidly and accurately process complex applications such as making three-dimensional maps or predicting the behavior of molecules. (Courtesy of Thinking Machines Corporation)

fully utilized because appropriate software has not been developed. Silicon microchips are currently the most used technology for processing and handling data in the computer. But other types of circuits are being developed and tested that can provide greatly improved performance. Too, the overall architecture of computers has been based for many years on a single central processing unit, but recently, multiple processors have been used in several designs that call for parallel processing. In addition, advances are being made in input and output technologies as well as in storage. Increasingly, input and output capacities are being built into the same devices—including devices, such as robots, that have other capabilities as well.

New microchip technologies.

Advances in chip-making technology are leading to microchips with many times more circuits, or switches, than those of similar size in common use today. In the mid-1980s, a chip the size of your thumbnail contained perhaps half a million switches; in the 1990s, more than 20 million switches may occupy the same amount of space. Micros that use these superminiaturized circuits could have the same processing capacity as many of today's mainframes. Mainframes in the future could similarly increase their power and storage capacity to exceed that of today's supercomputers. And supercomputers, if needed at all, would work with unprecedented amounts of data at astronomical speeds.

To increase the capacity and speed of microchips, manufacturers are experimenting with the use of new materials and techniques. These materials may soon lead to machines that are fundamentally different from today's models in the way they operate.

One experimental material is **gallium arsenide,** which may someday replace silicon as the conducting material for chips. Gallium arsenide chips work five times faster than silicon, and they use up to 100 times less power. Already used in communications hardware and high-speed computers, they may soon appear in portable computers, lessening the battery requirements and also prolonging the amount of work that can be done on one set of batteries.

Other experiments involve the **Josephson junction,** a microswitch that operates at extremely low temperatures. Because there is virtually no resistance to electricity at these temperatures, Josephson junctions can switch data even faster than gallium arsenide—up to 20 times faster, in fact. The problem is to maintain the extreme cold necessary at a reasonable cost. If this is solved, Josephson junctions may be used in the electrical circuits of many high-performance computers. Using Josephson junctions, a computer with the capacity of a mainframe could be the size of a book.

The Josephson junction is made of superconductors, or materials that offer no resistance to electrical current. Very recently, scientists have made dramatic breakthroughs in the development of superconductors that operate at less extreme temperatures. Their goal is to develop superconductors that operate at room temperature.

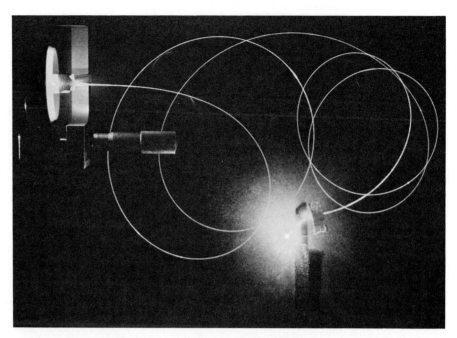

Figure 15-5 Lasers
Laser light transmitted over fiber optics cable is increasingly being used to transmit large amounts of data, replacing electronic transmissions. By the 21st century, laser technology may also be used to process information inside the computers themselves. (Courtesy of AT&T/Bell Laboratories)

Other technologies being explored today may mean that the electrical components of computers are replaced altogether. Scientists are experimenting with the development of **biochips** to process information. Biochips would be developed using techniques of organic chemistry, the study of carbon-based molecules that are the basis of living tissues. And a related subject of experimentation involves lasers: with biochips, the digital circuits would be switched using microlaser beams rather than electricity. Such chips would be faster and less prone to errors and would cause no electronic interference. And, like fiber optics for data communications, they would be more secure from outside surveillance.

Parallel processing. Most computers today interpret instructions and process data in single, continuous streams, one instruction at a time. This is called **serial processing.** Because serial processing computers are based on a design developed in the 1940s by John von Neumann and his colleagues, they are known as **von Neumann machines.** Scientists are now developing computers that perform **parallel processing.** Using multiple central processing units, these machines can handle several instructions simultaneously. With parallel processing, a computer can execute many instructions in the time it takes to execute one with serial

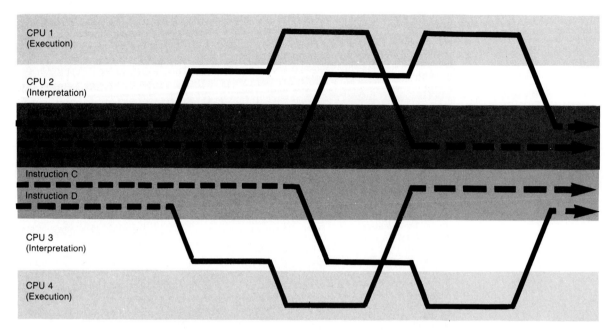

Figure 15-6   Parallel Processing
In one of the simpler kinds of parallel processing, each instruction is handled by a
pair of processors, one to interpret it and one to execute it. By overlapping the
instructions, the processors can do their work in half the time—or less if there are
more than two processors. The four instructions shown above could be from different programs, or from the same program. More complex parallel processing may
use several processors for each instruction.

processing. Parallel processing has the potential of allowing computers
to execute thousands of billions of instructions per second.

New input technologies.   As suggested already, tomorrow's computers may require less keyboarding, because they could be equipped to
accept other kinds of input. More and more systems will accept spoken
commands and data as input, because voice recognition devices can handle
increasingly larger vocabularies and are becoming more dependable and
less expensive. Optical character recognition (OCR) could also play a
bigger role in input. As manufacturers develop lower-priced, more versatile OCR scanners able to handle images as well as text, more computer
systems will be equipped to read input directly from typewritten or handwritten drafts and forms.

Other input devices are also likely to be integrated into more computer systems. As you read in the previous chapter, several organizations
have systems that allow employees and customers to use telephones for
keying in data. The industry is also experimenting with the use of tele-
visions for both input and output. As input options expand, people will
become more able to use computers without purchasing keyboards and
special equipment.

External storage. In addition to firmware chips mentioned earlier, other powerful storage media are under development. These include the **optical disk,** which has already gained popularity as the compact disk for recording music and could soon replace the floppy disk for external storage of software and data. So far, there are several users' devices for reading data from optical disks: **CD-ROM,** for compact disk—read-only memory, offers digital signals; **CD-I,** for compact disk-interactive, offers graphics and audio as well as software storage. But the technology for recording on them is only just starting to develop. It will result in much greater external storage capacity for computer systems.

Output technology. In addition to superminiature circuits, another factor that is helping to reduce the size of micros and terminals is the use of liquid crystal display (LCD), electroluminescent gas plasma, and other technologies to produce flat panel displays that don't require the bulky cathode ray tubes (CRTs) now used in most monitors. LCDs have been used in pocket calculators and digital watches for years. So far, computer manufacturers have incorporated flat panel displays primarily in laptop models, and users have complained of poor image contrast. Recent developments such as super-twist LCDs, however, have produced flat panel screens that are easier to read and more adaptable to different light conditions. In fact, they can be much sharper than the screens on CRTs.

Eventually, computers may even display **holograms,** which are three-dimensional images created with laser technology. (You may have seen small holograms on some credit cards or clothing labels, where they're being used to prevent unauthorized reproductions.) Because they are 3-D, holographic images could lend a greater sense of personal presence to teleconferences. But, perhaps more important, they could greatly enhance computer-aided design and other graphics applications.

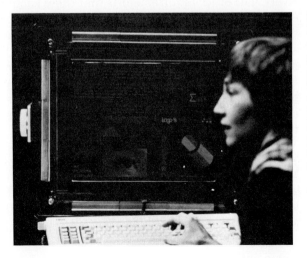

Figure 15-7   A Gas Plasma Screen

Gas plasma screens consist of three sheets of glass, the middle one containing tiny holes filled with luminescent gas. Each pocket of gas can be made to glow independently by electrical conductors in the outer sheets. Unlike CRTs, gas plasma displays can be flat and of unlimited size. (Courtesy of International Business Machines Corporation)

Robots. According to a study by the Rand Corporation, factory workers might make up 2 percent of the work force in the year 2000, as compared with about 20 percent today. One important reason for this forecast is the likelihood that computerized robots will perform more and more manufacturing jobs. So far, most of this country's "steel-collar workers," as robots have been called, are used in automobile factories for simple, routine operations such as welding.

Until now, robots have not played as significant a role in the processing of information as they have in more mechanical operations. This may change, however, as robots are linked into networks so that they can share information and transmit data to central computers for processing. At the Automated Manufacturing Research Facility in Gaithersburg, Maryland, the National Bureau of Standards tests machinery and information systems that it expects to be widely used in the twenty-first century. The facility includes **automated workstations,** or robots, that not only perform basic manufacturing tasks but also inspect products and monitor inventories.

What will the new technology bring?

Computer systems seem likely to become more powerful, more versatile, and easier to use. But what will this do for organizations and individuals? There are many possibilities. A major question is, what is it that determines whether a new idea will catch on and be accepted on a large-scale basis?

In essence, there are two requirements for an idea to succeed. One is that it must fill a widely felt need. Many organizations, or many individuals, must sense that procedures and products based on the new idea will solve a problem for them, and solve it effectively and not too expensively. The other requirement is that there should not be side effects that cause major problems for organizations or for large numbers of individuals.

Depending on the cost of the technology needed, some ideas may succeed on a limited basis. If the software and hardware are relatively inexpensive, an idea can be successful even when it does not have a wide following. However, if a technology involves a considerable expense, it probably needs wide use if it is to succeed and be developed further. And only if it has wide use is it likely to have a major impact on the way that the future develops.

COMPUTERS IN THE WORKPLACE

Already, computers have had a profound effect on the workplace. Their influence is likely to continue to be strongly felt over the next decade or two as still more systems are installed. As in the past, computer technology could eliminate some jobs and change many others. But how extreme will the changes be?

Figure 15-8   A Missing Element?
Setting your own hours and working fairly independently are two advantages of telecommuting. However, to overcome the isolation of working at home, many of today's telecommuters try to schedule regular vists to the office to maintain business and social ties with co-workers. (Courtesy of International Business Machines Corporation)

Telecommuting.   Consider the case of telecommuting. **Telecommuting,** or working at home and communicating with the office by modem, has been technologically possible for several years, but it hasn't really caught on. With the increase in distributed information processing, will the number of telecommuters grow? To answer this question, you must think about the needs of a variety of people and groups.

For the worker, there are pros and cons to telecommuting. Not having to commute to work would probably seem a real advantage to most people. Most people would also feel more relaxed without a supervisor continually checking their work. But telecommuting provides little personal contact with co-workers—including little opportunity for praise from the supervisor. Promotions would become totally dependent on an ability to communicate electronically. And the distractions of home may be very frustrating on occasion; some people need help to keep their minds focused on a job.

For the organization, telecommuting may appear to offer several benefits. The employer does not need to provide a desk, a parking space, and other facilities for the worker at home. Because interoffice communications would be severely limited, the home worker is unlikely to be as easily sidetracked by office social life. However, workers at home have other distractions. And supervision of work done at home is less direct, leaving managers with a feeling of loss of control.

Society as a whole would probably benefit from many aspects of telecommuting. Fewer cars would be jamming the roads at rush hour, and there would be less air pollution from automobile commuters. However, if telecommuting does not gain clear support from either workers or employers, or if either objects strongly to the idea, telecommuting is unlikely to catch on in a big way.

To date, telecommuting has not become really popular. Some organizations allow a sampling of workers to work at home for a portion of their hours. But support for the idea is not so great that it is changing the way that America works; organizations and workers both seem to favor a workplace away from the home. Employers prefer to supervise work directly. And employees value the social life and the directedness of the workplace. However, this may change.

Continued automation.   Automation in the workplace is somewhat different. To date, automation has had considerable success, particularly

Figure 15-9   Robots
Today's robots make use of artificial intelligence technology to perform highly complex and skilled tasks. The experimental robot shown here can "see" by means of a camera on its wrist, and it can perform some complex manufacturing tasks usually handled by skilled workers. (Courtesy of the National Bureau of Standards)

in manufacturing. As discussed already, computerized robots have joined the production line and can perform tasks that formerly were performed by people. This is partly because they are more consistent than people and partly because they are more economical in the long run—they do not have to be given a paycheck each week. This allows American business, for example, to be competitive with companies abroad that have lower labor costs.

However, one cannot predict how far this trend toward use of robots will continue. Already there is considerable opposition to robots from people whose jobs are threatened. Many workers, even in dangerous and hazardous jobs, dislike the prospect of having to learn and find new occupations. And society as a whole is upset when many workers become unemployed. Responding to these pressures, organizations often incur considerable expense helping workers whose jobs will be automated. They may retrain these employees to do other work or help them to find new jobs with other employers. Working together with labor unions, they may slow down conversion to a new system so that the job market is not flooded with hundreds of displaced employees at one time. But such concern with displaced workers costs money and could affect the further acceptance of this new technology.

Will robots ever move into the office in a big way? So far office automation has done more to change the nature of office jobs than to make them obsolete. But is this always going to be so? Computerized robots could take over simple tasks like photocopying and document assembly. If controlled by expert system software, they might even be able to handle initial screening interviews for job applicants, releasing personnel department workers from the most routine interviewing tasks.

Once again, these changes could well occur, but only if people see the benefits outweighing the disadvantages. Computerized screening interviews might be more objective, less biased by personal likes and dislikes. However, if interviewees will not submit to computer interviews, the idea would not succeed. And personnel managers may be unwilling to trust the judgments of a computerized expert system over human intuition. Everyone who thinks about the future has different predictions, based on how they think people will react to new uses of the computer.

User-created systems. One interesting development, already mentioned in Chapter 12, is the growing number of user-created systems. Because of the new user-friendly fourth- and fifth-generation languages, computer users can now often simplify their work by developing software tools of their own. They can thus bypass the involved traditional process of systems development.

Many people believe that this will lead to far greater use of computers in the workplace. They argue that traditionally developed systems are often underutilized. Reasons given for this are that misunderstandings frequently arise between systems users and developers; that business changes occur so frequently that when a desired system is finally implemented correctly, it may no longer be needed; and that even if a new

Figure 15-10 User-Created Systems
User-created systems need not be large and complex. Using widely available hardware and off-the-shelf software such as spreadsheets, databases, word processing, and graphics, many users have already created systems that are tailor-made for their needs. (Courtesy of Wang Laboratories)

system is needed, users may well become impatient with it as they see in use how it might have been improved. With the new languages, these thinkers believe that major systems will be created more quickly, more accurately, and with greater flexibility, so they can be adapted to new ideas.

Once again, however, this prediction depends on the assumption that enough potential systems users have time or patience to develop their own systems and that they have the insight to do it right. Also, such users will need assurance that their systems are kept compatible with other organizational systems. Can this be arranged conveniently, or will it impede the development of new systems? The actual future of systems development will depend on issues such as these.

The safety issue.   An important consideration for many organizations planning future computer uses is safety. The possibility of computer malfunction or errors in software code or data input can pose hazards. If a CAD (computer-aided design) system is used to design a bridge and the stress calculations are a little off, the bridge could collapse. Or suppose a government missile detection system had a major error in its software. The error might prompt it to "detect" a hostile nation's missiles when, in fact, none had been fired. The seriousness of the consequences are almost unthinkable. In weighing the effects of a system on society, organizations and individuals must take into account the adequacy of the system's safeguards against such errors.

COMPUTER TECHNOLOGY AT HOME AND IN SOCIETY

The future of computers in the home and in society is just as unpredictable as their future in the workplace. They will probably have a considerable impact, but what that impact will be is quite uncertain.

Computers at home. In many homes of the future, a computer's presence may not be obvious. More and more appliances and other household devices will probably be controlled by microchips. But these controllers could be linked to microcomputers that sit inconspicuously on or under desktops and end tables. A voice-controlled security system could monitor a home's doors and windows, turn lights and appliances on and off, and even dial prearranged telephone numbers to inform the owner and the fire department if the smoke alarm is set off. In other homes, micros could also be used more actively, for household finances, home research, and expert advice. But precisely what applications will be most used in tomorrow's homes is impossible to predict.

Perhaps homemakers will welcome the computer more readily when expert systems are available to help people with do-it-yourself plumbing, electricity, or carpentry projects. There could even be expert systems that monitor the behavior of children and warn their parents about the approach of behavior problems. The number of different services that computers could provide for households is vast. But there is no way of knowing which application will be the Visicalc of the home computer market—the application that finally brings the computer into a majority of homes.

Computers for society's needs. Computers are likely to change not only the workplace and the home but also many aspects of the overall social and physical environment in which we live. You have already read about some of the uses of computer systems for law enforcement—to trace stolen cars and credit cards. Obviously, law enforcement is one area in which computer use could increase greatly, and not only for crime detection. A new idea being tried today, home confinement, outfits a prisoner with a nonremovable bracelet that contains electronic components. A computer calls the prisoner's home at random times, and the prisoner responds by holding the bracelet to the telephone speaker so the bracelet can transmit signals to the computer. If the prisoner leaves without permission and doesn't respond to the call, the computer alerts the authorities immediately. Home confinement reduces overcrowding in jails. By enabling prisoners to hold down jobs, it may also reduce the chance that they'll break the law again.

There are so many other areas in which computers are being used today, or are likely to be used in the future, that it would be impossible to comment on them all. Specific problems like traffic control, weather forecasting, and national defense as well as general problems like environmental pollution, control of the economy, and world hunger stand to be solved or made less urgent by the use of information systems and computers.

Figure 15-11 Forecasting the Weather

Today's meteorologists rely on the communications abilities of complex computer systems to predict the weather. Accurate forecasting requires the rapid input of data from many remote locations, speedy processing, and quick communication of the resulting predictions. (Courtesy of NOAA)

For example, the political process could be revolutionized by allowing legislators and other politicians to consult electronically with all of their interested constituents before they vote on a bill or sign a new law. For another example, education could be transformed by the use of sophisticated educational software, which could convey important information with infinite "patience" and consistency. Classroom teachers would become far more conveyors of enthusiasm and motivation for learning, able to personalize learning for particular students.

In fact, use of the computer will probably lead to the creation of many new organizations—businesses, government agencies, and political groups. Such organizations will provide new types of goods, services, and information. They are likely to have significant influence on the economy, the social and political climate, and employment opportunities.

Preparing for change in the workplace

Though details of what the future will bring are unclear, one thing *is* certain: there will be many changes in the workplace and in the rest of the world during your lifetime. Perhaps you feel apprehensive about this. People are often afraid of change. They tend to feel safer in familiar, stable environments. But change isn't necessarily threatening, especially if you're prepared to make the most of it.

Unlike workers of previous generations, many people today can expect to have more than one career. Computers will continue to take over some tasks, change the way others are done, and create new ones. Because of this, you may well face the challenge of retraining for a new career once, or even several times, during your working life. This may be difficult for some people. But if you are willing to retrain and learn new skills, it will be almost impossible to remain stuck in a single, boring job for all of your life. In fact, you may spend much of your work life in novel careers that don't exist today.

On and off the job, a flexible attitude will be essential. You'll adjust to change more easily if you don't resist it and if you are mentally and emotionally adaptable to new situations. Not long ago, those who fared best in the workplace were specialists—people who were educated and highly skilled in one area but who didn't necessarily have other skills. This is no longer true. Now, the advantage seems to be with those who are well educated but not narrowly specialized. These are the people who can best adapt to the retraining and career changes that will soon become the norm.

Influencing change

So far in this chapter, you have read about the likely influences of computer technology on people. Somewhat less obvious, but equally important, is the influence of users and other people on the development and use of that technology. As people depend on computers to perform more and more tasks, it may seem that their day-to-day lives are being increasingly controlled by machines. But you should not lose sight of the fact that it is people who control computers, not vice versa. People decide what information systems should be developed and how computers should be used.

INFLUENCING THE DEVELOPMENT OF COMPUTERS

The likes and dislikes of users are critical to computer manufacturers. The economics of the computer industry depend in the end on the purchaser and the user. If users dislike software or hardware, they won't purchase more or make recommendations to other prospective buyers. Satisfied users, on the other hand, can mean dollars to the successful manufacturer—dollars that will be invested in the production of more units and in the development of new ideas. So computer manufacturers are careful to listen to the needs of their customers.

Users can express their opinions by writing letters directly to manufacturers or by responding to questionnaires that companies often enclose with new products. Service representatives will often pass on customers' opinions. System analysts for large organizations may also convey users' thoughts to the manufacturer; they have considerable influence because they make decisions about computer system purchases.

You can also influence the development of computer technology by participating in a **user group.** User groups gather to discuss particular

Figure 15-12 User Groups
User groups can meet face-to-face to discuss common interests or they can meet electronically. Major on-line information services such as Compuserve offer equipment users the opportunity to share ideas and solve problems by means of electronic "bulletin boards." (Courtesy of Wang Laboratories)

products, sharing techniques and pinpointing problems. They are often directly affiliated with a hardware or software manufacturer. Many employers sponsor user groups during regular working hours. In addition to serving as a source for invaluable tips from more experienced users, these groups can handle and pass on complaints. New versions of software often incorporate improvements sought by user groups. Manufacturers are more likely to listen to suggestions from user groups than those from individuals, simply because user group comments represent a consensus rather than a single opinion.

INFLUENCING THE USE OF COMPUTERS

Just as users can influence the development of computer technology, they can also have an influence on what is done with it. The mere existence of new technology does not necessarily justify its use in all situations. Benefits provided by particular computer applications may not always be worth their long-term cost to society. On the other hand, some of the problems associated with computer technology may be worth enduring because the related benefits outweigh them. You can make your own opinions known by exercising your rights as a citizen.

Your votes for local school board candidates can affect the way that opinion about computers is shaped in your community. You can vote and campaign for state and national candidates who take responsible positions on the use of government databases—and against those who don't. Moreover, you can contact legislators and other government officials to convey your views on laws and government policies that relate to computer technology and database security.

The process of weighing long-term benefits of technologies against problems they pose is known as **technology assessment.** Increasingly,

THE HUMAN SIDE
Views of the Future

How will computers affect our lives in the future? Most experts predict that within the next few years, scientists will perfect a fifth generation of computers, machines with artificial intelligence that can understand natural language, learn to handle new situations, and master new tasks. These computers could become the "brains" of robots that will take over many jobs now performed by humans in factories, offices, and homes. Thus, they may soon drive cars, teach children, nurse the elderly and sick, fight wars, explore the planets, perform dangerous and unpleasant jobs, and run household appliances.

These developments would make life easier, but would it necessarily be better? Here is what some prominent thinkers have to say on the subject:

John Naisbitt, author of *Megatrends* and *Reinventing the Corporation*, predicts that America will become an information economy that no longer grows food or manufactures material goods but imports these products from other countries. The number of available jobs will shrink substantially, but those who continue to work will enjoy tremendous job benefits and opportunities for creativity and personal growth. Naisbitt's wife and coauthor, Patricia Aburdene, believes that people will compensate for the changes

in the workplace with a renewed interest in artistic accomplishments, such as the theater, painting, and poetry.

Alvin Toffler, in *Previews and Premises*, predicts that more people will work at home or at neighborhood work centers rather than commute to centralized workplaces. Toffler says widespread telecommuting will open new work options for many elderly and physically handicapped people. Because workers will spend more time at home, Toffler says, they will form stronger bonds with their families and become more involved in their communities.

On the other hand, Robert Theobold, author of *Avoiding 1984*, predicts a grimmer future. He believes computer technology will cause massive permanent unemployment. Because people place such high value on their jobs he predicts that this will lead to widespread depression and feelings of worthlessness.

One thing these futurists and others agree on is that, for better or for worse, dramatic changes are coming. And they agree that the best way to prepare for life and work in the future is to acquire a broad education in the sciences and liberal arts—to discover how to learn and adapt.

technology assessment is involved in decisions about the use of computers. Organizations are beginning to establish technology assessment teams to consider the social consequences of proposed systems, not just the financial costs and benefits. Congress has also established the Office of Technology Assessment to deal with these issues on a national scale.

STAYING INFORMED

A final key to influencing change—and, indeed, preparing for it—is to follow developments in computer technology and its uses. The more attention you pay to technological developments, the better able you'll be to make sound judgments about the costs and benefits of particular applications. You'll also be more able to position yourself in jobs that are lucrative, relatively stable, and otherwise rewarding. Newspapers and magazines are full of articles that focus on new trends in the world of computers. In addition, as you read other articles and books about trends in business and technology, you will become more able to draw your own conclusions about what the new developments will mean.

Being able to work comfortably with computers and having some understanding of how they work and affect people's lives is called **computer literacy.** Computer literacy is important in today's workplace. In the future, as computers play a greater role both in your jobs and in other aspects of your lives, it will be even more important than it is now. However, because computer technology is developing so rapidly, computer literacy can quickly become dated. Reading this book should have helped you to become computer literate. But to maintain your literacy, you must keep on learning about information systems technology as it continues to develop. Only by keeping aware of the continuing changes in this field,

Figure 15-13   Information Resources
Libraries are excellent sources of up-to-date information on computer technology, and many of them use that technology as well. While many libraries still use card catalogs, many others have begun to computerize their catalogs, and to use computerized reference works. (Courtesy of Anne Day/The New York Public Library)

and of how they are affecting lives, will you be able to influence computer technology and have some say in shaping the world of the future.

SUMMARY

- The rapid change that computer technology has brought to the workplace and to overall society is likely to continue and even accelerate. You will see many more changes in the coming decades in computer applications, and in computer technology itself.

- Tomorrow's software will be more reliable, more integrated, more flexible, and easier to use. Language software will be easier to use, and many new programs will employ artificial intelligence: both natural languages to communicate with users and expert systems to apply human-like reasoning skills to solve problems.

- Microchips will become a viable alternative to disks as removable storage media, and many new approaches will be tried, including gallium arsenide, Josephson junctions, other superconducting devices and materials, and biochips. Parallel processing will be more widely used, and new input and output technologies will become commonplace.

- The exact changes that will occur as a result of computer technology are, however, highly unpredictable. They depend as much on the needs of organizations, individuals, and society as they do on the capabilities of tomorrow's computers.

- Some changes that might occur are a greater reliance on telecommuting, development of robots for office use, and employment of user-friendly languages for customized systems development. Perceptions of safety factors will affect the use of computers in the future.

- Computers are also likely to be relied on more in the home, to perform automatic functions such as controlling appliances and providing security and perhaps to supply expert help for various household projects and needs. Wider societal needs like crime control, traffic congestion, and political and military communication will also be increasingly served by computers.

- People entering the work force today can expect to change careers several times. The workers best positioned to benefit from technological change will be those who are well educated but not overly specialized, who have well-developed basic skills, and who remain flexible and well informed.

- The precise direction of developments in this field can be influenced by individuals, both as users who communicate needs to manufacturers via letters, work channels, and user groups and as citizens working through the political process. To exercise this power responsibly, individuals should remain informed about developments in technology.

TERMS FOR REVIEW

artificial intelligence
natural language
expert systems
gallium arsenide
Josephson junction
superconductor
biochips

serial processing
von Neumann machines
parallel processing
optical disk
CD-ROM
CD-I
flat panel displays

holograms
automated workstations
telecommuting
user group
technology assessment
computer literacy

TERMINOLOGY CHECK

For each of these definitions, choose the correct term from the list of Terms for Review:

1. Organization of people who discuss techniques and problems associated with particular computer products.

2. Using computers and modems to keep in contact with fellow workers rather than traveling to the office.

3. Use of multiple central processing units to handle several instructions simultaneously.

4. Conducting material that is faster than silicon and uses less power.

5. Process of weighing the benefits of developments in computers and systems against the problems they may pose.

6. Computer that handles instructions one at a time.

7. Medium that can store billions of bytes of information recorded with laser technology.

8. High-speed electrical switch that operates at extremely low temperatures.

9. Three-dimensional image that might be produced as output from future computers.

10. Software concept that encompasses both natural language programming and expert systems.

INFORMATION CHECK

1. What changes seem likely in the development of integrated systems as hardware becomes more powerful?

2. Does artificial intelligence enable computers to think the way human beings do? Explain your answer.

3. Name two ways in which chips made with gallium arsenide are superior to those made with silicon.

4. How will biochips differ from today's microchips?

5. In what ways is parallel processing different from serial processing? How does this relate to the computers of the future?

6. Why are optical disks not widely used today for computer storage? Is this likely to change? Explain.

7. What are employers doing to lessen the negative consequences of automation? How might this affect the acceptance of new technology in the workplace?

8. Give an example of how robots may soon be used in offices as well as on production lines.

9. How are new developments in computer languages likely to affect systems development?

10. What does safety have to do with the use of computer technology? Give an example.

11. How might computerized control systems be used in homes of the future?

12. How might expert systems be used in homes of the future? Give two examples: one from this chapter and one from your imagination.

13. Why is an attitude of flexibility important for people entering the work force today?

14. How do user groups influence the development of computer technology?

15. What is the Office of Technology Assessment? What does it do?

PROJECTS AND PROBLEMS

1. Joan Warner is disturbed by a news report she read about a proposal to merge the databases used by various agencies in her state so that they can share information. She believes this could lead to serious invasions of privacy and misuse of information. Is there anything she can do about this? What would you suggest?

2. Write a few pages describing your activities on a typical day 10 years in the future, discussing each direct or indirect encounter you are likely to have with a computer system. Relate your expectations about computer systems to technological developments that are already under way. Use your imagination as well as the information provided in this chapter.

3. Let your imagination loose, and describe a computer application related to work or home life that seems appealing to you and that you think would be useful to others. Base it on science fiction you have read, if you wish. Then try to evaluate the likelihood that it would really happen. What advantages does it offer to people? To organizations? To society? What negative consequences might it bring? Could it ever be inexpensive enough that users would find it a good investment?

Appendix:
Programming in BASIC

Introduction

As you have been reading, there are many different types of programs, ranging from word processing and database software to systems programs. Each has been written by one or more skilled programmers. But just what is programming, and how is it accomplished? In this Introduction to the Appendix you will take a look at what a programmer does and the tools used in preparing a program.

A program is a list of directions for the computer to follow to complete a specific task. Because the computer does not understand English, these directions must be written in special codes or languages. As discussed in Chapter 7, a programmer may use many types of computer languages to write programs. The computer must first translate all of these languages into the particular code that it can understand—its machine language—so that its own CPU can execute the directions. The software that translates the programming code to machine language is called a compiler or interpreter for that code.

Because computers require each step of a process, no matter how small, to be explained in great detail, programmers spend much of their time planning their programs. The first phase in planning a program is to specify what the program should do. This is called the systems definition or program specification phase. As Chapter 12 explained, definition should include information about input (data that will be supplied by the user), processing (the steps that the computer will follow), and output (the information that will be produced by the program).

Once program specification is complete, the next phase is to break the plan down into separate parts. This is called program design. Most programs have separate sections to handle input, each of the major processing steps, and the different types of output. Each section must be broken down until all its details have been laid out. This process of refinement continues until every ambiguity is removed, to ensure that the program will produce the desired results.

Only after the refinement process has been completed can the program itself be written. Because programs are called code, writing the programs is known as **coding.** In coding, the steps defined in the program design are translated into the appropriate computer programming language instructions.

422

Once coding is complete, the program must be tested to verify that it works as required. If mistakes are found, the design and coding phases may have to be repeated. This is called "debugging" or program verification. Ideally, no program is complete until it has been tested by the people it was designed for. This final stage is called **beta-testing.**

TOOLS FOR PROGRAM DEVELOPMENT

The following discussion will show how an applications program can be developed to simulate a weekly payroll. The program will allow any user to enter the number of hours worked by each employee, and it will then create a set of paychecks to cover the weekly payroll. Reading this Appendix should by itself help you understand how computer programs work. However, if you have an IBM-PC, or a compatible MS-DOS computer, you can also try to follow the program by entering the material in BASIC.

If you decide to code as you read, there are a few things you should do. First, study your user manuals to learn how to load BASIC into your computer. Second, use only the versions of the checkwriter program that are presented as figures; the lines presented in the text itself may on occasion add unwanted instructions for the final program. Third, follow the examples very carefully; misspellings, wrong punctuation, and even wrong spacing could make your program fail.

Before programmers start coding, they must plan the program. Several tools can help them do this.

Pseudocode. Because each phase in the development of a program is complex and involves increasing amounts of detail, programmers have developed several tools to help them avoid errors. Each tool adds more detail about the program being written. The first tool is pseudocode. **Pseudocode** uses English phrases to represent computer processing. The pseudocode for a checkwriting program might read:

```
For each employee:
    A. Read in the employee's data
    B. Calculate gross pay, deductions, and net pay
    C. Print the paycheck
```

Each task listed in the pseudocode can be refined, adding more detail about the processing that the computer performs:

```
    C. Print the paycheck
        1. Print a top border for the check
        2. Print payee's name
        3. Print the amount earned
        4. Print a bottom border
```

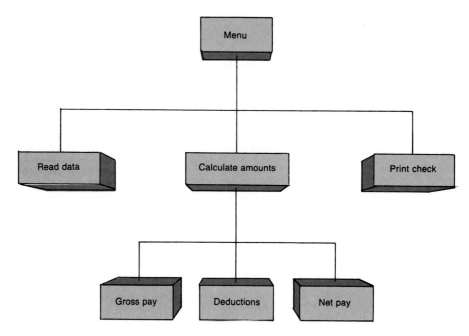

Figure A.1   Hierarchy Chart
Notice how the "calculate amounts" box is subdivided into three further stages, providing greater detail—just as in the pseudocode, where the check printing procedure was broken down into smaller steps. This is in fact a HIPO (Hierarchial Input Processing Output) chart, as you can see from studying the first level of the chart.

Other necessary steps can be added, and steps can be broken down into even smaller tasks if further detail is needed to write the correct program.

Hierarchy Charts. For large programs, a **hierarchy chart** can be used to show graphically the different parts of the program and their relationships. Each box in a hierarchy chart represents a separate process to be completed by a section of the program. A hierarchy chart for the checkwriter program is shown in Figure A.1. As you can see, a hierarchy chart is similar to pseudocode, but the relationships between different parts of the program are clearer.

Flowcharting. One of the oldest tools for program development is **flowcharting.** Using special symbols, a flowchart shows the actions of each part of the computer program. For example, the portion of the flowchart to calculate gross pay in the checkwriter program would look like the diagram shown in Figure A.2. Because of the amount of detail that can be included, a complete flowchart is very close to the language that the programmer would use.

The purpose of all these tools is to bring the programmer from a very general description of the program's action to a specific explanation of what individual sections of the code should accomplish. Moving from the general to the specific in this manner is called "top-down design"—a method that has proved to produce the best programs in the smallest amount of time.

DOCUMENTING PROGRAMS

For a program to be truly useful, it must be documented. That is, the processes that it performs and how it performs them must be explained so that they can be easily understood. There are two basic types of documentation: programmer and user. As you know, user documentation describes the actions of the program and explains the set of commands that the user is expected to give. The user manual that comes with a word processing program is one example of user documentation, and help messages provided by the software are another type.

Programmer documentation is for programmers, who may have to modify the program. The hierarchy diagrams and flowcharts described

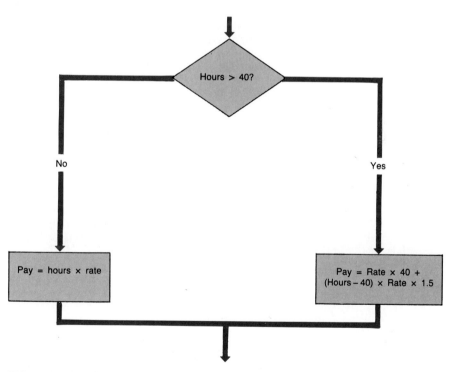

Figure A.2   Flowchart

This section from a flowchart shows how a program might handle overtime calculations. The diamond-shaped box represents a decision, over whether overtime is owed. If the answer is no, one calculation is used to calculate pay. If the answer is yes, another calculation is needed. Flowcharts put processes like calculations in rectangular boxes. Other shapes are also used, to represent different functions, as you will see later.

previously are important parts of programmer documentation. Much programmer documentation also exists within the program's code itself, as you will see. Such documentation is often known as comments or remarks. User documentation is usually prepared after a program has been completed and debugged. Programmer documentation is prepared before and during the coding of a program.

Programming in BASIC

BASIC is a third-generation programming language that is used by many small businesses because it is easy to learn. It was originally developed at Dartmouth College for teaching introductory programming on mainframe computers. The name stands for **B**eginner's **A**ll-purpose **S**ymbolic **I**nstructional **C**ode. BASIC was designed to be used as an interpreted language (see Chapter 7). However, it is occasionally found in compiled versions.

Because BASIC is easy to learn and use, it is very popular. Almost every microcomputer comes with a version, either built in to its ROM chips or on a diskette with the operating system. However, each version has some slightly different commands because each manufacturer has "improved" on the Dartmouth BASIC to make it work better on its computer or to compensate for a perceived deficiency in the original.

Most versions of BASIC follow a minimal standard that allows a careful programmer to work on different computers with little difficulty. The BASIC used in the following examples is the version found on the IBM-PC. However, it will be noted when this BASIC differs from other common versions.

IMMEDIATE MODE: OBEYING COMMANDS

Because BASIC is interpreted, it can make the computer respond immediately to commands that you keyboard. For example, keyboarding

```
PRINT "Pay to the order of Bill Freitas"
```

will cause the computer to display the phrase *Pay to the order of Bill Freitas* on the screen. This is called **immediate mode** because the computer executes the command immediately. PRINT is a BASIC command that tells the computer to display something on the screen.

The BASIC interpreter indicates to the computer that anything following a PRINT command is to be displayed on the screen. But exactly how it is to be displayed must be specified by the programmer. Words or phrases, usually termed **strings** by programmers, need to be placed between double quotation marks as shown in the preceding example. BASIC can also handle numbers, and numeric expressions that it will compute:

```
PRINT 20 + 40
```

will cause the computer to display a *60* on the screen. When numbers are used for calculation, they are called values and are *not* placed in quotes. You may realize that this is similar to the distinction between labels and values on a spreadsheet, mentioned in Chapter 5.

The use of quotes tells BASIC whether to print a string or a numeric value. This allows the programmer to mix strings and values in the same PRINT statement. For example,

    PRINT "20 + 40 =" 20 + 40

prints *20 + 40 = 60* on the screen. The computer treated "*20 + 40 = *" as a string: it merely printed the expression. However, when not enclosed in quotes, the expression was taken as a set of values and the calculation was actually performed. Modern business programming requires that a program be able to process both string data and numeric data. BASIC uses the quotes to differentiate between the two.

(Some forms of BASIC require that you separate different elements of a command with semicolons. The preceding print command would be written PRINT "20 + 40 = "; 20 + 40. This was part of the original BASIC developed at Dartmouth. When punctuation is required in a programming language, programmers *must* supply it; otherwise the program they are writing will malfunction.)

An asterisk (*) is used in most programming languages to represent multiplication and a slash (/) to represent division. Therefore,

    PRINT 20 * 40

causes *800* to be printed and

    PRINT 20/40

prints a *.5* .

When strings and numeric expressions are placed in the same PRINT command, BASIC will leave one space between them. Any other spaces wanted must be included within the quotes. Thus,

    PRINT " $" 20 * 40

causes *$ 800* to appear on the screen, offset three spaces from the left margin.

PROGRAM MODE: FOLLOWING INSTRUCTIONS IN SEQUENCE

BASIC allows groups of commands to be executed in a specific order. This is the sequence operation of a structured programming language (see Chapter 7). The commands, more often called instructions or **statements** when they are not in immediate mode, are stored in the computer's memory until the computer is commanded to execute them as a program. For an entry to be stored as a statement, it must start with a line number that indicates its position in the sequence. For example, keyboarding

```
10 PRINT "Pay to the order of Bill Freitas"
```

does not immediately print anything; instead it stores the PRINT statement at the 10th instruction address in an area of the computer's memory. Positions in the sequence that do not contain instructions (i.e., 1 to 9 in this example) are ignored.

More statements can be added by specifying new line numbers:

```
20 PRINT "    $" 20 * 40
9999 END
5 PRINT "*********************************"
30 PRINT "*********************************"
```

(The END command indicates to the CPU that it need not look for any more statements.) The computer now has five statements stored in its memory. To execute them in order by line number, the immediate command RUN must be keyboarded. This will produce the output:

```
*********************************
Pay to the order of Bill Freitas
    $ 800
*********************************
```

Notice that in this Appendix, output from the computer is printed in italics. It does not appear in this way on the screen; it is merely for your convenience, to enable you to differentiate between the instructions a programmer enters and the output generated as a result of them.

RUN causes BASIC to execute the statements in order of their line numbers, without regard for the order in which they were entered. We have now created a small, five-line BASIC program to print a paycheck for Bill Freitas, who worked 40 hours for $20 an hour. Though the line numbers in this program go up to 9999, there are only five commands stored in the computer's memory. Most versions of BASIC allow line numbers from 1 to 65,000 to allow for large programs to be written.

USEFUL IMMEDIATE COMMANDS FOR PROGRAMMING

In addition to RUN, there are some other immediate commands that are useful when programming in BASIC. One is SAVE", followed by a file name of your choice. This saves all the numbered statements onto diskette, under the file name you selected. Another is NEW, which erases all the numbered statements from the computer's memory (though not from the diskette), allowing a fresh start for a new program. A third is LOAD" followed by a file name, which loads the selected program into the statement area of memory (and also erases what was there before). Check your BASIC manual for further information about these commands.

A fourth immediate command to know in BASIC is the LIST command. BASIC will display the program in memory when LIST is typed:

```
LIST
5 PRINT "********************************"
10 PRINT "Pay to the order of Bill Freitas"
20 PRINT "     $" 20 * 40
30 PRINT "********************************"
9999 END
```

This allows you to examine the sequence you have created, even if you entered the lines in a different order.

Most BASIC programmers number their lines by multiples of 10 to leave room for additional lines to be inserted should the program need modification later. They may leave larger gaps if they have planned the program beforehand and know that a long sequence of instructions precedes the ones they are working on currently.

MAKING CHANGES IN A PROGRAM

If the line number of an existing statement is entered again without any following instruction, the old statement is erased. This allows programmers to delete statements when they wish to. New commands can be added, as you have seen, by giving them a line number that does not already exist. And whenever a new statement is typed that has the same line number as a previous one, the old statement is replaced by the new one. For example, if the preceding five-line program is in the computer's memory, keyboarding

```
10 PRINT "Pay to the order of Bob Waterhouse"
RUN
```

produces

```
********************************
Pay to the order of Bob Waterhouse
    $ 800
********************************
```

The new PRINT statement command is stored in memory in place of the old line 10. In this way, programmers can make changes and corrections in BASIC programs without having to type them in from scratch.

Using variables

The paycheck printing program written previously is limited because it works only if Bill Freitas (or Bob Waterhouse) has worked 40 hours.

BASIC also provides a method for storing information that will need to be altered as the program proceeds. The programmer sets up a name for the information, creating a **variable.** The variable is used to store the information, to change it, or to access it later.

A variable's name can be used in an immediate command or in a statement. For example,

    RATE = 15

immediately places the value 15 at a memory address in the computer's active memory (though in an area different from where the program statements are stored). This value can be accessed at any point by using the name RATE. Similarly,

    1 RATE = 15

will set up the value 15 at this same address if the RUN command is entered.

NUMERIC VARIABLES

RATE is called a variable because the information stored at that address can vary. It is further described as a **numeric variable** because it is used to store numbers. Whatever information is held there, the name RATE will always bring it into the calculations. (The equal sign [=] is used to assign a value to the variable. Some versions of BASIC require you to write LET RATE = 15.)

Variables are especially useful if a particular piece of information is needed several times in a program. Instead of changing each statement that depends on the information, you can use a variable name (for example, RATE) in each of these statements, and then only change the statement where the information is first assigned to the variable.

Information currently stored in a variable can be checked immediately by using the PRINT command. Thus, if you enter PRINT RATE, you will see *15* on the screen (rather than the name of the variable). And if you now change the value assigned to RATE:

    RATE = 20

and then enter PRINT RATE, the screen will show you the new value, *20*.

Variables can be treated just like values; not only can they be printed but they can also be used in calculations. Look at this immediate sequence:

    RATE = 20
    PRINT RATE * 40
    800

As you see, the computer has taken the value in RATE and has multiplied it by 40. And you can take this one step further; as you can see in this program sequence:

```
1  RATE = 20
2  HOURS = 40
20 PRINT "$" RATE * HOURS
RUN
$ 800
```

Here the computer has taken the value of two variables and multiplied them together.

Variable names are one of the most difficult incompatibilities between different versions of BASIC. Using meaningful variable names (such as RATE) simplifies programming and makes it easier to understand previously written programs. However, some computer languages, for example, one version of Apple BASIC, only allow variable names to be one or two letters long. IBM BASIC allows them to be up to 40 characters long—the first must be a letter and the rest may be letters or digits. Other versions of BASIC allow variable names of up to 255 characters or even more. They are usually required to start with a letter, followed by letters or digits, though the underscore (_) is commonly also permitted.

STRING VARIABLES

RATE and HOURS are variable names. Note that they are clearly different from strings. That is why strings have to be enclosed in quotes—otherwise the computer will try to interpret strings as variables, or as commands like PRINT. To get the computer to print the name of a variable, you have to treat the name as a string and enclose it in quotes. PRINT RATE will print the value currently held in RATE, but PRINT "RATE" will print the word RATE. Thus, the following is possible

```
PRINT "RATE * HOURS =" RATE * HOURS

RATE * HOURS = 800
```

The names are printed because of the string portion of the command, which is in quotes; the answer is produced by the part that is not in quotes.

The situation gets more complicated because there is a second type of variable known as a **string variable.** This is a variable in which you can store, not a value, but a string. Look at the following command:

```
PAYEE$ = "Bill Freitas"
```

It assigns the string "Bill Freitas" to a variable called PAYEE$. The $ sign at the end of the variable name is always used in BASIC to indicate when a variable is a string variable, because the computer treats these rather differently—as strings rather than as values. Thus,

```
PRINT "Pay to the order of " PAYEE$
```

will produce

Pay to the order of Bill Freitas

(Notice the space after "of". This is needed to separate the variable's string, *Bill Freitas,* from the command's string, *Pay to the order of.*)

We are now in a position to add to the checkwriting program that was started in the last section. To add the variable assignment statements, however, we will need to move the statements to new memory locations. We will make room for all of the future program by using high line numbers, irregularly spaced to allow for the different statements we plan to add later. This will not matter to the computer system. All that the BASIC interpreter requires is that the numbers be in the order in which the instructions need to be executed. The new version of the program is listed in Figure A.3.

DOCUMENTING PROGRAMS AND VARIABLES

As noted in the first section of this Appendix, programmers often place notes about the operation of certain parts of a program within the program itself. These notes are called remarks and are part of the programmer documentation. Each remarks statement begins with the command REM (short for **REM**arks).

A typical REM statement looks like this:

```
60 REM RATE The employee's hourly wage
```

```
1050 PAYEE$ = "Bill Freitas"
1070 RATE = 15
1090 HOURS = 40
2010 PAY = RATE * HOURS
3080 PRINT "********************************************"
3110 PRINT "Pay to the order of " PAYEE$
3120 PRINT "    $" PAY
3170 PRINT "********************************************"
9999 END
```

Figure A.3 Checkwriter, Version 1

Here is the checkwriter program with variables added. Notice that in addition to those described in the text, a new variable, called PAY, has been created. The programmer does not assign the value to this variable. Instead, it is assigned in line 2010, which represents the central calculation of checkwriter.

```
10 REM Program to process paychecks.
20 REM Written by: Bill Freitas 03/19/87
30 REM Environment: IBM PC BASIC
40 REM  ** Variables **
50 REM PAYEE$       The employee's names
60 REM RATE         The employee's hourly wage
70 REM HOURS        Hours worked by the employee
80 REM PAY          Pay due to the employee
160 REM
1000 REM  ** Enter employee data **
1050 PAYEE$ = "Bill Freitas"
1070 RATE = 15
1090 HOURS = 40
2000 REM  ** Do calculations **
2010 PAY = RATE * HOURS
3000 REM  ** Print paychecks **
3080 PRINT "*********************************************"
3110 PRINT "Pay to the order of " PAYEE$
3120 PRINT "   $" PAY
3170 PRINT "*********************************************"
9999 END
```

Figure A.4 Checkwriter, Version 2

This version shows programmer documentation added to checkwriter. These REM statements will make it easier for you to see how this version matches up with those presented in the following pages. Note that the REM at line 160 merely serves to space the program itself, so that it is easier to read when listed.

reminding the programmer what the variable RATE is used for. Another REM statement might read:

```
3000 REM ** Print paychecks **
```

informing the programmer what action the code will perform in the section that follows.

When a program is run, the BASIC interpreter ignores anything on a line starting with REM. For example,

```
1050 PAYEE$ = "Bill Freitas"
1060 REM PAYEE$ = "Bob Waterhouse"
3110 PRINT "Pay to the order of " PAYEE$
RUN
Pay to the order of Bill Freitas
```

The computer takes no notice of Bob Waterhouse in line 1060, even though he is the latest PAYEE$ mentioned. It writes the check to Bill Freitas because line 1060 was a REM statement, meant only for the programmer. Therefore, the value stored by PAYEE$ is unchanged. REM commands are thus ideal for documenting programs.

It is usual for programmers to use REM statements to identify the program itself, to identify and explain the variables that will be used, and to identify the different sequences in the program, explaining what they do. This is very helpful if another programmer has to make changes to the program later. You can see the checkwriter program with internal documentation added in Figure A.4.

INPUTTING VALUES FROM THE USER

Another way of assigning values to a variable does not involve rewriting program statements. In BASIC, a program can request information from the user while it is running; it will store that information in a specified variable. The command to accomplish this is INPUT. INPUT prints a prompt (a question mark in this case), waits for the user to type information, and then stores it away as directed. This is the next item to introduce into the checkwriting program, so that you do not need to rewrite the assignment statements every time the program is used to pay a different person.

In place of each of the assignment statements (RATE = 20), we place a pair of PRINT and INPUT statements. These can be combined, but for simplicity they are being kept separate in this Appendix. Thus, for

```
1050 PAYEE$ = "Bill Freitas"
```

we can substitute

```
1050 PRINT "Enter employee name"
1060 INPUT PAYEE$
```

This sequence instructs the computer to display the message, then on the next line to display a question mark and wait for the user to supply a string to store in the variable. (The computer "expects" a string because the variable name ends with a $.) Similarly,

```
1070 PRINT "Enter payrate for " PAYEE$
1080 INPUT RATE
```

will produce

```
Enter payrate for Bill Freitas
?
```

or for whoever's name was inserted in response to the earlier input statement. It will then wait for the user to enter a value (because RATE is a numeric variable).

THE CLS COMMAND

When running a program, it is often necessary to clear the screen of any old listings or output. This will be true in the latest version of the present

```
10 REM Program to process paychecks.
20 REM Written by: Bill Freitas 03/19/87
30 REM Environment:  IBM PC BASIC
40 REM  **  Variables  **
50 REM PAYEE$        The employee's names
60 REM RATE          The employee's hourly wage
70 REM HOURS         Hours worked by the employee
80 REM PAY           Pay due to the employee
160 REM
1000 REM  **   Enter employee data  **
1050 PRINT "Enter employee name"
1060 INPUT PAYEE$
1070 PRINT "Enter payrate for " PAYEE$
1080 INPUT RATE
1090 PRINT "Enter hours worked by " PAYEE$
1100 INPUT HOURS
2000 REM  **  Do calculations  **
2010 PAY = RATE * HOURS
3000 REM  **   Print paychecks  **
3010 CLS
3080 PRINT "**********************************************"
3110 PRINT "Pay to the order of " PAYEE$
3120 PRINT "    $" PAY
3170 PRINT "**********************************************"
9999 END
```

Figure A.5   Checkwriter, Version 3
Here is a version of checkwriter that loads the variables by using INPUT state-
ments. In addition to PAYEE$ and RATE, HOURS is also entered by the user.
PAY is still calculated by the program, however.

program; otherwise the input statements will remain on the screen when
the check is displayed. This may be acceptable, but if it isn't, IBM BASIC
has the CLS (**CL**ear **S**creen) command to provide a blank screen for the
next output. Other versions of BASIC use different commands. For example, HOME is used on the Apple. In our program we can insert a CLS
command as a new line 3010, between the input statements and the check
print commands. Now the program will first clear the screen and then
print a paycheck. For the current version of the developing program, see
Figure A.5.

More complex operations

If a computer language could perform instructions only in sequential
order, it would be of limited use. For example, a typical business pays
overtime; if employees work more than 40 hours, they are paid the extra
hours at one and one-half times their usual rate. This requires two separate options, one to be followed if HOURS are less than or equal to 40,
the other if HOURS are greater. This was shown in the flowchart segment

shown as Figure A.2. The program must follow two alternative routes, depending on the value in HOURS. A straight sequence is no longer enough.

THE SELECTION OPERATION

Chapter 8 explained that a computer's ALU (**A**rithmetic **L**ogic **U**nit) can compare data items logically as well as calculate with them mathematically. (Figure A.6 shows a table of the comparisons that can be made.) Comparison instructions in BASIC are often used in IF. . . THEN statements, which say: evaluate a comparison. If the comparison is true, do what follows immediately; otherwise proceed to the next statement. A typical IF. . . THEN statement has the form:

```
2020 IF HOURS > 40 THEN PRINT "OVERTIME"
```

This particular statement will display the word OVERTIME on the screen whenever HOURS is greater than 40. Otherwise it merely continues to execute the next program line—OVERTIME will not appear. This would be useful to alert the user that this check needed special treatment.

But the computer can do better. Look at the following sequence:

```
2010 PAY = RATE * HOURS
2020 IF HOURS > 40 THEN PAY = RATE * 40 + (HOURS -
     40) * RATE * 1.5
```

These two commands work as follows: the first one assigns to PAY a value equal to RATE × HOURS. The second instruction makes the value in PAY equal to the more complex expression if *and only if* HOURS is greater than 40. Thus the computer calculates PAY in two different ways, depending on the value of HOURS that has been stored by the program. To see this at work in the checkwriter program, look at Figure A.7.

Symbol	Meaning	Example
<	Less than	3 < 4
>	Greater than	2 > 1
=	Equal to	1 = 1
>=	Greater than or equal to	2 >= 1
<=	Less than or equal to	1 <= 1
<>	Not equal to	3 <> 1

Figure A.6   Comparison Operators in BASIC
As you see, comparisons are expressed using the same operators as in algebra. In fact, you will have noticed that much of computer programming is like algebra, though with full-word variables rather than x's and y's.

```
10 REM Program to process paychecks.
20 REM Written by: Bill Freitas 03/19/87
30 REM Environment: IBM PC BASIC
40 REM  **  Variables  **
50 REM  PAYEE$        The employee's names
60 REM  RATE          The employee's hourly wage
70 REM  HOURS         Hours worked by the employee
80 REM  PAY           Pay due to the employee
90 REM  GROSS         Gross pay
100 REM TAXES         22% Taxes
160 REM
1000 REM    **  Enter employee data  **
1010 CLS
1050 PRINT "Enter employee name"
1060 INPUT PAYEE$
1070 PRINT "Enter payable for " PAYEE$
1080 INPUT RATE
1090 PRINT "Enter hours worked by " PAYEE$
1100 INPUT HOURS
2000 REM  **  Do calculations  **
2010 GROSS = HOURS * RATE
2020 IF HOURS > 40 THEN GROSS = (RATE * 40) + ((HOURS - 40) * RATE * 1.5)
2030 TAXES = GROSS * .22
2040 PAY = GROSS - TAXES
3000 REM. **  Print paychecks  **
3010 CLS
3080 PRINT "*********************************************"
3110 PRINT "Pay to the order of " PAYEE$
3120 PRINT "    $" PAY
3170 PRINT "*********************************************"
9999 END
```

Figure A.7   Checkwriter, Version 4

To calculate overtime, the calculation section of checkwriter has been amended here with the selection routine described in the text. Note the new statements 2030 and 2040, which take care of tax deductions. GROSS has been defined as a variable to store results from the selection process, and PAY is now defined by deducting TAXES from GROSS. See also the new REM statements to describe these new variables.

CREATING A MENU

IF. . .THEN can be used with INPUT to create a menu of choices that the user of the program can select from:

```
220 PRINT "Do you want to:"
230 PRINT "  1) Enter employee data"
240 PRINT "  2) Print paychecks"
260 PRINT "  3) Exit from program"
270 PRINT
280 PRINT "Enter (1-3):"
290 INPUT CHOICE
```

(Notice the blank PRINT statement in line 270, which makes the output leave a blank line on the screen.)

CHOICE is being created here as a variable to hold the user's selection. The variable can be later consulted by a sequence of IF . . . THEN statements to direct the computer on which course to follow:

```
400 IF CHOICE = 1 THEN GOSUB 1000
410 IF CHOICE = 2 THEN GOSUB 3000
430 IF CHOICE = 3 THEN 9999
440 GOTO 200
```

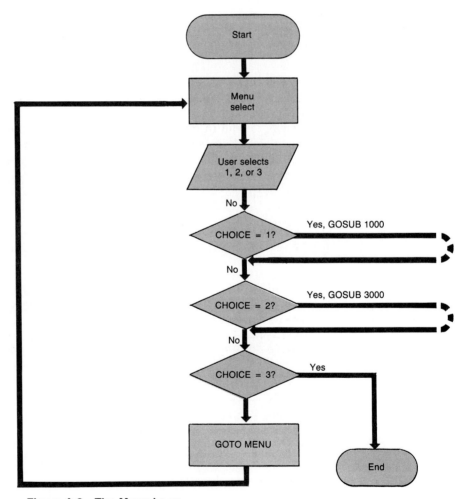

Figure A.8 The Menu Loop
This flowchart demonstrates how the menu described in the text operates. On the basis of user input (the parallelogram is used to indicate where user input occurs), this program routes the computer into one of the GOSUB routines, to the END of the program, or back to the menu again. This is a very simple loop structure. Note also the ovals used in flowcharting to indicate where a program starts and ends.

Each IF. . . THEN statement directs the computer to move immediately to a different line number, ignoring the lines on the way. The two GOSUBs indicate that the computer will be required to return to this menu portion of the program after fulfilling the instructions that it was directed to follow. (GOSUBs are explained in more detail later.) Line 430 tells the computer to go directly to line 9999, which is the end of the program so that there is no need to return.

The instruction listed in line 440, GOTO, is a command that must be used carefully. Here it simply tells the computer to return to the menu display lines in case the user fails to enter one of the responses called for in the menu (for example, if the user entered 5.) It also makes sure that the computer will show the menu again after the user has gone through a GOSUB routine. The flowchart shown as Figure A.8 should help you to understand the full structure of how this menu works—it is a kind of loop, executed over and over again until the user selects "three" to end the program.

In general, use of too many GOTO statements is problematic. If a programmer needs to make changes, it can be difficult to figure out how such a program works. The term *spaghetti code* is sometimes used to describe programs with lots of GOTOs, because, like cooked spaghetti, they appear to lead in many random directions. At the end of this Appendix, you will learn that many versions of BASIC are provided with complex commands, which can allow creation of menus without using GOTO. Structured programming is in fact sometimes called GOTO-less programming, and there are versions of BASIC that allow you to avoid using this command altogether.

MAKING THE MENU WORK—GOSUB ROUTINES

The GOSUB statements we have placed at lines 400 and 410 are useful because they help create subroutines, or sections of code that can be used several times to accomplish specific tasks within the overall program. By setting CHOICE to "one" or "two" through the menu just created, the user directs the computer to begin a subroutine and follow its instructions. In this case, these subroutines are made up of sections of the code we have already written.

The menu will take users who choose "one" to line 1000, the start of the employee data section. There they will be invited to enter their data, and then the rest of the program listed in Figure A.7 will be completed, including the writing of the check itself, which we don't want.

To prevent this from happening, a RETURN statement must be inserted before the statements for writing a check:

```
2999  RETURN
```

This statement indicates that the subroutine is completed and directs the computer to go back to the statement that started the subroutine going— line 400. (The subroutine is thus a second loop structure, which can be

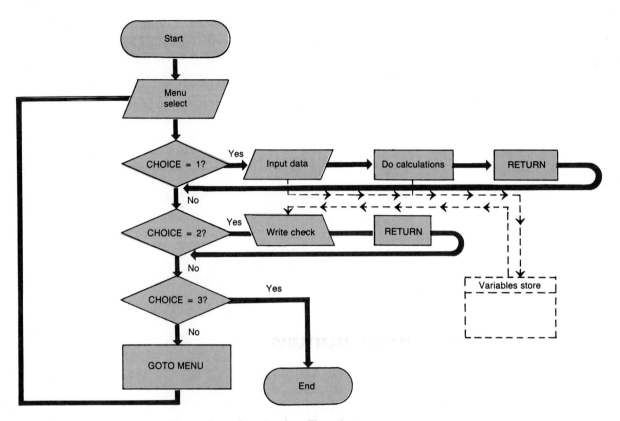

Figure A.9   Checkwriter Flowchart
This is a very general flowchart showing the overall structure of the program as it currently stands. In addition to the menu loop, notice that each of the two GOSUB routines forms a loop and that the first GOSUB routine includes the main INPUT statements for the program. The variables are defined during the first loop, and some of them are used during the second checkprinting loop.

entered only from the menu loop.) From here the CPU proceeds as you might expect, passing through 410 and 430 (because CHOICE is still equal to "one") and then back to display a new menu on the screen (statement 200 again).

Figure A.9 should clarify how these subroutines will work. This flowchart could be made more detailed, showing every step in the menu and the subroutines, but here it is used to demonstrate the overall flow of the program. You will see that the actual display of the check is made into a second subroutine. To operate this program, the user selects "one" from the menu, enters the first subroutine loop, and inputs the data for the variables. (Note that the calculations for PAY are included in this subroutine.) Then the user returns to the menu loop and back to the menu itself. Next the user selects "two" to enter the second subroutine loop and display the check itself, with the calculated variable in place. The RETURN statement that is used at 3999 prevents the program from ending after a single check and causes the program to return to the menu loop again, at which point the user can either start over by entering new data or else, by selecting "three", go to the END of the program.

If you are successfully entering these statements and running the programs you are creating, you will find this particular version has a severe flaw. As soon as the check is displayed, the RETURN statement whisks the computer back to the menu, clearing the screen (line 210) in the process. One more element is needed:

```
3180 PRINT
3200 PRINT "to continue, press RETURN"
3210 INPUT A$
```

This small sequence uses an INPUT statement to make the computer wait for a user response, thus holding the displayed check on the screen. Only after the RETURN key has been pressed will the CPU continue on to the RETURN statement at 3999 and from there back to the menu. A$ is merely a token variable, set up to allow the INPUT statement to be used to create a pause.

Making the program handle more data

The latest version of this program is now shown in Figure A.10. It has become quite complex. However, it still requires considerable work from the user each time a check is to be displayed. Every piece of data must be entered for each employee, then a menu choice must be made, and the checks must be printed one at a time. The remainder of this Appendix will add features enabling the program to create the checks with less and less work for the user.

LOOPING WITH READ . . . DATA STATEMENTS

You have seen how a BASIC program uses variables to store information and how INPUT allows a running program to request information from the user. However, often a program should have certain information available without requiring the user to enter this information each time. For example, a payroll program should "know" the names of the employees and their hourly wages. This would mean that the user wouldn't have to enter this information for each week's payroll.

BASIC allows such information to be stored in a DATA statement. A DATA statement consists of the word DATA followed by the information to be stored. For example, a DATA statement to contain the name and pay rate of an employee would look as follows:

```
9000 DATA "Bill Freitas", 20
```

Information is transferred from a DATA statement to a variable using

```
10 REM Program to process paychecks.
20 REM Written by: Bill Freitas 03/19/87
30 REM Environment: IBM PC BASIC
40 REM  **  Variables  **
50 REM  PAYEE$      The employee's names
60 REM  RATE        The employee's hourly wage
70 REM  HOURS       Hours worked by the employee
80 REM  PAY         Pay due to the employee
90 REM  GROSS       Gross pay
100 REM TAXES       22% Taxes
130 REM CHOICE      User's selection from menu
140 REM A$          Token variable for pause
160 REM
200 REM  **  Menu  **
210 CLS
220 PRINT "Do you want to:"
230 PRINT "  1) Enter employee data"
240 PRINT "  2) Print paychecks"
260 PRINT "  3) Exit from the program"
270 PRINT
280 PRINT "Enter (1-3):"
290 INPUT CHOICE
400 IF CHOICE = 1 THEN GOSUB 1000
410 IF CHOICE = 2 THEN GOSUB 3000
430 IF CHOICE = 3 THEN 9999
440 GOTO 200
1000 REM  **  Enter employee data **
1010 CLS
1050 PRINT "Enter employee name"
1060 INPUT PAYEE$
1070 PRINT "Enter payrate for " PAYEE$
1080 INPUT RATE
1090 PRINT "Enter hours worked by " PAYEE$
1100 INPUT HOURS
2000 REM  **  Do calculations  **
2010 GROSS = HOURS * RATE
2020 IF HOURS > 40 THEN GROSS = (RATE * 40) + ((HOURS - 40) * RATE * 1.5)
2030 TAXES = GROSS * .22
2040 PAY = GROSS - TAXES
2999 RETURN
3000 REM  **  Print paychecks  **
3010 CLS
3080 PRINT "*******************************************"
3110 PRINT "Pay to the order of " PAYEE$
3120 PRINT "    $" PAY
3170 PRINT "*******************************************"
3180 PRINT
3200 PRINT "To continue, press RETURN"
3210 INPUT A$
3999 RETURN
9999 END
```

Figure A.10 Checkwriter, Version 5
Compare this program with the flowchart shown in Figure A.9. You will see that though the program has now grown quite long, it is still possible to follow what is being accomplished by consulting the flowchart and the REM statements.

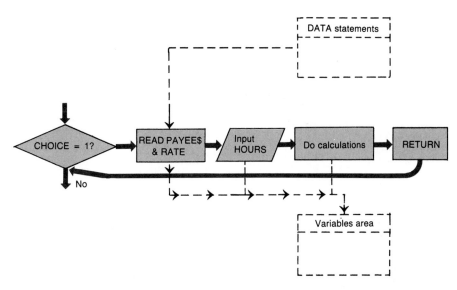

Figure A.11   READing DATA
This amended section of the checkwriter flowchart shows how the DATA statements substitute for two of the INPUT statements in the Figure A.9 version. Each time the program passes through the first subroutine, it reads a different set of data from the DATA statements.

READ. For example, to incorporate this new data into the current program's variables, you would use:

```
1080 READ PAYEE$, RATE
```

Line 1080 tells the program to read PAYEE$ and RATE from the DATA statement, thus making PAYEE$ = "Bill Freitas" and RATE = 20.

DATA statements usually come in groups, presenting several sets of data. Each statement can also contain more than one set. Thus, there could be two lines containing four sets of data.

```
9000 DATA "Bill Freitas", 20, "Bob Waterhouse", 20
9010 DATA "Marly Bergerud", 25, "Tom Keller", 25
```

Each time a READ statement is performed in a program, it reads from the next set of data presented in the DATA statements. Thus, in the checkwriter program, this new line 1080 would enter "Bill Freitas" and 20 into the variables the first time the first subroutine loop is entered; it would enter "Bob Waterhouse" and 20 on the second pass through this loop; the third time it would yield the information "Marly Bergerud" and 25, and it would continue until it had read all sets of data. (At that point it would print a message saying that there was no more data to read.) The BASIC interpreter automatically keeps track of which item of data in the statements was read last, and thus which is to be read next. This arrangement is shown graphically in Figure A.11. The program itself is

**Figure A.12
Checkwriter,
Version 6**
Here is the check-
writer program with a
full set of data includ-
ed at the end of the
program (though the
location of DATA
statements is entirely
up to the program-
mer). In this version,
note also the lines
added between 290
and 400. These em-
ploy a complex com-
parison: unless the
user enters 1, 2, or 3,
a message is dis-
played indicating that
these are the only
correct responses.

```
10 REM Program to process paychecks.
20 REM Written by: Bill Freitas 03/19/87
30 REM  Environment: IBM PC BASIC
40 REM   ** Variables **
50 REM   PAYEE$        The employee's names
60 REM   RATE          The employee's hourly wage
70 REM   HOURS         Hours worked by the employee
80 REM   PAY           Pay due to the employee
90 REM   GROSS         Gross pay
100 REM TAXES          22% Taxes
130 REM CHOICE         User's selection from menu
140 REM A$             Token variable for pause
160 REM
200 REM   ** Menu **
210 CLS
220 PRINT "Do you want to:"
230 PRINT "  1) Enter employee data"
240 PRINT "  2) Print paychecks"
260 PRINT "  3) Exit from the program"
270 PRINT
280 PRINT "Enter (1-3):"
290 INPUT CHOICE
300 IF CHOICE >= 1 AND CHOICE <= 3 THEN GOTO 400
310 PRINT
320 PRINT "You must press 1, 2, or 3"
330 PRINT
340 PRINT "To continue, press RETURN"
350 INPUT A$
400 IF CHOICE = 1 THEN GOSUB 1000
410 IF CHOICE = 2 THEN GOSUB 3000
430 IF CHOICE = 3 THEN 9999
440 GOTO 200
```

shown in Figure A.12. As you will see, the user is now called upon to enter only the hours worked by each employee each week. Employee names and pay rates are supplied by the DATA statements.

USING ARRAYS TO MAKE DATA ACCESSIBLE

DATA statements are very useful for holding standardized data, but they can be accessed only once during a program. For DATA statements to be used more than once, data must be transferred to variables or held through similar techniques. This seems to imply that, to handle any large amount of data, a huge number of different variables would be needed. Storing information for 10 employees would need 10 sets of variables, one set for each employee. Thus, you might define PAYEEONE$, PAY-EETWO$, RATEONE$, RATETWO$, HOURSONE$, HOURSTWO$, and so on.

Once all of these variables were filled with the appropriate information, you would also have to find a way of extracting the appropriate

```
1000 REM  **  Enter employee data    **
1010 CLS
1080 READ PAYEE$, RATE
1090 PRINT "Enter hours worked by " PAYEE$
1100 INPUT HOURS
2000 REM  **  Do calculations  **
2010 GROSS = HOURS * RATE
2020 IF HOURS > 40 THEN GROSS = (RATE * 40) + ((HOURS - 40) * RATE * 1.5)
2030 TAXES = GROSS * .22
2040 PAY = GROSS - TAXES
2999 RETURN
3000 REM  **  Print paychecks  **
3010 CLS
3080 PRINT "*******************************************"
3110 PRINT "Pay to the order of " PAYEE$
3120 PRINT "   $" PAY
3170 PRINT "*******************************************"
3180 PRINT
3200 PRINT "To continue, press RETURN"
3210 INPUT A$
3999 RETURN
9000 DATA "Bill Freitas", 20, "Bob Waterhouse", 20
9010 DATA "Marly Bergerud", 25, "Tom Keller", 25
9020 DATA "Claire Thompson", 23, "Cheryl Morrison", 18
9030 DATA "Sheera Stern", 17, "Paula Harris", 16
9040 DATA "Amy Eppelman", 7, "Steve Rohrman", 12
9999 END
```

information for each check. This would be difficult with separate variables, because instructing the computer which variables to use for which check would be very complicated. However, it is made far simpler by the concept of **arrays.**

An array is essentially a stack of variables that are numbered with subscripts. An array called PAYEE$ contains a set of variables—PAYEE$(1), PAYEE$(2), PAYEE$(3), PAYEE$(4), and so on up to a set number. That number is defined by the programmer with a DIMension statement, in the form

```
170 DIM PAYEE$(10), RATE(10), HOURS(10)
```

More than one array can be defined in a single dimension statement.

Each variable in an array is called an **element.** Array elements can be accessed for both storage and retrieval, by using their full names—PAYEE$(1), PAYEE$(2), and so on. They can also be accessed by using the array name together with a marker variable. Thus,

```
1080 READ PAYEE$(I)
```

will enter information into PAYEE$(1) if I = 1; it will read information into PAYEE$(2) if I = 2; and so on. All that is needed, therefore, is some technique to make I, the marker variable, increase regularly from 1 to 10.

FOR . . . NEXT LOOPS AND PROCESSING ARRAYS

One very convenient technique for increasing, or **incrementing,** the marker variable is to use a FOR . . . NEXT loop. This happens to be the final element needed for series checkwriting. A FOR . . . NEXT loop is set up by two statements, much as a subroutine is created by GOSUB . . . RETURN statements. But, unlike the GOSUB loop, it is a **definite loop** because the programmer specifies how many times the loop is to be performed; this number is defined by a loop counter variable.

A FOR . . . NEXT loop starts with a FOR statement, which specifies the counter variable and its two limits:

```
1060 FOR I = 1 TO 10
```

It then performs all statements that follow until it reads the NEXT statement, which also mentions the counter variable:

```
2070 NEXT I
```

The first time that the FOR . . . NEXT loop is executed, the loop counter variable is assigned the low limit value—1. Any program statements between the FOR and the NEXT statements are executed in the normal way. When the NEXT statement is encountered, the loop counter variable is incremented by 1, and the program checks to compare its value to the high limit. If the loop counter variable is less than or equal to the high limit value (10 in this case), the computer goes back and starts executing the line under the FOR statement again (line 1070). But if I is greater than 10, the computer executes the line that follows the NEXT statement—in this case line 2999.

FOR . . . NEXT loops, and similar loops that can be created with other languages, represent a versatile programming technique. They can be used with any counter variable that you define and can be used for several purposes. A very simple use is merely to slow down the operation of a program so that a display does not write itself onto the screen too fast for you to read. A set of statements such as

```
3200 FOR J = 1 TO 50
3210 X = X * 1000
3220 NEXT J
```

would make the computer take time out to perform 50 calculations between the display of each check and the time the menu is displayed. It would thus be an alternative to the token INPUT statement currently in the program. Though the answers to the 50 calculations are never seen on the screen, and are not directly useful to the program in any way, they would slow down the operation for long enough to allow users to see each check displayed.

The main use to which we will put FOR . . . NEXT loops in the check-writer program is, however, to feed information into, and then to read information from, the arrays that are dimensioned in the program. FOR . . . NEXT loops are perfect for processing arrays because the loop counter variable can also be used as the subscript variable for the arrays. Thus, the first time the loop is executed, when I is set to 1, all processing of data can be done using the first element in each array— PAYEE$ (1), RATE (1), HOURS (1), and so on. When I is incremented to 2 on the second pass through the loop, the array elements used are PAYEE$ (2), RATE (2), and so on.

This continues until all array elements have been filled. You can perhaps visualize this better if you look at Figure A.13, which shows how each pass through the loop addresses a different set of elements. The program that accomplishes all of this is shown in Figure A.14. You will see that the variables have now become array elements, addressed by using the subscript I—PAYEE$ (I), RATE (I), and so on. The subscript variable I is the same as that used for the FOR . . . NEXT loop counter, enabling the FOR . . . NEXT loop to read each element in turn.

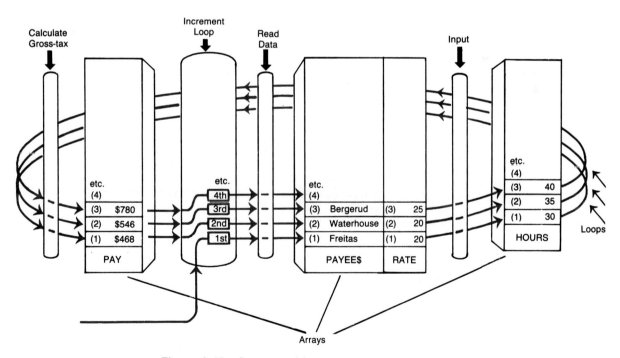

Figure A.13 Arrays and Loops
This diagram shows how arrays can be used with a FOR . . . NEXT loop. The loop incrementer changes the value of the counter variable by 1 each time the loop is executed, until it reaches the maximum value. This controls the number of loops performed. On each loop, a different element in each array is accessed, because the counter variable is the same as the subscript variable.

```
10 REM Program to process paychecks.
20 REM Written by: Bill Freitas 03/19/87
30 REM Environment: IBM PC BASIC
40 REM   **  Variables  **
50 REM   PAYEE$()      The employee's names
60 REM   RATE()        The employee's hourly wage
70 REM   HOURS()       Hours worked by the employee
80 REM   PAY()         Pay due to the employee
90 REM   GROSS()       Gross pay
100 REM TAXES()        22% Taxes
130 REM CHOICE         User's selection from menu
140 REM A$             Token variable for pause
150 REM I              Increment for counter
160 REM
170 DIM PAYEE$(10), RATE(10), HOURS(10), PAY(10), GROSS(10), TAXES(10)
200 REM  **  Menu  **
210 CLS
220 PRINT "Do you want to:"
230 PRINT "  1) Enter employee data"
240 PRINT "  2) Print paychecks"
260 PRINT "  3) Exit from the program"
270 PRINT
280 PRINT "Enter(1-3):"
290 INPUT CHOICE
300 IF CHOICE >= 1 AND CHOICE <= 3 THEN GOTO 400
310 PRINT
320 PRINT "You must press 1, 2, or 3"
330 PRINT
340 PRINT "To continue, press RETURN"
350 INPUT A$
400 IF CHOICE = 1 THEN GOSUB 1000
410 IF CHOICE = 2 THEN GOSUB 3000
430 IF CHOICE = 3 THEN 9999
440 GOTO 200
```

Figure A.14 Checkwriter, Version 7
In this version of checkwriter, notice the array dimension statement at line 170 and how throughout the program most variables in the earlier version have been replaced by array elements with the subscript (I). As the FOR . . . NEXT loops increment, the subscript also changes, causing different elements to be used each time a loop is performed. This occurs both in the data entry/calculation loop and in the check printing loop.

Completing the program

Many other features can be added to the checkwriter program that will make it closer to a workable business tool. Thus far, the checks look very primitive. There is nowhere to sign them, they are rather small, there are no check numbers, and dollar fractions are displayed only as optional decimals, rather than consistently as cents. Also, the checks are displayed only on the screen. No attempt has been made to allow them to be printed on paper. These defects should obviously be remedied. In addition, it would

```
1000 REM  **  Enter employee data   **
1010 CLS
1060 FOR I = 1 TO 10
1070   REM This loop loads the arrays with DATA, HOURS input, and PAY
1080   READ PAYEE$(I), RATE(I)
1090   PRINT "Enter hours worked by " PAYEE$(I)
1100   INPUT HOURS(I)
2000   REM  **  Do calculations  **
2010   GROSS(I) = HOURS(I) * RATE(I)
2020   IF HOURS(I) > 40 THEN GROSS(I) = (RATE(I) * 40) + ((HOURS(I) - 40) * RATE * 1.5)
2030   TAXES(I) = GROSS(I) * .22
2040   PAY(I) = GROSS(I) - TAXES(I)
2070 NEXT I
2999 RETURN
3000 REM  **  Print paychecks  **
3010 CLS
3060 FOR I = 1 TO 10
3070   REM This loop uses the arrays to print all checks in sequence
3080   PRINT "*********************************************"
3110   PRINT "Pay to the order of " PAYEE$(I)
3120   PRINT "   $" PAY(I)
3170   PRINT "*********************************************"
3180   PRINT
3190 NEXT I
3200 PRINT "To continue, press RETURN"
3210 INPUT A$
3999 RETURN
9000 DATA "Bill Freitas", 20, "Bob Waterhouse", 20
9010 DATA "Marly Bergerud", 25, "Tom Keller", 25
9020 DATA "Claire Thompson", 23, "Cheryl Morrison", 18
9030 DATA "Sheera Stern", 17, "Paula Harris", 16
9040 DATA "Amy Eppelman", 7, "Steve Rohrman", 12
9999 END
```

be useful if the program could create a printed record of checks written for the accounting department.

These defects are all taken care of in the final version of the check-writer program, presented as Figure A.15. The first part of the program is almost identical to the previous version, except that the menu is expanded to include the option of printing a check record (see lines 250 and 420); and a new array, CHECKNUM(I), is added to accommodate check numbers. See if you can understand how lines 2050 and 2060 cause the starting check number (CHECK) to be incremented by one each time the FOR . . . NEXT loop is performed.

The output end of the program is considerably expanded. The user is invited to activate the printer (in line 3040) by pressing a combination of the CONTROL and the PRINTSCREEN keys. (This also deactivates the printer in line 3200.) The check itself is considerably enlarged, as you will see by inspecting the program (lines 3080 to 3170). The caption for Figure A.15 describes the PRINT USING statement and explains how the semicolon is used to let a line of output be split between two or more program statements. In addition, notice the TAB specifications included

```
10 REM Program to process paychecks.
20 REM Written by: Bill Freitas 03/19/87
30 REM Environment: IBM PC BASIC
40 REM  **  Variables  **
50 REM  PAYEE$()      The employee's names
60 REM  RATE()        The employee's hourly wage
70 REM  HOURS()       Hours worked by the employee
80 REM  PAY()         Pay due to the employee
90 REM  GROSS()       Gross pay
100 REM TAXES()       22% Taxes
110 REM CHECKNUM()    Check number for each check
120 REM CHECK         Starting check number
130 REM CHOICE        User's selection from menu
140 REM A$            Token variable for pause
150 REM I             Increment for counter
160 REM
170 DIM PAYEE$(10), RATE(10), HOURS(10), PAY(10), GROSS(10), TAXES(10),
200 REM  **  Menu  **
210 CLS
220 PRINT "Do you want to:"
230 PRINT "  1) Enter employee data"
240 PRINT "  2) Print paychecks"
250 PRINT "  3) Print checks record"
260 PRINT "  4) Exit from the program"
270 PRINT
280 PRINT "Enter (1-4):"
290 INPUT CHOICE
300 IF CHOICE >= 1 AND CHOICE <= 4 THEN GOTO 400
310 PRINT
320 PRINT "You must press 1, 2, 3 or 4"
330 PRINT
340 PRINT "To continue, press RETURN"
350 INPUT A$
400 IF CHOICE = 1 THEN GOSUB 1000
410 IF CHOICE = 2 THEN GOSUB 3000
420 IF CHOICE = 3 THEN GOSUB 4000
430 IF CHOICE = 4 THEN 9999
440 GOTO 200
1000 REM  **  Enter employee data **
1010 CLS
1020 PRINT "Data Entry"
1030 PRINT
1040 PRINT "What is the first check number"
1050 INPUT CHECK
1060 FOR I = 1 TO 10
1070    REM This loop loads the arrays with DATA, HOURS input, and PAY
1080    READ PAYEE$(I), RATE(I)
```

Figure A.15   Checkwriter, Final Version

This version of checkwriter improves on many features of the earlier versions. Note especially the new line 3120, a PRINT USING statement, which here makes the program print out all numbers to two decimal places, with a dollar sign in front. This is a complex command, as you will see if you check your BASIC user's manual. It is included in IBM-PC BASIC but not in many other versions. Notice also how the statement ends with a semicolon (;). This ensures that the following print statement, 3130, continues outputting on the same line.

```
1090    PRINT "Enter hours worked by " PAYEE$(I)
1100    INPUT HOURS(I)
2000    REM  **  Do calculations  **
2010    GROSS(I) = HOURS(I) * RATE(I)
2020    IF HOURS(I) > 40 THEN GROSS(I) = (RATE(I) * 40) + ((HOURS(I) - 40) * RATE * 1.5)
2030    TAXES(I) = GROSS(I) * .22
2040    PAY(I) = GROSS(I)    TAXES(I)
2050    CHECKNUM(I) = CHECK
2060    IF I > 1 THEN CHECKNUM (I) = CHECKNUM(I - 1) + 1
2070  NEXT I
2999  RETURN
3000  REM  **   Print paychecks  **
3010  CLS
3020  PRINT "Check Printing"
3030  PRINT
3040  PRINT "Be sure printer is online, and press CTRL-PrtSc, then RETURN"
3050  INPUT A$
3060  FOR I = 1 TO 10
3070    REM This loop uses the arrays to print all checks in sequence
3080    PRINT "**********************************************************"
3090    PRINT "* National State Bank" TAB(48) CHECKNUM(I) TAB(55) "*"
3100    PRINT "*" TAB(55) "*"
3110    PRINT "* Pay to the order of " PAYEE$(I) TAB(55) "*"
3120    PRINT USING "*   $$####.##";PAY(I);
3130    PRINT TAB(55) "*"
3140    PRINT "*" TAB(55) "*"
3150    PRINT "*" TAB(25) "_____" TAB(55) "*"
3160    PRINT "*" TAB(25) "I. M. A. User, President" TAB(55) "*"
3170    PRINT"**********************************************************"
3180    PRINT
3190    NEXT I
3200    PRINT "To continue, press CTRL-PrtSc, then RETURN"
3210    INPUT A$
3999    RETURN
4000    REM  **   Print Checks Record for Accounting  **
4010    CLS
4020    PRINT "Checks Record"
4030    PRINT
4040    PRINT "Be sure printer is online, and press CTRL-PrtSc, then RETURN"
4050    INPUT A$
4060    PRINT "Ch #" TAB(10) "EMPLOYEE" TAB(32) "NET PAY" TAB(44);
4070    PRINT "GROSS" TAB(54) "TAXES"
4080    PRINT
4090    FOR I = 1 TO 10
4100    REM This loop uses the arrays to create a complete list of checks
4110    PRINT CHECKNUM(I) TAB(10) PAYEE$(I) TAB(30);
4120    PRINT USING "$$####.##";PAY(I);
4130    PRINT TAB(40);
4140    PRINT USING "$$####.##";GROSS(I);
4150    PRINT TAB(50);
4160    PRINT USING "$$####.##";TAXES(I)
4170    NEXT I
4180    PRINT
4190    PRINT "To continue, press CTRL-PrtSc, then RETURN''
4200    INPUT A$
4999    RETURN
```

```
9000    DATA "Bill Freitas", 20, "Bob Waterhouse", 20
9010    DATA "Marly Bergerud", 25, "Tom Keller", 25
9020    DATA "Claire Thompson", 23, "Cheryl Morrison", 18
9030    DATA "Sheera Stern", 17, "Paula Harris", 16
9040    DATA "Amy Eppelman", 7, "Steve Rohrman", 12
9999    END
```

in the PRINT statements (though not in PRINT USING). These act like the typewriter Tab key, moving the print head of the printer to the specified point. Thus the TAB(55) "*" sequences in lines 3090 to 3160 cause a vertical line of asterisks to be printed 55 spaces in from the left margin.

The check register subroutine (lines 4000 to 4999) is totally new in this version. It is performed by another FOR . . . NEXT loop and uses several of the new features described in the preceding paragraphs— CONTROL/PRINTSCREEN for printing, TABs, semicolons, and PRINT USING to supply a dollars and cents format. See if you can figure out the new subroutine, using your BASIC user's manual or consulting with your instructor if you are having difficulty. You will find that the subroutine prints a check register, which includes employee's gross pay and taxes owed in additional columns.

BASIC has many more commands than have been presented here, enabling programmers to make the computer perform complex tasks. Some of these commands simplify jobs that can be performed in other ways. For example, INKEY$ statements allow a far simpler menu to be constructed—the user is not required to press RETURN after the selection key is pressed. Other features of the language make totally new operations possible: arrays can be designed with multiple subscripts, creating multidimensional matrices that can be used for very complex data processing.

However, these commands are well outside the scope of this Appendix, which is in no way intended to substitute for a course in BASIC. What it should have done is show you something of the clear, logical thinking that goes into working with computers. This logical thinking, when saved in the form of programs, enables the computer to perform many versatile operations over and over again, efficiently and productively. Programming is how the computer is instructed in what to perform—it is the heart of software. And software is what enables computers to manage information so effectively.

Glossary

4GL
Another name for fourth-generation languages.

accounting
Methods by which organizations manage financial information using standardized techniques to track billing, inventory, accounts payable, accounts receivable, reporting, and payroll.

accounts
Records of various areas of financial activity.

accumulator
Register which stores data calculated in the ALU is stored.

acoustic coupler
Type of modem that generates an audible signal that is fed into a telephone receiver.

acoustic panels
Modular sheet of material that absorbs sound inside and outside a workstation.

acoustics
Qualities of a room dealing with how clearly sounds can be heard or transmitted.

active memory
Memory in computer, as opposed to on storage device such as a disk, where computer's work is laid out and results stored as work is performed.

Ada
Third-generation computer language sponsored by the U. S. Department of Defense for large-scale projects.

administrative assistant
Person in an office responsible for various duties, some of which may be reception work, word processing, and filing.

administrative support supervisor
Person responsible for overseeing the work of a group of administrative assistants and other office support staff.

ALU
Arithmetic/logic unit.

ambient lighting
Indirect, overall lighting in an office environment which minimizes glare.

analog
Continuous, wave-like signals of telephone transmission.

analytic graphics software
Software that converts numerical data to graphs for easy understanding.

APL
Third-generation computer language that is particularly economical in handling complex instructions.

applications development language
Type of fourth-generation language that enables people to create their own applications software.

applications software
Software programs that direct the input, processing, and output functions of a computer to meet the needs of a particular application.

architecture
Structure of a computer system.

area-by-area conversion
Strategy of redesign and renovation that implements changes in an office one area at a time.

arithmetic/logic unit (ALU)
Part of the microprocessor that handles mathematical calculations and logical comparisons.

array
Stack of variables numbered with subscripts (numbers in parentheses).

artificial intelligence
Computer's ability to approximate human intelligence, especially including the ability to respond to natural language and to simulate the judgment of human experts.

ASCII
Common transmission code that assigns a seven-bit binary sequence to represent each of 128 numerals, letters, and other symbols.

assembler
Assembly language program that translates source code to object code.

assembly language
First language developed to write computer pro-

grams, expressing instructions in letter sequences and numbers rather than zeros and ones.

asynchronous
Slowest transmission mode; characters are transmitted as the user types them.

audit trail
Automatic record used to trace the origin of errors or sabotage, shows exactly what was done to a file, when and with what password.

authoring system
Software program that enables trainers without programming experience to create customized lessons.

automated teller machine
Computer at a bank that allows users to make deposits and withdrawals on their accounts.

automated workstation
Robots that perform basic manufacturing tasks, inspect products, and monitor inventories.

automatic logging
Record of computer activity showing who was on a system, for how long, and what files they used.

backup
Copy of a file stored as a security measure in case the original diskette is lost or damaged.

balance sheet
Statement that shows the financial position of a company in terms of assets, liabilities, and owner's equity at the end of an accounting period.

bandwidth
Range of frequencies available for transmission through a particular medium.

bar code scanner
Device that reads retail codes from labels on consumer products.

baseband
Medium that carries only one set of signals at a time, such as a twisted pair.

BASIC
Stands for Beginners All-purpose Symbolic Instruction Code; easy-to-learn, common program sometimes used by small businesses that want to develop their own programs.

batch file
Simple computer program for a microcomputer that enables a sequence of commands to be executed in order by the operating system.

batch processing
Single stream of input of accumulated data and prepared programs into a computer.

baud rate
Number of information bits the datacom transmission medium can carry per second.

Baudot code
International alphabet used primarily for telex transmissions that represents each of its characters with five data bits.

beta-testing
Final stage of testing in which the program is used by the people a program was designed for test it.

binary
Refers to the two states—on and off—characteristic of digital computer circuits.

binary digit
Smallest measure of computer memory and activity, the single zero or one; also called a bit.

biochip
Experimental microchip that would use processes developed with organic chemistry; these would be switched with microlaser beams rather than electricity.

bit
Smallest measure of computer memory and activity, the single zero or one; another name of binary digit.

block move
Function in word processing that allows the user to move large or small blocks of type from one position to another anywhere in a document.

boilerplate
standard word processing document that can be used repeatedly.

bridge
High-speed switch used to connect ring networks.

broadband
Medium, such as microwave or coaxial cables, that can carry many communications channels.

bubble memory
Type of memory chip that can hold data even after the computer is turned off, useful with portable computers.

bug
Malfunction or mistake in a software program or system.

bus
Connection between any two electronic elements of a microcomputer.

bus network
Network that uses a single transmission medium with several nodes, comprised of terminals and printers, attached to it that intercept signals addressed to them.

byte
Unit containing eight bits groups to measure memory.

C
Computer language that embodies structured programming concepts and is well suited to both business and scientific applications.

caption
Name or number written on a file folder to help locate it.

CAR specialist
Records management employee specializing in using

a computer to retrieve microfilmed documents for other employees.

CARTS principle
Standard set up by the federal government that requires that personal information in federal files be Complete, Accurate, Relevant, Timely, and Secure.

catalog
Record of information files and where they are located on a diskette.

CD-I
Stands for Compact Disk-Interactive; device for reading data from optical disks that offers graphics and audio as well as software storage.

CD-ROM
Stands for Compact Disk—Read-Only Memory; device that uses digital signals to read data from optical disks.

cell
Place on a spreadsheet where a row and a column intersect.

central processing unit (CPU)
Part of the computer that interprets instructions and controls processing of data into information, the heart of the computer.

centralized structure
Organizational plan in which specialized workers perform information processing tasks in a central area for several departments.

chain printer
Most popular type of line printer with characters mounted on an endless chain loop.

character code
Standardized code that allows different CPUs to communicate with each other despite different machine languages.

character printer
Impact printer that prints one character at a time.

chief information officer (CIO)
Member of top management who sets information resource policy.

circuit switching
Method of telephone switching in which a communications circuit is kept open until the caller hangs up, regardless of whether any signals are being transmitted.

coaxial cable
Wire mesh tube made from an electrical conductor that encloses a single insulated, high-capacity wire.

COBOL
Common Business-Oriented Language; the tranditional language used for business, with instructions that resemble English sentences.

coding
Another name for writing programs, so called because programs are known as code.

column
Vertical section on a spreadsheet where data is entered.

COM operator
Person who uses computer-output microfilm recorder to create and index microfilm from computer output.

comb
Disk drive with one read/write head for each surface of each disk.

command
Specific instruction given to the computer entered by the user through the keyboard.

command consistency
Uniformity of commands from one application to another.

command-driven software
Software package that is guided by specific instruction or commands, entered by the user.

command language
Sets of commands for communicating directly with large operating systems for file maintenance and other instructions.

common carrier
Telephone company or other organization that provides public communications service.

communicating information processor
Allows individuals in different locations to work together on a single document, exchanging words, phrases, and paragraphs as they create the document together.

communications protocol
Rules and standards that must be agreed upon for successful data transmission.

communications software
Enables users to send information electronically over telephone lines before it has been printed.

compiler
Programming tool for translating a complete program from a Third-generation language into object code, this process speeds running time.

computer-aided design (CAD)
Graphics software that enable engineers to design objects on a microcomputer.

computer-aided manufacturing (CAM)
Software that helps in organization inventory and assembly on the factory floor.

computer-aided retrieval (CAR)
Technique used to locate microforms within memory of a computer.

computer-based message system
System that enables the high-speed distribution of information through linked computers.

computer-based training (CBT)
Process of teaching and testing new procedures to employees using a computer.

computer conference
Linking of computers that allows individuals to confer via computer and have a permanent written record of their interaction.

computer input microfilm
Technique in which a computer reads data directly from microfilm and enters it into its own memory.

computer language software
Translates instructions that a programmer writes into electronic code.

computer literacy
Ability to work comfortably with computers and understand how they work and affect people's lives.

computer operator
Person who performs many of the manual tasks necessary for running a mainframe computer.

computer output microfilm (COM)
Technique used to produce a microform image of a computer document without having to produce a paper document first.

computerized mail cart
Automated cart programmed to move through large offices picking up and delivering internal mail.

concurrency
Running two programs in a computer simultaneously.

console
Command terminal for a mainframe computer.

consultant
Professional who advises others for a fee from his or her own knowledge of or expertise on a specific subject.

control unit
Part of the microprocessor that directs sequence of operations, interprets coded instructions, and initiates proper commands.

coordinate
Pair of numbers that define a dot's position so that a computer can create an image with graphics software.

copy protected
Furnished with programming codes, or encryption, or technical means that can be incorporated into software to thwart software piracy.

corporate solution
Centrally controlled approach to information management policy, most appropriate for organizations dependent on centralized mainframe computers.

corporation
Organization that exists as a legal entity in itself, with assets belonging to the entity rather than to owners or managers. Often formed to protect owners from loss.

cost-effectiveness
Quality of something producing enough benefits to make it worth its cost.

crash conversion
Approach to converting an old system to a new one by abruptly stopping the old system and quickly implementing the new one.

critical path
Line in a CPM chart that represents the minimum and maximum amounts of time it will take to complete tasks in a particular project.

critical path method (CPM)
Chart used in project management that estimates the minimum and maximum time it will take to complete each task in a project.

cross-index
A list that enables the user to search for stored data in more than one way.

CRT
Cathode ray tube; the most common monitor, usually displaying 25 lines of text with 80 characters per line.

cursor
Movable and often blinking symbol on a display screen that designates the position of the next character or command to be entered.

cursor pointing
Feature of spreadsheet software that uses cursor movements to highlight blocks of numbers that are to be entered into a formula elsewhere.

cylinder
Set of tracks with which the heads of a disk drive are in contact at any one time.

daisy-wheel printer
Printer with precast type element, with characters arranged in a circle at the end of the wheel's many spokes, produces letter-quality copy at slower speed than dot-matrix printer.

DASD
Direct access storage devices.

data
Raw material fed into a computer.

data bank
Several databases joined together that can store enormous amounts of cross-referenced information that is instantly accessible.

data communications network
Linking of computers to maximize the availability of stored information within one organization.

data compatibility
Allows data to be transported from one application to another.

data dictionary
List of fields being used in a database.

data diddling
Criminal technique used to modify data as it enters or leaves a computer system without affecting the internal processing of that system.

data entry clerk
Person who keys raw data into a computer.

data flow diagram
Chart that depicts input, output, documents, and

procedures as they flow through an organization; also called flow charts.

data processing (DP) system
Computers used to handle many basic forms of company transactions automatically rather than manually.

data security
Methods of protecting information stored on ʹcomputers.

database
Collection of systematically organized data on magnetic tapes or disks.

database administrator
Trained specialist who controls access to the information that is stored in databases.

database file
Full collection of data about a specific subject, often the database itself.

database management system (DBMS)
Software system that can create and give access to a database.

datacom network
Abbreviation of data communications networks.

debugging
The process of isolating and correcting malfunctions or mistakes in a system.

dedicated word processor
Computer used specifically for preparing written documents.

dedicated workstation
Work area in an office intended for one person's continual use.

default value
Preset instruction on a word processor, assumed in the absence of other instructions, that creates a standard page format.

definite loop
Loop for which the programmer specifies how many times it is to be performed.

delete
Function in word processing that allows the user to remove words, sentences, or whole blocks of type from anywhere in a document.

departmental solution
Approach in organizations with traditional MIS/DP structures in which each department is responsible for managing its own internal information systems with a MIS/DP group that processes and regulates information moving from department to department.

desktop accessory program
Supplement to a software program that features typical desktop tools such as an appointment calendar, notepad, and calculator.

desktop publishing
Preparation of documents directly on a computer screen.

desktop publishing software
Program that enables the user to combine text and graphics to produce reports and newsletters of nearly the same quality as those from professional print shops.

diagnostic aid
Software program used in the medical field to help manage the large amount of information available on diseases and drugs.

digital
Most common type of computer, using two numerical units to operate, zero and one.

digitizer
Device required on many types of software that converts physical movement into digital input that a computer can understand; an example is the mouse.

direct access storage device
Disk drive that can go quickly to any file or piece of data, even if it is in the middle of a disk—such as comb device or cylinder.

directory
Record of information files and where they are located on a diskette.

disk address
Spot on a disk where a particular file is located.

disk drive
Slot on the front or side of a microcomputer where flexible disks are loaded; disk drive may be a separate unit.

disk pack
Airtight container holding six or more disks used by large computers.

diskette
Flexible magnetic disk used for data entry to a computer; also known as a floppy disk.

documentation
Manual that accompanies a software package to explain its operation.

DOS
Initials standing for Disk Operating System that are frequently included in the names of operating systems for microcomputers.

dot-matrix printer
Common type of printer that creates characters or graphics through a series of dots, faster than printers with precast type elements but of poorer quality.

download
To transfer whole sections of a database from a central data bank into the memory of another smaller computer.

draft printer
Fast, inexpensive printer used for printing rough drafts of documents.

driver
Part of an applications package that enables it to work with particular peripheral hardware such as a printer.

drum plotter
Output device in which paper moves under pens.

drum printer
Line printer with characters on a drum that rotates vertically behind the paper on which it prints.

duplex
Two-way transmission.

EBCDIC
Data transmission code, developed by IBM, that uses eight bits and can represent more symbols than ASCII.

editing
Correcting and altering text in word processing.

Education Privacy Act
1974 law intended to ensure the privacy of student records kept by schools that receive federal funds.

effectiveness
Degree to which what is produced is as well suited to the purposes of an organization as possible.

efficiency
Production of goods and services with a minimum of waste and expense.

EL
Elector-luminescent monitor displays text by means of electrodes sealed in a flat gas-filled panel.

electronic bulletin board
Computerized list of messages that can be posted and read by many computers in different locations via telephone lines.

electronic conferencing
Means by which communications software allows users in different locations to exchange information quickly and efficiently.

electronic mail
Written messages sent over telephone lines from one computer to another.

electronic typewriter
Typewriter with a memory for making multiple copies, checking spelling or performing other repetitive tasks.

electrothermal printer
Nonimpact printer that uses a combination of heat-sensitive paper and a heatable print head to etch characters.

element
Each variable in an array, stored under its full name including subscripts.

encryption
Security technique that involves scrambling of data by a special program and unscrambling only for users who enter the required code.

enhancement application
Software program that allows users to customize general-purpose programs to meet their specific needs.

environment
Context in which an information system works.

EPROM
*E*rasable Programmable Read-Only Memory; chips that can be erased by special processes after they are programmed.

equity
Current worth of a business; assets minus liabilities.

ergonomics
Study of the worker and workplace environment with the principal focus of designing the work space and equipment so that they can be used as effectively as possible.

error trapping
Built-in control in software that alerts a user to mistakes made in data entry.

evaluation grid
Chart used in the selection of components for a new system that indicates all the needs that must be met and which vendors can meet those needs.

executive program
Element of a multi-user computer's operating system that acts as a priority manager.

expanded memory card
Utility that adds more memory space to a microcomputer.

expense
Money that flows out of a business.

expert system
Very advanced database that can simulate the judgment and advice of a human expert by using human-like reasoning skills to solve problems.

external modem
Standalone piece of equipment connecting an output port of a computer and a phone line.

facsimile (FAX)
Electronic transmitting system that uses telephone lines to send exact copies of original documents to distant locations.

Fair Credit Reporting Act
1970 law that allows individuals to examine the credit records that businesses keep about them.

feasibility study
Study that examines problems with an existing computer system and suggests viable changes.

Federal Copyright Law
Law that prohibits the copying or sale of written materials without consent from their authors, publishers, or other copyright owners; 1976 revision specifically protects computer software and related materials.

Federal Privacy Act
1974 law intended to prevent the misuse of information about individuals kept by the federal government.

feedback
Process by which a computer checks results and au-

tomatically makes adjustments or waits for commands from the user.

fiber optic
High-speed, noiseless transmission medium comprised of long, thin glass filament sheathed in plastic bearing pulses of light flow.

field
Category for the grouping of related data in a database.

fifth-generation languages
Natural programming languages, allows computer to adapt its understanding of human language.

file
Pieces of work stored on a magnetic diskette as a single unit from word processing software.

file name
Name given to a set of records stored on magnetic disks; used for retrieval.

file structure
One of the fundamental structures of databases, essentially keeping a single list or file, with different records each containing several fields.

firmware
Instructions built into a computer that enable it to interpret other instructions.

fixed-head disk drive
Fastest type of disk drive for a large computer that has one head for each track of each disk, fixed in position so that it can read data instantaneously.

flat panel display
Type of monitor which does not require bulky cathode ray tube technology, for example, liquid crystal displays (LCD) and electroluminescent (EC) displays.

float
Lag between when a check is written and when the funds are deducted from the check writer's account.

floppy disk
Flexible magnetic disk used for data entry to a computer, also known as a diskette.

flowchart
1. in systems development, a chart that depicts input, output, documents, and procedures as they flow through an organization; also called a data flow diagram.
   2. in programming, a tool that uses special symbols to plot the actions of each part of a computer program.

flowcharting
Technique used in planning computer programs that enables the programmer to see how all the elements and steps fit together and whether they will lead to the desired results.

formatting
In word processing, designing the appearance of a document for printing; disk drive's process of preparing a new disk so that the computer can interact with it.

formula
Mathematical or algebraic expression which can direct a particular calculation, used in programming or in spreadsheet cells.

FORTRAN
Stands for Formula Translator; the earliest third-generation language that is useful to the scientific community.

fourth-generation language
Recent language program with built-in problem-solving strategies.

Freedom of Information Act
1966 law that allows individuals to examine the information that federal agencies have gathered about them.

frequency-division multiplexing
Type of multiplexing used with broadband media, in which different signals travel on different frequencies at the same time.

front-end processor
Special-purpose computer in a large system which contains a multiplexor and many output ports to handle communications tasks before sending signals to the central processor.

full-duplex
Transmissions that can carry signals in both directions simultaneously.

full-text retrieval
Ability to obtain the complete text of any document in a database by entering a keyword under which the document is indexed.

function
Special operation performed in a word processing program.

function key
Special key on a computer keyboard set aside for commands.

gallium arsenide
Experimental conducting material being tested in microchips; it is five times faster than silicon and uses up to 100 times less power.

Gantt chart
Simple table used in project management for scheduling project activities over time.

gateway
Computer that can connect a network with outside networks with different protocols and incompatible operating systems.

general ledger
Where separate records are maintained for amount received or paid for each account.

general-purpose software
Software programs that can be used in many different industries and situations.

glare
Bright light reflected on a computer screen which

hinders a user's ability to read material and results in eye fatigue.

glossary
Collection of macros.

graphics software
User-friendly analytic tool available on the micro that pictorializes numerical data.

graphics tablet
Pressure-sensitive pad that enables users to create images on a display screen.

half-duplex
Transmissions in which data travels in both directions, only one direction at a time.

hands-on evaluation
Assessment of a proposed system by potential users, who test it for such qualities as speed, flexibility, reliability, capacity, and security.

handshake
Initial connection of two computers ready to transmit data to one another by telephone.

hard disk drive
Sealed disk drive with disk that can retrieve information faster and can store far more information than a flexible disk.

hardware
Mechanical and electronic devices of a computer, including keyboards, screens and printers, as well as the main units that contain computer circuitry.

help message
On-screen explanation of how to perform a selected task, obtained by striking certain keys.

help screen
On-screen explanation of how to perform certain tasks in a software package.

hierarchical database
Database particularly good for speed of access and certain types of modification; it works by progressively limiting a search.

hierarchy chart
Tool used for large programs to show graphically the interrelationship of different parts of a program.

hierarchy of needs
Five levels of human needs as postulated by the psychologist Abraham Maslow; 1. physiological needs, 2. safety and security needs, 3. social needs, 4. esteem needs, 5. self-actualization needs.

high-level design
First step in the systems definition process, in which a detailed document outlining the requirements of a new system is produced.

hologram
Three-dimensional image created with laser technology.

horizontal application
Software program that is useful across a broad range of organizations.

host computer
Central computer which controls a network, most usually a star network, and which often offers database and other information services to the other computers and terminals.

HVAC
Initials that stand for heating, ventilation, and air conditioning used when discussing office design.

immediate mode
Immediate execution of a command in BASIC.

impact printer
Printer that strikes a ribbon to transfer ink to a page much in the same way as a standard typewriter does.

income statement
Lists the revenues and expenses of a business and shows whether there was net income, or profits, or whether a business suffered a loss during an accounting period.

incrementing
Technique for increasing values in an array.

inference engine
Component of an expert system that compares data entered by the user with the knowledge base to suggest a possible solution to a problem.

information center
Place in an organization where employees can go for help in using computers in their jobs and that provides such services as training and systems analysis and development.

information resource management (IRM)
Approach to information management in which responsibility for management of all information resources is centralized in one department but the resources are distributed throughout the organization.

information service
Service that charges a fee to make commercial databases accessible to users.

information system
System in which important information is generated and passed between individuals, departments, and even organizations.

initializing
Disk drive's process of preparing a new disk so that the computer can interact with it.

ink-jet printer
Nonimpact printer that places an electrical charge on paper to receive magnetized ink to form each character.

input
Data that is fed into an information system.

input buffer
Small memory that can hold a few signals at a time until the central processing unit can process them.

input port
Connection of an input device, usually a keyboard, with the computer.

insert
Function in word processing that allows the user to add new words, symbols, or paragraphs anywhere in a document.

integrated
Combined.

integrated operating environment
Software that allows the user to load independent software packages into the computer together and to transfer data between them.

integrated package
Large program that incorporates several software applications into one package.

integrated series
Set of related software packages that can read the same user-created data files but that cannot be used concurrently.

integrated software
Software in which different applications programs are designed so they can work together, sharing commands or data.

intellectual property
Software publisher's or author's ownership of ideas and logic on which particular computer programs are based.

interactive
Two-way communication between user and computer.

interface
Place where two information systems relate to one another.

internal modem
Modem installed inside the computer housing.

INTERNIST/CADUCEUS
Medical expert system that covers about 500 diseases and more than 3,500 symptoms of those diseases.

interpreter
Software that translates certain computer language instructions line by line.

JCL
Job Control Language.

Job Control Language.
Another name for command language.

Josephson junction
Microswitch that operates much faster than conventional microchips but requires extremely low temperatures.

junk mail
Unwanted mail; its volume has been increased by word processing and simple generation of mailing lists.

keyboard
Input device resembling a typewriter used for entering numerical and alphabetical data.

keyboarding
In word processing, the initial entering of words into memory through the keyboard.

keypunch machine
Early data entry machines that physically punched holes in different locations on cards to represent data.

keyword
Term commonly used in documents on a specific subject used for speedy computer searches through databases, including full-text retrieval.

kilobyte (K)
Group of 1,024 bytes to measure memory.

knowledge base
Database that contains the information of an expert system.

label
Word entered in the cell of a spreadsheet.

laser printer
Very high speed and costly printer that creates high-quality characters and graphics through a process similar to photocopying.

LCD
Liquid crystal display; a type of monitor that displays a black image on light gray and usually fewer than 25 lines at one time.

letter-quality printer
Printer that produces documents with high print quality, suitable for sending to clients.

Lexis
On-line database serving the legal profession.

liability
Amount of money owed by an organization.

library
Feature of a word processor that stores often-used documents or repeated paragraphs; sets of files that provide working help to applications programs by providing special "expert" help.

light pen
Input device that allows users to make changes or additions to material directly through the display screen.

line printer
Impact printer that prints many characters together.

LISP
One of the earliest languages, suited to developing expert systems.

local area network
Group of computers and terminals linked together in a very small area.

log on
To follow a special start-up procedure that usually includes entering a password as a security measure.

LOGO
Language mainly used to teach programming in elementary schools but can also handle complex applications.

machine code
Language expressed in zeros and ones in varying configurations that is understood by computers.

machine language
Language expressed in zeros and ones in varying configurations that is understood by computers.

macro
Feature of a word processor that allows representation of a term, phrase, or series of commands by one or two keystrokes.

magnetic ink character recognition (MICR)
Input technology involving the printing of a bank and account number on a check to aid in check processing.

mainframe computer
Large and versatile computer run by computer professionals and primarily used by large corporations and government agencies.

management information system (MIS)
Computerized system that processes day-to-day activities and produces reports for managers to analyze productivity, performance, and other trends that affect the decision-making process.

management objective
The goal management hopes to achieve with a system.

management system
Coordinates the work of an organization's other systems through lower, middle, and top levels of management.

marketing support representative
Vendor employee who helps customers in the maintenance and use of vendor's equipment and systems.

mechanical
Layout sheet containing photos, graphics, and type for printing.

megahertz (MHz)
Indicator of computer power and processing speed, it represents one million cycles per second.

memory
Area within a computer where data is arranged and stored.

memory address
Position in computer's memory where information is located.

memory resident
Type of software designed to remain in memory while other programs are loaded.

menu
List of instructions or commands that appear on the display screen to help users operate software, thus eliminating the need to memorize commands.

menu-driven software
Software package in which command options are presented on a menu at each point where the user must make a decision.

merging
Feature that enables the user to combine two files automatically.

message switching
Economical means of switching in which an entire message is stored in a computer's memory and then forwarded as a single block, not appropriate for interactive use.

MICR
Magnetic ink character recognition.

microchip
Small silicon wafer etched with thousands of microcircuits, attached to computers with metal legs.

microcomputer
Smallest and least expensive personal computer.

microfiche
Microform on a sheet of film about the size of an index card.

microfilm
Microforms on a continuous roll of film.

microforms
Film of reduced paper documents that can be viewed on special readers and stored efficiently.

micrographics
Photographic reduction and storage of documents as tiny images on film.

microwave
Communications signal or frequency that travels through the air without wires and have larger capacity than wires.

million instructions per second (MIPS)
Measure of processing speed for larger computers.

minicomputer
Computer more powerful and larger than a microcomputer that can usually accommodate several users, handle more data, and be linked to more external devices.

mnemonic
Shortened or abbreviated word used as an aid to remembering commands and programming code.

modem
Hardware device that converts the digital (on/off) signal of a computer into the analog signals required for datacom transmission and *vice versa*.

module
Section dealing specific functions of a system that may be used to implement a system gradually.

monitor
Display screen of a computer.

mouse
Input device that enables users to move words and images across a display screen.

movable storage medium
Storage device that can be removed or replaced, an example being a diskette.

MS-DOS
Operating system family for the microcomputer originally prepared for IBM but later used by other computer manufacturers.

multi-user system
Computer system having the necessary power, management, and speed to work with many users.

multiplexing
Technique that allows one medium to carry many transmissions at the same time.

multiplexor
Device that divides a medium so that it can carry several channels at once.

multiprocessing
Technique that allows a single computer to have more than one CPU, all coordinated to reduce processing time.

multiprogramming
Technique used to enable one CPU to handle many programs simultaneously by arranging active memory into partitions.

multitasking
Kind of multitasking that uses applications program to perform more than one task at the same time.

MYCIN
Medical expert system that performs diagnoses on blood and meningitis infections.

National Crime Information Center (NCIC)
Data communications system used by the police, for example to trace stolen cars or to detect fraudulent credit cards.

natural language
Commands for software that are similar to language spoken by human beings.

natural programming language
Language under development that would instruct the computer in natural, English sentences.

network
In data communications, large system which link several computers.

network controller
Monitors traffic on a ring network by polling the nodes to determine which is ready to transmit.

network database
Powerful database that combines the speed of a hierarchical system with the flexibility of a relational system.

network topology
Specific arrangement of computers, terminals, and other elements of a data communications network.

node
Junction unit that monitors traffic along a bus network, comprised of computers, terminals, and printers.

noise
Electrical interference in data communications.

nonimpact printers
Type of printer that does not strike an inked ribbon to produce characters on paper, but employs other non-contact, techniques.

numeric variable
In BASIC, a variable for storing numbers.

object code
Version of a computer program that is translated by the computer into its familiar strings of zeros and ones.

office management program
Program developed for managing the business aspects of a variety of professions.

open office
Office with work areas defined by partitions instead of walls, allowing for a free flow of ideas and information among workers.

open pair
Early wiring arrangement in which uninsulated telephone lines were strung over telephone poles resulting in much interference with signals.

operating system
Program which performs tasks essential for operating applications programs on particular hardware.

operational objectives
What a system is supposed to accomplish in day-to-day operation.

optical character reader
Input device that can read some typewriter and printer typefaces, enabling whole documents to be entered into computer memory.

optical disk
Storage medium using rigid disk with vast capacity, etched by laser.

optical mark reader (OMR)
Scanner that reads marks written in pencil in numbered boxes on a card for input into a computer.

organization chart
Depicts the formal lines of authority within an organization.

organizational system
Systematic approach for accomplishing repetitious tasks efficiently.

outliner
Program resembling traditional outline that helps users organize their thoughts and main ideas when using word processing.

output
End result of data processed in an information system.

packet switching
Type of message switching that stores a complete message, then breaks it into small packets of data.

page composition program
Another name for a desktop publishing program.

page printer
Another name for a laser printer printing full pages at once.

parallel
Connection to an output device in which bytes of data travel over 8, 16, 32, or more separate wires at the same time, with each wire carrying a single bit.

parallel conversion
Safe but costly approach to converting an old system to a new one by running both systems simultaneously until the new one is running smoothly.

parallel processing
Simultaneous processing of several instructions made possible by the coordination of multiple central processing units.

parity check
Test to detect interference in transmission by adding a bit to each character's ASCII code.

partnership
Business owned and controlled by more than one person.

Pascal
Computer language well suited to structured programming for math and science applications.

peripheral
Device such as a keyboard and printer attached to a computer in order to perform particular tasks.

phased conversion
Approach to converting an old system to a new one in which parts of the new system are introduced incrementally while most of the old system remains in place.

pilot conversion
Approach to converting an old system to a new one in which one designated division of an organization uses the new system while other divisions continue to use the old one.

plotter
Output device used in computer graphics that can move a pen across paper to produce a fine line.

point-of-sale terminal
Input device now used in households for purchasing merchandise seen on cable television; computerized machine used by stores to adjust accounts and inventories and then print a sales slip.

point-to-point link
Linking of only two computer systems in a communications network.

poll
Process of checking to see which equipment in a star network is ready to transmit data and to determine the order in which the signals can be transmitted.

presentation graphics packages
Software used to design attractive visuals for a wide variety of purposes, requires some artistic talent.

printer
Output device that produces copies of documents created on a computer.

printing
In word processing, the creating of a printed document.

private branch exchange (PBX)
Centralized telephone switching system used internally by most organizations.

problem-oriented language
Language, such as RPG, directed at one type of problem.

procedural language
Third-generation language that allows the programmer to tell a computer what procedures it must follow to achieve objectives.

processing
Stage in an information system during which data is converted into usable information.

processor
Area of a computer that uses stored instruction to work on data and produce usable information.

productivity
Producing as much work as possible for every hour worked for achieving overall goals.

program
Set of instructions or procedures used by computers in order to handle a problem—the program is sometimes called the software.

program generator
Type of fourth-generation language that enables people to create their own applications software.

program librarian
Person who controls, backs up, and catalogs the storage media for the daily work of a mainframe computer.

programmer
Trained specialist who writes computer programs or software.

programmer documentation
Forms, charts, and other documents pertaining to a systems design and function; also known as systems documentation.

Project Evaluation and Review Technique (PERT)
In project management, method of estimating resources necessary to complete each task throughout a project.

project management software
Programs that help users control project schedules and budgets by breaking down each project into individual actions and events.

PROM
Programmable read-only memory; chips that can be programmed only once and thereafter only read.

prompt
Message appearing on a display screen that is created by a software program to guide the user.

pseudocode
Tool that organizes the programming task using English phrases to represent computer processes.

query language
Type of fourth-generation language used for searching, entering, and manipulating information in a database.

RAM
Random-access memory.

random-access memory (RAM)
Section of memory that stores instructions and data and is continually added to and altered by the user.

read-only access
Safeguard that allows users to see and work with information on their computers but prevents them from changing the central record.

read-only memory (ROM)
Section of memory that holds permanent instructions needed by the computer to function.

read/write head
Movable electromagnetic unit that can be directed to read any part of a diskette or record on the diskette instantaneously.

real-time computing
When a user at a remote workstation is connected to a computer by asynchronous communication.

record
Individual entry in a field of a database.

records management
Controlling an organization's records.

records management center
Place in an organization where paper and microfilm documents are stored and retrieved.

records management specialist
Person who controls access to an organization's centrally stored paper and microfilmed documents.

register
Temporary memory device that stores small amounts of unprocessed information.

relational database
Database made up of several lists or files related by shared fields.

relative reference
Feature of spreadsheet software for copying formulas while automatically adjusting cell references.

relay
Device that amplifies or repeats signals as they travel.

request for proposals (RFP)
Formal document used by an organization to define systems needs and invite vendors to submit bids.

reservation ticket terminal
Computer used by travel agents to record tickets sold and then print the ticket.

resident storage device
Hard disk that is built into a computer and allows data stored on it to be continually on-line.

revenue
Money that flows into a business.

Right to Financial Privacy Act
1978 law that gives individuals the right to review information about themselves kept by financial institutions.

ring network
Network in which nodes are linked to each other in a circle instead of individually to a line.

robotics
Computer-aided mechanical devices that can perform repetitive tasks with precision.

ROM
Read-only memory.

row
Horizontal section on a spreadsheet where data is entered.

RPG
Very early language developed specifically to produce business reports.

salami crime
Criminal technique of slicing small amounts of money from several accounts for deposit in an illicit account.

save
Hold information or documents in an electronic file.

scrolling
The movement up, down, or sideways of data on the display screen.

search
Feature of a word processor that allows the user to locate a specific word or symbol.

search and replace
Feature of a word processor that allows the user to locate and substitute one word or symbol for another automatically.

second-generation language
Category into which assemblers fall; although assemblers are the oldest language translation software, machine languages came even earlier.

secondary storage
Device such as disk drive that can supplement the active memory of the computer.

sector
Part of a track on a diskette.

serial
Connection to an output device that responds to streams of bits in series, necessary for printers or modems more than six feet from the CPU.

serial processing
Processing of instructions by a computer in a single, continuous stream, one instruction at a time.

shared system
Linking of several microcomputers and/or minicomputers to a mainframe.

shareholders
Joint owners of a corporation. They elect a board of directors to oversee the business.

simplex
Transmissions that carry signals only one way—from sender to receiver.

software
Set of instructions or procedures, usually stored in magnetic form, needed to operate a computer.

software piracy
Unauthorized copying of computer programs.

sole proprietorship
Business owned and controlled by one person.

sorting
Arranging of data in a particular sequence in a database.

source code
Original version of a program as it is written by the programmer in assembly language or a higher order language.

special-purpose software
Applications software packages targeted at specific business problems.

spelling checker
Feature of a word processor that checks misspellings against an internal dictionary and alerts the user.

spooling
Process that allows users to work on another file while printing out work on a word processor.

spreadsheet
Worksheet or type of table displayed on a computer screen used to create, process, and analyze numerical information quickly.

spreadsheet software
Programs that enable users to create tables of figures on the screen and that enable the computer to perform all the necessary calculations and place the answers in the correct positions in the tables.

star network
Network with lines leading from a central host computer to other equipment, terminals and peripherals or smaller computers as well, each component being directly linked to the host computer.

statement
In BASIC, a command not in immediate mode but stored in the computer's memory to be executed in sequence according to its line number.

static RAM
Memory chips that require only low levels of current, useful with portable computers.

storage hierarchy
Range of storage technologies from microchips and bubble memory on the top through less accessible tapes and cassettes at the bottom.

string
Word or phrase placed between double quotation marks following a PRINT command in BASIC.

string variable
In BASIC, a variable for storing strings, string variables are differentiated from numeric variables in code by means of a dollar sign ($).

structure programming
Programming that uses only the three structures of sequence, selection, and repetition and is considered the most efficient way of producing software.

subsystem
Smaller division within a larger system.

supercomputer
Most powerful and expensive computer frequently made up of several mainframes designed to work together and used to do very specialized work.

supermini
Very large minicomputer that is faster and more powerful than regular minicomputers and even some mainframes.

synchronous
Efficient, fast transmission mode of storing characters so they can be sent *en masse* and processed without delay.

system
Any set of related components that work together as an integrated whole, usually for a specific purpose.

system objective
The goal the system will be designed to achieve.

systems analyst
Trained specialist who designs information-handling computer procedures to increase efficiency and productivity.

systems development cycle
Cycle for establishing, maintaining, evaluating, and revising computer systems.

systems documentation
Forms, charts, and other documents pertaining to a system's design and functions; also known as programmer documentation.

systems implementation
Phase of systems development that includes installing a new system, testing it, documenting its operations, training people to use it, and converting from the old system to the new one.

systems maintenance
Part of a systems development cycle following implementation that involves continuous debugging and modifications and the ongoing evaluation of a system to ensure that it is still meeting organizational needs.

systems software
Software that helps the computer system to perform its operations more efficiently.

systems support software
Software packages that supplement the features provided by a computer's operating system to perform certain specialized tasks.

systems vendor
Company that sells software and hardware.

table plotter
Output device using pens that move across the surface of a page.

task lighting
Bright lighting focused on paperwork or other non-computer tasks.

task/ambient lighting
Carefully designed lighting scheme that provides general, diffuse lighting at the same time it provides focussed light on work areas.

technology assessment
Process of weighing the long-term benefits of technology against the problems they pose.

telecom
Telecommunications.

telecommunications
General term for long-distance communications of electronic signals.

telecommunications manager
Person who manages the planning, installing and operating of a large company's telecommunications system.

telecommuting
Working at home and communicating with the office by modem.

teleconference
Conference of several people at scattered locations involving the telephone or more sophisticated equipment to exchange written and graphic information.

telex
System using keyboard terminals to send and receive information over telephone lines.

template
Diskette for a specific spreadsheet design that includes labels and formulas but no data.

thesaurus
In word processing, a feature that allows user to replace one word with a substitute taken from a prepared list.

third-generation language
Computer code that is closer to English than assembly languages; also called procedural language.

time-division multiplexing
Type of multiplexing used by baseband media in which a narrowband wire first carries one signal and then another.

time line
Defines time limits for each of the steps needed in a development process.

time-sharing
Information processing system in which a mainframe host computer allocates time to many users at terminals in different locations.

token
Distinctive pattern of bits that one type of ring network passes around the system to restrict access to only one computer at a time.

touch screen
Display screen that allows computer users to move through a series of menus by touching the screen with a finger.

tracks
Circular configuration into which information on a diskette is inserted.

transaction processing
Instantaneous and interactive processing of data in which one transaction is fully completed before the next is started.

transmission media
Wires, frequencies, and devices that transmit data.

Trojan horse
Criminal technique of adding illegal functions to a computer program that otherwise acts normally.

tutorial
Instructional disk or portion of a disk that teaches users to operate a software package.

twisted pair
Common modern wiring arrangement for telephone lines that involves thin, insulated wires twisted together.

UNIX
Operating system originally developed for larger computers and adapted for more powerful microcomputers and for interfacing with larger computers.

user
Person who uses a computer.

user documentation
Nontechnical procedures manual, may also include a user's handwritten notes.

user friendly
Easy to use; usually referring to software that does not require specialized computer skills to operate.

user group
Group that gathers to discuss particular computing in order to share techniques and pinpoint problems with specific products.

user interface
Point of contact between the user and the computer.

utility
Part of an operating system that performs various support functions.

value
Numerical data entered in the cells of a spreadsheet.

variable
In BASIC, a name for information stored at a certain address that is created for the purpose of providing for change.

vendor
Seller of computer equipment and systems.

vendors' conference
Meeting for the exchange of information about a proposed system between the development team and vendors under consideration.

vertical applications
Software programs that are intended for the special needs of a particular profession.

virtual memory
Memory retrieved from storage to active memory only as needed, thus vastly expanding the total available memory.

voice mail
Computerized system for sending and receiving voice messages.
von Neumann machine
Name for serial processing computers that are based on a design developed by John von Neumann in the 1940s.

wand
Portable reader that picks up retail product codes from price tags.
white sound
Steady, low-level noise, used to mask individual voices or machine noises.
wide area network
Group of computers and terminals linked together over long distances, possibly different continents.
windowing
Feature of spreadsheet software that allows users to view different parts of a spreadsheet side by side on the same display screen.

word
Number of bits that the central processing unit handles at one time.
word processing software
Computer program that allows the user to enter text into the computer memory using a keyboard and then edit and format the material before it is printed onto paper.
word processing specialist
Person whose job it is to produce written documents through the use of a word processing system.
word processing supervisor
Person who monitors the word processing staff's workload and distributes the work among the word processing specialists.
word wrap
In word processing, automatic movement of words to the next line when the right margin is reached.
worksheet
Ruled paper form with rows and columns set up for the entry of numbers, especially dollar amounts.

Index

Color photo credits

Frontmatter (Page x) Hewlett-Packard Company, International Business Machines Corporation; (Page xi) UNISYS; (Page xii) Hewlett-Packard Company; (Page xiii) International Business Machines Corporation, International Business Machines Corporation; (Page xiv) Hewlett-Packard Company, Haworth Inc.; (Page xv) Hewlett-Packard Company; (Page xvi) International Business Machines Corporation, Hewlett-Packard Company.

Computers at work photo essay (between pages 64 & 65) (Plates 1–2) Hewlett-Packard Company; (Plate 3) Burroughs Corporation; (Plate 4) International Business Machines Corporation; (Plate 5) NASA; (Plate 6) NOAA; (Plate 7) Phil Portlock/WMATA; (Plate 8) Apple Computer, Inc.; (Plates 9–11) Hewlett-Packard Company; (Plate 12) International Business Machines Corporation; (Plate 13) Jack Ward Color Service, Inc.; (Plate 14) Apple Computer, Inc.; (Plate 15) International Business Machines Corporation; (Plate 16) Hewlett-Packard Company; (Plate 17) Apple Computer, Inc.; (Plates 18–19) Hewlett-Packard Company; (Plate 20) Texas Instruments.

Computer graphics photo essay (between pages 128 & 129) (Plate 1) Apple Computer, Inc.; (Plate 2) International Business Machines Corporation; (Plate 3) Tom Hollyman/J.P. Morgan & Company; (Plate 4) TRW, Inc.; (Plate 5) Hewlett-Packard Company; (Plate 6) Apple Computer, Inc.; (Plate 7) NASA; (Plate 8) Hewlett-Packard Company; (Plate 9) Tom Hollyman/J.P. Morgan Company; (Plate 10) Intergraph; (Plate 11) Hewlett-Packard Company; (Plate 12) Hewlett-Packard Company; (Plate 13) Apple Computer, Inc.; (Plates 14–15) Computer Associates; (Plate 16) NASA; (Plate 17) Paul Meakin/E.T. Dupont de Nemours & Company; (Plate 18) Apple Computer, Inc.; (Plate 19) Haworth/Advanced Dimensional Displays, Inc.

Computer manufacture photo essay (between pages 240 & 241) (Plate 1–2) International Business Machines Corporation; (Plate 3) ITT Corporation; (Plate 4) Hewlett-Packard Company; (Plate 5) Monsanto; (Plate 6) Hewlett-Packard Company; (Plates 7–8) Intel Corporation; (Plates 9–20) Hewlett-Packard Company.

Offices and computers photo essay (between pages 352 & 353) (Plates 1–2) Metropolitan Life Insurance Co. archive; (Plate 3) Metropolitan Life Insurance Co.; (Plates 4–6) Hewlett-Packard Company; (Plate 7) UNISYS; (Plate 8) NASA (Plate 9) International Business Machines Corporation; (Plates 10–11) Kodak KIMS System; (Plates 12–13) United States Department of Agriculture; (Plate 14) Tom Hollyman/J.P. Morgan & Company; (Plate 15) Gary Kufner/Steelcase, Inc.; (Plate 16) Tom Hollyman/J.P. Morgan & Company; (Plate 17) Steelcase, Inc.; (Plate 18) ACCO International, Inc.; (Plate 19) Steelcase, Inc.; (Plate 20) Hewlett-Packard Company; (Plate 21) Environetics International, Inc.

Part and chapter opener photos

Part one Wang Laboratories, Inc.
Part two Wang Laboratories, Inc.
Part three Hewlett-Packard Company
Part four International Business Machines Corporation
Part five NCR Corporation